BOBBED HAIR AND BATHTUB GIN

ALSO BY MARION MEADE

BIOGRAPHIES

Free Woman: The Life and Times of Victoria Woodhull
Eleanor of Aquitaine
Madame Blavatsky: The Woman Behind the Myth
Dorothy Parker: What Fresh Hell Is This?
Buster Keaton: Cut to the Chase
The Unruly Life of Woody Allen

NOVELS

Stealing Heaven: The Love Story of Heloise
and Abelard
Sybille

BOBBED HAIR AND BATHTUB GIN

WRITERS RUNNING WILD IN THE TWENTIES

MARION MEADE

NAN A. TALESE

DOUBLEDAY
NEW YORK ■ LONDON ■ TORONTO
SYDNEY ■ AUCKLAND

PUBLISHED BY NAN A. TALESE
AN IMPRINT OF DOUBLEDAY
a division of Random House, Inc.

DOUBLEDAY is a registered trademark of Random House, Inc.

Book design by Marysarah Quinn

Library of Congress Cataloging-in-Publication Data
Meade, Marion, 1934–
Bobbed hair and bathtub gin : writers running wild in the Twenties /
by Marion Meade.— 1st ed.
      p.   cm.
Includes bibliographical references (p.).
1. Authors, American—20th century—Biography. 2. Women and
literature—United States—History—20th century. 3. United
States—Social life and customs—1918–1945. 4. Women authors,
American—Biography. 5. Millay, Edna St. Vincent, 1892–1950.
6. Fitzgerald, Zelda, 1900–1948. 7. Parker, Dorothy, 1893–1967.
8. Ferber, Edna, 1887–1968. 9. Nineteen twenties.   I. Title.

PS151.M43 2004
810.9'9287'09042—dc22
[B]
2003064585

ISBN 0-385-50242-7

PRINTED IN THE UNITED STATES OF AMERICA

May 2004

FIRST EDITION

1   3   5   7   9   10   8   6   4   2

FOR MY DAUGHTER, ALISON

CONTENTS

BOBBED
HAIR
AND
BATHTUB
GIN

1920

Publisher Condé Nast (center) surrounded by his staff: Vanity Fair *editor Frank Crowninshield,* Vogue *editor Edna Chase, theater critic Dorothy Parker, and managing editor Robert Benchley.*

CHAPTER ONE

IT COULDN'T BE WORSE.

Twenty-six, and she was losing her job. *Vanity Fair*'s editor in chief broke the news in the grandeur of the Tea Court at the Plaza Hotel, beneath the Tiffany glass dome, amid the Caen stone and Breche violet marble, the Baccarat crystal and gold-encrusted china, the handwoven Savonnerie rugs. He had to fire her, Frank Crowninshield said, because his former theater critic was planning to return to the magazine and of course he needed his old job back. She said she didn't know that. He hoped she would work at home and do little pieces in her spare time. She said she really couldn't. She had no idea how to change a typewriter ribbon.

Vanity Fair had no cause to fire her, thought Dorothy Parker. And so what if every producer on Broadway hated her. It was Sunday afternoon on Central Park South, the carriage horses dozed standing up at the curbs, the leafless trees across the street were dark against the dusky sky. When Dottie emerged from the hotel, she went straight home, round Columbus Circle, up Broadway, back to the Upper West Side, where she grew up. From an early age she knew a thing or two about misfortune: a dead mother (*E. coli*), a dead stepmother (stroke), and a brother who vanished without a trace (amnesia, homicide, possibly pique). And not only them but her uncle Martin Rothschild, a first-class passenger on the unsinkable *Titanic*—Martin the family martyr. Sometimes it seemed as if her whole life had been spent waiting for something terrible to happen. Even so, to be canned over tea and scones, with the accompaniment of harp and violin, was the absolutely worst. She had spent four years with the Condé Nast publishing company, her first and only real job.

Her husband was waiting when she walked into the apartment. Edwin Pond Parker II, scion of Congregational clergymen and once a Wall Street broker, had served during the war in the muddy trenches of France as an ambulance driver. His van hurtled into a bomb crater, and Eddie spent two days buried with the dead and the wounded before being rescued. Handsome, blond, a Connecticut thoroughbred, he had appeared to be an ideal husband before the war. Since the armistice, he'd been devoting himself, almost full-time, to alcohol and morphine.

Not surprisingly, Eddie had little practical advice to offer, and so for counsel and comfort she turned to her best friend. Robert Benchley was the managing editor of *Vanity Fair*, and while everybody called him Bob or Rob, she never did. With her impeccable manners, she addressed him, ladylike, as "Mr. Benchley" (or "Fred," or in times of very bad trouble "Dear Fred"), and he in return called her "Mrs. Parker." The day he walked into the office for the first time, Dottie knew that she and Bob Benchley were kindred spirits sharing a similar sense of humor. For example, he subscribed to *The Casket*, an undertakers' magazine that published everything you always wanted to know about subjects such as embalming ("sometimes in the fresh body of a robust suicide the descending colon may be contracted to the thickness of the thumb"). Dottie had never known anyone who thought it necessary to be well informed about embalming. Immediately she ordered her own subscription. Each month she leafed through the *Casket* ads for hearses and giggled over the humor column (From Grave to Gay). Then she clipped the most interesting anatomic plates to hang above her desk. Over the months her office friendship with Mr. Benchley had deepened steadily (and platonically, despite gossip to the contrary), until now they were practically inseparable.

In the early evening of January 11, Bob left his home in Scarsdale and hurried into town on the seven o'clock train. It was easy to see that Crownie shared none of the responsibility for dismissing Dottie, since he was little more than a hired hand in the Condé Nast empire (*Vanity Fair, Vogue, House and Garden*). The man behind her firing was Nast himself. Recently he had denied her a raise and squawked about several pieces, but she'd never given it a second thought. By every reasonable standard, she had done nothing wrong. Unfortunately, the publisher had never figured out that the duty of a critic was to determine what is of high artistic quality—and what isn't. After several hours spent loudly damning Nast for stupidity—the man ought to be horsewhipped, at the least—both of them fell back on personal principles. She knew everything bad happened to her. He always believed the greatest sin was disloyalty. And so the next morning he went to the office and quit.

With evident glee, the New York papers reported the upheavals in Nast's staff—a third editor, Robert Sherwood, also quit—and took the side of the editors. F.P.A. (né Franklin Pierce Adams), the city's most widely read columnist, wrote in the *New York Tribune*, "R. Benchley tells me he hath resigned his position with 'Vanity Fair' because they had discharged Mistress Dorothy Parker; which I am sorry for." The *New York Times* also ran a sympathetic account under the byline of its theater critic, Alexander Woollcott. (Woollcott held court at the Algonquin Round Table, a group of friends—a dozen or so humorists, journalists, and playwrights, including Dottie and Bob—who regularly lunched together at the Algonquin Hotel—the "Gonk"—on West Forty-fourth.) That week the walkout remained Topic A over publishing luncheon tables.

At *Vanity Fair,* Frank Crowninshield continued to shake his head. When Bob submitted his resignation, Crownie concluded that he had lost his mind. Bob's wife, Gertrude, stuck in Scarsdale with their two boys, thought so, too. But to Dottie his willingness to walk away from his job would forever be treasured as "the greatest act of friendship" she could imagine.

D OTTIE SOLD HER FIRST poem to *Vanity Fair* in 1914, before the war, when learning the tango and the turkey trot was the biggest thing on some people's minds. Her verse had appeared earlier in F.P.A.'s Conning Tower column, but this was her first publication for money (the sum of twelve dollars). She felt so tremendously confident that she presented herself at the offices of the new Condé Nast magazine, on West Forty-fourth Street, to apply for a writing job. At that time she was playing piano at a dance school and thinking about a new line of work, but, to be on the safe side, she told Frank Crowninshield that she was an orphan, an exaggeration.

The tall, silver-haired editor would always remember his first glimpse of Dorothy Rothschild: dainty manners, well turned out in a smart suit and bowed black patent pumps, drenched in perfume, brandishing a verbal switchblade. No openings were available, but Crownie, with his gift for spotting talent, directed her to *Vogue,* where for ten dollars a week she was indentured, writing captions for drawings of underwear ("Brevity is the soul of lingerie"). *Vogue* was a fossilized place, manned by lizardy-skinned Victorians wearing lorgnettes. But the job was a good deal better than slaving at the dance studio and living with her sister's family. In a fit of mischief, she once tried to sneak past the proofreaders a caption suggesting that a peekaboo mousseline de soie nightdress would be perfect for a night of debauchery. She was bored, barely managing to stay out of trouble, when Crownie rescued her from peonage in the undies department. In the autumn of 1917 he engineered her transfer to *Vanity Fair*, where she was assigned to write features and comic verse. It took only a few months before she replaced the English humorist P. G. Wodehouse as theater critic.

To Dottie, who had always loved the stage, the chance to become New York's only woman drama critic was incredible good luck, the first she'd ever known. But she soon discovered a tiny worm in the apple: *Vanity Fair* prided itself on being a magazine of no opinion, and she had nothing but opinions. Nevertheless, she tried her best to please by adopting the attitude that her job was to be a sort of weather forecaster. Faced with mediocre shows, she dutifully proceeded to issue regular gale warnings along with solid information theatergoers needed to know: bring knitting, sneak out for "a brisk walk around the Reservoir," go home, or, a favorite of hers, no need to show up at all. Unlike other critics, who confined their reviews to plot and performance, Dottie complained about the locations of her seats, smacked producers for low taste, and pilloried chorus lines for looking motherly. She one time reviewed the performance of a woman seated next to her who'd been searching for a lost glove. Not surprisingly, her columns pleased quite a lot of readers as much as they enraged an awful lot of producers.

In the January issue Dottie was critical of a comedy by Somerset Maugham. She thought that the leading lady, Billie Burke, had overacted badly and compared her performance to that of a well-known vaudeville dancer famous for wild gyrations. After objections from Crowninshield, Dottie toned down the review of *Caesar's Wife* and mildly observed that Burke, at thirty-five, was too old to play an ingenue—and her impersonation of Eva Tanguay ("The I Don't Care Girl") also seemed ill-advised.

Billie Burke happened to be the wife of Florenz Ziegfeld, not only a powerful Broadway producer but also an important *Vanity Fair* adver-tiser. Affronted, Ziegfeld made a fuss about Mrs. Parker, and within days Condé Nast fired his wiseacre critic.

DURING THEIR remaining weeks at the magazine, Dottie and Bob made a point of expressing their disdain for Nast. They pinned on red discharge chevrons and marched around the office in a conspicu-ous display of scorn, even hung a sign in the lobby of the building re-questing CONTRIBUTIONS FOR MISS BILLIE BURKE. As soon as Dottie left, the same week that Prohibition began, the company hastened to can-cel her *Casket* subscription and rip down her anatomic art, but could do little about the odor of her favorite perfume, Coty's Chypre, which must have seeped into the upholstered antique chairs. Around the wa-tercooler, secretaries in high-heeled morocco slippers gossiped that the whole office could stand fumigating. What's more, Mrs. Parker had asked to be punished for daring to write something quite vulgar about Billie Burke's having "thick ankles." But Mr. Nast insisted that was not dramatic criticism and ordered it cut. And that was the real story on her dismissal.

By February, Dottie and Bob had begun to share a tiny office in the Metropolitan Opera building at Broadway and Thirty-ninth. Actually, it was not an office but a corner of a corridor that had been glassed off, so cramped that "an inch smaller and it would have been adultery," she joked. There was room for two scuffed tables, three chairs (one for vis-itors), two typewriters, and a hat rack. They laughed about maybe get-ting their door lettered UTICA DROP FORGE AND TOOL CO., ROBERT BENCHLEY PRESIDENT—DOROTHY PARKER PRESIDENT. Luckily, she began receiving freelance assignments from magazines such as the *Saturday Evening Post*. Getting fired, she guessed, wasn't the end of the world af-ter all. It might even be for the best. Still, she doubted if she would ever again feel quite so foolishly happy as she had at *Vanity Fair*.

That winter, weeks after leaving the magazine, Dottie and one of her friends bumped into Condé Nast in the lobby of the Algonquin Hotel.

Nast, as congenial as he could be, had the gall to tell her that he would be going on a cruise shortly and wished she could join him.

Dottie gave the publisher her brightest smile. If only she could, she replied very politely.

As soon as he had walked on, she turned to Bunny Wilson. "Oh, God," she whispered. "Make that ship sink."

THE TYPEWRITER was a featherlight shiny black Corona No. 3 portable, a real beauty whose carriage folded trimly over the keyboard. It even came with a special leather carrying case. Regrettably, Edna St. Vincent Millay could not afford the pedigreed Corona, because she was a poet and poetry didn't pay. Vincent loved beautiful things but never had money, which was why her own typewriter was an ugly workhorse with a lumbering carriage and sticky keys.

This particular Corona, as it happened, was not for sale. The machine belonged to one of Vincent's beaus, actually to his employer, and had come to her notice by accident one day while she was visiting James Lawyer at the office of the American Red Cross. A decorated war hero who had seen action in France, Jim was a construction engineer who lived in Washington and had to make periodic business trips to New York. At first he was grateful just to have company for the evening. But then he fell in love with Vincent, and she with him, and they began talking about marriage. Only one thing stood in the way: his wife.

During Jim's visits they mainly spent their time in out-of-the-way hotels, and when he went back to Washington, he wrote passionate letters. Although he was devoted to his wife—a fantastic woman, he said—he could not help loving Vincent too and had begun thinking about divorcing Louise. He told Vincent that there was "nothing I wouldn't do for you, My Darling."

A few weeks into the affair the Corona somehow found its way from the American Red Cross to a dilapidated house on West Nineteenth Street, near the waterfront, where Vincent was living with her mother and two sisters. Having mastered the touch system, she was an excellent typist who could play the machine like Paderewski. Her sister Norma marveled at the sight of Vincie's fingers "going like hell" across the keyboard. Never had Norma known anybody to type so fast. The sudden appearance of an expensive typewriter was a bit strange, but nobody in the family questioned Vincent very closely—miracles had a way of happening around big sister.

Vincent was the oldest of three daughters of an insurance agent and an ambitious mother, who divorced when she was eight. She grew up in the coastal villages of eastern Maine, a land of brief summers and endless winters, and spent her childhood writing poems, which were published in a children's magazine, *St. Nicholas*. When she was twenty, she wrote a long narrative poem in which an adolescent girl finds herself being raped by Eternity and begins screaming. The sins of the world are crushing her ("Ah, awful weight! Infinity / Pressed down upon the finite Me!"). Begging God to revive her, she suddenly springs up from the ground, miraculously reborn. Cora Millay found "Renascence" deeply moving and urged her daughter to submit the poem in a competition for a literary anthology, *The Lyric Year*. Despite Vincent's conviction that she would win first prize, all she received was honorable mention. It was enormously disappointing, but there were a number of poets who noticed the poem and began to champion "Renascence," insisting it was much better than the winners.

A short time later, this poem about loneliness and fear of death attracted the attention of certain well-to-do older women who stepped forward and offered to underwrite Vincent's college education. As a result of this charity, she was able to enroll in Vassar College at the age of twenty-one. No question, it was an extraordinary opportunity for a small-town girl whose mother supported the family as a practical nurse and wig maker. On the other hand, such amazing good fortune only proved what Cora had always said: Vincent was brilliant.

With her college degree (Vassar '17) and her excellent typing skills, Vincent could easily have found employment. But she would never think of working in a business office. Back in Camden, her sisters,

Norma and Kay, earned pocket money by waiting tables and selling books door-to-door after school. Vincent didn't. (And Kay never forgot it: "Oh, no, not you. What did you care how mother worked. You wouldn't do anything manual, [even] to pay for your music lessons. Not you!") In Vincent's opinion, menial jobs were for people such as her sisters. It was different for her. She was an artist—and supremely proud of it.

In New York, Vincent earned money by selling fiction (under the pseudonym Nancy Boyd) to various second-rate magazines. Aside from these stories, two collections of her verse (*Renascence* and *A Few Figs from Thistles*) had been issued by obscure publishers but did not produce royalties. Otherwise, she had performed a few unpaid acting roles at the Provincetown Playhouse, which had produced her play *Aria da Capo* and where Norma was employed sewing costumes. In short, she was barely keeping her head above water. Most of the time, she prayed her checks wouldn't bounce and was quick to accept when a nice man invited her out for dinner.

Vincent's affair with Jim Lawyer continued for three months, until one night, in bed at the Hotel Judson on Washington Square, they heard the telephone ringing. When Jim finally answered, a Washington doctor reported the awful news that his wife had tried to kill herself by swallowing a quart of bad bootleg whiskey. Vincent, trying to remember what her coolheaded mother would do in a crisis, got him on the next train home. He looked frightened to death. In a short time Louise recovered, but her suicide attempt shook Jim so badly that he made up his mind to remain in Washington for a while. He needed to do the right thing by his wife.

A blizzard shut down New York City in February, leaving people trapped indoors. Mounds of snow and rubbish sprawled over the sidewalks. After six days without garbage collections, Vincent's friend Frank Adams worried in the *Tribune,* "I hope we shall not have a plague." Vincent, meanwhile, waited for news from Jim. She had no way of knowing when—or even if—he was coming back. Impatient, she began referring to him, pityingly, as a "poor fish." Another lover took her to the Biltmore, an especially nice hotel, with its famous clock and house detectives and guests who checked in with luggage. She finally received a letter. He was heartbroken, Jim said, but had to stop seeing her. Nothing, of course, would ever dim his memories of their love. Would she please remember to return the Corona to the Red Cross?

Fɾᴏᴍ ᴛʜᴇ ᴡɪɴᴅᴏᴡs at *Vanity Fair*, Bunny Wilson, the new managing editor, looked out at the roofs of office buildings blurring into the winter skies. Outside the tramcars were moving slowly through rivers of gray slush left behind by the blizzard. It was getting dark, and the yellow electric lights blinked like "fiery handwriting"—flat-footed prose, but Wilson liked it well enough to jot it down in his notebook. Bunny, whose real name was Edmund, was a red-haired, moonfaced, highly nervous young man. At twenty-four, he'd never had a sexual experience, much less a girlfriend. As preparation for success, however, he carried in his pocket a condom purchased at a drugstore on Greenwich Avenue.

Born in Red Bank, New Jersey, he was educated at Princeton, class of 1916, and served in the Army Intelligence Corps. After the armistice he visited *Vanity Fair* in hopes of selling some of his undergraduate essays. It was Dottie Parker who came out to the reception area and shook his hand. The whiff of her extremely strong eau de cologne was impossible to ignore. Even though she was awfully pretty, "and although I needed a girl, what I considered the vulgarity of her too much perfume prevented me from paying court," he recalled afterward. In reality, he found himself gently shooed away like a slobbery puppy. All day long his hand smelled of her perfume, as if it had been pickled in Chypre, until he forced himself, reluctantly, to wash.

Recruited on an emergency basis to fill in for Dottie and Bob, he was first assigned to reading manuscripts. Benchley, calling him a scab, offered nonetheless to show him the ropes. Once Bob had left, Crownie offered Bunny a staff job with Benchley's title and duties, for less than half of his hundred-dollar-a-week salary. Since *Vanity Fair* was an influential publication—and because Bunny needed the experience—the position of managing editor represented a perfect stepping-stone into the publishing business.

Before long he found himself doing all Benchley's work and quite a bit more. When additional help became necessary, Crownie gave permission to hire a Princeton friend, John Peale Bishop, an aesthete whose taste for luxury rivaled his distaste for work. A self-styled poet, John looked the part with his languid manner and blue eyes watery as a fish. (In a novel just published, *This Side of Paradise*, F. Scott Fitzgerald had modeled his elegant patrician poet Tom D'Invilliers on John.)

Bunny felt uncomfortable around Crowninshield. He viewed him as an unsympathetic person whose peculiarities included smelling his mail before opening it and who liked to declare he was not as "genial" as he appeared. (Bunny agreed.) To certain visitors the sight of Crownie mincing around the office in his frock coat brought to mind "the manager of some exclusive seaside resort," an apt observation because his type must have sustained Gilbert and Sullivan through numerous operettas. His fey mannerisms fed rumors that the forty-seven-year-old bachelor was a homosexual. But Bunny disbelieved these stories because Crownie told him in confidence that a prostitute made regular house calls to his apartment.

Still, he never really came to trust his boss. Crowninshield once invited him to lunch—a free lunch—at the Coffee House, his private social club, where he held forth to the long table of diners about Dottie Parker and Bob Benchley in the most tasteless language. Then he turned to Bunny and warned him not to listen. But Bunny was already offended.

As the weeks passed, gaining self-confidence, Bunny loosened up. He began sporting a flashy yellow necktie with his Brooks Brothers suits. He rented an apartment in the Village with three friends and hired a West Indian woman to cook. At the office he and John Bishop horsed around playing "The Rape of the Sabine Women," a game in which they galloped about holding aloft Condé Nast's secretaries.

B UNNY FELL IN LOVE with Edna St. Vincent Millay on an April evening in Greenwich Village. He and John met her at a party given by one of their Princeton friends, Hardwick Nevin, who had raved about her brilliance. Nevin explained that she would be arriving late, because she was performing a few blocks away, in a small role, at the Provincetown Playhouse. But they should be sure to wait. She was worth it. Bunny, who knew the poet by reputation for her admirable antiwar play *Aria da Capo*, needed no urging.

The party was crowded, and it was almost midnight before he spied her settled on the divan with a drink and a cigarette. Her slender body was draped in a brightly colored batik-print dress, her mass of un-bobbed red hair spilling around flushed cheeks. Not a true beauty—her features were far from perfect—she conveyed the impression of being "almost supernaturally beautiful," he decided, and she had the aura of a person of importance.

Invited to recite, she replied that she was tired. Nonetheless, the room had already hushed. For some reason, she began offering infor-mation instead of poetry, telling the crowd how, after a reading in Ohio, a member of the audience had the temerity to ask her questions. Inter-rogating a serious poet was shocking, she thought. What did they think? Since she did not wait for a reply, all of this appeared to be patter with a purpose, a bit of stage setting. She finally took a last puff of her ciga-rette. With a theatrical instinct for timing, she suddenly straightened her neck and threw back her head. Then she began to recite. The lovely, long throat, the fake British accent, the way she pronounced every syl-lable distinctly, even her cigarettes, transfixed Bunny and John and everyone else in the room.

Afterward, observing her flanked by admirers, Bunny pondered the best approach. He finally stepped over and introduced himself as an ed-itor at *Vanity Fair*, which got her complete attention. There were better showcases for her material than *Ainslee's* and *Current Opinion*, he said. Had she considered a magazine of high literary quality?

SLEEPING WITH THE BOY from *Vanity Fair* was probably a bad idea. But Vincent did it anyway. The chance to get "Dead Music—an Elegy" published in the magazine's July issue was too tempting. Even better, the poem was accompanied by a plug for *Aria da Capo* and a paean to her brilliance—"One of the most distinctive personalities in modern American poetry"—although she knew herself to be a tiny fish swimming in a vast literary ocean.

Bunny, poor sweet Bunny, so naive about the opposite sex, had fallen in love with her. To prove it, he turned into a pest, penning very poor love poems and fussing over various strategies to advance her career. Complicating matters, his friend John Bishop had begun chasing her, too. Before long, she was resenting both of them. Why couldn't they understand the complexities of the artistic temperament? A poet needed to be alone.

When she accompanied Bunny to his apartment one day to play the piano, he was enraptured. Glancing around his parlor, she complimented him on the handsome hand-carved mantelpiece.

It wasn't hand-carved, he corrected her.

Well, she replied, the old mantel was just like life, "so much work and care put in on it, and then look at it!" Following these preliminaries, she relieved him of his virginity, because sex meant little to her and he was obviously dying to do it. She would not deny having a great fondness for sex, and she also enjoyed being in love, although not quite as much as she liked men and women falling in love with her. Once that happened, she soon got bored and wished they would disappear. Fortunately, most of her adventures ended fairly quickly, sometimes after a single encounter.

Bunny, however, refused to go away. Would she marry him? She didn't want to hear it. She was three years his senior, she told him, and no Madonna to boot, having had more sexual partners than she could count on both hands, eighteen, give or take a few, by her calculation. (Her accounting methods may not have included the women, though.) But he insisted that neither age nor history made any difference; he still wanted to make her his wife.

ZELDA SAYRE was going to be married in Saint Patrick's Cathedral. She stepped off the train at Pennsylvania Station with her older sister Marjorie Brinson on Good Friday, April 2, the day before the wedding. Waiting for them were Goofo and his best man and also Zelda's sister Rosalind, who lived in the city with her husband, Newman Smith. From the station the sisters went to the Biltmore Hotel, where rooms had been booked so they could freshen up and rest, but Zelda was too excited to relax. Montgomery, Alabama, where nothing had happened since the Civil War, lay behind her. So did Mama and the Judge and being the baby of the family. Nobody in the wide world could tell her what to do now.

Zelda did not expect to accomplish grand things in life. As she saw it, this was less about laziness than from a complete lack of ambition. To hell with a career of her own. Being Zelda was quite enough. For girls such as herself, girls who believed in miracles, fame would come through a man. All she wanted was to be nineteen always. To find her soul mate. To be madly in love. To be horribly irresponsible. Who cared about the rest?

In February, when Zelda's period was late, Goofo mailed her a handful of pills from New York that were supposed to get rid of the baby. Disgusted, she threw them away, because everyone knew that only prostitutes had abortions. "God—or something" would make it turn out right, she told him. Sure enough, due to the grace of God or something, she was not pregnant after all. That very same month Metro Studios purchased a story of Goofo's for twenty-five hundred dollars, and Charles Scribner's Sons—the prestigious publisher of Edith Wharton and Henry James—prepared to release his novel. Undoubtedly, *This Side of Paradise* would become an enormous success. With the arrival of a platinum-and-diamond wristwatch, engraved FROM SCOTT TO ZELDA, it was all settled. She was going to marry Scott Fitzgerald.

The third of April was a cold spring morning that felt more like Christmas than Easter to Zelda, accustomed to Montgomery's heat and humidity. At noon the wedding party gathered in the vestry of Saint Patrick's. Zelda, carrying a bouquet of orchids, wore a dark blue suit and matching hat trimmed with leather ribbons. The attendants were Scott's best man, Ludlow Fowler, and Rosalind Smith, the matron of honor, and her husband. Still to appear was Zelda's third sister Clothilde, who was coming from Tarrytown with her husband, John Palmer. But Scott began to grow restless after a few minutes of waiting. Before anybody realized what was happening, he impatiently brushed off Zelda's protests and hurried the priest into performing the ceremony. By the time Clothilde and John arrived, it had ended. Worse yet, Scott had neglected to plan a luncheon. There was no reception of any kind, not even a wedding cake to slice. The bridal couple simply turned and marched away from the cathedral, vanishing into the Easter crowds on Fifth Avenue. Zelda was nineteen, Scott a few years older, but even so, nothing excused such shocking rudeness. (The sisters would never forgive Scott and find any number of additional reasons to hate him.) Left to celebrate alone, Zelda's relatives found themselves shivering on the sidewalk and wondering where to eat lunch.

A cold drizzle fell in the days after the wedding. But to Zelda, who had never seen a building taller than ten stories, never ridden a subway or a taxi, the metropolis seemed like a Babylonian circus where everything and everybody was in a hurry. She could hardly wait to explore the town. On Fifth Avenue she climbed on the hood of a cab and discovered that riding on top of a taxi costs more than inside, and in Washington Square she did not hesitate to jump into the fountain. She and Scott got themselves chased out of *George White's Scandals* after they began giggling and he stood up and pretended to undress in the middle of the theater. To their room high above the city on the twenty-first floor of the Biltmore, which to her smelled sweetly like marshmallows, they were constantly inviting people over for all-night parties. She could not have been more surprised when the hotel management, seeing its room being trashed, insisted that they leave. They checked out—and then immediately checked into the sleek new Commodore with its two thousand rooms, where they spun madly in the revolving door, did cartwheels down the rose-carpeted corridors, and continued to make a ruckus with Scott's friends.

Acting like a couple of nuts was perfectly natural to Zelda. She'd always been different, a girl whose brain did not work in the same way as others'. At home, where she stood out as a cutup, some people called her wild; others just said nobody had more guts than the Judge's daughter.

DURING THE WAR Montgomery was overrun with soldiers from Camp Sheridan. At the country club one night, Zelda danced with a boy who introduced himself as Francis Scott Key Fitzgerald, a Yankee who immediately said one of his ancestors (a second cousin three times removed) had written the words of "The Star-Spangled Banner." Never would she forget her first glimpse of him strolling around the club as if angels' wings were lifting him off the ground. His canary-colored hair and light green eyes were like no other boy's she had ever seen. His features were as pretty as a girl's. Dancing with him, she thought that "he smelled like new goods," as exciting as an unwrapped Christmas package. Before long, the lieutenant from Minnesota was camping on her front porch on Pleasant Avenue. He was a writer, he said; indeed, he talked nervously and incessantly about a novel he had written, a tale inspired by his experiences at Princeton, a school he had flunked out of. *The Romantic Egotist*, twice rejected by Scribner's, was being revised. Someday he was going to be terrifically famous.

Without any way of judging his ability, Zelda was almost tempted to take his word for it, but what she did know—and this was her main concern—was that this Romeo had no money. Her purpose in life was to be a wife, preferably a rich and pampered wife. While she could never marry a man unable to support her, Scott Fitzgerald and his wild ideas were intriguing. Montgomery girls did not usually meet writers; they more often brought home football players from Georgia Tech.

DOTTIE GLANCED at Scott's bride. No, she decided, Zelda was not particularly beautiful.

They were lunching at the Algonquin. To avoid the clubbish atmosphere of the Rose Room, the backdrop for daily gatherings of the Round Table, they met in the small Oak Room restaurant next to the lobby. Same $1.65 blue-plate special—same broiled spring chicken, cauliflower hollandaise, buttered beets, fried potatoes, same free popovers—but no celebrities. At a narrow table they snuggled shoulder to shoulder on a banquette with their backs propped against the wall, Dottie, Bunny, Scott, and Zelda. The seating arrangement made conversation a bit awkward.

"This looks like a road company of the Last Supper," Dottie said.

Listening to Scott's goofy ideas, his enthusiasm, and, above all, his unshakable confidence in the future made Dottie smile. He seemed much younger than his twenty-three years—"God! How I miss my youth," he once cried to Bunny—and everything about him was small-town. There was, however, nothing provincial about his ambitions. No sooner had Scribner's accepted *This Side of Paradise* than he began predicting sales of twenty thousand.

Some of the editors laughed. Face facts. First novels were lucky to sell five thousand.

Not sell twenty thousand? he replied. Why of course it would.

Scott's editor was a quiet young man in his mid-thirties, guarded, sensitive, and shy. Maxwell Perkins had put his job on the line for Scott Fitzgerald, or, as he wished to call himself, F. Scott Fitzgerald, because of an overwhelming feeling that the boy from St. Paul had talent worth fostering. Perkins was perhaps the only one at Scribner's not surprised when the novel sold twenty thousand copies within two weeks of publication, transforming Fitzgerald into the most-talked-about author in town.

Success made Scott giddy. At lunch he talked about nothing but himself, his sales figures, his ads ("WERE YOU EVER UNDER THIRTY? Then Read This Side of Paradise"), his state of mind ("manic depressive insanity"). But he was also itching for this chance to show off his new wife, all fresh and pouty-lipped, like a baby being wheeled along in a pram by a doting daddy.

For months Scott had been bragging about the most beautiful girl below the Mason-Dixon Line, and so Dottie had imagined the kind of fiddle-dee-dee coquette found on her veranda by Sherman's army. It was surprising to discover that this person with the odd name Zelda was anything but frivolous. Her hair, honey-colored, was bobbed daringly around her ears in the lastest fashion. She was chomping gum and speaking in an Alabama drawl. As for the face, Dottie had seen it any number of times on various chocolate tins: the tiny, petulant bow mouth and the girly-girl pout. (A spoiled brat who thinks she's "queen of the campus," sniffed one of the Round Table regulars.)

In his optimism over the book, F. Scott Fitzgerald was cute, Dottie decided. But the Kewpie-doll bride was a bit of a bumpkin.

DURING LUNCH Zelda had an opportunity to take the measure of "Mrs. Parker," whose shadowy husband was never seen and for all Zelda knew may not even have been alive. She was not particularly impressed. To Zelda, who had perfected the gift of smiling politely without listening (so that you wondered what she was really thinking), Dottie was one of those older professional women, no doubt pushing twenty-five, who continued to wear old-fashioned long hair and Merry Widow hats. Her condescension, the almighty superiority of the native over the foreigner, could not have been more obvious. But Zelda didn't mind. In fact, she showed so little curiosity about others that she sometimes appeared indifferent if not slow-witted. Unlike Scott, she wanted people to like her, but if they didn't it was no concern. She found women especially boring. "The only excuse for women was the necessity for a disturbing element among men," she was made to say in

Scott's novel, a cheeky statement but nevertheless an accurate summation of her feelings. Most women were cowards, she thought.

In Montgomery, Zelda's father was a circuit-court judge, later associate justice of the Alabama Supreme Court, where he was known as "The Brains of the Bench," and she was her father's daughter. Graduating from Sidney Lanier High School, class of 1918, she had more formal schooling than Dottie, whose higher education ended at fourteen, when she dropped out of Miss Dana's School after one semester, for reasons she declined to explain. But while Dottie, a prodigious reader, educated herself and could recite Shakespeare from memory, Zelda made no pretense of being a scholar, let alone a reader. She had never finished a serious book in her life. Where she came from, girls washed their hair and powdered themselves and slipped into dainty dresses. Each afternoon was "a garden party and the whole town bathed and dressed and set out in the summer sunshine smelling of talcum powder and orris root," she would write. Nobody was the slightest bit interested in memorizing Shakespeare.

"NO EVENING CLOTHES," the man mumbled.

On opening night Edna Ferber was standing at the back of Ford's Grand Opera House in Baltimore next to a beefy, neckless fellow with a dead cigar pasted to his lips. $1200 *a Year* was practically over, but Sam Harris had yet to utter a single comment. Knowing him to be slightly deaf, she took care to speak distinctly.

"Well, Mr. Harris?" She waited.

Finally the Broadway impresario turned and glanced at her. "Needs a lot of work," he said.

What made him think so?

"No evening clothes," he repeated.

But her play had nothing to do with evening clothes, she objected. $1200 *a Year* wasn't mindless fluff. It was about teachers' salaries, please. There were insights.

Harris shook his head.

Edna shook her head back at him. For one thing, this was a comedy. For another, there was plenty of food for serious thought. (An economics professor struggles to make ends meet on twelve hundred dollars a year, while the town's mill workers are earning twenty to thirty dollars a day. He gives up his job to work as a laborer.)

Harris did not look overly pleased. Where are the laughs? he said.

Where indeed. But she knew what he meant. The dialogue had sounded hilarious when she and her collaborator, Newman Levy, were blocking out the script, but the opening-night audience sat there like mourners at a funeral Mass. Clearly, they just didn't get it. And neither, apparently, did the Baltimore critics, who next morning would call it a propaganda play about capital and labor, which made no sense to Edna.

Ford's Grand Opera House offered its patrons a full season of shows bound for Broadway. Productions opened every Monday, and closed every Saturday, with some pushing on to fame in New York and the rest meeting their demise at Ford's. At the end of the week Sam Harris dispatched $1200 *a Year* to the graveyard.

In overwhelming disbelief, Edna went home to New York, back to the hotel suite she shared with her mother. She had failed.

HANGING ABOVE the edge of Central Park and Seventy-second Street, opposite the Dakota, was one of those lofty hotels that Edith Wharton described as a fleet of battleships moored "along the upper reaches of the West Side." The lobby of the battleship in which Edna lived, the Hotel Majestic, was a palette of palm fronds and red carpet. On the tenth floor she sat hunched over the Underwood all day. She was in the habit of working in her bathrobe, stockings rolled at the knees, hair drooping, fingernails as chipped as a charwoman's. No telephone calls. No cigarettes either. No food except water and chewing gum. Sometimes her mind wandered downtown, to Aleck Woollcott and the rest of them around the big lunch table at the Algonquin. Edna, who never bothered with lunch, found it a bit ridiculous that the Round

Table would continue to hum well into mid-afternoon. When did those people work? To Edna, writing involved a combination of "ditch-digging, mountain-climbing, treadmill and childbirth," not hanging around the Gonk trading wisecracks. She waited until afternoon to read her morning mail and warned people never to telephone "unless someone in the family is murdered."

Fond of presenting herself as a humbly born daughter of the soil, Edna actually came from a family of shopkeepers. When a kid, she was shaped by prairie anti-Semitism in a succession of whistle-stops such as Ottumwa, Iowa, a coal-mining burg where "there was [not] a day when I wasn't called a sheeny." Far more pleasant was Appleton, Wisconsin, with its forty Jewish families, where her mother ran a dry-goods store. Julia Ferber, a shrewd businesswoman who supported the family after her husband lost his sight, had become the real-life prototype for many of Edna's characters.

For months Edna had been struggling with a novel about three generations of Chicago women. Each morning she would station herself religiously at the Underwood and shove fresh sheets of paper into the machine, but the writing only inched along until she was frantic. She was a successful writer of short fiction for magazines such as the *Saturday Evening Post* and *Woman's Home Companion*. She had also published a half-dozen collections of stories and two novels. Several movies and a Broadway play, *Our Mrs. McChesney*, starring Ethel Barrymore, were based on her work. After ten years, shouldn't she be in her prime? She expected fiction to be easy by now.

It wasn't. Interminable hours at the Underwood sometimes produced a mishmash of awkward sentences and dumb metaphors. She found herself taking wrong turns and wandering down blind alleys, until finally *The Girls* just squatted there like a stubborn child. Edna was sensitive to criticism, and she was painfully aware of belittling remarks made by certain other writers. In an offensive recent novel a Princeton boy named Fitzgerald had laughingly lumped her with Zane Grey, the popular writer of Westerns. Edna did not like being laughed at.

A latecomer to fiction, Edna published her first short story when she was twenty-four. It was more or less an accident. After a half-dozen years as a newspaper reporter, she suddenly fell into depression, quit her job, and spent her time in bed staring at the wallpaper, going steadily downhill. She was on the verge of becoming a real basket case when she bought a secondhand typewriter and decided to try writing. The story she began pecking out was about a fat girl who weighs two hundred pounds, "ugly, not only when the story opens, but to the bitter end"—not your ordinary heroine. Pearlie Schultz was Edna, who always believed herself ugly. (Everyone said so, she told a friend, "except mother and even she has moments of doubt.") When *Everybody's Magazine* accepted "The Homely Heroine" and sent her a check for $50.60, Edna had mixed feelings. She never did figure out the sixty cents, but it made her so furious—"the old stingy-guts!" she thought—she never sent *Everybody's* another story. For her first novel, published by Frederick A. Stokes a year later, she used her own experiences as a newspaperwoman. The heroine of *Dawn O'Hara, the Girl Who Laughed* is not homely or fat. She is beautiful, thin, and Irish, and her adventures sold ten thousand copies.

By 1920 Edna had built a loyal audience, fans who appreciated good storytelling above great literature, but this didn't satisfy her. She was still sitting in the cheap seats, without a "literary" novel that would ensure her a decent obituary in the *New York Times*. Why kid herself?

The failure of *$1200 a Year* was a bitter disappointment. Her trouble starting the new novel was another blow to her confidence, and so she grumbled about everything: the city that she normally loved ("I hate New York"), the new fashions that put grown women in skimpy schoolgirl skirts, the writers who earned more than she did. "Everybody who is writing," even those with tin ears for language, was earning a minimum of $100,000 a year. Every writer except herself, she fumed.

"Stop it," scolded her good friend Bill White. (William Allen White, a well-known political journalist, was editor and publisher of the *Emporia Gazette* in Kansas.) She should quit worrying about other writers' bank accounts.

Of course, hardly anybody was earning $100,000 ($1 million in current dollars)—plenty of writers were living on beans—and she knew it. Several years earlier, a big-money literary agent asked to represent her. She gave Paul Reynolds a cool reception. What was in it for her? Why should she throw away her earnings on commissions when she could place her own writing?

Could he have just fifteen minutes of her time to talk it over? Reynolds asked.

Why not? she replied. "There are heaps and shoals, and floods of money in this country that I might get, and don't. I know that."

So did Reynolds, which was why he continued his pursuit.

Edna usually took out her frustrations on Bill White. Another close friend to whom she regularly complained was F.P.A. Frank Adams was an experienced journalist, a wit who wrote a weekly diary in the style of Samuel Pepys, but he also happened to be a superb editor, a purist when it came to language. For many years he had been married to a handsome showgirl (a former member of the famed Floradora sextet), their only offspring a large white cat, and his column constantly mentioned both Minna and Mistah, giving the impression of conjugal happiness, deliberately leaving out conjugal warfare. Frank, probably the sexiest homely man in the city, had a roving eye for long-legged beauties, but he also got along famously with smart women such as Edna, and it was not unusual for the two of them to spend several evenings a week together. Frank, though sympathetic to Edna's writing paralysis, had no idea how to help her get unstuck.

Edna's goal was to complete "three pages if possible—a thousand words a day—a thousand words a day—a thousand words a day, day after day, week after week, month after month." On her worst days she could manage to squeeze out only fifty or a hundred words, on a good day as many as three or four thousand, enough for her to feel satisfied when she left the typewriter. What was the secret to decent writing? Sitting there until you got it right? As she knew, this was not a trivial question. Throughout the spring Edna spent hours in her bathrobe each day. There really was nothing else to do.

. . .

ALL ZELDA MANAGED to do some days was soak in the tub and lunch on tomato sandwiches. By this time the Fitzgeralds had begun to feel so exhausted they had to get out of the city. Hopefully, peace of mind could be found in Westport, Connecticut, a shorefront town on Long Island Sound where they rented a shingled colonial cottage on Compo Road. They hired a Japanese servant to cook and keep house, and Zelda joined a beach club. While writing short stories for the *Saturday Evening Post* and *Metropolitan*, earning up to nine hundred dollars a piece, Scott made plans to work on his next project, *The Flight of the Rocket*.

Within weeks, however, Zelda began to chafe at being stranded in the suburbs. Scott spent long stretches at the typewriter and wearily insisted that bills were giving him the jitters. His withdrawal into work during the day left her alone with nothing to do but baby her hangovers and sip lemonade. When the weather warmed up, she went swimming in the afternoons.

Despite her moaning and groaning about feeling useless, she was in fact contributing more than she realized to the family business. In *This Side of Paradise,* the Rosalind character was originally modeled on Scott's rich Chicago girlfriend Ginevra King, but by the final revision he had spliced in the unmistakable traits of the far more unconventional Zelda Sayre. His book immediately immortalized the "flapper," a word now being used for trendsetting young women with short hair and short skirts who smoked, drank, and used powder and rouge, everybody hot to defy traditional female roles. In stories such as "The Ice Palace" and "The Jelly-Bean," Scott reproduced the thoughts and behavior of his own flapper, until eventually he would have trouble creating a female character who was not a portrait of his wife. Around friends, he made no effort to hide how much he owed Zelda for supplying the content of his current stories as well as *The Flight of the Rocket*.

Beyond borrowing Zelda's personality and ideas, he had begun to appropriate her writing as well. Before her marriage Zelda kept a diary so original that Scott took the liberty of copying whole passages verbatim, without any attempt to paraphrase, as if it were his own work. Typed extracts went to his editor. "You'll recognize much of the dialogue," he told Max Perkins. "Please don't show it to anyone else." Zelda saw nothing wrong with being her husband's muse. It was flattering.

Newly settled on Compo Road, the Fitzgeralds started giving out their number, Westport 64 Ring 4, and consequently the telephone never stopped ringing. Even though Westport was only an hour from New York, it was considered the country. "They filled the house with guests every weekend, and often on through the week," as Scott would write in *The Beautiful and Damned*, because they "hated being there alone." The visitors were largely Scott's bachelor friends from Princeton, and soon the gray house began to resemble a fraternity where Zelda was the only woman, a situation that made her happy. In Montgomery she had always sought the company of boys, who were more willing than her girlfriends to serve as accomplices for stealing a streetcar or begging change at the train station. In Westport there were plenty of men, drunk or sober, willing to drive her down to the city whenever she felt like getting away from Scott.

Despite good intentions, it was turning out to be a summer of a thousand giant orange blossoms, with their biggest household expense the bootlegger. On a single night in July, Scott dropped forty-three dollars for booze (an enormous sum equal to almost five hundred dollars today). For both him and Zelda evenings were spent getting drunk, and mornings feeling like hell.

Westport, a peaceable village characterized by lawn mowers and cocktail shakers, was infested with marital land mines. A good deal of petting and patting of other men's wives took place. After Scott became flirtatious with Tallulah Bankhead's sister Eugenia, Zelda retaliated with George Jean Nathan, co-editor with Henry Mencken of *The Smart Set*. Nathan had become friends with both of them, and Scott was basing a character in his new novel on the editor. "Dear Blonde," George began letters to Zelda, and wittily concluded them "A Prisoner of Zelda." Certainly he admired her sass, and she in turn was pleased by his attention. One of her favorite stops in the city became his apartment in the Royalton Hotel, on West Forty-fourth across the street from the Algonquin. A debonair bachelor of thirty-eight, a sophisticated man-about-town, he was known for his absinthe cocktails and affairs with married women. When Zelda showed some of his amorous letters to Scott, George became alarmed. She was a bewitching creature, he told her, but she was also an idiot. Why didn't she rent a post office box? At one of Nathan's parties, she told a friend, "I *cut* my *tail* on a broken bottle and can't possibly sit on the three stitches that are in it now—The bottle was bath salts—I was boiled—The place was a tub somewhere." What she could not remember was exactly how she wound up naked in George's bathtub. "It's been a wild summer, thank God."

Everybody, in fact, was wild and boiled and never cared what he or she did. The Boston Post Road between Westport and New York roared with drunks running their motorcars into stone walls and fireplugs. It didn't matter, because nobody would arrest them. The police minded their own business.

Zelda wrote, much later, about the sights and sounds of that first summer of her marriage: the roadhouse where they always stopped to stock up on gin, George Nathan playing "Cuddle up a Little Closer" on the piano, the upsetting quarrels with her husband—and her need for him too. "Without you, dearest, dearest I couldn't see or feel or think—or live—I love you so . . ." Scott, too, was to look back later. But in contrast to Zelda's cool, dry-eyed recitation of details, he would become overwhelmed with nostalgia. On one afternoon, he recalled, he rode through midtown in a taxi and "I began to bawl because I had everything I wanted and knew I would never be so happy again."

To a great extent, *This Side of Paradise*, which went through nine printings in its first year, appealed to the younger generation. Scott was being compared to Rupert Brooke, the British soldier-poet who had died in France. (His title was from a poem of Brooke's.) While the book was extensively reviewed, and praised for its originality, not everybody liked the writing, and some detractors were inclined to view the novel as an example of crass commercialism having nothing whatsoever to do with literature. Heywood Broun, the *New York Tribune*'s most important reviewer, found it so juvenile that he wondered if this F. Scott Fitzgerald could actually be twenty-three. His writing was "complacent," "pretentious," and "self-conscious"; the unlikable characters, Amory Blaine and his snobbish Ivy League friends, were effete creatures, best described as "male flappers." Scott, bristling over this slap in the face, had dismissed Broun, who was thirty-one, as an old codger. As if Broun weren't bad enough, Frank Adams scorned *This Side of Paradise* as "sloppy and cocky." Every chance he got, Frank printed lists of mistakes and spelling errors—"flambuoyant," "Ghunga Dhin"—to the amusement of *Tribune* readers. It was embarrassing for Scott, though. "FPA is at it again," he complained to Max Perkins.

Scott's admirers, oblivious of his atrocious spelling, continued to snap up the book. They were crazy about the story, the author, and the author's wife. By this time Zelda had earned a national reputation as the ultimate flapper, a figure of extreme glamour personifying the new image of "flaming youth." In interviews Scott proudly announced, "I married the heroine of my stories," while Zelda posed for rotogravures with her skirt inches above her knees. A few months ago she had been living in Montgomery, and nobody knew her name. Now she had her picture in magazines. And this was her real life, no fairy tale.

THREE HUNDRED MILES north of the city the June sun beat down at midday and turned the sand the color of burned sugar, and the mosquitoes whizzed all through the salty nights. Vincent and her family left behind the furnished rooms on Nineteenth Street to spend the summer in a borrowed bungalow near the tip of Cape Cod, in Truro. It was a weathered two-story cottage on Old King's Road, just behind the dunes, the kind of house that lacked indoor plumbing and electricity.

But a hedge of wild roses studded with whining bees bloomed along the front porch, and there was a nostalgic resemblance to the homes of her Maine childhood, wrong-side-of-the-tracks places with a few sticks of furniture and no electricity or heat.

Despite minor discomforts, Vincent had her Corona portable, which was everything she needed to work. She was happy to be away from the noise and speed of the city, where crossing the streets petrified her sometimes. Gone, too, were the people who had cluttered up her life. With a borrowed Victrola, on which she continuously played Beethoven's Fifth Symphony, she wrote sonnets such as "Pity Me Not Because the Light of Day" for *Vanity Fair* and short stories for the dependable *Ainslee's* magazine. Unfortunately, this idyllic state did not last. Before many weeks had passed, men she left behind in New York, the ones who could not live without her, began nipping at her heels. Bunny, for one, had encouraged her leaving, but his enthusiasm was far from genuine. He became cranky after learning she would be gone four or five months. Sometimes, though, she couldn't help missing him and remembering how sweet he'd been to her. More often she lost patience with his doglike mooning.

He no longer knew what to say to her, Bunny moaned.

That made two of them, she said. "What would you like me to write?"

Another morose lover was John Bishop, who had spent the spring attempting to lure Vincent to his midtown apartment as often as possible. At their last meeting she breezed in late and did not hesitate to admit that she had just come from another man's bed. What's more, she was pressed for time because she was meeting someone else (her third sexual encounter of the day). Where two-timing treatment of this sort might have cooled most men, it only stoked John's ardor. (She behaved like a man, he decided.)

She had barely unpacked when he pleaded to visit. Her suggestion of the Fourth of July brought no reply, however. Obviously he was being ornery. "Damn it, gimme a little information, boy."

John turned up at the end of July and hung around for a week. No sooner had he left than Bunny arrived.

Bᴜɴɴʏ's ᴡᴇᴇᴋᴇɴᴅ got off to a shaky start. Stepping from the train at Wellfleet, he found a cart and driver willing to transport him to Truro, but, inexplicably, the man made a detour and dumped him some distance from the cottage. Night having fallen, lost and hungry, Bunny was left to stumble around in the dark, dragging his suitcase through a field of scrub oak.

Apparently, no preparations had been made for his arrival, but a bottle of whiskey and something to eat were set on the table. Inside the house it was stifling and noisy with the Millay women talking relentlessly. Bunny, seeing for the first time the entire family together, thought that the three sisters—a redhead, a blonde, and one exotically dark—were extremely attractive. The scene recalled *Little Women*, but in contrast to Alcott's fictional creations, and rather incongruously, these sisters behaved like high-strung children who lapsed into baby talk and addressed each other by silly nicknames: Titter Binnie or Sefe (Vincent), Hunk (Norma), and Wump (Kathleen).

Of the four women, however, the mother (variously called Mothie, Muvver, Muddie, or Mumbles)—a bespectacled little old lady— seemed most unusual to Bunny. Cora, to whom Vincent bore a strong physical resemblance, appeared older than her fifty-five years, and Bunny imagined that she must have had a hard life. Sitting up ramrod straight in her chair, like a New England schoolteacher taking atten- dance, she followed the conversation with a stern expression as she sipped her whiskey. The schoolmarmish air and the granny glasses proved deceptive, however, because she soon began making "raffish" re- marks to him. She used to be such a "slut," she said between drags on a cigarette, so it was no wonder her girls should be, too. A mother styling herself a prostitute! He nearly died.

To escape the chaperonage of Cora and the sisters, Bunny and Vincent went out to huddle in the dark on the porch rockers but were soon driven inside by flurries of wicked mosquitoes. In addition to bug bites, he would suffer during the weekend from a variety of afflictions, including diarrhea and eczema. He was not prepared for the lack of modern conveniences—the outhouse, the makeshift outdoor shower, the oil lamps. No proper meals were served except suppers, and those were slapdash. Poor boy, the Millay women began to cluck, poor Bunny.

Being alone with Vincent was not easy, but he finally found an opportunity to sit her down and bring up the subject burning in his mind. Like the young gentleman he was, he asked her formally to be his wife. To his dismay, she threw cold water on the proposal. Even her promise to think about it rang false, and afterward he could not help remembering her exact words.

"That might be the solution," she said.

Her withering remark, with its mercenary implications, flustered him more than he cared to admit. Probably it was the idea of marriage that bored her, he decided, and not him.

Next morning, nothing more was said about marriage, and they decided to go to the beach. Still upset, Bunny tried to keep the conversation bright. As they were coming back to the house, he kissed her behind a bush, and she grinned and gave him a "summer girl smile."

"By the time we're fifty years old, we'll be two of the most interesting people in the United States," he said.

"You behave as if you were fifty already," she answered.

Bunny left Truro on Sunday close to tears. In a rush of misery, he confided to John his problems being a guest of the Millays, making clear how unnerving he found the lack of plumbing. Not surprisingly, John replied that he knew exactly how Bunny felt. As a matter of fact, he had "stopped defecating" for a whole week. After leaving Truro, he immediately checked into the YMCA in Boston and took a bath.

Back in New York, Bunny reflected that his amorous achievements had been limited to a single kiss. Edna St. Vincent Millay had turned him into putty, he told himself. Yet he continued to pine for her.

. . .

I̶F TRURO proved an ordeal for Bunny, it was becoming a struggle for Vincent too. The summer started off splendidly, but her concentration fizzled. So did her writing. Although she bobbed her hair and learned to drive a car, it turned out to be mostly a fruitless period in which she treaded water with Nancy Boyd potboilers banged out quickly for cash and entertained visitors from New York. Eventually her family also began to get on her nerves, especially the snakebites of sisterly jealousy.

For Vincent's youngest sister, Kay, the summer had been "stupid, hot, lonesome." Tormented by mosquitoes and a miserable cold, she wrote grouchy letters to her boyfriend, Howard Irving Young. Otherwise she spent her time sniffling and sulking and watching Titter Binnie play games with John and Bunny. (They were not the only visitors. The editor of *Ainslee's* also appeared.) For the first time, despite an abundance of clues, Kay understood that the interest of the New York editors was not entirely professional. Shocked, she concluded that Vincent must have plotted to figure out "who was the editor of what magazine," and then "deliberately met and slept with him until he published her work and then she went on to the next editor." Sister was not a poet at all, only "a very clever woman with a definite gift for jingle," she thought.

Kathleen Kalloch Millay, twenty-four years old, a budding writer of grace and some small talent, felt underappreciated. For as long as she could remember, her mother doted on Vincent, even bestowing a theatrical name custom-made for applause. With the household organized around little Vincie's genius, Norma and Kay took for granted that she owned all the space, artistic and otherwise. Kay, at the age of sixteen, worshiped "my Vincent," and when influential women generously arranged her sister's Vassar education, Kay whooped for joy. "Glory Be!" she wrote in her diary. "Did ever such fairy-tale-like things happen to anyone before?" But living in her sister's shadow eventually became onerous, and now, behind Vincie's back, Kay sarcastically called her "Edna St. Jesus."

Kay griped mostly to her boyfriend, a personable young man from

Rutherford, New Jersey, who planned to become a playwright. Howard Young worked as a production manager at Famous Players–Lasky movie company, which occasionally allowed him to write a scenario but otherwise paid him pennies. Hoping to further his career by rubbing shoulders with important people, Howard had turned into an enthusiastic partygoer and name-dropper. His letters to Kay were full of news about various celebrities he'd met: George Jean Nathan at his Royalton suite playing pop tunes on the piano; F. Scott Fitzgerald and his engaging wife, whose name escaped Howard; Henry Mencken, with whom he had just dined. As Howard was quick to inform Kay, Mencken had raved about Vincent as "the only worthwhile poet" published by *The Smart Set*. Wasn't that incredible?

When Vincent returned to New York in September, she was pleased to find that her prestige had grown. Village bookshops were selling *A Few Figs from Thistles*, her collection of saucy peep-show verses that pictured all-night sprees on the Staten Island Ferry, candles burning at both ends, lovers discarded like yesterday's papers. Thanks to Bunny, *Vanity Fair* ran an entire page of her verse and called her "the Most Distinguished American poet of the Younger Generation." It was thrilling to see herself becoming "very famous," she confided to a friend. All over town everybody was talking about Edna St. Vincent Millay. To another Edna—Edna Ferber—fame was a motion picture, about none other than herself, in which she was portrayed as a raving beauty.

OVER THE SUMMER Edna Ferber had gone to Hollywood, where Universal was shooting the film version of her second novel, *Fanny Herself*, a book so autobiographical it might have been called *Edna Herself*. (The movie would eventually be titled *No Woman Knows*.) While secretly pleased that she was being played by a gorgeous young actress (Mabel Julienne Scott), Edna sniffed at the vulgarity of the movie capital, which struck her as both boring and offensive. Hiking around Beverly Hills, she noticed that she was the only person on foot. From their windows people peered as if she were "some strange animal loose in the streets." Relieved to leave an unreal place where "the sun came up, day after day, day after day," she continued her traveling summer with trips to Chicago and San Francisco to attend the Republican and Democratic political conventions. With Bill White and Jay "Ding" Darling, the Iowa cartoonist, she'd been hired to supply team coverage for United Press. In August she turned thirty-five (all she admitted to was thirty-two), and in September she was back at the Hotel Majestic. Soon she was immersed in her regular routine: writing in the mornings, meeting various editors at the Cosmopolitan Club, and looking ahead to Christmas and wondering what she could buy her friends (a trombone-flute might be the thing for Frank Adams). There was no better city anywhere than New York in winter, she thought.

A few blocks from the Hotel Majestic, Dottie and her husband were preparing to abandon their apartment on West End Avenue and Seventy-first. After months of agonizing, they were going to spruce up their wartime marriage by giving it what amounted to a fresh paint job and new curtains. Eddie had just lately pulled out of his morphine addiction (he still drank heavily) and returned to work at Paine Webber. They rented an apartment the size of a teacup on the top floor of a red-brick building at the corner of Fifty-seventh Street and Sixth Avenue. To brighten it, they bought a canary and a dog. The building, full mainly of artists' studios, stood adjacent to a branch of the Sixth Avenue El, and so the apartment quaked every time a train rumbled by. The real problem was the Boston terrier, Woodrow Wilson, who had never been housebroken. Nobody remembered to walk him, and the hardwood floors soon began to warp.

A short stroll from the Parkers lived Zelda and Scott, who had left Westport for a brownstone apartment on Central Park South. The Fitzgeralds were now conveniently located a few doors down the street from the Plaza, their favorite hotel. Sometimes they ran up extravagant tabs by ordering meals from the hotel. When they were broke, however, they dined on homemade olive sandwiches washed down with Bushmills whiskey. Working furiously on his novel, Scott was periodically forced to stop and knock out short fiction. Still, money remained tight, and he once borrowed a hundred dollars from Dottie, only to find that the cash mysteriously disappeared. Considering the turmoil in his relationship with Zelda—there was a bruised eye and a broken door—the money could easily have been lost or misplaced in any number of ways. Scott, though, blamed his wife. Of course she took it, he muttered, because she wanted to squander his earnings on clothes. There was no way to prove this theory one way or another. But that fall, she did have her sights on a darling squirrel coat.

AFTER WINNING a hundred-dollar poetry prize for "The Beanstalk," Vincent decided to spend every cent of it on clothes. She splurged on "the sweetest new evening gown you ever saw, and shoes with straps across them and stockings with embroidery up the front." The new outfit was devilishly sexy. Unfortunately, it did nothing at all to help her work or lighten her mood. Back in the city, she began to feel "sad so much of the time." The obvious solution, she thought, was to shake free from her family and find a place to write without the watchful gaze of her mother or the sound of Norma's sewing machine whirring in the next room. Soon thereafter, she took a lovely big room in a brownstone on West Twelfth Street, a block from the hospital for which she was named. That the building frequently ran out of hot water didn't bother her a bit. She simply arranged to bathe over at Bunny's, raising the eyebrows of his roommates the first time they saw her sail naked out of the bathroom. She was in her new home only a few weeks when Kay spoiled things by moving into a room down the hall. And her mother, still puttering around the Truro house by herself, kept pushing problems on her. What should she do with the kittens? Who was going to pay the summer bills? Vincent "better settle with the gas company by money order."

Her family was not the only distraction. As usual, she simply could not escape the men who interrupted her work. She had begun seeing a cherubic English writer, Llewelyn "Lulu" Powys, who whipped himself into a lather over her. In one of his swooning letters he likened himself to "some wretched child under a spell." In addition to Lulu, there was the besotted John Bishop continuing to trail at her heels like a dog begging for table scraps. "For God's sake, Edna," he implored, "don't forbid my seeing you this week—I can't stand it." After dinner one night Vincent found herself entangled on her daybed with John and Bunny and playfully began making love with both of them. To be fair, she assigned her upper half to John and gave the bottom to Bunny, who amid the giggling decided his was the "better share." Vincent was hugely entertained by the sexual theatrics of the Princeton Brahmins, whom she dubbed "the choir boys of Hell." By one of her lovers—the choirboys, Lulu, someone else—she became pregnant in November and had to have an abortion. The cause was more carelessness than ignorance; she had just recommended a Margaret Sanger birth-control manual to Kathleen's boyfriend. To make matters worse, she wound up with an incompetent doctor who botched the abortion.

The week before Christmas, still weak from loss of blood, Vincent arrived at the Brevoort Hotel on Fifth Avenue to attend Kathleen's wedding to Howard Young. It was a modest affair witnessed by only the sisters and Howard's roommate. Standing next to her bridegroom, Kay appeared unusually jittery, as if she were having second thoughts. (Several photographers had approached her about modeling, and she had prospects, she said later, but "I gave it all up to marry you.") Unquestionably "Lil Ho'wid," as Vincent called him, was cookies and milk, as sweet as the boy next door. Yet he did not seem to be especially well equipped for a successful career, and neither did Charles Ellis, a sexually confused actor whom Norma had met at the Provincetown and was thinking of marrying.

To Vincent, who was twenty-eight, nearing the dreaded age of thirty, Kay's choice of a husband was a little upsetting. Was marriage, even to a nice but weak man such as Lil Ho'wid, better than being single?

Several days after the wedding, she wrote her mother to say she'd been "quite sick." There was a bout of bronchitis and "a small nervous breakdown," but she was on the mend now. She then lobbed a piece of startling news at Cora: she was going to Europe in two weeks. *Vanity*

Fair had made her a foreign correspondent, and she naturally accepted, as would any "business woman" ambitious to see the world, and not because of "any love affair, past or present." For another thing, Crownie agreed to pay a regular stipend for the Nancy Boyd stories she had been selling to *Ainslee's*. Anticipating that Cora would throw a fit while reading the letter, Vincent emphasized that the new job was too exciting an opportunity to pass up.

Besides, she went on, she desperately needed to get away. New York drained her of artistic inspiration, making her feel old and "sterile." In a place like Paris or Rome everything would be different. She longed for a drastic change, ideally a castle with a moat and a drawbridge, where she could be alone and find "fresh grass" to feed her muse. In short, she had made up her mind to go, and nothing Cora might say could stop her.

Impatient to embark on her new life, she began packing her trunks with her favorite things: a pair of fur-trimmed velvet galoshes, a blue silk umbrella, and her Corona of course. She could hear the clock ticking.

"I'll be thirty in a minute!" she told Bunny.

1921

Dottie lunching with her gang at the Algonquin Round Table: (clockwise) Bob Benchley, Alfred Lunt and Lynn Fontanne, Frank Crowninshield, Aleck Woollcott, Heywood Broun, Marc Connelly, Frank Case (hotel manager), Frank Adams, Edna Ferber, George S. Kaufman, and Robert Sherwood.

CHAPTER TWO

O N CENTRAL PARK WEST, palm trees rustled in the vast plush lobby of the Hotel Majestic, while outside the park was covered with snow. It was a gray Wednesday afternoon, and Edna Ferber came home from shopping with bunches of jonquils and new candles, "tall, thin, greasy looking dark blue ones," for her pewter candlesticks. The yellow blossoms, arranged so prettily on a table in the parlor, gave her an idea. Why not invite Aleck Woollcott for cocktails and a candlelit meal? That evening, with her mother out for dinner and the opera, she would be alone. Company would give her an opportunity to dress for dinner. But when she telephoned, there was no answer.

Disappointed, she scribbled a note to Woollcott instead. Daffodils and beautiful candles helped to banish the wintry gloom, she said, but he of course was the one she had really wanted to see. Too bad, although they'd probably have quarreled.

Alexander Woollcott and Bunny Wilson came from the same hometown, Red Bank, New Jersey. Not only that, but Bunny's maternal grandfather, a homeopathic physician, had delivered Aleck. This coincidence, however, did not alter Bunny's view of Aleck as a "disagreeable" fellow with an "uncomfortable" personality.

It was just as well because had Aleck been a little more agreeable— a little less uncomfortable—Edna might have fallen in love. (Aleck, a bachelor, was evidently still a virgin because, he said, a case of mumps had left him sexually impotent, but some people didn't quite believe it.) Edna met him through Frank Adams (the two men served together during the war on the Army newspaper the *Stars and Stripes*) and liked him at once, even though Aleck was extremely high-strung and they were often at odds. Soft and pudgy, wearing owlish spectacles, he walked like a tubby auntie, a "New Jersey Nero" in a pinafore, Edna teased. He hated exercise and sports (except croquet) and favored fatty, creamy food washed down with more than forty cups of coffee a day, habits that caused a physical-fitness zealot like Edna to shudder.

Most of the time she managed to forgive his irritability. She delighted in shopping for gifts of brocade lounging robes and dreaming up playful pet names, her favorite being "Amoeba." Making puns on his surname, with its double o's, l's, and t's, which people invariably misspelled, she mailed letters to his *Times* office addressed to "Mr. Aaron Woolstein." Or "Wormstock," or a half-dozen other aliases. Herself she signed as "E. Feldman," sometimes "Fannie Hurts." (Fannie Hurst was a rival novelist.)

Now in his mid-thirties, one of the best-known people in the country, Woollcott was the Zeus of Broadway critics. In his cape and opera hat, he was a standard fixture in the city's playhouses. The romance of opening nights never ceased to thrill Edna, and she eagerly accepted his invitations to dress up and join him on the aisle. The price she paid was that after the performance, when she wanted to enjoy an après-theater cocktail, he had to race back to the *Times* to write his review. It was annoying to be dumped into a taxi and sent home.

Aleck appeared to be a lovable butterball on first-name terms with the rich and famous, but he could also be a backbiting gossip full of cruel barbs. Unfortunately, it was hard to predict which Aleck would pop up. There was the time Edna planned a formal dinner at the Coffee House on West Forty-fifth in honor of her sister Fannie, visiting from Chicago. She went to great lengths to make sure Aleck would be free. The hour was specifically set for 7:30. Aleck, however, made an entrance forty-five minutes late. Chugging up the narrow staircase, he shrugged off his tardiness. A delay at a cocktail party, he said.

She was burning. The dinner was ruined.

Don't be ridiculous, he said. She didn't have to wait on him.

A week later they continued to feud. Aleck refused to apologize. He had done nothing wrong. It was she who, in his opinion, was unreasonable and really ought to snap out of it.

She called him "rude," "inconsiderate," and "unkind."

He had no idea what she was talking about.

Did she mention that she hated him? In fact, she could tell him precisely how she felt: "utterly bewildered and disappointed, and sorry, and sick."

Tardiness was not a terrible crime.

"Don't think that I didn't hug to myself the idea of a friendship with you," she told him. "I did."

A couple of weeks later, still not ready to drop the squabble, she began to soften and found it "harder and harder to work up my daily hate toward you."

It took her months to get over it; in fact, she kept Aleck in the doghouse until he sent a peace offering, a letter from France containing the dearest pressed flower. She replied, all business, that she planned to save his letter, not from sentiment, but as a financial investment. Who knew? It might be a collector's item someday.

. . .

IN A LATIN QUARTER CAFÉ Vincent met a striking man with a reddish beard. Unable to help herself, she "breathlessly and ruthlessly" turned her back on the man who introduced them (one of her lovers) and promptly transferred her attention to George Slocombe, special correspondent for London's *Daily Herald*. With his beard and tawny coloring, George presented a lordly figure not unlike a character from a historical novel. Looking as if he should be mounted on horseback, always seen in a wide black hat and spiffy ascot, Slocombe exuded testosterone. His smile revealed two missing teeth, lost in the war, he explained. Only twenty-seven, Slocombe was a well-known journalist who covered front-page news of international politics and had just managed to obtain an important interview with Mussolini.

From the first day Vincent and George were inseparable. It was a fine spring, and they took walks through the Bois de Boulogne, she talking of Maine and her mother, he looking adoringly at her, admiring her knees, and calling her sweet nicknames. Not surprisingly, George was accustomed to getting his way. He was a demanding lover who wanted his women on call—his job was important. But he also went out of his way to make sure Vincent lacked for nothing. By May she had begun wearing expensive dresses and had moved to a nice hotel on rue de l'Université. It wasn't long before they were making plans to be married. They might live in France, or move back to England, whatever he wished, and she would have babies, of course.

In the meantime, George was wrestling with a painful problem: how he could get a divorce when he had a wife and three children in the suburbs. To Vincent, in love, a father walking out on his family was distressing but surely not the end of the world.

VINCENT HAD NOT seen her own father in ten years. A few days before leaving New York, she received a letter, however. Someone had just told him she was going to France to be a foreign correspondent, he wrote. Certainly he could vouch that she would be "a great success at work of that kind," but the job did strike him as "a big undertaking for such a little girl." Most of the letter, however, concerned his fear of missing the next mail pickup.

If Henry Millay appeared to forget that his daughter had grown up, that was understandable. Vincent was seven years old when drinking and gambling led to his banishment from her life. They were living in the farm village of Union, Maine, before they moved to Camden, in a white frame house next door to the common. Vincent remembered seeing him walk away, taking the shortcut to the train station, down through the cranberry marsh, after her mother warned him to "go and not come back." For the children's sake, Cora tried to cushion the blow by saying that their father could return if he would "do better," although she never wanted to lay eyes on him again.

No doubt relieved to escape Cora's rage, Henry made sure he did not do better. After moving to a small town in north-central Maine, he worked for the Northwestern Mutual Life Insurance Company. He lived a bachelor's existence in rooming houses and hotels and turned into a ghost father, vaguely remembered but unmissed. Every so often, when Cora found herself unusually hard up, all three girls wrote him pleading letters, and then the ghost would slip a five-dollar bill into an envelope, asking for confirmation of its arrival because he worried about postal thieves. When her father died in 1935, Vincent confessed regret for the "hundred other false and rotten things" she had said about him. His death left her "terribly upset," even though probably nobody would believe it "because I can't bear to show my feelings in front of people."

The distance between Camden and the piney woods of Kingman— 140 miles—was more than geographic. It may have been a bad marriage, but Cora did her best to kill it.

WHEN BUNNY ARRIVED in Paris that summer, he hoped and prayed that he was over Vincent. In the past six months she had written him only one letter. It contained a poem ("Nuit Blanche") and an apology for mistreating him. Since this was small consolation for his suffering, and since she continued to call him "poor Bunny," it was clear where he stood. At home he'd begun seeing an actress, a woman who respected him, and felt the relationship growing serious.

Vincent, however, continued to exert an irresistible pull, and no sooner had he put down his bags at a pension near her hotel than he scooted around the corner to see her. The elegance of her hotel was unexpected, and so was her manner. It was as if a stage had been set for his visit, he thought, stepping into her room. Surrounded by tidy piles of manuscripts, she was seated at her typewriter and greeted him aloofly without rising. Looking older, more mature, she was outfitted in a decorous black dress, the kind of garment usually seen on Sunday-school teachers, that seemed to have been carefully selected to create an earnest impression. Soon, however, she relaxed, and they began chatting nostalgically about *Vanity Fair,* as well as Bunny's departure for a job at *The New Republic.*

After a short while, though, Vincent was eager to shift the conversation to herself. She had great news, a secret, but knew she could trust him. She had fallen in love, she confided. She was going to marry and live in England, and they hoped to start a family. Love had transformed her. No longer was she the devil-may-care good-time girl famous for breaking hearts. She had been younger then. Couldn't he see that she had become a different person?

Astounded, Bunny took all this in without comment. As luck would have it, Vincent went on to say, there was an unpleasant complication—her fiancé was married and had a family living nearby in Saint-Cloud. Knowing that she had wrecked a home was sad, she said, but this was real love, and George was just going to have to work it out as best he could. She sounded genuinely happy. Now that she belonged to George, everything would be taken care of.

Belonged to George? Bunny couldn't ever remember Vincent's wanting to belong to anybody. He could hardly imagine this new compliant woman who did as she was told. Obviously George was the one defining the terms of their relationship.

Continuing to meet Vincent over the next week or so, Bunny realized that she was taking no chances by cautiously describing him to George as an old friend from home. Apparently he was a jealous old-fashioned man who would not tolerate any foolishness. For that reason, Bunny was puzzled to hear her propose, while walking in the Bois one day, that they tour the south of France together. Did she suddenly care about him? He thought not. She would turn her back on him the first time she ran across a man more sexually attractive. And what about George? Making excuses, Bunny said he had other plans—his girlfriend from New York was joining him—and wished her luck. He did offer to bail her out *if ever* she ran into financial trouble. *If ever* that should happen, she certainly would, she said. A few weeks later he received a letter, postmarked Dieppe, reminding him of his offer. *If ever* had just come. Could he spare six hundred francs? Vincent was to be pitied, he told himself.

But he also continued to worry that she might "throw bombs into my soul." Being around her was like leaning into "the crater of an extinct volcano," thrilling but dangerous, because it might erupt at any second.

IN NEW YORK, Zelda's apartment on Central Park South reeked of cigarette smoke and stale alcohol. In the living room, white rings embossed the veneer of the table tops, and the kitchenette was piled with empty bottles and trays of dirty plates belonging to the Plaza. The closets hid piles of unwashed shirts. Scott's disapproving friends whispered it was entirely Zelda's fault that the place had turned into a sty. She was oblivious, though. What in the world could she do to kill time, she would groan. "A little housework," thought one visitor.

Living out of suitcases and ordering meals from room service made it difficult to organize a proper household, but even so Zelda couldn't be bothered with mundane tasks such as dusting. After nine months of marriage she loved nothing better than parties and speakeasies, and of course shopping. She had the most glamorous dancing dresses, one with diaphanous panels of Scheherazade froth in the palest shade of pink, another a glittery silver gown, slinky and theatrical. Who cared if her apartment was a wreck? She always stepped out the door knowing that she looked gorgeous.

Scott, however, was not feeling quite so happy. For a few months he had been soaring above the spires of the venerable house of Scribner, wheeled on high by a hurricane of success. Without warning, however, the wind died down, and he plummeted to earth with a rather nasty thud. He naturally assumed that once the literary capital of the world bestowed love, it would last forever, like being knighted, but New York was turning out to be remarkably fickle.

A T A PARTY on 105th Street the previous fall, a red-haired drunk lurched up to the editors of *The Smart Set* and draped his arms familiarly around their necks. So they were critics, Sinclair Lewis declared to Henry Mencken and George Jean Nathan. Well, he was the greatest writer in the goddamned country, and his new book was the best damned novel they'd ever read. When Lewis began addressing the editors as "Hank" and "Georgie," they made a quick beeline for the street.

"Can you imagine such a jackass writing a book worth reading?" Mencken said indignantly to Nathan. The man was an idiot.

The next day on the train going back home to Baltimore, Mencken began reading a set of review proofs from Harcourt, Brace. Superficially, it was the story of an intelligent woman who marries a dull man—what could be more clichéd?—and moves to her husband's small town, but the novel was also about the town itself and what happens when Carol Kennicott attempts to cultivate the boors of Gopher Prairie. It looked as if Don Quixote, reincarnated as a tightly strung library-science graduate, was tilting at windmills on the main streets and back roads of America. When the train pulled into Philadelphia, Mencken called a Western Union boy and sent a telegram to Nathan. Grab the nearest bar rail and brace for a shock, he warned, because "that idiot has written a masterpiece."

Sinclair Lewis's five previous novels never quite clicked with readers. So who could have predicted that his sixth would sell a stupendous 295,000 copies during its first year? Promptly heralded as the book of the year, if not the decade, *Main Street* caused some to conclude there would be no surpassing it, and Bunny Wilson believed it easily "the best of modern American novels."

For Scott, who had trouble understanding the economics of publishing, releasing a first novel the same year as *Main Street* was unfortunate timing. Having outstripped Scribner's underestimation of his sales, he continued to believe himself the exception to the rules and expected the money to keep rolling in. (In reality, *This Side of Paradise* sold seventy-five thousand copies and never made *Publishers Weekly's* bestseller list, which in 1920 and 1921 was dominated by Lewis and Zane Grey.) Watching reviewers slather Lewis with adoration made Scott extremely unhappy, naturally. He did an excellent job of pretending not to mind and sent respectful congratulations to the fellow Minnesotan who had generously praised him as "the equal of any young European" author.

With sales of *This Side of Paradise* just better than respectable, Scott hurried to finish *The Flight of the Rocket*. In his second novel, a character study of a man warped by the promise of inherited millions, Scott divided himself into two individuals—weak, talentless Anthony Patch (Scott living beyond his means) and Richard Caramel (the creative Scott publishing a "highly original, rather overwritten" bestseller). By winter he had revised the first draft and turned it over to Bunny for editing. At first the story struck Bunny as "rather silly" because it seemed to be a literal account of Scott and Zelda, during their summer in Westport, fighting and acting tiresome. But further reading revealed unexpected maturity and emotional power.

Completion of *The Beautiful and Damned*, as it was retitled, came at the right time as Scott and Zelda found themselves in serious financial trouble. In 1920 he had earned approximately $21,000 from books, short stories, and movie options (which had the purchasing power of $200,000 in current dollars). Although this was a fortune compared with the previous year, when his income had been exactly $879, neither of them understood how to handle money, and everything quickly evaporated. But then serial rights to the novel fetched seven thousand dollars from *Metropolitan Magazine*, and they had money galore. The future, they happily decided, had a way of taking care of itself.

In February, Zelda discovered she was pregnant, which required her to think differently about the future, worry about losing her figure, dread the horrible pain of childbirth, and consider how she would take care of another human being. She wasn't really happy about the baby, but she wasn't unhappy either. For months she had been joking with Scott about the difference between good babies and bad babies. A good baby would have Scott's eyes and her mouth, a bad baby her legs and Scott's hair. Her husband, emotionally an adolescent, hadn't a bit of interest in good or bad babies. Neither in her heart did she, at least not at this time. But efforts to avoid pregnancy—if any—had failed to work.

The first plan they made after the sale to *Metropolitan* was to travel abroad. It was the popular thing to do these days, and many of their friends had already made the tour. Now, while they had no responsibilities, they could take advantage of the favorable exchange rate against the dollar and get a bargain tour of Europe, starting in England, where *This Side of Paradise* was just being published. When the *Aquitania* docked at Southampton in the second week of May, Zelda was feeling queasy but determined to enjoy four or five months of leisurely travel.

London treated the Fitzgeralds like movie stars. Yellow-haired Zelda wearing her squirrel coat and yellow-haired Scott swinging his silver-headed walking stick—looking like a pair of daffodils—cut amusing figures for the British. There was no shortage of invitations to drink champagne with a polo team, or to lunch with Lady Randolph Spencer Churchill and her son Winston at Hyde Park and dine on strawberries the size of tomatoes. One night a friend of Scott's from prep school offered to take them slumming on East London's waterfront, the kind of adventure that Zelda relished. She disguised herself in a tweed cap and men's trousers and went off to Wapping hoping to see a few pickpockets.

A good deal less interesting was a formal dinner, in Hampstead, at the home of John Galsworthy. Parties with a bunch of old guys failed to stir Zelda's enthusiasm, but Max Perkins had specially arranged for them to pay their respects to the author of the Forsyte chronicles. In the company of the eminent Nobelist and some of his friends, Scott went haywire. Introduced sometime earlier to the patrician Edith Wharton in the Scribner office, he had overreacted and knelt at her feet. With Galsworthy he committed a similar faux pas and began gushing like a schoolboy, perhaps thinking his host expected to be buttered up. But his moronic theatrics made for a tense evening.

From London they headed across the Channel, only to discover that the French had never heard of Scott Fitzgerald. Without friends in Paris to keep them busy—no polo or society teas organized in their honor—the excitement of the trip quickly began to wear thin. Guidebook in hand, they fell back on the standard sight-seeing; they rubbernecked at the Folies Bergère and shopped for souvenirs like ordinary tourists. Setting off for Italy by train, they stopped in Venice at the Royal Danieli and strolled around Piazza San Marco; in Rome they toured the Forum and the Colosseum. Unfortunately, museums and ruins left them cold, just as they took no interest in knowing the people (or in learning French or Italian). Scott wrote to Bunny in disgust that Europe felt like a big antiques shop and France, in particular, made him ill. It was hard to imagine a duller place. But it was not only Europe that aggravated him, because, more to the point, he and Zelda were getting on each other's nerves.

She blamed him for drinking.

No, no, he said. It was she who never stopped whining.

After barely eight weeks they decided to call it quits. However, months of first-class hotels—in fact, a failure to economize in any fashion—had depleted their funds. To cover their passages from Liverpool, Scott was obliged to wire his agent, Harold Ober, for a thousand dollars. For most of the trip Zelda had battled fatigue and the queasiness of morning sickness. She was not sorry to sail for home in early July.

. . .

IN THE MIDDLE of July, George Slocombe told Vincent that he could not marry her after all. He could not even continue to see her. The reason, he explained in a letter, was that "I love you too much." Should they marry, he would inevitably try to dominate her, and, he predicted, she could never be happy living in subjection to a spouse. And then there was his family. Leaving them would be dishonorable.

What must have happened was clear to Vincent: George's wife finally learned about her. Before the war he had married a Russian woman, the daughter of a prominent attorney who was *homme d'affaires* of the grand duke Michael. By this time Marie Karlinskaya had grown accustomed to her husband's philandering—Vincent was not his first mistress—and felt disinclined to step aside for another woman. But, more likely, George himself must have realized that he was about to make an enormous mistake. He needed a wife who would run his household and look after the children while he covered the big public-policy stories and came home whenever he pleased, which was exactly the situation he already had.

As soon as Vincent received George's letter, she fled Paris by joining some people she knew who were going to the seashore. On the beach in Dieppe she lay in shock and stared at the water full of bathers having a good time. Writing to her sister Kay, she admitted being in bad shape, without saying what had happened to her. She felt knocked out, upside down and inside out, "all shot to pieces." Despite four-mile walks, she had not managed "a natural movement of the bowels for over six weeks" and now had to depend on laxatives. If she could only get a plain slice of toast, instead of the awful half-baked bread and coffee without cream, she'd be just fine. Unlike other Americans rhapsodizing over fantastic edibles for pennies, the escargot, the *gâteau maison* drenched with marsala, Vincent turned up her nose at French food. Kay was left with the impression that Vincent's pain was physical, not emotional.

At Dieppe, in a fog of grief, she recovered by hardening her heart. Hiding away her only picture of George, a passport photo showing him young and clean-shaven, she composed a lamentation for the dead. In

"Keen" she drowned her feelings. The words were carefully chosen. An idyll "sweet" for a month, she wrote, would eventually dissolve into a "harsh and slovenly" domestic sewer.

Vincent knew that her mother worried about her. In letters, careful to censor her bad luck, financial as well as romantic, Vincent always seemed to be working like the devil or traveling here and there. That summer, owing to unforeseen disaster, her letters home had been sparse. What she finally did send Cora was a poem, one of the few completed since her arrival in France, with instructions to show it to Kay and Norma.

With its simple Mother Goose rhythms, "The Ballad of the Harp-Weaver" brought to mind Clement Moore's " 'Twas the Night before Christmas." But Vincent's poem was not about Santa carrying toys down the chimney, nor were there parents in kerchief and nightcap. A son relating the death of his mother remembers crying himself to sleep, cold and hungry, while she weaves golden and scarlet threads on the strings of a harp. On Christmas morning he awakes to find her sitting there frozen, surrounded by piles of clothing fit for a prince. To Cora, the poet's self-sacrificing mother, who had eked out a living as caretaker for the dying and weaver of hairpieces for the living, the poem was profoundly disturbing.

The ballad depicted not just the outlines of Cora's struggle—certainly nothing was made explicit—but her ideas, her experiences, the essence of her being. It was piracy so surprising that she was incapable of replying for three months. Kay, always alert to shady motives in her sister, was aghast. "I cried when I got that poem," she said afterward, thinking Vincent had no right to use such painful family experiences and pass them off as her own. "Years of hard filthy labor on her part—and you get the Pulitzer Prize for such a pretty song you made of it."

That summer Cora was busy trying to become a professional writer while living in a house Kay rented for her in Morris County, New Jersey. After Vincent left, she used family connections to contact the agency handling her daughter's plays. She had already published a few verses in *Maine Farmer,* among the regular verse about Grandpa's pumpkin patch, but hoped to branch out into fiction for major magazines. Encouraged by the interest of the American Play Company, she was preparing several stories for submission to *Pictorial Review.* All of Cora's stories were rejected, however, partly because of her rural subjects and rustic dialect, partly because she was not much of a writer.

Weeks and then months went by before Vincent concluded that "The Ballad of the Harp-Weaver" had been lost in the mail and sent another copy. At last her mother answered by politely saying that she had passed along the "wonderful" poem to Kay and Non, who had loved it. Kay, in fact, did not love it. Embarrassed, she refused to show the poem to her husband. (Another person who disliked it was Bunny, who thought it belonged in a ladies' magazine.)

While Vincent took care to conceal her unhappiness from her family, one person knew more than he wanted to. Arthur Davison Ficke was a well-to-do Harvard-educated poet whose verse, like himself, was charming and intelligent but unfocused. At the time "Renascence" was published in 1912, Arthur and his friend Witter "Hal" Bynner wrote an encouraging note assuring Vincent that she had the makings of an exceptional poet. That was the start of a flirtatious correspondence in which she cast Arthur in the role of literary guru and all-purpose confidant.

The first time Vincent met Arthur was in 1918, when she was living in the Village. He, an Iowa friend of her lover Floyd Dell's, was an Army captain bound for France. "He's exceedingly handsome," she reported to Kathleen, "tall and curly-haired with a lovely voice and oh, my lord, everything!" She was "crazy about him, and he's gone, he's gone, and there's no comfort for me on earth." She began composing passionate sonnets for him. But after that single brief contact in 1918, all further communication took place in letters and verse. Despite her inability to see the man clearly, his deep timidity and insecurity, she never wavered from her initial impression. He would always be the ultimate romantic lover to her, the worshipful muse that no poet could live without.

Now thirty-eight, Arthur lived in Davenport, a family man, a non-practicing attorney in his father's law firm and living on inherited money. In Midwestern literary circles, he cut a dashing figure with his perfectly barbered hair, Savile Row suits, and cordovan shoes. His work tended to be intellectual and juiceless, and despite several books of verse he had never been anything more than a minor poet.

Desperate after the loss of George, Vincent turned to Arthur. For the rest of the summer she bombarded him with long, incoherent letters. She admitted feeling crushed and broken but did not intend to reveal what exactly was causing her anguish—the reason "didn't matter." It was Arthur and Arthur alone she desired. They had spent so little time together, she chided, as if he did not have a life in Davenport with his wife, Evelyn, and nine-year-old son, Stanhope. Why on earth couldn't he join her?

Judging by Arthur's replies, maddeningly lighthearted, he wasn't taking her rebukes a bit seriously. A jaunt to Paris would be impossible, he said, and "I don't know if I'd come if I could." He wondered if they could "bear each other for more than one hour and forty minutes talk every fourth year: that's all we ever had." Was she really a nice person? "I'm not!" Having been exposed to a tiny dose of the Millay family angst, he must have been secretly petrified by the intensity of Vincent's emotion, because he had successfully managed to avoid her for four years.

However, the real reason for Arthur's reluctance would have surprised Vincent. Only a few weeks after she left for Paris, he began having an affair with a young woman from New York, Gladys Brown. By this time he had taken to writing love poems for his "dirty little Gladys," signing his letters "Artiemouse" with phallic drawings of fat mice wagging long wiggly tails. Although Vincent remained unaware of the girlfriend, Gladys knew everything about her. The devious Arthur assured Gladys that he and Vincent "never have, and never could, be anything to each other." Just the same, he intended to keep Gladys's existence a secret from Vincent.

. . .

DOTTIE'S FAVORITE SPEAKEASY was shielded away on the street floor of a brownstone on West Forty-ninth. Its locked door with the requisite peephole was hidden behind an iron grille; its windows were shuttered against the daylight. Inside Tony Soma's were checkered tablecloths, heavy white coffee cups, and a bar running the length of one wall. Night or day, the air smelled of fried steak and whiskey. Establishments such as Tony's remained open until the last customer left—the beauty of being illegal.

One evening in July, the same Saturday that Jack Dempsey knocked out Georges Charpentier in the fourth round in Jersey City, Dottie was sitting in Tony's with Bob Benchley. Bob disapproved of drinking and, at thirty-two, had never tasted a drink. A "White Ribboner" who had taken the pledge, he had become the worst sort of prig. On this particular night he finally gave in to friends who said he should sample booze before condemning it. He ordered an orange blossom. After a few sips he turned to Dottie.

"This place should be closed down," he said. He emptied the glass and ordered another.

As the wife of a drinker, Dottie knew all about the domestic hell caused by alcohol. Most mornings Eddie stumbled off to work at Paine Webber, unless he happened to be on a binge, in which case she would call his office and lie for him. Five years earlier he had been fun, but the war left him a sick man. One time she came home, smelled gas, and had to pull his head out of the oven. They rarely shared a meal at home, Dottie insisting that saucepans were a mystery to her. In truth, it had nothing to do with saucepans. Eddie no longer seemed eager to be with her, and so she would seek company across the hall at the studio of Neysa McMein, the fashion-magazine illustrator.

Personally, Dottie disliked the taste of liquor, but everybody was going to speakeasies. People such as Mr. Benchley who had never tasted alcohol were ordering three or four drinks, and those who had been polishing off three were up to six. Dottie's childhood friend Heywood Broun carried a bar with him, whipping out a silver hip flask of home-brewed gin from a pocket of his rumpled suit. At first she drank Tom

Collinses and pink ladies, the cloying cocktails popular with women, then moved on to whiskey sours, sidecars, Manhattans, and eventually martinis. It was funny how much she loathed the taste of gin—and how quickly she had learned to love dry martinis. After sampling most of the bar, she discovered scotch.

Of course, the problem with getting tight was the mornings. Dottie's hangovers sometimes were not cured until noon. Although she had no office hours to worry about, she did have plenty of magazine assignments. Partly from hangovers, but partly from boredom, she became increasingly unreliable about deadlines and sometimes blamed Eddie. "My husband has had an attack of appendicitis," she told the *Saturday Evening Post*. When she submitted a humorous piece on apartment-house living, she warned the publisher that it was "rotten," in fact "too poisonous." Accustomed to her excuses, the famed and feared George Horace Lorimer agreed that the piece wasn't her best work, but "it's really not so rotten." And by the way, in future please submit the "short stuff" she was selling to *Life*.

AFTER SEVEN MONTHS away from New York, including a trip to her favorite summer vacation spot in Colorado, Edna was happy to be back. Despite her scorn for writers who lunched, she was curious about the Algonquin Round Table and asked Aleck if she might visit. Afterward she continued to show up occasionally, usually on Saturdays, invariably hatted, veiled, and dressed in a fashionable outfit.

Aleck noticed her tailored suit one day. "Why, Ednaaaa," he said, "you almost look like a man."

"So do you," she replied sweetly.

That fall saw the publication of *The Girls*, the book that had given her so much grief the previous year. It was her second novel, and the first with her new publisher, Doubleday, Page. *The Girls* is about three generations of a Chicago family: seventy-four-year-old Charlotte; thirty-two-year-old Lottie, the catalyst; and eighteen-year-old Charley, who studies business at the University of Chicago. All three women—the "girls" of the title—are unmarried. Like their author, by choice, not chance. While eager to distance herself from the organized suffragists, Edna had a lot to say about the subject of woman's rights. She considered herself a crusader on behalf of women who could take care of themselves, progressive women like herself. What could be more subversive than a story glorifying successful modern women who don't need men to be happy?

On the other hand, what could be more dreary? Edna's keen ear for storytelling warned her that the bare-bones plot, with its stereotypical images, might sound boring to readers, so she confronted the problem squarely on the opening page: "A story about old maids! You are right. It is." But the Thrift "girls" were no reclusive Miss Havishams, abandoned at the altar. Neither were they swans or ugly ducklings, only average women. During the war the straitlaced Lottie travels to France, where she has an affair with an American journalist and becomes pregnant. The lover is killed and, faced with aborting or giving up the newborn, she decides to do neither and comes home cradling a baby girl.

The story of an old maid and a baby out of wedlock may have been the subconscious regrets of an unmarried novelist, but with her next novel, when she again took up the subject of motherhood, Edna had quite a different tale to spin.

Given the novel's unorthodox ending, serialization of *The Girls* had proved difficult, and some magazines demanded a new ending. Finally, though, *Woman's Home Companion* accepted it as written. Henry Mencken praised the writing as her finest. Frank Adams commended her descriptions of Chicago. Even her mother, usually grudging with compliments, allowed it was so-so. But despite hearty drumbeating from friends, Edna was dismayed at the reactions of the literary establishment, whose opinion she most valued. *The Dial*, a highbrow magazine, ripped apart *The Girls* as a "flashily written" novel full of uninteresting details in the lives of three boring women. "Edna Ferber has sold her narrative gift for a mess of mannerisms." In general, critics deemed *The Girls* to be well-imagined storytelling, written in a popular style, but certainly not literature.

The problem was obvious. To command respect, a woman novelist had to be an untouchable like Jane Austen or Edith Wharton, whose book *The Age of Innocence* had just won the Pulitzer Prize. Edna was neither, but she knew what she needed to do: try harder.

She finally agreed to representation by Paul Reynolds, the high-powered agent who had spent the last decade hoping to handle her stories. On the brink of an agreement, she reminded him that they had not discussed his percentage. "I would like to hear from you on it." His request for a cut of all her earnings made her jump on him. "Ten per cent is, undoubtedly, the commission due you on all business transacted by you," she replied. She would gladly pay the standard fee on offers he brought to her. But why should she pay him 10 percent for work she had obtained herself? Five percent would be "fair enough," she said. Within days Edna was bossing Reynolds like a duchess breaking in a new housemaid. A story for *Woman's Home Companion* must be attended to immediately: "Whisk it right over to Miss Lane's office," she ordered. "This afternoon." She could not deliver it herself, because, "as usual, I'm broke." Ferber broke? What about her twenty-four-hundred-dollar story price (twenty-five thousand dollars in today's money)? Reynolds was not about to argue, however.

FRIENDS OF DOTTIE's, Ruth Hale and her husband, Heywood Broun, were hosting their annual New Year's Eve party. It was the biggest they'd thrown, because they had just purchased their first house, across the street from where Dottie had once lived with her father. "A great party and merry as can be," Frank Adams reported. Two hundred of the city's most interesting people packed the brownstone on West Eighty-fifth. Even H. G. Wells showed up. All furniture, except a couple of folding chairs, had been removed for the occasion, and there was no music or food, only a gigantic vat of orange blossoms. Almost lost in the crowd was little Woodie, the pale, thin son of Ruth and Heywood, trained to call his parents by their first names and to conduct himself like an adult.

Of all Dottie's woman friends, Ruth was the most unusual. Fiercely feminist, she wanted to change the world. Ruth was against traditional marriage and motherhood and housekeeping and deference to the male sex. In short, any custom that chained women to the home. But her anger centered on one particular legal issue: this was 1921, and a woman had to give up her name if she married, and a man didn't. Since this state of affairs practically went back to biblical Eden, most women took the situation for granted, but not Ruth. She had refused to take Heywood's name and kept on calling herself Ruth Hale. Continuing her fight, she applied for a passport in her maiden name, but the request was denied. A second application resulted in a document made out to "Mrs. Heywood Broun, otherwise known as Ruth Hale." A personal note from the Secretary of State explained that granting Ruth's request would constitute deception and place American consulates abroad in "a most embarrassing position." Ruth, of course, sent it back.

Dottie was all for equality. Still, she could not work up much enthusiasm for some of Ruth's causes, and neither could their friend Jane Grant. A *New York Times* reporter working in the women's department, Jane was regularly assigned weddings and society news and occasionally what passed for hard news in the ladies' ghetto, the activities of First Lady Mrs. Warren Harding. On Jane's wedding day, however, the rector's secretary happened to address her by her new, married name. Outside the church, her husband said that, frankly, he didn't know if he liked all that "Missus" stuff, and she replied that even the look of the words "Jane Ross" was corny. At the *Times* she followed Ruth's lead and went on using her maiden name.

Jane's new husband, a man who took everything personally, was fond of Dottie but found Ruth annoying. She, and now Jane, too, seemed to believe the oppression of women was all his fault.

"Why don't you two hire a hall?" Harold said, trying to be funny.

To prove inequality was no joke, they made up their minds to found a feminist organization whose goal would be giving women the choice to keep their names. The first meeting of the Lucy Stone League, so named in honor of the nineteenth-century fighter for woman's rights, drew an enthusiastic crowd of reformers to the Pennsylvania Hotel. The group adopted a statement of Lucy Stone's as its slogan: "My name is the symbol of my identity which must not be lost." All this fuss about names cut no ice with Dottie. Personally, she said, the reason she'd married Eddie was to get a nice American name like Parker, and she would rather die than be known as Dottie Rothschild. With her luck, however, she would not be surprised if her obituary read, "Dorothy Rothschild Dies."

On this New Year's Eve, Dottie showed up at Ruth and Heywood's by herself. Her friends took Eddie's absences for granted. He was "a nice quiet boy out of his element," one person decided, but others joked among themselves that she kept Parkie "in the broom closet." Dottie, careful to avoid the subject of her husband, got a drink and began exchanging wisecracks with Frank Adams, who looked like the happiest man in the world. His column the next morning would begin running alongside Heywood's on the opposite editorial page of the up-and-coming *New York World*. Having put away a few orange blossoms, Frank insisted that he loved Dottie more than anybody else there. That was hard to believe because his wife was standing right next to him, never mind the actress in a pink dress he was ogling. Ruth and Heywood liked to follow the old tradition of mounting a chair and jumping into the New Year. On the stroke of midnight, Dottie climbed and jumped along with those other guests still capable of doing so. Later, at five in the morning, the tub of gin and orange juice was empty and not about to be refilled. Upstairs in the quiet brownstone, Woodie Broun had fallen asleep. Minna Adams finally dragged her husband away. But Dottie was still there. What was there to go home to?

1922

Dust jacket for The Beautiful and Damned, *illustrated with Zelda and Scott look-alikes.*

CHAPTER THREE

VIENNA IN WINTER was chilly and overcast without "a shred of sunlight," so Vincent kept the lights on all day. Inside Zwiaver's rooming house, at 7 Floragasse, she was living with Griffin Barry, the American journalist whom she had thrown over for George Slocombe in 1921. Between her and the spurned Griffin remained more rancor than affection, but having him around was convenient because he paid his share of the expenses and it was more cheerful than being alone in a city where she knew nobody.

Luckily, living at Zwiaver's was cheap. The big, comfortable room with heat and electricity, accompanied by breakfast, luncheon, and tea, cost a pittance—$7.50 a month—and her main expenses were dinners and laundry. Even the $7.50 was a hardship, though. In the year since leaving New York, she had produced only one important poem, "The Ballad of the Harp-Weaver," and her creative impulse had dried up. For one thing, she did not anticipate finding herself virtually penniless. Unpredictably, the *Vanity Fair* stories did not begin to cover her expenses, nor had she seen a penny from the publication of her third volume of poetry, *Second April*, which contained several of her best poems ("Ode to Silence," "The Poet and His Book"). At one point she was dismayed to realize that she had fifty-three dollars to her name and owed thousands to various men.

In an effort to bail herself out, she came up with an idea for a novel that she successfully pitched to an up-and-coming publisher, Boni & Liveright, headed by a flamboyant dreamer named Horace Liveright. She explained that *Hardigut* would be a comic allegory about food and sex and, if packaged correctly as a daring work of art, could likely be suppressed on the grounds of obscenity. All this delighted Liveright, who was known for taking chances on unconventional ideas, the more eccentric the better. By fall, she had negotiated a contract with a five-hundred-dollar advance and a delivery date that would permit publication in the fall of 1922.

After the breakup with George Slocombe, she had grown a bit obsessive about Arthur Ficke, who seemed precisely the right sort of man. Throughout the summer and fall, she continued to think about him constantly. Did he ever think of her? she asked him. Couldn't he please leave Davenport for a while and join her in Paris? In response to her tearful letters Arthur never once offered a reproach. "No, dearest, I can't go over to you," he would reply patiently and enclose a check.

In November came a letter, gossipy and humorous as usual. But then he went on to relate how Witter Bynner was visiting him, how they had been talking about her, of course, and how Hal mentioned that he once asked Vincent to marry him, but she never replied to his letter.

What a splendid idea, Art reported saying. He should ask again. So to the letter Hal Bynner appended a casual postscript wondering why she had never responded to his offer.

This was absurd. Vincent had no idea what they were talking about. She had received no such proposal.

Over the years Vincent and Hal seldom had occasion to meet face-to-face, but they did manage to keep up a friendly correspondence. Hal, like Arthur, was a secondary poet. A Harvard graduate, he worked with Lincoln Steffens and Willa Cather at *McClure's Magazine*, where he championed the work of writers such as A. E. Housman and O. Henry. A man of means living on inherited wealth, he was able to indulge his love of Chinese literature and make several trips to China. Just forty, Hal had never married, because he was a homosexual.

That a middle-aged balding man she had not seen since 1913 would suddenly want to marry her was so lacking in credibility that the half-baked idea almost sounded believable. With each passing day she became more enthusiastic. The plain fact was both of her sisters were married, Norma recently to Charles Ellis, and she remained an old maid. There was no reason, she told herself, why she and Hal should not lead a perfectly contented life. He was hugely rich, manly enough in appearance, and in a way she did love him. Not as she loved Art, of course, but there were different kinds of love.

Several weeks passed without another word from Hal. By Christmas, patience thinning, she had written to him. Did he really want to marry her? She would love to marry him. Having known each other for so many years, perhaps they were fated to wind up together, her letter went. Would he please come to Europe and see her? "You will let me hear from you at once, Hal, won't you?"

Transatlantic mail was slow, and so a week later she wired her acceptance. The week after that, a bit frantic, she sent a one-word cable: "Yes." Meantime, she could not resist leaking the news to her sister. She was "sort of engaged," she confided to Kay, but couldn't mention the man's name, because possibly they would change their minds. Everything would be settled when they saw each other in the spring.

Shortly after the first of the year, with still no word from Hal, she heard from Arthur once more. In this letter, out of the blue, he explained that he had recently become involved in a "light" love affair, a completely meaningless fling, with a girl in New York. (They had been seeing each other for almost a year, but he was careful to edit the particulars.) Alas, the romance had not remained insignificant, because Gladys Brown, a girl from a good family, was not a person to be trifled with and dropped. Naturally, Gladdie wished to be married. To abandon her would be caddish.

Putting on a good show, Vincent pretended to know all about the affair, not specifics of course, and insisted that she had sensed someone else for months. It didn't matter, though. He could fall in love as often as he pleased. Girlfriends had "nothing at all to do with You and Me." She planned to marry Hal but wanted him to know that nobody could take his place because "we sit in each other's souls." In reality, she was stunned. Arthur was the unavailable married man whose wife would never grant a divorce. Lo and behold, some cunning little girl had figured out how to entrap him. For this Gladys person he was going to duck out on his marriage, something he had allowed Vincent to believe was impossible.

Finally, in early February, Hal's letter arrived, but certainly not the one for which Vincent had been waiting. He expressed surprise that she had made something out of nothing, taking the scheme seriously when it was only a vague possibility at best. What happened was this: he and Artie had been joking around, and, to be honest, he expected her to laugh, too. In theory it was a sensible idea, he supposed, because they had known each other for a long time. But, he went on to say, he was "a coward." Good heavens, it was incredible how easily a simple jest got blown out of proportion.

Never had she heard of anything quite like this. "Oh, Lord—oh, Lord—Oh, *Hal!*" she replied "apoplectically." She felt like wringing his neck. "The thought of you hits me on the head like a piece of lead pipe."

Never in her life had she felt so low, the sort of despair that made her want to hide under the bed. She had foolishly fallen for the dirty trick. As for Arthur, who had cooked up this nightmare, who had also betrayed her with another woman, she stifled criticism. (She refused to acknowledge the girlfriend.) Possibly his affair would come to nothing. In such circumstances men have been known to change their minds.

What a comedy of errors. Mortified, she did her best to be a good sport and laugh off her outrage as if nothing had happened. Poor fellow, she wrote Hal, those silly letters and wires of hers must have scared him to death. Surely, he hadn't taken her seriously.

ST. PAUL WAS DEAD as hell, Scott liked to say. It was also brutally cold with the temperatures plummeting to eighteen degrees below zero. Twenty winters in the South had not prepared Zelda for her husband's hometown. On Goodrich Avenue, in a leased house, with a nurse to mind the baby, she was still struggling to shed the pounds she had gained during pregnancy. Scott, claiming inability to work around a squalling infant, rented an office downtown. Instead of his usual bread-and-butter short stories, he began writing a satiric comedy about a clerk who gets drunk and imagines himself elected President. Scott was obsessed with the idea of becoming a playwright, and his months of tinkering with *Gabriel's Trombone* would mean writing off 1921 as a bad year in which he produced practically no new fiction.

What depressed Zelda more than the weather was Scott's disinterest in Scottie, now five months old. Her crying made him nervous, and her need for everyone's attention made him jealous. He was the first to admit his resentment, which he used as the basis for a short story about a father who sees his two-year-old daughter as an interloper in the relationship between himself and his wife. Therefore, when Zelda got pregnant that winter, it was not happy news. Given Scott's attitude, she could not bring herself to bear another child.

By early March, when they traveled to New York for publication of *The Beautiful and Damned*, Zelda had become determined to get an abortion. When friends arrived at the Plaza, she appeared distracted and didn't bother to hide her bad mood. Sore at Scott, she complained in front of company about his indifference to their baby left behind in St. Paul. The tension was obvious to Bunny. Not only was her "old jazz" missing, but so was her once-stylish appearance. She had not got her figure back, causing Bunny to describe her as "matronly and rather fat."

Zelda made an appointment to obtain abortion pills, a decision that disturbed Scott more than he let on. And that she took care of this business in such a matter-of-fact way—she wasted no time on tears—angered him even further. Eventually he would write in his notebook that she flushed his son down the toilet of the Plaza Hotel in cold blood. Scott, however, was back in the literary limelight, and his mind was on publication celebrations. In his expectations, the new novel was bound to generate the same kind of electricity, praise, and sales as his debut book. It took him a week or two to understand that his first success might not be so easily repeated. Furthermore, he was shocked to find hostile critics lying in wait to do a hatchet job.

Technically, *The Beautiful and Damned* was more polished than *This Side of Paradise,* but a surprising number of influential reviewers felt Scott had made a meal of describing the minutiae of his marriage. Who cared about his headaches with Zelda? What did it matter how she mishandled his dirty laundry? Among the detractors was *The Bookman's* Burton Rascoe, who pronounced the novel banal and "blubberingly sentimental" and its author a promising talent who had failed to mature in three years but now apparently took himself "seriously as a thinker." Bunny, who had liked the book on first reading, was sour, too. He gave Scott credit for possessing the gift of incredible expression but said he lacked intellectual control of his imagination. Frank Adams, reading on the train from New Haven, claimed he fell asleep over the book.

Perhaps the most interesting review was Zelda's, who wrote about *The Beautiful and Damned* for the *New York Tribune.* The book was "absolutely perfect," she said in "Friend Husband's Latest," and Gloria Patch's character "most amusing." Anybody buying the book would do her a favor, because it meant a platinum ring and the "cutest" cloth-of-gold gown costing only three hundred dollars. However, she was surprised to recognize passages from an old diary of hers that had mysteriously disappeared, not to mention scraps of letters that also looked vaguely familiar. The author, she went on, apparently figured "plagiarism begins at home."

Her cheeky tone was meant to be amusing. Who could have imagined it was true?

Zelda did not blame readers for thinking the book was a roman à clef, not when the jacket illustration showed a smart young couple who looked exactly like the author and his wife. She of course was less than thrilled with her fictional counterpart, because Scott had turned her into a spoiled, selfish, one-dimensional bitch. But more disturbing was the use he had made of her writing. Once undeniably happy to be his muse, she had changed her mind. For a person who never picked up a pencil, except to write letters, her life story, her view of the world, kept finding its way into books and magazines, just as if she were a writer herself. Scott had dumped verbatim her diaries and letters, one three-page passage actually labeled "The Diary," into his narrative. Exactly how much he rooked was not entirely clear until after publication. Complaints of literary theft seemed the height of foolishness to Scott, who felt justified in using the material. That's what all novelists did, he said, but she was not totally convinced.

Her *Tribune* review, for which she was paid fifteen dollars, the first money she'd ever earned, was nothing more than a stunt. Still, it turned out to have unexpected consequences because she began receiving assignments from other publications, among them *Metropolitan*, the glossy magazine that was a regular market of Scott's. She received fifty-five dollars for "Eulogy on the Flapper," a last hurrah for pioneers such as herself, smart girls who, by applying "business methods to being young," had provided an instructional manual for getting your money's worth out of being female. At the end of the year her earnings added up to nine hundred dollars, not bad at all for a novice.

Their stay in New York petered out in a round of speakeasies and parties. Generally Scott was a happy drunk, eager to be everybody's chum, buying rounds and leaving spectacular tips before passing out.

Once the euphoria dissipated, however, he was liable to turn belligerent. Following one all-night bash he blearily hailed a horse and carriage and pulled up to Bunny's doorstep, wanting him to wake up and come for a spin in the park. Bunny refused. In the harsh light of dawn Scott looked frightening. His face was drained of color, his complexion waxy, his eyes sunk into his head. It reminded Bunny of a John Barrymore deathbed scene. Before returning to a St. Paul winter, Zelda and Scott celebrated their wedding anniversary at the Biltmore. It was hard to believe they had been married only two years.

CORA MILLAY could have killed Vincent's new lover. The Frenchman was a slithery snake, a "dirty panderer," who slunk around like a person with "shit in his breeches." He reminded Cora of somebody, excuse her plain language, who had "pooped at meetin'." In her presence he "slinks like a whipped cur."

To make her mother happy, Vincent had arranged this trip to Paris at considerable trouble. When Cora arrived at Le Havre at the beginning of April, Vincent met the boat and brought her back to the Left Bank, where she had taken lodgings for them in a nice hotel. In the following days they visited all the sights—the top of the Eiffel Tower, Père-Lachaise to see Chopin's tomb, and the Russian ballet at the Opéra. In the evenings they joined friends for dinner at the Rotonde Grill. One night they went to Zelli's, the popular Montmartre club, where Cora, with her gray Buster Brown bob and folksy expressions, caused a minor sensation. A few men even tempted her onto the dance floor.

In an enthusiastic letter to Norma, Vincent reported that "mummie" was having a jolly time, even when low funds had forced their move to a cheaper, and not very clean, hotel near the Luxembourg Gardens. But Cora, indefatigable, visited every church and museum.

There was no mention of the Frenchman, whom Vincent had met shortly after Cora's arrival. One night a perfect stranger walked over to her table in a café and sat down. His background was rather obscure—he had no visible employment—and sometimes, down on his luck, he borrowed money from her. Nevertheless, he was well dressed, well-bred, and very good-looking in a suave sort of way, which even her mother could not deny. (Each of his glances was "almost an orgasm," Cora thought.) Sometimes she and her mother would be sitting in a café when he suddenly appeared at the table and wedged in next to her, pulling her arm and enticing her away. She could tell that Cora was upset, even though she said nothing. Unable to resist, Vincent would wander off and leave her mother sitting stock-still with her head down.

For reasons Vincent failed to comprehend, her mother took an immediate dislike to the Frenchman. Something about his manner or appearance—Cora later told Norma he resembled her former husband—may have bothered her, but even so there was no accounting for the intensity of her hatred. Perhaps she also felt abandoned, but spending every waking minute together was unreasonable, and anyway Cora was accustomed to entertaining herself.

Vincent never did record the Frenchman's name in her letters or diary. Years later, a friend recalled his name might have been Daubigny, but she could not be sure. She did remember him as a genuine layabout, a French fop with an irresistible accent, and that Vincent was smitten with him.

Appearing at the American consulate, Vincent filled out papers and made an affidavit attesting to her citizenship, marital status, and date of birth. In a second document she swore that she had attained her legal majority and therefore was free to marry without parental consent. That was at the end of June.

A T THE BEGINNING of July, Cora made Vincent leave Paris very suddenly. In a threatening letter she warned the "snake-headed fish"—as she termed her daughter's lover—to stay out of her way, undoubtedly describing the consequences if he disobeyed. Vincent had become ill, so badly constipated that not even castor oil helped, and she also suffered a host of other ailments ranging from severe abdominal pain to unexplained fatigue. But Cora soon realized that the real predicament was neither constipation nor anemia. It was morning sickness. As if Vincent's infatuation with the Frenchman were not upsetting enough, now his seed was growing inside her. Cora could not deny that her daughter was "child-like" and "lustful," but this was one time the piper would not be paid. After fifteen years as a practical nurse, she did not hesitate for a minute. What she needed could not be found on the streets of Paris, however.

Within a matter of days the Frenchman disappeared, and the Millays had crossed the Channel and were living in the south of England. The village of Shillingstone, nestled in the middle of the downs, was little more than a clump of thatched-roof cottages along an unpaved road, but their comfortable lodgings had a garden, even a piano. To explain their abrupt move from Paris to Dorset, Cora sent home excuses: Vincent was exhausted from the pressure of the *Vanity Fair* articles; French food disagreed with her; she was having such "a bad time" with her bowels.

Cora first tried to induce a miscarriage by dragging Vincent on twelve-mile hikes, climbing the downs or visiting neighboring villages. But primarily she spent her time scouring the fields for greens—dandelion greens, Vincent called them, but also milk thistle, clover, nettles, pigweed, and many more—all of which she brewed for hours in a big kettle. If Cora's grocery list of herbs sounded like the makings of a vegetarian lunch, they were anything but. To the pot she added herbs such as henbane, gentian, and particularly the blue-flowered alkanet of the Borage family to expel a dead fetus. Eventually the vile-tasting potions did their work.

For the rest of the summer and into the autumn, they remained in Shillingstone. In a nearby field of sheep and cows, Vincent found a straw-carpeted shed, where she retreated to write. At lunchtime Cora appeared with a basket containing a nutritious meal—meat, baked potato, prunes with cream—and waited until she had finished.

Now that Vincent was menstruating again, and with the constipation under control, her health problems should have cleared up. They did not. Vincent looked bloated and suffered from a recurrence of abdominal pain, more severe than ever. After caring for hundreds of patients, some of them leaving in hearses, Cora remained bewildered about the cause of her daughter's problems. But she was experienced enough to know that they might be serious. No amount of castor oil and senna, or scalded milk and brandy—her standard cure-alls—was going to help.

ONE EVENING in July, Dottie came home to find the bed piled with suitcases. What now? The open closet door revealed empty hangers. He was leaving, Eddie said. He was fed up with Paine Webber and going home to Hartford. She was welcome to the dog and the furniture.

The last place Dottie wished to be reminded of was Hartford, where the Parkers, blue-blooded clergymen for more than two hundred years, despised her father's German-Jewish pushcart forebears. While the right ancestors meant nothing to Eddie, no member of his family, or hers, attended their wedding in 1917.

As befitted ladies and gentlemen, neither she nor Eddie publicly acknowledged the separation. Divorce was not mentioned, and Dottie went on calling herself Mrs. Parker, as she would for the rest of her life. To those ill-mannered enough to question Mr. Parker's whereabouts, she treated the expired marriage as she might the death of an aged relative who'd slipped away in his sleep without undue suffering. Friends learned that Eddie had left the city for a new job, in Hartford, of all places. Who in her right mind would want to live in a town like that, where it was too quiet to sleep? The breakup did not surprise anyone.

Shortly after Eddie's departure, Dottie wrote her first short story. For years she had been publishing criticism, features, and poetry, but fiction of course was much different. She had never thought of great matters to write about, either inside or outside herself, and, besides, there was no point trying to turn yourself into a creative writer when you had no ability. But alone in the apartment, feeling empty, she noticed a story beginning to form in her mind. Incapable of writing directly about herself and Eddie, she tunneled into the lives of Bob and Gertrude Benchley. She could not help identifying with poor Mr. Benchley, trapped in Scarsdale with a dull wife, two little boys, and a mortgage on his house and white picket fence. In her story Mr. Wheelock is a suburban husband who commutes into the city each morning on the 8:12, in the same seat, and returns on the 5:17. On weekends he putters in his yard with garden shears and hose while his wife and daughter relax on the porch, a pretty domestic picture. Clipping his hedges one evening, Mr. Wheelock suddenly pauses and looks up at the porch, where Adelaide is sewing on buttons. What would happen if he laid down his shears and walked out the gate? "That would be the last they'd see of him." It is a delicious, terrifying idea. But Mr. Wheelock returns to his clipping, resigned like Mr. Benchley to serving a life sentence. (No, Bob once said, he would never consider divorce, because a man has his wife and that's the end of it.)

Through the summer and fall, Dottie tried teaching herself to write fiction. Frank Adams gave her a book of French poetry and advised sharpening prose by copying the design of the verses. Precision was the trick. When she realized that writing fiction on a typewriter wasn't working so well, she switched to longhand, correcting and tightening each sentence as she went along until she reached the end of a final draft.

There was no commercial market for "Such a Pretty Little Picture" because it was depressing and had no conventional ending, in fact no conclusion at all. It just stopped with Mr. Wheelock continuing to clip. But *The Smart Set* took the story for fifty dollars. Aside from literary quality, the story had gossip value for the initiated, since it was understood to be about Bob Benchley. Encouraged, Dottie would always think of the piece as her best work, high praise for someone who was her own toughest critic.

While struggling over the story, she met a recent discovery of Aleck's who worked on the *New York American*. Everybody adored Charlie MacArthur's company, and Aleck, completely enamored, imagined him to be some elfin storybook character, possibly one of Robin Hood's merry men. He may have been an imp to Aleck, but in reality Charlie was a six-foot, curly-haired, hard-drinking tomcat. Son of an Elmer Gantry–type evangelist, he saw action during the Mexican war and in France with the Rainbow Division. By the age of twenty-seven, a graduate of the hell-raising school of journalism, he, along with his friend Ben Hecht, had become the highest paid reporter in Chicago; later he and Hecht would use their misadventures as the basis for a stage comedy, *The Front Page*.

In New York that summer, estranged from his wife, Charlie was busy cutting a swath through midtown, hopping from bed to bed, claiming to hate the phony, self-conscious city. However, it was the only place to be for an aspiring playwright. "What a perfect world this would be if it were full of MacArthurs," raved Aleck. No kidding, laughed women who knew the score. Neysa McMein, Dottie's neighbor across the hall, presented the charming rascal with a convenience, a rubber stamp that printed "I LOVE YOU."

Being around Aleck's leprechaun, womanizer or not, made Dottie feel better. At his worst, Charlie picked subway fights by recklessly hurling curses ("God damn New Yorker!"), but at his best he was utterly enchanting. He one night pulled up in a taxi to the ASPCA pound carrying boxfuls of birthday cakes for all the lonely yipping dogs, exactly the sort of sensibility that might appeal to a dog maniac like Dottie. How could she resist? Before long, inseparable, they looked fiercely in love to everyone.

The basis of Dottie's relations with Charlie was pure and simple sex—and scotch. As a result, a number of misconceptions arose on both sides. Convinced he was entirely hers, she ignored his wandering eye and put her trust in love. Charlie, swept away in clouds of Chypre, decided that Dottie was a potted plant in need of watering. What he failed to notice was that secreted behind her helpless facade was, as

Ben Hecht put it, "a machine-gun nest capable of mowing down a town."

One day not too many weeks later, Charlie suddenly woke up and saw the artillery. He resumed sleeping with other women. As for Dottie, she realized that Aleck's leprechaun couldn't be trusted after all, which was just about the same time she discovered herself pregnant.

IT WAS TIME to settle down. For the sake of the baby and themselves, Zelda and Scott decided to lay off the booze and lead a quiet life in some pleasant suburb in Westchester or Long Island. Leaving Scottie in St. Paul with the baby nurse, they quietly checked into the Plaza and began contacting real-estate agents.

It was Indian summer in New York, the season Zelda loved best, when the daytimes felt crisp and the twilights veiled the skyline in a curtain of indigo, the air throbbed to the music of Vincent Youmans and Paul Whiteman, and hope seemed boundless after all. To her, the city's roofs looked like "tips of castles rising from the clouds in fairy tales and cigarette advertisements." The shops, stuffed with the choicest goods, catered to customers who needed nothing but spent lavishly because they were bored. After a year in St. Paul, Zelda felt almost like a tourist again. She delighted in the European luxuriance of the hotel lobbies, at the Biltmore, the Plaza, and the St. Regis, the girls waiting for taxis, wearing hats shaped like bathtubs, Charlie Chaplin in a yellow coat.

During the first days back, eager to negotiate a Broadway production for *Gabriel's Trombone*, Scott was preoccupied with business matters. Aside from meeting with theatrical producers, he worked on a story, "Winter Dreams," about a poor boy in love with a rich girl, one of his favorite themes. Having turned over a new leaf, he and Zelda stayed home and went to sleep instead of dashing out to clubs. After several days, however, sensible living turned out to be a lot more boring than they had counted on. To break the tedium, they could not resist telephoning Bunny and telling him to hurry over. They were on the wagon,

Scott announced. Neither he nor Zelda had had one drink since they got there, which came as surprising news to Bunny. He could never remember a time when Scott wasn't drinking.

That's right, Scott repeated. From now on there would be no alcohol, no nightclubs, no jealousy, only work and business.

To Bunny, they certainly did appear to be in good spirits. Zelda was noticeably mellow and mature, Fitz full of energy and sensible plans for their future. And both of them looked to be in dandy physical shape, healthier than he had ever seen them.

Several days after their reunion with Bunny, the Fitzgeralds decided there would be no harm in doing a little entertaining and invited guests for lunch. Sparing no expense, they ordered a main course of lobster croquettes (a trademark dish almost as famous as the Plaza's crispy French rolls and creamy sweet butter) and liquor from a first-class bootlegger. A table was set up facing the park, and a waiter hovered discreetly in the background to pour champagne and mix Bronx cocktails. (A Bronx is a mix of gin, vermouth, and orange juice.)

Their guests for this occasion had been carefully chosen. Sherwood Anderson, author of the much-admired *Winesburg, Ohio,* was an amiable man with curly gray hair and shaggy eyebrows. He turned up wearing a sartorial nightmare, a silk "Liberty" necktie that was not as stylish as it once was. Anderson, who had little respect for Scott, a lightweight writer of trivial subjects in his view, had accepted the invitation out of politeness. The other luncheon guest was John Dos Passos, a shy, balding man of twenty-five who recently published a first novel that Scott reviewed favorably for a St. Paul paper. Out of either awe or suspicion, Dos Passos surveyed the room bug-eyed. (He was wondering if the Fitzgeralds were really staying at the hotel "or whether they hired the suite just for the day to impress their guests.") As it turned out, the men had plenty to chat about, mainly writers' locker-room talk about how their publishers had dropped the ball on promotion.

John, known as Dos, had a long, puffy face that made him look like an "elongated squirrel," Zelda thought, and he suffered from a speech impediment that caused him to lisp slightly. She decided Dos was an odd duck, although kind of cute for a homely man. As lunch went on, however, it became clear that he was extremely straitlaced, a bookish fellow who took himself very seriously indeed. Unable to resist, Zelda began teasing him about his love life, nothing serious, just sociable banter, but he became flustered. His sex life was "nobody's goddamn business," he said stiffly, and got up to stare out the window.

After lunch Anderson immediately excused himself, and the rest of the party squeezed into a chauffeured touring car and headed for Long Island's North Shore. At a real-estate office in Great Neck, a salesman showed them a number of expensive houses, but nothing suitable. So that the outing would not be a complete waste, they decided to pay an unannounced visit to a writer living on East Shore Road overlooking Manhasset Bay. Ring Lardner was a mournful-faced man of thirty-seven, a syndicated sportswriter who managed to earn an annual income of about $100,000, which was why he could afford a Great Neck estate with tennis courts.

To Zelda, Ring looked "embalmed," and to Dos, who had longed to meet him, he was "out on his feet." He may have been the most venerated sportswriter of his generation, but that afternoon Ring was propped against the fireplace in his living room, trying not to fall on his face. His wife, coaxing him to speak, finally gave up. Ring's habit was to stockpile several weeks' worth of columns before embarking on a drinking binge. Normally a man of considerable wit, he was far from himself that afternoon, and after a few whiskeys the visitors took their leave.

On the way back to the city, they passed an amusement park whose colored lights and calliope music were tumbling onto the highway, a rollicking note to an otherwise frustrating day. It was late, and the fairgrounds practically empty, but Zelda insisted they stop. She wanted to ride the Ferris wheel. Grumpy, Scott said he would wait in the car with the driver, and so Dos volunteered to accompany her. With the fields of the North Shore below, and the rickety Ferris wheel tipping lazily through the night, he began talking about himself, how he would like to paint the scene, about memories from his childhood. He never stopped talking until Zelda became bored stiff and tried to change the subject.

Let's get off, he said.

No.

Why not?

Because she didn't want to get off, she said.

Angry, he stopped speaking. To Dos, looking back, Scott's wife had "good looking hair," but she was too outspoken for her own good. As for Scott, he lacked taste. No serious diner would have ordered the croquettes when the Plaza kitchen offered so many superior choices.

When they finally straggled back to the car, Scott was tippling whiskey from a bottle he had hidden under the seat.

A T THE END of September, Zelda moved into a shiny new home in Great Neck Estates, a leafy maze of twisting lanes just off Middle Neck Road. The cream stucco house sitting high on a triangular corner lot had a circular driveway and a smart red-tiled roof. A massive pine tree towered over the front lawn. Zelda called it a "nifty little Babbit home," a reference to Sinclair Lewis's latest bestseller and his real-estate-salesman hero, George F. Babbitt, who sells houses with gleaming tiled kitchens and fireless fireplaces for "more than people could afford to pay." Signing the lease while drunk, always a risky practice, turned out to be fine because 6 Gateway Drive could not have been more cheerful. Looking forward to a settled life at last, she left Scott in charge of hiring servants and an infant nurse and hurried back to St. Paul for little Scottie.

When she stepped off the train with the baby, adorable in her pink coat and bonnet, Zelda found Scott in the company of a nanny so obviously unqualified that she fired her on the spot. During the next weeks her attempts to set up a household resulted in "the wildest confusion," she wrote friends in St. Paul. By wild confusion, she meant screaming brawls. Slowly, she was learning a basic truth about life with an alcoholic. One way or another, when everything was going well, he would find a way to screw up.

For all his plans to spend the winter hard at work, Scott had difficulty adjusting to his new home in a community where temptations abounded. Great Neck was a commuting colony only twenty miles from Manhattan, a convenient forty-five-minute drive by car. But judging by the number of celebrities per square mile, and the number of parties they regularly hosted, it could have been Times Square with boats. So many flashy Broadway types were seen prowling the main street that Middle Neck Road looked to Zelda just like Forty-second Street after dark. A jaundiced Ring Lardner, feeling his town under siege, hated the visiting partygoers and called them riffraff who would turn the place into a "social sewer." But Scott liked the "very drunken town full of intoxicated people"—many of them genuine fourteen-carat celebrities such as Herbert Bayard Swope.

In the end, the fast-living celebrities and the drunken parties were beside the point. For the Fitzgeralds the main trouble with Great Neck was that they could not afford to live there. The total cost of basic expenses—rent, servants, laundress, and nurse—turned out to be almost six hundred dollars (six thousand dollars) a month, and hundreds more went for a country-club membership, theater tickets, hotel bills, restaurants, and a secondhand Rolls-Royce. Since money was Scott's responsibility, Zelda saw no reason why she should worry about economizing. Recently Warner Brothers had paid him twenty-five hundred dollars for movie rights to *The Beautiful and Damned*, and a prominent Broadway producer agreed to option *Gabriel's Trombone*, which was certain to make them "rich forever," Scott kept saying. Altogether that year he earned slightly less than twenty-eight thousand dollars, an exceptionally comfortable income for 1922. However, it was not enough. To make ends meet, they were obliged to rely on emergency loans from Scott's agent and Max Perkins at Scribner's.

. . .

AFTER YEARS of living in furnished apartment hotels, Edna moved from the Majestic to the Prasada, a handsome Beaux Arts–style building at Sixty-fifth Street and Central Park West that had a central open courtyard and a lobby domed with shimmery stained-glass skylights. Proud of having "a real home" at last, she felt as if she'd "got religion or fallen in love." The Prasada would have to carry her out in a wooden box, because she was never going to leave "this wonderful place. Never." By day, when the leafy treetops of Central Park were dusted in sunlight, she would not have been surprised to see a Jersey cow grazing. At night the park eight stories below turned into an inky blur of "purple and black with little gold balls of light." But the best part of all was having her own bed with a mattress nobody else had slept on, a mattress "fresh from the factory with its paper wrappings still unbroken."

Edna was a homebody at heart, and her first step was hiring a crew of contractors and decorators to transform the six-room apartment into "my own darling place." For the twenty-nine-foot living room, its walls painted a soft green, she splurged on everything she ever wanted: a thick-pile carpet, a Steinway grand piano, a red moiré armchair, custom-made lemon-yellow curtains of French-glazed chintz with flame-colored taffeta frill, a sofa covered in green silk rep and piped with flame taffeta, and an eighteenth-century writing desk. She replaced a mantelpiece tarted up in cupids and writhing serpents with a simple one that was perfect for displaying her favorite pewter candlesticks. For the master bedroom, decorated in candy colors of buttery yellow and mint sea green, she ordered an apple-green-painted bedroom set. The only spartan room in the apartment was her working space. Fearing the park view might prove too distracting, she placed her desk and typewriter in a dark back bedroom.

While much of her time was passed in that back room, Edna gladly spent her evenings out on the town, sometimes returning tipsy after staying out much too late. Her alcohol consumption—a few glasses of red wine, a cocktail or two—was modest. Even so, some mornings she woke with a sore throat, her euphemism for feeling hung over. At the

Barrymores' party one evening, she met a banker-architect type who invited her to a dance at the Ritz-Carlton. Since Marc Connelly and his girlfriend, Margalo Gillmore, were also going, she accepted. When it was time to leave, however, she noticed that the banker-architect type was unmistakably "soused." Hat in hand, he was slumped at the top of the stairs, weaving slightly, and so she decided to avoid trouble and sneak out.

Three years into Prohibition, there was nothing uncommon about the sight of falling-down drunks. People in various stages of inebriation, conducting themselves in ways that would have been unimaginable a few years earlier, had become a fact of city life. And that was hardly the only sign of changing times. After returning from a vacation in Europe, Edna was startled to see New York had turned into the mecca of the shopping world. Along Fifth Avenue flowing five abreast whipped a torrent of powerful motorcars shimmering with "thick rich enamel." Stutzes at $3,250 were selling briskly to people normally driving Fords. The homes of ordinary people were becoming mini cathedrals to vacuum cleaners, toasters, and electric ranges, while the grand estates on Long Island were stocked with Pierce-Arrow cars, Worth gowns, and premium-brand radios, not to mention all manner of custom-made bibelots.

Considering that just last year New York was teetering out of the wreckage of war, and the economy still remained shaky, the changes were astonishing. It had become a city of "silk stockings and no runs," Edna thought. Both Wall Street financiers and average working people were looking for the fast buck and snapping up stocks and bonds. Most surprising, twenty- and thirty-year-olds were rolling in money. All over town, she noticed these nouveaux riches youngsters in Brooks Brothers speeding in fast cars and savoring expensive after-dinner cigars. Where did all these rich kids come from? What sort of values had they been taught? No subject fascinated her more than money and power.

That winter, caught up in a whirl of theater dates and parties, Edna kept observing the attractive, prosperous young men and decided that one such person might make a good story. No sooner had she begun writing, however, than something curious happened. Almost against her will the story insisted on changing as a stronger figure muscled in and shoved the youngster aside.

Three years earlier, while writing a story about a farmer whose wife nags him into moving to the city, she was riding around the produce market on Chicago's South Side, looking for color. Suddenly she noticed a woman wearing a blue serge suit sitting alone between crates of turnips and beans and chickens, the only female among the scores of wholesale grocers and truck gardeners unloading their wagons of vegetables. What struck Edna was the woman's face, middle-aged yet as exquisite as a cameo. Her expression was that of a person who could squeeze triumph out of failure, a type Edna knew well. It was her fictional saleswoman Emma McChesney—as well as her mother and herself. A moment later Edna had driven on, and the woman in blue, only a face in the crowd, was gone.

The image of this woman somehow managed to float to the surface of Edna's consciousness. Soon her story was taking place on a farm near Chicago, not on the streets of Manhattan, and the handsome young man had become the woman's son. The trouble was that Edna knew nothing about truck farming. Obviously, legwork would be necessary to investigate the subject, if nothing else to revisit the Chicago market in the hours before dawn, when farmers brought in their vegetables. But Edna, ordinarily the most professional of researchers, never got around to it despite her good intentions.

More worrisome than sketchy research, she suspected that a greater fault lay in the story itself. Nineteen-year-old Selina Peake is a naive girl when she arrives to teach school in High Prairie, Illinois, and marries an ignorant Dutch farmer. After her husband dies prematurely, she is forced to take stock. Her youth is gone, "but she had health, courage; a boy of nine, twenty-five acres of worn-out farm land, dwelling and outhouses in a bad state of repair; and a gay, adventuresome spirit that was never to die, only a trackless waste from which she had to retrace her steps painfully." Determined to transform a mud hole into a business, Selina becomes a slave to the soil and takes as much pride in red and green cabbages as she would have "jade and burgundy, chrysoprase and porphyry. Life has no weapons against a woman like that," Edna wrote. Any amount of drudgery is worth her son's having the advantages Selina missed. But the sacrifices for her precious little "So Big" turn out to be in vain because Dirk grows up to be one of the black-tie bankers Edna sees at the Ritz, a flush young man addicted to the best clubs, restaurants, and women. Practically every quality Selina Peake holds dear has been cast aside.

With a novel that had no plot to speak of, and a theme hidden between the lines, Edna could not help feeling nervous. Nothing much happened. Probably the most exciting scene, she supposed, was a description of Selina hauling a load of cabbages into the city. Even the working title—*Selina*—sounded lame. Was such a flimsy novel even publishable?

To DOTTIE'S FRIEND Ruth Hale, marriage and motherhood were not necessarily a woman's destiny. It had taken her years to get from Rogersville, Tennessee, to the city rooms of papers such as Philadelphia's *Public Ledger* and the *New York Times*, and Ruth had no intention of sacrificing her career for dish washing. One day, however, she and her future husband were sitting on a bench in Central Park when a squirrel scampered up and stationed itself in front of them. Begging and chattering a mile a minute, it was clearly a brainy little beast who seemed to be conversing with them.

Ruth laughed. "He wants a peanut," she said. "Why don't you go and get some?"

Heywood smiled lazily. "I'll tell you what," he said. "I'll give him a nickel and he can go buy his own."

Ruth laughed so hard that she changed her mind about marriage. But that didn't mean she was going to have children. On the other hand, a son meant so much to Heywood.

They named the baby Heywood Hale Broun.

Dottie, unlike Ruth, did want children. Nobody believed her. No, no, she told Bunny, he didn't understand. The ability to make another person is a miracle, surely. But he decided she must be pulling his leg. For crying out loud, she once referred to his newborn daughter as "it." Another skeptical friend doubted she could have anything in common with children, maybe because "they didn't drink."

Now she had to choose: a fatherless baby or an abortion. After weeks of procrastination, by which time she had passed the first trimester, she finally made arrangements for a dilation and curettage with a "Doctor Sunshine." Either she misjudged the time of conception or the doctor neglected to examine her beforehand, but during the procedure he was annoyed to discover she was further along than assumed. For whatever reason, he made certain she got a view of the fetus, which looked to her exactly like a real baby, with its tiny hands perfectly formed. She was sickened.

Afterward, recounting the experience at length to anybody willing to listen, she made the regulars at Tony's uncomfortable when she started nattering about fingers and toes, the sadistic doctor, and so forth. Her nastiest insults, however, were reserved for the despicable Charlie MacArthur. Any gentleman would have paid the whole cost of the abortion, but he handed her thirty dollars and made himself scarce as "Judas making a refund." Of course it was stupid of her to get involved with such a stingy shit in the first place, she said. She should have known better than to put "all her eggs in one bastard."

Eventually her moaning got on people's nerves. Friends such as Marc Connelly who wished she'd shut up reminded her that everybody has troubles. One day Marc pitched forward to his knees in Tony's. Please cheer up, he begged. Please count her blessings.

What for?

Didn't she have friends?

That's right, Dottie agreed, she was on velvet.

Didn't she have her health? Her talent?

If he said so.

So what was wrong with her? She had a wonderful life.

It was an awful life.

After he got to his feet, she called him a "silly old fool." You'd almost think he was born yesterday. No woman had worse luck than she did.

It wasn't Marc's performance that warned she must be in trouble. Not even the lack of any blessings worth counting. It was life weighing her down. Shortly before Christmas she condensed her life into a three-stanza poem, a confession of a woman contemplating a cut flower. The woman's adoring lover chooses the most romantic of gifts, a single exquisite rose, fragile, dewy, sweetly scented. In the language of love the bud is perfect. What more could anyone want? And yet she can't help wishing for something a bit more substantial, a gift that would not be drooping the next day and flushed down the toilet the day after that. Instead of flowers, how about a perfect Rolls-Royce? But damn it, it was just her luck to get a stupid rose.

"One Perfect Rose" appeared in *Life* magazine the first week of January. People said how amusing, and Marc said yes, she was "as tough as a muffin," and wasn't it wonderful how she could laugh at herself again.

1923

Vincent's wedding to Eugen Boissevain, Croton-on-Hudson, New York. Her sister Norma is the matron of honor. Her mother, Cora, and sister Kathleen were not invited.

CHAPTER FOUR

ON THE GROUND FLOOR of Dottie's building was a restaurant, the Swiss Alps, known in the neighborhood for its perfectly vile food. Usually she avoided the place, but she was famished that January evening. After telephoning the Swiss Alps and ordering a meal to be sent up, she walked into the bathroom, where her eye fell on a safety razor left behind by her husband. Gone, his tube of shaving cream. Gone, the brush and the packet of blades. All that remained was a fossil from the ruins of a marriage. For six months Eddie's razor had been lying in plain view without her noticing.

Standing in front of the sink, she plucked out the blade; she deliberately cut along the bright blue line on the underside of her left wrist. Blood jetted up over her hand and clothes, gushed into the sink, spattered the wall. Then she tried to slit the opposite wrist, not so easy because the blade in her fingers had become wet and slippery.

VINCENT RETURNED to New York in January. When the *Rotterdam* docked at Hoboken, she and her mother were met by Esther Root, a wealthy young woman they knew from England who had arranged an apartment for them downstairs from her own in the Village. Two years had passed with very little to show for it, except that Vincent was thirty—almost thirty-one—and still alone. Not only stone-broke, not just depressed and demoralized, she was severely ill. When Esther Root gave her a homecoming party, she made an effort to look cheerful and confident, but there was no possible way to hide her haggard, feverish appearance. Friends overjoyed to see her again ignored the flushed cheeks, and Frank Adams, celebrating her return in the Conning Tower, carefully chose his words and complimented her as the picture of "high bright gaiety." Bunny, however, could not help being shocked at her physical deterioration since their last meeting in Paris. Vincent, reticent, said nothing to explain her appearance. After spending an evening together, he came away thinking that her hollow-eyed looks must be the result of dissipation and "considerable recklessness."

In reality, she was ill and terrified. After the abortion her health had continued to go downhill as she suffered from a variety of medical problems, including gastrointestinal pain, irregularity, fatigue, fever, and loss of appetite. Separately, these were all common ailments; together they had become disabling. (The cause was probably inflammatory bowel disease, either ulcerative colitis or Crohn's disease, disorders of unknown origins that result in acute inflammation of the large or small intestine.) She lacked the stamina for work of any kind. Bunny, temporarily back on the staff of *Vanity Fair* after a year at *The New Republic*, failed to pry a single poem out of her. When Horace Liveright wanted to know how the novel was coming along, she replied, "[b]eautifully," but not one page had been written. Taking care of herself was all she could do, and in truth even that was beyond her capability.

After Cora left, Esther Root devoted herself to looking after Vincent. A member of an old WASP family, a Smith graduate, and a talented amateur pianist, Esther was a large, handsome woman who happened to be financially independent. (Her father had given her $100,000 on her twenty-first birthday.) While Vincent considered her a loyal friend, and certainly appreciated her care, both emotional and financial, she soon began to feel hobbled by being told what to do all the time. Some of her friends took a dislike to Esther, who now appeared to be running Vincent's life. From the start Bunny sized her up as a "rich amiable discontented girl," unbearably bossy, with nothing to do except attach herself to Vincent as a combination nurse and social secretary.

Giving her the slip became easier for Vincent because Esther suddenly had her hands full with Frank Adams. On the night of Vincent's homecoming party, Esther had invited him upstairs to have a look at her apartment. "It's nice here," he said. "I'd like to move in." It was the kind of remark that got women into Frank's column, and Frank into their beds. While not exactly a sexual conquistador, Esther happened to be a single woman of twenty-eight, and Frank, married or not, showed unmistakable interest; he started stopping at Waverly Place on his way home from work. Before long, the name "Miss E. Root" began cropping up in his column with regularity, as someone he had run into at the theater or tennis court, even once as a dinner guest at his home when she showed up on the arm of an obliging beard, Marc Connelly.

With Esther romantically occupied much of the time, Vincent had opportunities to seek other company, and she began renewing relationships with old friends. Among these was Arthur Ficke, who had left Davenport and was living practically around the corner with Gladys Brown, waiting out the months until he could obtain his divorce and remarry. Resigned to the situation, even going so far as to befriend Gladys, Vincent nevertheless seduced Artie one afternoon when Gladys was out. He was reluctant of course—it would be disloyal to Gladdie—but Vincent managed to convince him otherwise. Afterward he came by her apartment with a postcoital bread-and-butter note that he quietly slipped under the door. "You were so right to give me that unforgettable beauty," he wrote, because the images were burned into his brain. All along he had tried not to think of her sexually, but, honestly, he had no idea that "I should love your body so much."

As might be expected, sex with Artie failed to make her happy. It did not alter his decision to marry Gladys. And she was too sick to care anyway.

IT WAS HARD to understand. She should be in Woodlawn lying alongside J. Henry and Eliza Rothschild, under a white tombstone that said, EXCUSE MY DUST, DOROTHY PARKER, 1893–1923. Yet she was alive, saved by the Swiss Alps waiter bringing her dinner, rushed by ambulance to the Presbyterian Hospital on East Seventieth Street, and finally obliged to make polite conversation with puzzled long-lost relatives. Gathered around her bedside were all the Rothschilds and Drostes, behaving as if they had been summoned to an unexpected family reunion.

Why did she do it? they asked.

But she had no idea.

She had botched the job but learned from the experience: dying was harder than advertised, razors need to be really sharp, and the cut has to be deep—none of which she had ever thought about. The truth was, her biggest mistake was ordering from a greasy spoon such as the Swiss Alps, with its speedy delivery service.

Shortly after her release from the hospital, Dottie faced a ticklish situation when it was her turn to host an evening of her women's bridge group, which met almost every week to drink cocktails and play cards. The regulars included Jane Grant of the *New York Times;* Peggy Leech, the writer, who was going to marry Ralph Pulitzer of the newspaper-owning Pulitzers; and Winifred Lenihan, the actress, who had been cast to play Saint Joan in Shaw's new drama. Dottie, her wrists bound with yards of gauze, knew they would ask questions that couldn't be answered. The night of the card game, she decorated the bandages by tying black velvet ribbons into giant bows. As each guest arrived, she announced, "I slashed my wrists."

Taking a direct approach was a mistake. The entire evening the bridge players struggled to find appropriate words of sympathy, which was the last thing Dottie desired. In fact, none of them knew exactly what to say because they, like all Dottie's friends, were not acquainted with people who slashed their wrists. The sole authority on the subject seemed to be Dottie herself, and eventually she wearied of trotting forth overpolite apologies and started making wisecracks about her erstwhile husband.

It was all his fault, she said. "Eddie doesn't even have a sharp razor."

Altogether it was not a cheerful evening.

The funny thing was, the sight of Dottie's bandaged wrists actually aroused more suspicion than pity. After leaving that night, Jane Grant began thinking about Dottie and her husband's razor and how she had laughed too much. Of course it was no secret that the Parkers' married life had been "far from tranquil"—Dottie constantly mocked poor Parkie's inadequacies—but to make him responsible for the failure of her suicide attempt was rather unfair. The whole thing didn't make sense, Jane decided. A smart woman would not allow a bad love affair (a "setback," Jane called such things) to drive her to "the depths of despair." In Kansas, where she came from, setbacks made smart women show some backbone.

Later, Jane began to wonder if Dottie's attempt might have been a stunt. After all, she failed to kill herself, didn't she? Even fishier was the melodramatic last-minute rescue by a delivery boy, from the Swiss Alps of all places, that suggested a *Perils of Pauline* two-reeler. The thought crossed Jane's mind that Dottie might have staged the whole thing for attention, possibly to get back together with her husband or even Charlie MacArthur.

But Jane kept her suspicions about Dottie to herself. That winter she remained preoccupied with her husband, whose problems had dominated their marriage these past four years. Harold Ross was thirty-one, a high-school dropout from Colorado who had bummed around as a hobo newspaperman and probably would have remained in the boondocks if not for the war. In Paris, working on the *Stars and Stripes* with Frank Adams and Aleck Woollcott, he met and fell in love with Jane, a friend of Aleck's from the *Times*. When Harold informed her that he could never live in a sissy town like New York, she immediately set him straight about her own plans: she was returning to her job at the paper when the war ended.

Harold had always dreamed of owning a publishing company. The big question was what kind of publication, because New York already had a dozen dailies along with a great many other periodicals. Jane favored a weekly magazine about the city, but her husband was holding out for a shipping paper that he wanted to call the *Marine Gazette*. Among the other ideas he considered were cheap paper books, a syndicated comic strip, and a high-class tabloid. For the longest time there was quite a bit of talk but no action. Her husband's insecure personality and lack of business sense made it necessary for Jane to do "a great deal of prodding." Consulting the *Times's* managing editor, she learned that the amount required to start a tabloid could be as high as $5 million. That was the end of that scheme. In the meantime, they continued to live on her newspaper salary—and freelance pay from the *Saturday Evening Post*—and to bank his earnings from the *American Legion Weekly*.

The first time Edna Ferber met Harold, at Frank and Minna's house, she figured he must be a vagrant Frank had dragged home as a joke. With his thatch of mouse-colored bristles, a tongue hanging over his lower lip, tiny gray eyes, and a gap between his two front teeth, Harold looked like a plucked woodchuck. Even Jane admitted that her husband was downright funny-looking, "the homeliest man" she'd ever met. He seemed completely out of place among the streetwise New Yorkers at the Algonquin Round Table. A born complainer and paranoid, constantly bemoaning everything from his dental problems to the world conspiracy against him, he naturally became the butt of Round Table jokes.

At lunch one day, he wondered if anybody had dental floss.

"Never mind the floss," Aleck snorted. "Get him a hawser." Ross resembled his grandfather's coachman, Aleck taunted.

Coachman or not, Ross happened to be a master of grammar and syntax. Sentence structure was his passion, commas and semicolons his obsessions, H. W. Fowler's *Modern English Usage* his bible. The one thing never questioned by the Round Table writers was his editorial skills, which were considerable. What they greeted with incredulity was his wacky idea of becoming a publisher. He had no business running a company.

Tired of living in a cramped apartment on West Fifty-eighth Street, Jane and Harold were determined to buy a place of their own that year. The twin buildings were located west of the Ninth Avenue El in Hell's Kitchen, a slum of the worst rotting tenements and warehouses, known for gang wars and prostitution. It was not the kind of neighborhood where people such as themselves usually lived, but the properties at 412 and 414 West Forty-seventh Street were relatively cheap and would be ample for living and working. To afford the price of seventeen thousand dollars, and the cost of extensive renovations, they sold a one-half interest to Aleck Woollcott and one of his college friends. Everybody would live together, along with two rental tenants, and share a living room, dining room, kitchen, and garden.

Including Aleck was a mistake, Jane soon realized. Not only did he fuss about the service, carrying on as if he were in the presidential suite at the Plaza, but he also behaved like a child. Meals became difficult because he existed almost entirely on meat, potatoes, rice pudding, and gallons of coffee. Whenever Jane served nourishing soup or green vegetables, he sulked and refused to come to the table.

Naturally, it was Jane, not Harold or Aleck, who got stuck running the household and finding reliable bootleggers to deliver ten-gallon cans of pure grain alcohol. It was Jane who manufactured the gin by adding drops of juniper oil, shaking and stirring over thirty-six hours, then pouring in distilled water. And it was Jane who received a grand-jury subpoena for violating the National Prohibition Act. On weekends, faced with feeding twenty or thirty unexpected guests, she began to feel like tearing her hair out. Did people think it was a boardinghouse? Worst of all was her husband's Saturday poker gang (the Thanatopsis Literary and Inside Straight Club), whose players behaved like utter pigs, leaving behind spilled drinks and a filthy bathroom. Even with two servants it was impossible to keep up.

One day at the hairdresser's Jane asked for a short bob.

More, she urged, cut more.

She would be sorry, the stylist warned.

When Jane walked out of the salon, her head was shorn "just like a boy." And, no, she was not sorry.

By the time renovations were finished, the houses had been transformed into a stylish cooperative, complete with a courtyard and fountain, so inviting that members of the Round Table began treating it as a western annex of the Algonquin Hotel.

AFTER WEEKS OF NAGGING, Esther Root persuaded Vincent that it would be healthy to spend a weekend in the country. Croton-on-Hudson was a town thirty-four miles up the river that had become a popular retreat for certain Village bohemians. At a small party on Mount Airy Road, the guests turned out to be mostly Vincent's ex-lovers and their women: Arthur Ficke and his fiancée, Gladys Brown; Floyd Dell and his wife, B. Marie. Everyone was happy to see Vincent, the women perhaps a bit less so. Examining her with keen interest was a rather splendid-looking man, a widower who lived in the neighborhood. When the guests began playing charades, she found herself paired with Eugen Boissevain. She probably did not remember, he said, but they met once, years ago, in the Village. She did remember, sort of.

Floyd Dell, who still could not look at Vincent without thinking that her mouth was shaped just like a valentine, noticed how quickly the two of them clicked. Soon they were playing their parts so well, he said, "it was apparent to us all that it wasn't just acting."

Floyd was right. That weekend Esther took the train home alone, and Vincent moved into Eugen's house on Mount Airy Road.

EUGEN JAN BOISSEVAIN, some years before, had been married to Inez Milholland, the feminist heroine known for leading a parade down Washington's Pennsylvania Avenue on a snow-white horse. In 1916, however, she lay dying in a Los Angeles hotel room. Thirty years old, a graduate of Vassar College and New York University law school, she was a figure of Amazonian brains and beauty who had become the great hope of the suffragist movement. A spellbinding speaker, an enthusiastic walker of picket lines, the champion of laundry workers and factory children, indeed an activist on behalf of almost every wrong in the world, she inspired women as readily as she terrified most men. For all her leftist opinions, cackled Max Eastman, editor of the radical *Masses*, she remained an idle "opera-going" rich girl who drove up to picket lines in a chauffeured touring car and busied herself with meaningless appointments. Max Eastman's sour grapes had more to do with their broken engagement than with her political causes.

During the fall of 1916, an election year, Inez was suffering a variety of symptoms associated with pernicious anemia. Nonetheless, she set out on a lecture tour supporting a boycott of the Democratic Party, which had failed to endorse a federal suffrage amendment. In Los Angeles, wearing a blood-red-lined cloak, she was addressing a rally—"How long shall women wait for liberty?" she said—when she collapsed.

Trembling at her sickbed sat her husband of three years. "Shall I come with you?" he said, understandably overwrought.

"No, you go ahead and live another life," she replied.

Eugen (known also as Ugin or just plain Gene) was a tall, solidly built man with dark hair and the complexion color that looked like a year-round tan. The picture of masculinity, he had a hearty laugh, a huge appetite for fun and food, and an equally huge emotional hunger to be needed. An expatriate from the Netherlands, he had never been obliged to work. The Boissevain family made its fortune operating a shipping line between Holland and Java, and his father published a leading Amsterdam newspaper. Irish on his mother's side, Gene could boast a grandfather who'd been provost of Trinity College, Dublin. He was introduced to Inez on a steamship between New York and London; their elopement soon afterward made front-page news in the *New York Times*.

Seven years after Inez's death, forty-three years old, Gene remained unmarried, although there had been a romance with one of Isadora Duncan's adopted dancers. Finding another famous woman was important to him. Until one came along, he preferred to remain a boulevardier and adventurer who had supposedly hunted big game in Africa and explored his psyche with Carl Jung in Switzerland. When not traveling, he operated a trading company in lower Manhattan near the seaport. He imported sugar and coffee from the Dutch East Indies and lived with his best friend, Max Eastman, in the Village.

Although Max found him endearing, he would get annoyed when Gene's "feminine" side took over and he started to fuss over meals and household decoration. With the pained expression of a Dutch housewife, Gene once bawled him out for wiping a razor blade on a white guest towel. (Max denied doing it.) The trouble with Gene, Max decided, was that he cared intensely "about everything that belonged to him."

VINCENT WROTE an affectionate little verse about a man obsessed with his flower bulbs. At night, lying awake next to his lover, he imagines the damage field mice are doing to the precious bulbs outside his window. She slipped the first draft of "Hyacinth" into a sealed envelope containing a photo and lock of her hair and gave it to Gene.

There was no need to tell him she was ill, perhaps even needed to be hospitalized. At his house in Croton he insisted she stay in bed and be nursed by him and his servants. Several days a week he drove her into the city for examinations by specialists. When stomach and bowel X rays turned out to be inconclusive, he advised her to undergo the exploratory surgery being recommended by the doctors.

In Croton with Gene, Vincent had to rely on good-hearted friends such as Bunny to shop and run errands for her in the city. To Arthur Ficke she sent an itemized list: "walking-stick in left-hand back corner of closet"; Macy's soap, the "big brown hexagonal ones"; and "bunch of typed poems for new book." Sounding relieved at the prospect of Vincent safely married, Art joked to Kay, "Aren't you glad she isn't going to die a virgin? I am." Gene, he said, was the only man on earth, except Charlie and Howard, "who could possibly marry a Millay without paying for it with his life and liver."

Several days after meeting Gene, Vincent learned that she had won the Pulitzer Prize for poetry. The prestigious awards, still in their infancy, had been established in 1917 by a newspaper publisher, Joseph Pulitzer, to recognize excellence in journalism, letters (both fiction and nonfiction), and drama, with the poetry prize added as an afterthought five years later. Having published nothing in 1922, and consequently technically ineligible, Vincent was a surprise winner. Her most recent book, *Second April*, was released in time to be a 1922 finalist but the prize had gone to Edwin Arlington Robinson. The Pulitzer jury continued to find her deserving, however, and bent the requirements in order to assemble a package of her work: an expanded edition of *A Few Figs from Thistles* and a pamphlet edition of "The Ballad of the Harp-Weaver," together with eight sonnets that had been published in *American Poetry, 1922: A Miscellany*. She was the first woman to win the prize, whose purse of one thousand dollars seemed like a fortune.

When news of the award was announced in the *Portland Evening Express*—"Maine Girl Wins Pulitzer Prize for Book of Verse"—an immensely excited Cora bought stacks of papers and sent clippings to everyone she knew. Vincent, however, had little energy to write anyone, including her mother, but when she did, in June, it was not to talk of literary prizes. Did Cora remember meeting a man named Eugen Boissevain in Waverly Place? Well, she was going to like him because "I love him very much & am going to marry him. *There!!!*"

Before they tied the knot, sometime during the summer, she planned to bring him to Maine. "Won't that be fun?" Gene had given her a car, a "beautiful big Mercer."

The letter offered little clue about Eugen. Was he young or old, single or married? A poet or a plumber?

Vincent was perfectly happy to let Norma supply the details, including the pronunciation of her new boyfriend's name (you-gin, not you-jean). Norma, in turn, told Cora that he was over forty but looked youthful, in fact acted like a kid. Tanned from cavorting in his garden wearing only a batik loincloth, he was good-looking, in Norma's opinion. Compared with some of the skunks in Vincent's past, this one seemed the best of the lot and might turn out to be a "bully good husband." As for assets, he was not really, really rich, but he had run through a couple of fortunes and conceivably could make another. He could, on the other hand, buy just about anything he wanted—houses, cars, the best medical treatment—and certainly would be able to support "our Ed St. Bincent" in the manner she deserved.

L IKE ANY YOUNG WIFE in Great Neck, Zelda was eager to entertain and show off her sweet Babbitt house. She invited the movie scenarist Anita Loos to come out from the city. When dinner was announced, Scott was nowhere about, and so Zelda and Anita took their places at the candlelit table and began eating without him. During the meal Scott, without warning, bounded into the dining room.

"I'm going to kill you two!" he yelled. A lit candelabra sailed through the air.

He was obviously drunk. The wine cooler was next, followed by the leg of lamb on its silver platter, which persuaded Anita and Zelda he might be serious. They sprang up and beat a hasty retreat.

They returned to the house some time later to find Scott sitting quietly outside near the road and eating dirt. He was "a swine," he said.

The two women offered no argument. After that Anita Loos steered clear of the Fitzgeralds.

It was the hottest June on record, with temperatures brushing one hundred. Zelda wheezed and broke into eczema, but she never knew why. With Scottie leading a separate life in the care of her nurse, Zelda quickly fell into a leisurely Southern routine of lazy days she had known as a teenager. Mornings, she woke late and ate peaches for breakfast before going off to the country club for golf and swimming. In the grueling heat of the afternoon she had a fine time being lazy. No eating, no reading, just solitude and pleasant sounds. She invented a refreshing lemon cooler, three parts gin to one part water and the juice of a lemon. A reporter from the *Louisville Courier-Journal* made an appointment to interview her, and she got dressed up in country-club clothes and seated herself in the living room. As it turned out, the questions could not have been more lame. How did it feel to be "the heroine of her husband's books"? Was it fun being "the living prototype" of the liberated American flapper?

"I like to write," she said. Not only did the reporter find this statement bewildering, but he soon ran out of questions, and so Scott had to be called in.

"What would you do if you had to earn your own living?" Scott teased her.

When pressed, Zelda replied seriously. Before marriage her only accomplishment was dancing, a talent that had been highly praised in Montgomery. Those years and years of ballet lessons might qualify her to be a Follies dancer; her second choice of profession would be a film actress. If both of those failed, "I'd try to write."

There were no more questions from the reporter. The idea of Zelda's writing for a living sounded absurd to Scott, too.

ON THE ROAD connecting Great Neck and midtown Manhattan were mountainous ash heaps, dotted by filling stations and peeling billboards, and dusty craters suggesting some Martian Main Street.

Through this powdery industrial terrain, the Fitzgeralds traveled back and forth that summer to their favorite playground. Making movie-star-like entrances, sometimes with a Hearst photographer at their heels, they spent the evenings in crowded cabarets where the tables were wedged so tightly they sat penned in the laps of strangers. As grade-A celebrities, they were invited to the best parties and sometimes found themselves in penthouses of people they didn't know, strangers who had merely telephoned to say they were having people in and wanted Zelda and Scott to join them.

Not that there was any need to visit the city for a good time. On just about any night of the summer, Great Neck turned into a vast cocktail party. At dusk the sky began to slowly jell into the color of brandy, and by the time the moon rose, the whole area, all the swimming pools and even the Sound itself, was reeking of gin and light wines, as Zelda joked about it. From Manhattan the night crawlers rolled up, uninvited, to the Victorian houses overlooking the bay. They danced, they drank, they used the pool, they thrashed around in the bushes having sex. Many, Scott was shocked to note, did not know or care to know the names of their hosts. Fascinated, he began cataloging the species of gate-crashers, just as his fictional character Nick Carraway jots down the names of career party guests on an outdated Long Island Rail Road timetable: the man who got his nose shot off in the war; the woman who ran over the right hand of a drunk on the gravel drive; the quintessential leech named Ewing Klipspringer; the varieties of whoopee girls with names such as Jacqueline or Consuela. By midsummer Zelda had noticed that her husband had withdrawn and wanted sex even less often than usual. He had an idea for a new book.

IN THE OVERGROWN YARD of a Croton neighbor, Vincent married Gene on July 18. Before the ceremony, in a grove of trees, Floyd Dell took snapshots of the wedding party: Gene's brother Jan, Arthur Ficke and Gladys Brown, and Norma and Charlie Ellis. Norma had only learned about the wedding the previous day. Kay was not told at all. Neither, for that matter, was Cora.

There was no love lost between Norma and Gene, who on better acquaintance had come to dislike each other. Twenty-four hours earlier they had been screaming and fighting over the hasty ceremony that mostly excluded Vincent's relatives. "I'm not marrying the family, you know!" he shouted at her.

Norma turned to Vincent. "Are you really going to marry this low, cheap son of a bitch?" Was he the man she really wanted to live with? She stamped off in tears. Vincent made Gene apologize.

Even though the morning was unusually warm, guests came bundled up in suits and hats. Only Vincent looked cool in a dark green silk dress with a peasant skirt, an outfit that straddled the line between Halloween costume and Bleecker Street chic. Draped over her hair were an improvised veil and train, a piece of white mosquito netting that Norma had found after poking around the porch. Vincent, who could hardly drag herself about, didn't give a damn what she was wearing. In a close-up, Dell's camera caught her radiating a look of feverish intensity, her cheeks flushed—too flushed—and her eyes rimmed by dark circles.

The ceremony was over quickly. No sooner had the justice of the peace finished than Gene and Arthur helped Vincent into Gene's Mercer and they sped back to the city, where she entered New York Hospital that afternoon to prepare for surgery. As she was being wheeled into the operating room, she turned to Arthur. "I shall be immortal," she said, if she died on the table.

But she did not die. Instead, an announcement appeared in the *New York Times* that the Pulitzer-winning poet Edna St. Vincent Millay had secretly wed a wealthy importer a few hours before entering New York Hospital to have her appendix removed. It was like Gene to substitute a more presentable ailment.

In the weeks after returning from the hospital, Vincent mailed a letter to Kay describing the obstruction in her digestive tract and how the surgeon "cut holes in my intestines and sewed them together in such a way to make a new channel." She was happy to report that the doctors had performed "a very wonderful and skillful piece of surgery." If she imagined Kay would be grateful for a firsthand account, she was mistaken. Left to read about her sister's wedding and hospitalization in the newspapers, Kay felt miserably snubbed. Titter Binnie didn't care a fig about her.

That fall, the family was surprised when Vincent proposed a family reunion in Camden. It would be an opportunity for everyone to get acquainted with Gene, and, besides, the sisters had not been home together in a long while. Kay—and probably Norma, too—dreaded it. Nevertheless, it was arranged that Gene would drive the three of them to Maine in October. The other husbands—Charlie Ellis and Howard Young—skipped the trip. Kay made a point of warning Howard he'd be "bored to death," and Charlie was on the road with a play. In the backseat of the Mercer with Norma, Kay discovered against all expectations that Gene was "a lot of fun," a person with whom you could have "a real laugh." During the ten-hour drive to Camden, they were "howling" their "heads off."

Preconceived notions notwithstanding, the visit turned out to be enjoyable. The best part, Kay thought, was when they left Gene with Cora and the three of them piled into the Mercer and took a nostalgic drive up to Penobscot Bay, almost as far north as Belfast. And yet, observing the stolid Dutchman among the four of them, with their endless girlish yapping, their Bincents and Titter Binnies, Kay could not make up her mind about her new brother-in-law. She guessed that he was "a nice strong healthy man who would like to be decent and laugh a lot." But like the proverbial man with the silver spoon, he was as naive as "a puppet floundering about in the midst of the Millays," and she doubted him capable of ever understanding her family.

Not in question, though, was Gene's love for Vincent, his unabashed pride in being her husband. He beamed like the handler of a prize boxer. In Camden he took care of Cora's personal debts, just as he had quietly repaid money Vincent had borrowed from Arthur Ficke and others, altogether laying out thousands of dollars. Before returning to New

York, they continued north to Montreal, where he treated Vincent and her sisters to a weekend at the luxurious Ritz-Carlton.

Bringing together her family and new husband would establish the foundation for peaceful relations, Vincent hoped. Everyone in the family understood that. They also could see that the bad times were over for Vincie. Gene's taking care of her meant she would never have to worry about money again. Her Galahad had bestowed lavish gifts: a diamond watch, an emerald ring worth forty-two thousand dollars (almost half a million dollars today), clothing from the best shops, her own house on a leafy street in the Village, long-overdue dental work. From now on Gene would nominally be in charge. Even so, nobody doubted that Titter Binnie was going to call the shots.

DOTTIE DOTED ON her male friends—Mr. Benchley and Bunny and Frank and Aleck—and expected them to exhibit common sense. Most of the time they did, of course. But every so often one of them skidded off the deep end and started acting like a lunatic.

For Bob Benchley romance began with a chance encounter. One morning he came into Grand Central on the train, crossed the main concourse, and took a shortcut out the side entrance onto Vanderbilt Avenue. At the corner, in the Biltmore Hotel, was a Western Union office, where he sometimes stopped before going to work. Messages were printed on a yellow form and handed to the telephone operator.

Carol Goodner was a sociable girl with brown hair and gray eyes, a little above medium height, not yet out of her teens, and she was exceptionally pretty. Living in Hell's Kitchen with her mother (an ex-dancer in Victor Herbert operettas), Carol had been a typist and a waitress and sometimes a movie extra. She didn't intend to spend the rest of her life sending telegrams for seventeen dollars a week. Before Bob realized it, he was stopping at Western Union every morning.

Bob's life had already taken a curious turn when, months earlier, the Algonquin Round Table staged an amateur comedy revue for their friends. After agreeing to perform a monologue, Bob came unprepared and had to improvise. His material, about a nervous suburbanite unaccustomed to public speaking, stole the show. Afterward Sam Harris and his partner Irving Berlin asked him to perform "The Treasurer's Report" in their next *Music Box Revue*.

Bob smiled. He was drama critic for *Life* magazine, not an actor.

How much do you want? Harris said.

"Five hundred dollars a week," said Bob, naming the most ridiculous sum he could think of.

Harris fell silent for a moment. Very well, he said, "but for five hundred dollars you'd better be awfully good."

In September, Bob became a headliner in the third *Music Box Revue*, and Carol Goodner made her Broadway debut as a showgirl. In the opening number, "The Calendar," she played the month of November.

Dottie found it disgraceful. Not that she blamed Mr. Benchley for cheating on Gertrude—a frump who always looked like she was rushing from a burning building—but a Western Union girl was so tacky.

Carol entered a room with the royal bearing of a duchess, Bob said.

A royal gold digger was more like it, Dottie thought but refrained from saying.

Dottie and Bunny were in complete agreement about Bob's dime-store girlfriend.

"Very inferior," sniffed Dottie.

"Thick ankles," said Bunny. The worst part was her eyes, hard like a streetwalker's.

Despite everything, Dottie continued to believe in the sanctity of marriage. Once wed, you entered into a state in which any action no matter how heinous could be committed except leaving it—and now it appeared that marriages were collapsing all around her. After twenty years, and countless discreet infidelities, Frank Adams was being openly unfaithful to Minna with Esther Root. Mr. Benchley was lovesick over a telephone operator. Even Ruth's husband was gossiped to be unfaithful, although Dottie felt sure that Heywood must be more talk than action.

Seeing her male friends suddenly acting like horny teenagers was a bit scary, but not so frightful that she failed to notice the literary possibilities. What about a domestic comedy making fun of sex-starved husbands and the home wreckers to whom they fall prey? Everybody else she knew was writing a play, why not her?

In her short story "Such a Pretty Little Picture," Bob Benchley appeared as a confused, hedge-clipping Westchester County commuter, a persona that had once approximated his true character and that he continued to inhabit on the stage of the Music Box. But in less than a year's time Dottie's Mr. Wheelock had tossed aside his clippers and broken out of his yard.

Evenings at 8:50, dressed in a business suit and tie, Bob sauntered onto the stage of the Music Box and began speaking to the audience, almost absentmindedly, as if making up his comments as he went along. Eight minutes later he turned and walked off, generally heading for his aisle seat at another theater. After the show he would return to the Music Box to pick up Carol. Suddenly leading a double life, confounded by the same dilemma as a sailor with a wife in every port, he developed crippling arthritis, which necessitated crutches and a bachelor apartment in town. He made sure to telephone Gertrude at least once a day and tried to show up for Sunday dinner in Scarsdale, but sometimes he missed the train.

Meanwhile, Dottie was busy writing scenes for a play with the working title *The Lady Next Door*. In revamping the plot of her short story, she decided to bestow on her miserable suburban husband a love affair with a beautiful neighbor, an ex–chorus girl. On Saturday afternoons Ed Graham and Belle Sheridan play duets on mandolin and piano. Then what? How the play might end remained unclear. Mr. Benchley would never walk out on his family, would he?

"FOR GOD'S SAKE," Scott pleaded with Max Perkins. If he didn't deposit $650 in his bank by Wednesday morning, the furniture would have to be pawned. He was in "a terrible mess."

Mess or not, Scott and Zelda could not have been more elated, because by the looks of it they would soon be on easy street. In a couple of weeks Scott's play was trying out at Nixon's Apollo in Atlantic City before opening on Broadway—and it was supposed to be a smash hit. With the recent death of Warren Harding, the worst President in memory, and his replacement by Calvin Coolidge, nothing could be more timely than a political satire on the presidency. For two years Zelda had lived with *Gabriel's Trombone*, now rebranded with the cumbersome title *The Vegetable; or, From President to Postman*. She had watched the script written and rewritten, published as a book because no producer would touch it, and finally accepted by Sam Harris and cast with first-rate actors. Those who saw the rehearsals predicted it would run for a year.

Over the weekend of November 17, Scott had accompanied Ring Lardner to the Princeton-Yale game, an event that predictably led to sleepless nights and a drinking binge. On Monday evening, however, a sober and proud Scott took his seat at the Apollo and watched the curtain rise on his debut play. At first everything went smoothly. Jerry Frost, a railroad clerk, falls into a gin-induced hallucination in which he imagines having been elected President of the United States and living in the White House. But during the second act, when Jerry is impeached and wants to become a postman, the audience at Nixon's Apollo began an unseemly whispering and rattling of programs.

Scott was shocked. Around him people were noisily leaving their seats and walking out. There was no booing or catcalling, but they obviously hated the play. Never had he seen anything like it before. He had the urge to ring down the curtain and invite the poor actors to join him at the nearest speakeasy.

After *The Vegetable* closed, Scott walked around the house like a zombie. Suddenly he hated New York. For all its majesty, the city had turned out to be a heartless place, full of "careless people" who smashed dreams with absolutely no regard for the lives destroyed. Zelda, trying to downplay his devastation, wrote a friend that he was "terribly disappointed." Nobody could figure out why the show had unaccountably flopped like "one of Aunt Jemima's famous pancakes." Unfortunately, she had made the mistake of spending a week's worth of anticipated royalties on a dress to wear opening night and could not exchange it. Every day Scott holed up in his workroom over the garage and drank pot after pot of coffee as he ground out short fiction to pay his bills. After earning almost twenty-nine thousand dollars that year, he had nothing left.

During the weeks in September when her husband was busy in the city with rehearsals and rewrites, Zelda had completed three short stories. One of them, "Our Own Movie Queen," tells the story of a tough working-class woman living in a small Midwestern town. Gracie Axelrod is a cook at her father's fried-chicken stand until she gets a job at the local department store. Winning a company beauty contest, she is crushed to discover the contest is rigged. Instead of the promised starring role in a movie, she gets a measly walk-on, but Grace, like her author, takes no guff from anybody.

After his drubbing in Atlantic City, low on cash, Scott decided the Gracie story might be good enough to sell if he pruned the underbrush and added a decent climax. Although it was rejected by *Cosmopolitan*, and quickly written off by Scott as "a complete flop," Harold Ober kept sending it out. Eventually "Our Own Movie Queen" was purchased by the *Chicago Sunday Tribune* for one thousand dollars and published in June 1925, under Scott's byline. Nobody wanted a story by Zelda Fitzgerald, at least not for one thousand dollars.

BY THIS TIME Bunny had become a husband and the father of a three-month-old daughter. He had married Mary Blair, a Provincetown Playhouse actress, in February, when she was two months pregnant. Not particularly maternal, Mary was eager to return to the stage, and so baby Rosalind was shipped to Red Bank, where Bunny's mother assumed her care—permanently.

After Christmas, for the first time since Vincent's marriage, he received the kind of wicked letter that used to make him crazy, a perfect example of what John Bishop called her habit of "going out the door and leaving it unshut behind her." Of course she'd been a "swine" for ignoring him these many months, she said, but would he please think of her as a small pig, an elegant pink-and-white "truffle-sniffer." She was settled in a new house and wanted to see him. If he came by on Thursday at four, she'd give him a cigarette and a rosy apple, because she loved him "just as ever." Bunny could not resist.

Tucked away in the West Village, 75½ Bedford Street was half a house that could have been custom-built by P. T. Barnum for Tom Thumb. The tiny brick row house, a relic dating back to the mid-nineteenth century, measured eight and a half feet wide by thirty-five feet deep. Aside from a bathroom, the three-story building contained no rooms, only open floors connected by a staircase. There was a sense of claustrophobia, even though the top floor, converted into a skylighted studio, gave a little light and air.

Bounding upstairs, Bunny found Vincent alone drinking gin and reading the verse of William Morris. Since she appeared far from robust, he was surprised to learn she planned to undertake a strenuous monthlong reading tour of the Midwest, followed by a year's journey around the world, a kind of belated honeymoon. She seemed relaxed as she chattered of her husband and those friends of hers he had sent packing: the acolytes, the sycophants, and the hangers-on. Bunny thought she seemed eager to convince him that she was happily married.

To a businessman? Bunny could not accept the idea.

That annoyed Vincent. Gene was as "irresponsible" as the next person, she scolded. He was no different from Bunny.

Only when it was time for him to go did Eugen Boissevain come in. As Bunny reported afterward to John Bishop, he seemed to be "a very nice honest fellow," although not "overwhelmingly clever." Bunny, struck by Vincent's "withdrawal from the world," left the house feeling faintly disturbed. Despite what appeared to be a complete reversal of fortune, she gave him the distinct impression of being a princess in a tower, so grateful for a clean, well-lit cell with kindly jailers that she failed to notice the bars. John, however, far less romantic, thought she had made a practical choice. This amiable nobody would make possible all the luxuries "for which she longed in the old days."

O N THE EIGHTH floor of the Prasada, Edna gazed around happily at the floral arrangements. Her living room resembled the dressing room of an Italian diva, because there were bouquets of roses next to half a dozen huge poinsettias, no fewer than twenty potted plants. For all her considerable pessimism about the new book, she felt "popular and happy." Among her Christmas gifts that year was a velvet bed jacket, much too grand for bed, but it would look stunning over a black evening dress. And somebody gave her one of those dog-collar necklaces that were all the rage, just the thing with her newly bobbed hair.

On New Year's Eve she attended Ruth and Heywood's annual party on West Eighty-fifth Street, where a mob had gathered as usual. Presiding over the big punch bowl, ladle in hand, stood five-year-old Woodie Broun, happily slopping gin and orange juice into cups. Most of the evening Edna spent with Frank Adams, who for months had been turning to her for advice—not that she had any to give—about whether he should divorce Minna. It was a painful decision, made even more difficult because some of his friends were taking Minna's side and blaming him for succumbing to a rich young adventuress. In his column that very week, in an unusually personal comment, he admitted feeling "as low hearted as ever I was in my life." At the party, however, he did not appear particularly guilty. Giddy, making bad puns, one funnier than the next, he looked positively boyish in his tuxedo, Edna thought.

Good heavens, he looked as if he'd just been confirmed, she told him.

"I am a confirmed admirer of you," he replied.

All things considered, it would have been one of her best Christmases had it not been for *Selina*, now retitled *So Big*. There was nothing to do now but wait and worry. Luckily, *Woman's Home Companion* had accepted the novel for serialization, but there were ominous signs:

the typist had returned the last batch of pages of her final draft without a single comment, confirming Edna's worst fears that the story was tiresome.

Before sealing the manuscript package, she enclosed a rather unusual note: Doubleday, Page should not expect too much, she warned. It was possible that *So Big* would harm her career because nobody would read it. In that case she would prefer not even to publish the book. Several days went by before Russell Doubleday replied. She was dead wrong about *So Big*, he told her. It was wonderful. As for himself, he cried.

A weeping publisher? Edna could hardly have been happier.

1924

Oh, you beautiful doll: Broadway babies Betty Block and Carol Goodner from Irving Berlin's Third Music Box Revue with John "Daddy" Corrigan, the show's master carpenter. Carol's lover, Bob Benchley, is one of the headliners.

CHAPTER FIVE

On a raw morning in January, Edna was trotting around the reservoir with Frank Adams. Was something wrong? he asked.

What made him think something was wrong?

Because she looked awfully low. What happened?

Nothing happened.

What was the matter, then?

Well, she had no ideas.

Frank was quick—too quick—to laugh. Was that all? Her situation was nothing compared with his. He had a daily column to fill. If she had no ideas, nobody knew it except herself, and "when I have none it is patent to a vast number," he said.

Frank ought to have at least tried to understand. "No ideas" were two of the scariest words in the English language to Edna.

In the months that followed, she continued to feel spent as she waited to learn the fate of her novel. Doubleday, Page, which promised a big spring push with marketing and publicity, was betting it could reasonably expect to sell as many as fifty thousand copies. Yet she remained skeptical.

When *So Big* finally appeared in bookstores that spring, readers and critics alike were more enthusiastic than Edna could have imagined. The *Tribune*'s Burton Rascoe said that he could only "genuflect in homage," while the *Times* called it "a novel to read and to remember." One admiring reviewer wrote that the book was a sterling effort but was likely to sink without a trace by Christmas, a remark that enraged Edna given her insecurity about the subject. For several months, however, from March to September, *So Big* continued to sell. But Edna was frustrated and cranky, and her head was empty of ideas.

Earlier the drama editor of the *New York Times* had complimented her on a short story about a man whose residence with his son and daughter-in-law breeds predictable friction. The funny geezer in "Old Man Minick" might make a good comedy, remarked George Kaufman, who wrote for the theater in his spare time. Would Edna like to try to work together?

No thanks, she said without hesitation. Who's going to watch a play like that? But another story of hers, "The Gay Old Dog," might be suitable.

No kidding, Kaufman insisted, the old man is a play. His new show, *Beggar on Horseback*, had recently opened at the Broadhurst to excellent reviews. Edna thought about that. George had been around the block a few times. Could he be right about Minick?

. . .

I N HER COSTUME of royal green silk, her halo of bronze hair, and the flame-colored scarf she draped around her neck, Vincent had the look of some exotic specter from the bygone times of the troubadours. Her audiences were dazzled. In mid-January she felt strong enough to embark on a monthlong road tour of twenty cities—as far west as Omaha—to promote *The Harp-Weaver and Other Poems*, which had been issued by her new publishers, Harper & Brothers. The secret of surviving such a horrible trip, she wrote Kay from Columbus, Ohio, was resting as much as possible. Gene, who needed to remain in New York for business, felt lost without Vincie and turned to Kay for companionship. "Call me up and have dinner, tea, or a cocktail" because "I'm as lonely as hell."

Vincent was lonely, too. Traveling from Chicago to Cedar Rapids, squeezed into a parlor-car chair, she hated every minute of the six-hour ride, which reminded her of the IRT subway line when "it comes up for air at 137th Street," she wrote Gene. In Chicago she was insulted to discover that one of her bookings was in a private house in Evanston because a bunch of rich people wanted to see what she looked like. Feeling like a prostitute, she went through with the reading as scheduled but kept repeating to herself, "Never mind—it's a hundred & fifty dollars."

Despite such unpleasant moments, the tour was worth any amount of discomfort in that it helped to establish her reputation as a leading poet. Onstage, Vincent grabbed her audience like an opera star reaching for a high C. Making a sensational entrance, using her considerable acting talent, she began to declaim in a highly dramatic manner more suited to theater than to literature. Between recitations she dropped the stagy British accent and began to chat smooth as butter with the audience. A few minutes later, however, she could frown and turn into a lofty prima donna, making a scene over a latecomer or a cougher. Her adoring public loved it. Invariably, the climax of the performance would be the celebrated "Renascence," in which she pulled out all the stops, followed by an encore of her greatest hits, the naughty little verses about burning her candle and riding the ferry, which her audiences knew by heart. Reading engagements were nothing new for poets in need of money, but Vincent figured out how to transform bookish library oratory into literary entertainment.

Back home, a final reading was planned for a Sunday evening at the Plymouth Theatre. Filling a Broadway house was not easy. To ensure a sellout, Gene began scrambling weeks in advance to round up customers. "Tell as many people as you can," he urged Kay, "and make them buy tickets." He was thinking about giving up his business so that he could devote himself full-time to managing Vincent's career. As a start, he proposed raising her reading fee to six hundred dollars.

When Frank Adams asked Edna Ferber if she'd care to be his date, she eagerly accepted because her favorite things were "lamb chops and money and ambition and Edna Millay and the rosettes on my curtains." The night of the performance she cooked supper for Frank, who would rave to his readers about her sausages as the best he'd ever eaten: no wonder she wrote so brilliantly about food when she was such a splendid cook. As it turned out, he enjoyed Edna's sausages a good deal more than Vincent's theatrics. Notwithstanding his enormous affection, he criticized her for using unnatural speech "with too little variation of tone, using, meseemed, a range of only three notes." Reading her verse was better than listening to her mannered poetry voice, he advised. Afterward he and Edna stopped by the home of George and Beatrice Kaufman on West Fifty-eighth, where they ran into Dottie Parker and spent the remainder of the evening playing cards and gossiping.

In April the Boissevains set out on their belated wedding trip, journeying first to San Francisco, then boarding a ship bound for Honolulu and the Far East. After nine months of marriage Vincent was happily luxuriating in security she could scarcely have imagined. The care of their house was entrusted to Kay and her husband, who were living in New Jersey with his parents. Free rent did nothing to alter Kay's dislike of Titter Binnie's dollhouse, which she found claustrophobic and uncomfortably drafty. The wind "whistles around these floors like the deck of a ship."

The success of Vincent's poetry readings was not lost on her mother, who wondered if she might do something similar in Maine. While Vincent was away, Cora made her lecture debut in Belfast, her birthplace, a shipbuilding town of waterfront wharves and Victorian mansions. The Belfast Business Women billed her as the mother of Edna St. Vincent Millay.

To open her program, Cora recited "The Ballad of the Harp-Weaver," the poem that had pained her so much in 1921, before turning to her own poetry, which she called "of an entirely different nature." She read from a series of poems about a small boy, Little Otis, who after visiting Europe comes home to live on his grandparents' farm. Her plan, she said, was newspaper syndication followed by book publication. Cora turned out to be an entertaining speaker. Adopting Vincent's technique of digression, she talked intimately about her married daughters, who kept their own names, girls who had grown up to be poets, novelists, actresses. She called them "talented and artistic" and described how once all four of them lived together in Greenwich Village. Just as Vincent's stage ensembles conveyed an image of Renaissance style, Cora, too, devised a novel look for herself, but about as far removed from fancy dress as one could get. She attired herself as a male, with a tie, shirt, and trousers; she wore rimless glasses, and her brown hair was severely cropped. Even for the businesswomen of Belfast, this masculine Cora must have been startling to behold.

Her very first lecture yielded an enthusiastic account in the *Portland Sunday Telegram*, followed by publication two weeks later of a poem about Indian summer in the *Rockland Courier-Gazette*. By the time Vincent returned from her trip, Cora had begun to assemble her own file of clippings.

. . .

I T WAS PRACTICALLY NOON when George Kaufman appeared at Edna's door. Looking like a businessman on his way to the office, which was actually the case, he was nattily dressed, as always, in an expensive suit and tie. He was a good-looking man, sexy, tall, and supple as a stalk of celery, with a leafy pompadour of dark hair. In the course of six years he had co-authored a half-dozen successful plays, fattened his bank account, and acquired a sprawling apartment near Central Park. Something of a dandy, he owned a collection of gorgeous ties that rivaled the shirts in Jay Gatsby's closet. Nevertheless, every afternoon he continued to show up at the *New York Times*, where he performed his duties and collected a paycheck of less than seventy-five dollars a week. George at thirty-four behaved like a clerk saving for a rainy day.

To the amusement of his friends, he was scrupulous about keeping his two jobs separate and refused to give special consideration in the *Times* to his own projects or to their stars. In the case of *To the Ladies* the frustrated press agent asked him what he must do to get a story printed on Helen Hayes. "Shoot her," George said.

George, insecure about working alone, had always collaborated with Marc Connelly, the Pickwickian balding reporter who covered show-business news for the *Morning Telegraph*. A pair of transplanted Pittsburghers who had wound up on the theater beat, Kaufman and Connelly made a perfect team. But despite their successes (*Merton of the Movies, Beggar on Horseback*), the partnership was heading for the rocks. Unlike George, miserable unless every hour of his day was full, preferably with work, Marc was a carefree type who quit his newspaper job after their first hit. All he wished to do was take it easy, have a good time, and travel to Europe with his mother. Although George remained friends with Marc, who would win a Pulitzer in 1930 for his biblical drama *The Green Pastures*, he could never resist making digs about his ex-partner's purported laziness. When a Charles Dickens novel was published posthumously, he said sarcastically, "Charles Dickens, dead, writes more than Marc Connelly alive."

To replace Marc, George scrambled to find a workhorse like himself, man or woman, and he began canvassing the Round Table. The first person he approached was Dottie, whose wit was unmatched but who was obviously not going to work eighteen hours a day at anything. Their collaboration, limited to a one-act play (*Business Is Business*) presented live with the film version of *Beggar on Horseback*, proved to be an experience he did not care to repeat. Aside from Dottie's habit of showing up late, or not at all, there was her annoying practice of pretending to be a WASP when she was half Jewish. At the Round Table one day, when Aleck made an anti-Semitic remark in jest, George threw down his napkin and exclaimed that he was disgusted enough to walk out. He expected Dottie to "walk with me—halfway."

Naturally, the Round Table poked fun at the new Edna and George coupling—a literary roll in the hay, somebody called it—but Edna was not amused. She could not possibly be interested in a man so neurotic, so borderline pathological, that he made Aleck Woollcott seem almost normal. George was a simple hypochondriac, an advanced phobic, and a food fetishist who ate mainly meat and candy. For six years he had not slept with his wife, Beatrice, not since she gave birth to a stillborn son and he became incapable of getting an erection with her. Even more curious, marital celibacy had not derailed their marriage, each had extramarital romances, and now they were talking about adopting a baby.

George had no shortage of women. Edna, however, was never his type. "I'm fond of her," he told Marc Connelly, but that didn't mean he liked her very much.

Professionally, it was another matter. ("Daddy and Edna got on," said George's daughter, Anne.) George would show up punctually at Edna's, and they would head for her office at the back of the apartment. After a few minutes of gossip she rolled paper and carbon into the typewriter, which was the cue for him to untie and tie his shoelaces, whether they needed it or not. While they worked, he paced. He jiggled the curtain cord, played tunes on his cheek with a pencil, flopped on the couch, wandered about the apartment. He constantly fussed with his shoelaces. At one-thirty on the dot, they stopped for sandwiches and coffee.

All this hyperactivity didn't bother Edna a bit; she was having too much fun. The only thing that provoked her annoyance was George's disagreeable habit of reading her mail. No letter or telegram, not even a page of manuscript, was safe, and scolding had no effect. It was harmless curiosity, she guessed, but decided to punish him anyway. On a Western Union form she typed a message—"GEORGIE KAUFMAN IS AN OLD SNOOPER"—and slid the telegram under a stack of papers on her desk.

IN THE HOPE THAT a change of scenery might improve their lives, Zelda and Scott were preparing to leave Great Neck. The paraphernalia they'd accumulated during twenty months at Gateway Drive formed a pyramid of seventeen pieces of luggage, several crates full of Encyclopaedia Britannicas, and copies of Scott's books bound in pale blue leather with gold lettering. At the last minute they tucked in a hundred-foot roll of copper screen in case of flies. Six months of hard labor, working on "trash," Scott told Bunny, had not only extricated him from debt but also produced a surplus of seven thousand dollars and the freedom to work on serious fiction. In early May Scott and Zelda sailed for Europe, previously scorned but enticing again because of the favorable exchange rate. Their destination was the south of France, where living cheaply could make their nest egg last a long time. Whether this plan would work remained to be seen.

June found them settled in Saint-Raphaël, a seaside town of red-roofed pastel buildings and an especially good beach, the swimming facilities always an important consideration for Zelda. On a hill two miles above the town they leased a cream-colored villa facing the sea for seventy-nine dollars a month. Villa Marie, nestled in a terraced garden scented with roses and honeysuckles, overlooked the town Fréjus, with its crumbling Roman aqueducts. Nightingales sang in the umbrella pines. Two cooks were included in the rent, along with a gardener who insisted on addressing Scott as "Milord." On the gravel driveway Scott posed for a snapshot swinging a golf club and wearing a classic Brooks

Brothers wool suit with vest and knickers. Zelda dressed in cotton dresses and straw hats, attire a good deal more appropriate. To complete the picture, they purchased a beat-up Renault—a French Ford, Scott called it—for $750.

Zelda found Saint-Raphaël enchanting. For hours and hours she sat at the beach attempting to learn the language by reading French novels with the aid of a dictionary. In enthusiastic letters home she praised the incomparable scenery and urged everybody to hop the next boat. They were going to be very happy in Saint-Raphaël, she reported to Bunny. Never could she have guessed that "incompetency"—whose she left unsaid—could triumph against all odds and transport her to this idyllic setting. What she most craved was order, which finally seemed, on the bright shores of the Mediterranean, to be within her grasp.

Before arriving at the Côte d'Azur, during a stopover in Paris, they hired a nursemaid. Compared with Great Neck help who charged the outrageous sum of ninety dollars a month, Lillian Maddock seemed to be a bargain at twenty-six dollars, or under a dollar a day. The middle-aged Englishwoman was a professional with decent references and an upper-class accent that they expected Scottie would surely emulate. By the time they reached the Riviera, however, they had begun to feel less pleased because the "wonderful" Lillian Maddock was turning out to be a shameless snob, not above boasting about her previous employers, invariably families of the better class. She made clear that the Fitzgeralds were not up to her usual standards. Judgmental and condescending, she sized up Zelda as incompetent and easily pushed around. She repeatedly lectured her on deadly sun exposure and the dangers of permanent skin damage.

The novel that Scott started in Great Neck in the summer of 1923—partly discarded, partly revamped, partly cannibalized for "Absolution"—was moving forward again. As always he discussed his writing with Zelda, seeking her opinion on titles and endings, because her instincts were sound. When he had trouble visualizing the physical details of a character, she would sometimes sketch a picture for him. Soon "the book," as Scott called it, completely took over their lives. James Gatz, like Scott himself a poor boy from the Midwest, believes that nothing is impossible if you want it badly enough. Inventing a new self at the age of seventeen, he rejects his parents, mediocrities whom in his imagination he "had never really accepted," and begins his metamorphosis into the legendary millionaire Jay Gatsby of West Egg, Long Island.

Scott's trouble was in separating himself from his fictional characters, who had become more real to him than his own family. He found Scottie's presence particularly distracting, and after ten minutes Miss Maddock would be summoned to take her away. Drifting over his story was the motionless presence of Scott himself, not just writing autobiographically about Scott Fitzgerald of Minnesota but also narrating the events in the form of a memoir. His stand-in, greatly modified to be sure, is a trustworthy but otherwise unexceptional young man, Nick Carraway. Another transplanted Midwesterner, Nick makes his living as a Wall Street bond salesman and rents a house in Great Neck, where he gets mixed up in the grand notions of the millionaire next door. Jay Gatsby, whose affectation is to call men "old sport," is an odd character. His obsession turns out to be Daisy, Nick's rich, beautiful second cousin once removed. As Nick eventually learns, Jay is actually a white-collar criminal whose wealth probably comes from bootleg liquor and stolen securities, although Scott never makes clear the source of his money.

Drinking moderately, carefully husbanding his time, Scott got into the routine of sequestering himself all day. Mornings he wrote, and when he took a break, he'd read André Maurois's new biography of Shelley or chuckle over French magazines with their brothel ads and homosexual personals offering seashore sex weekends. Typically he kept to himself until the late afternoons, when he would drift down to the beach for a quick dip. At night he felt drained and rather monastic, which meant he and Zelda rarely had sex. He was completely absorbed in his book, which he could not resist bragging about, in a letter to Max Perkins, as "the best American novel ever written."

. . .

SAINT-RAPHAËL in the off-season, Zelda wrote Bunny, was crowded with so many British consumptives and Sunday afternoon watercolorists that she felt "quite alone." All this changed after a week or two, however, when she was befriended by a group of gregarious naval fliers from the local air base. Swimming and sunbathing every morning with Scottie and Nanny, she would leave them with the sand buckets and stroll up to one of the beach cafés. While sipping a glass of port on the terrace one day, she struck up a conversation with the Frenchmen, cocky young flyboys in crisp white duck uniforms who were immediately attracted to a flirtatious American blonde. Since the men were no more fluent in English than she was in French, conversation sometimes had to be conducted in sign language. But all of them hit it off, and soon Zelda invited them to the villa to meet her husband, who also enjoyed their company. They reminded Zelda of Montgomery during the war, when pilots from Taylor Field used to buzz their flying machines over her house.

The one Zelda liked best was Lieutenant Edouard Jozan, the youngest of seven children from a Provençal family of modest means, who had enlisted in the Navy and graduated from flying school after the war. Stationed at the Fréjus airfield, he was a chase pilot whose duties, mainly providing escort and support for other aircraft, must have been a humdrum assignment for an impatient twenty-four-year-old. In Zelda's autobiographical novel *Save Me the Waltz*, Edouard Jozan (Lieutenant Jacques Chèvre-Feuille) is built like a god, "bronze and smelled of the sand and sun." Irresistibly slim and muscular, he apparently wore no undershirt, because her heroine thrills to the touch of his back muscles rippling "naked under the starched linen." Zelda began meeting Edouard so regularly that people who noticed them whispering at the beach or pressed together on the dance floor of the smoky casino began to form conclusions.

At Villa Marie, Scott ceased to pay close attention to anything except the life of his fictional bootlegger. While not completely oblivious of Edouard, he found nothing really objectionable about his attentions to Zelda because all of them had become friends. It never occurred to him that the youth three years his junior might have the bad manners to overstep the boundaries of gentlemanly behavior when nobody was looking. Zelda, throughout their marriage, had enjoyed being the center of attention among Scott's college gang. Knowing that his friends, even the randy George Jean Nathan, found her desirable brought him a great deal of pleasure. With the frolicking safely under his control, he knew, as John Dos Passos remarked, that nobody dared to "make a pass at Scott's girl." No matter how coquettish Zelda might appear, the idea that she could be tempted into adultery was unthinkable.

Despite a passionate emotional bond, sex between Zelda and Scott had never been good. He was prudish in bed, never as eager to do it as she was. What's more, it had to suit his schedule, something she strongly resented. If he thought she was going to "sit around on my ass" until he had finished writing, or "lie on the bed waiting," he was very much mistaken, she would tell him.

"Wasn't sex satisfactory?" he was to ask her in later years. Zelda did not mince words.

"No," she said sharply.

Primarily she blamed their mediocre sex life on the size of his penis—too small to give any woman pleasure, she said. Atop his list of complaints was the suspicion that she was not a virgin the first time they slept together. She was acting, but happened to be a poor actress. Owing to her mother's negligence, the son of a rich cotton broker had seduced her at the age of fifteen. (Zelda refused to confirm or deny any of it.) Eventually Scott became so upset about the size of his penis that a friend took him into the toilet of a Parisian brasserie for an inspection. He was average, the friend told him. Scott had been examining himself from above, when he should have turned sideways and looked in a mirror. Even so, Scott never felt reassured.

It was the middle of July when Scott noticed Zelda's cozy behavior with Edouard. His suspicions were aroused, and one Sunday, around her birthday, he took her to task for unbecoming behavior. Unintimidated, she said that he could think whatever he liked. Increasingly angry, he resorted to threats and orders, which she ignored. (She never said she had sex with Edouard; she never said she didn't.) It would serve her right, he yelled, if he went back home and left her. Fair enough, but she loved Edouard. In fact, she wanted a divorce. In future she would run her own life.

Scott did not believe her for a minute. He certainly didn't suppose that Edouard wanted to run away with her. That was ridiculous. Let the boyfriend say all that to his face, he blustered. The two of them would fight it out like men. In the meantime, she was not to meet Edouard again.

"I was locked in my villa for one month," she said later, to prevent her from seeing Edouard. Although such a jail sentence would have been hard to enforce in a busy household with a child and several servants, the villa, figuratively, must have felt like a jail cell.

Trouble, when it came, was not easily blown away. Zelda refused to apologize, and although later she granted, reluctantly, that Scott's anger was justified, she failed to show a scrap of repentance. Her silence ensured that he would never be completely certain whether he was cuckolded, hence the lingering bile over her betrayal. In his ledger, where the Edouard incident was labeled "Big Crisis," he predicted that the damage to their marriage could never be repaired. For years afterward he punished her by mocking her feelings for the French flier in front of others, using her intimate experiences as the basis for misty cocktail-party talk, embellishing the details as he saw fit, milking her passion for pathos. In both the short and the long term, Edouard Jozan left footprints all over their marriage.

In a cheerful letter to John Bishop at this time, Scott pretended to be satisfied with his marriage. He and Zelda (like Tom and Daisy Buchanan in his novel) were soul mates, he insisted. Quarreling constantly did not mean any lessening of their affection, because they were the only completely happy couple he knew. It was a lie, of course. What he really felt was complete and utter isolation. He lived in a household with "no one I liked."

Eventually life swung back to normal, at least on the surface. Although Zelda sensed herself under house arrest, she continued to swim every day. In his ledger Scott noted that she was "getting brown." In the presence of visitors from home, they behaved as if nothing extraordinary had happened. John Dos Passos and Ring and Ellis Lardner noticed no particular tension; neither did Gilbert Seldes and his wife, Amanda, who apparently failed to connect a certain unnerving experience to marital discord the day all four of them drove down to the beach from Villa Marie. As the Renault approached a treacherous hairpin turn, Zelda said, "Give me a cigarette, Goofo." Struggling to keep the steering wheel steady, Scott pulled a cigarette out of a pack. While Zelda calmly lit up, the Seldeses huddled terrified in the backseat.

By this time Edouard had disappeared from Zelda's life, although not from Saint-Raphaël. As a naval officer, he lacked the freedom to come and go at will and would remain stationed at the local airfield for another two years, until September 1926, when he was transferred to sea duty aboard the aircraft carrier *Béarn*. For a man in his position, an aviator earning military wages, a summer beach fling with an attractive married woman, no matter how good the sex, was never meant to be serious. Despite indiscreet behavior, he had no intention of interfering in the Fitzgerald marriage, still less of assuming financial responsibility for a foreigner with a child. (Decades later he chivalrously declined to acknowledge any sexual relations had taken place.)

Although Zelda never saw Edouard again, she would relive the erotic details of their relationship in two novels, thus endowing the romance with more substance than it might have had. Her vivid descriptions were the results of the intense visual memory she brought to all her writing—and of the fact that this was the first and only occasion in her life that she experienced swooning sex.

With the lease on Villa Marie about to expire, Scott mailed off his typescript to Scribner's. In October they loaded up the sagging Renault with Scottie, their seventeen suitcases, the blabby Miss Maddock, and what Zelda called "germs of bitterness" and went to spend the winter in Italy. For the first time in her life Zelda suffered from serious illnesses.

An attack of colitis, which is an inflammation of the colon caused by a virus or an abnormal immune response (but may also be psychosomatic), was followed by inflammation of the right ovary. The ovarian infection made her so "horribly sick" that she spent five weeks bedridden with abdominal pain, fever, and vaginal discharge. Over the next year or two her gynecological problems persisted.

Nineteen twenty-four, in Scott's ledger, was recorded as "the year of Zelda's sickness and resulting depression." Actually, it was the other way around. But whichever one came first, she was beaten, and they both knew it. As she would write later, in an attempt to convert pain into philosophy, "You took what you wanted from life, if you could get it, and you did without the rest."

EDNA HAD NEVER been so happy. Writing a novel was work, filthy work, like "plodding along a dirt road ankle deep in mud." By contrast, writing a play made her feel as if she were strolling "down a country lane on a sunshiny day in early May." Despite her miserable experience with $1200 *a Year* four years earlier, she found everything about the theater pleasurable. After returning from Europe in August, she boycotted her typewriter and began spending her time at *Minick* rehearsals. The producer, Winthrop Ames, was a Boston Brahmin millionaire who used his family's hand-tool fortune to back Broadway shows. Edna knew of no classier person in show business than Ames, who talked business on the top floor of a theater he owned on West Forty-fourth, in an apartment decorated with priceless tapestries where a butler in white coat served cocktails and canapés on silver trays. Rehearsals were conducted with equal style. Every day at one, Ames's chauffeur and butler marched through the stage door bearing picnic baskets full of the most delicious salads, gourmet sandwiches, fruit, and hot coffee. When it came time for the company to depart on road tryouts, Edna decided to go along.

In Connecticut, *Minick* first opened in New Haven and Hartford, before moving to an old Shubert Theater in New London, the historic harbor town of the tall ships. On opening night the dimming of the houselights was a cue for bats roosting in the chandeliers to dive and dart into the orchestra. Shrieking, the audience used programs as umbrellas and ran toward the exits like rats fleeing a sinking ship. Onstage the actors were laughing hysterically, while Edna, sitting in a box, helplessly watched the bat ballet through opera glasses. The evening was a disaster.

Afterward the cast assembled for highballs and sandwiches in Winthrop Ames's hotel room. Edna, depressed, slumped against a cushion on the floor. To cheer up his cast, Ames remarked that the traditional system of out-of-town tryouts had become useless. It made more sense to charter a showboat and drift down some river, playing towns without ever getting off the boat.

Edna bolted upright. "What's a showboat?" she said.

A T THE END of August, Scott told Max Perkins that he had time for reading once more. Could Max recommend any good novels? No bestsellers, nothing like Joseph Hergesheimer's latest, which he could tell must be "vile."

Heading the list of Max's picks was *So Big*, "the most popular, and one of the best," and second was E. M. Forster's *A Passage to India,* which he had not yet finished, because of his hay fever.

Contrary to the predictions of some critics, *So Big* did not sink like a stone. Through the summer, sales kept creeping upward, and by Christmas the novel had galloped to number one on the bestseller list. During its first year the book would sell 318,000 copies, exceeding *Main Street.*

Despite Max's enthusiasm, Scott refused to read *So Big*. Ferber's books, he told Max, were beyond bad; they were "inferior" and "cheap," a lesser version of Willa Cather. He took the position that stories about "flip Jewish saleswomen" and an "earthy carrot grower" must be trash. Ferber and Fannie Hurst, pulp writers in his opinion, were "the Yiddish descendants of O. Henry."

Edna, however, had an equally unflattering view of Scott. She thought his novels were larky smarty-pants cartoons about silly flappers, his characters soft, anemic types. Clever young writers such as F. Scott Fitzgerald were, she predicted, the type to "peter out."

By THE EARLY 1920S Frank Nelson Doubleday had transformed his company into one of the country's leading publishing houses. Under the stewardship of his son Nelson, the family business would go on evolving into an even more successful operation, but for the time being the sixty-two-year-old patriarch still dominated Doubleday, Page. "Effendi," as he was known in the trade, liked to boast that he didn't read books. He sold them. Since Effendi's list sparkled with superstars—Rudyard Kipling, Joseph Conrad, O. Henry—literary honors were nothing new. Evidently, it never occurred to Effendi that *So Big* might also qualify as a contender for the Pulitzer Prize; at least the book was never submitted to the board.

Serving as one of the Pulitzer fiction jurors that year was Edna's dear friend William Allen White. The minute Bill saw the list of entries, he noticed the absence of *So Big* and began cracking the whip. Dear Frank, he wrote to Effendi. What about *So Big*? Why hadn't it been submitted? Never mind sending him a copy. He knew the book so well that he could practically "sing it."

A few days later Bill got in touch with the Pulitzer administrator. Dear Mr. Fackenthall, he said, Doubleday evidently neglected to enter *So Big* in the fiction contest. Surely it deserved a place among the top candidates, in his opinion qualifying as one of the final three shortlisted books. White's annoyance continued. Bad enough he was forced to remind Effendi about *So Big*, but then Doubleday, disorganized, sent a chintzy single copy to the Pulitzer board when it should have issued books to all three judges. In the end, he had to take care of buying and mailing the copies.

In a textbook case of von Clausewitz strategy, White commenced to spread his own fog of war, or at least a heavy mist, as he angled to steer his fellow judges toward *So Big* by a steady barrage of mail. Dear Dr. Fletcher. My dear Mr. Firkins. Dear Mr. Fackenthall. Everybody got letters. White, candid, made it clear that *So Big* was his first choice. On the other hand, he didn't feel so strongly that he would object to certain other titles. But then again, *So Big* was "outstanding." Figuring out precisely where he stood must have been almost impossible. (He failed to reveal an important conflict of interest: his twelve-year relationship with the woman he called "Angel Child.")

White's fellow judges, it turned out, had their own ideas about the best novel of 1924, and after numerous letters had passed back and forth, the panel agreed on three finalists: *So Big, Balisand,* and *Plumes.*

Balisand, like the other novels of Joseph Hergesheimer, portrayed decadence among the rich. Its author (along with James Branch Cabell) was considered the dean of American letters, and it was to Hergesheimer that a respectful Sinclair Lewis had dedicated *Main Street. Plumes* was a war novel by Laurence Stallings, co-author of the successful Broadway play *What Price Glory?* He and Edna fraternized with the Round Table crowd and attended the same parties, and both had allowed Harold Ross to use their names as window dressing on the editorial board of his new magazine, but otherwise they had nothing in common. Edna wrote about farmers, as if war had never happened, whereas Stallings, who got his leg blown off at the Battle of Belleau Wood, specialized in war. (*Plumes* would be turned into one of the greatest of all silent films, *The Big Parade,* starring John Gilbert.)

The chances of *So Big* winning were slim, not because Edna's competition was a pair of blood-and-guts males, but because only twice previously had the winning title also been a bestseller. From his desk at the *Emporia Gazette,* Edna's self-appointed fairy godfather made it his business to see this happened a third time.

Over the next four months White became shameless in manipulating his fellow jurors, along with the Pulitzer overseer. When the jury became deadlocked, and considered omitting the fiction award, he scolded the judges about wasting the prize money. He also suggested splitting the award between two of the entries (*So Big* and *Balisand*), an option that no previous jury had been permitted. In the end, thanks to White's determined lobbying, *So Big* won by default.

Following in the footsteps of Edith Wharton, Willa Cather, and Margaret Wilson, Edna was the fourth woman to be chosen. She was careful to mask her satisfaction and announced that the prize money would be turned over to the Authors' League fund for needy writers. Equally restrained in private, she brushed off her triumph by insisting she had no use for prizes but felt "pleased to have been the fortunate one this year." (Knowing Bill White's fingerprints were all over the award may have dampened her elation a bit.)

A Pulitzer did not guarantee respect, as Edna soon found out. Days after the prize was announced, the *New York Times* carried a derogatory item, about a Chicago society wedding, which claimed— inaccurately—that the bride and groom served as models for *So Big*'s main characters. Edna Ferber, the article went on to say, made the couple's acquaintance while convalescing at the bride's home "after having had her nose straightened." Such slurs were best left ignored.

B Y THE TIME Edna won her Pulitzer, *Minick* had opened on Broadway to enthusiastic reviews. Just about the only critics to pan the play were Edna and George's Round Table friends. An "interesting" play in which no character "came fully to life" was the verdict of Heywood Broun, while Aleck, who could be vituperative in the extreme, pronounced it "utter trash" for his *Sun* readers. Regardless, *Minick* ran 141 performances, followed by road-company and London productions, as well as a movie starring Warner Baxter.

But by now Edna had lost interest in Broadway because she stumbled, quite accidentally, on the subject for her next book. This time it was not a character, not even a story, but a setting. From Winthrop Ames she learned that a showboat was, as the name implied, a floating theater that tied up at towns along the river and whose acting company lived and worked on board. Fifty years earlier theatrical boats were commonplace along many rivers, especially the Mississippi, but Ames doubted if any still existed. Their era had ended long ago.

A few days after *Minick* opened, Edna left New York and rode the train south until she reached eastern North Carolina, where it was still summer. In the town of Washington she hired a car and driver for the thirty-mile trip to a landing on the Pamlico River, where she'd heard that a showboat was docked.

Luckily, the James Adams Floating Palace Theatre was still there. Pulling up to the gangplank, she called out to a man standing on the lower deck. "My name is Edna Ferber," she said. She had come from New York because she wanted to write about a showboat.

The man stepped forward. Was she the same Edna Ferber who'd written the Emma McChesney stories? The same Edna Ferber who'd written *So Big?*

To Edna's disappointment, the showboat season had just ended. She would have to go home and come back in the spring.

UNPLEASANT MEMORIES filled the Fifty-seventh Street apartment where Dottie had lived with Eddie and slashed her wrists. She was never good at keeping house, and the dinky flat had deteriorated alarmingly. It was time to move on. She thought it would be nice for a change to luxuriate in tidy surroundings where she never had to clean up after herself, where she could invite people in for cocktails, buy new lingerie, learn how to change a typewriter ribbon. Perhaps she would somehow manage to housebreak her dog. That spring, she'd transferred her belongings—typewriter, Boston terrier, a few good suits—to a furnished suite at the Gonk, which she had been treating like a home away from home for so long. The beauty of a hotel lay in its safety: the hubbub of chambermaids, the clerks behind the front desk, the certainty of a faux family around her day and night, an orderly, maintenance-free universe. Her suite—a sitting room and tiny bedroom—was spartan, but all she needed, she joked, was room to lay a hat and a few friends.

Happily ensconced in a new home, with the Rose Room and the

Round Table conveniently downstairs, Dottie found herself able to write with more focus and discipline. For most of the year she had been struggling with her play about Bob Benchley and his mistress, Carol Goodner, a comedy in which a suburban husband is tempted to run away with his next-door neighbor. Unfortunately, the first act was the length of *War and Peace*, and so she was obliged to enlist the services of an experienced playwright to help out with technique. Her collaborator, Elmer Rice, was best known for his drama *The Adding Machine* and could hardly be called the typical play doctor; in fact, he was being touted as America's Ibsen. Dottie, properly humble, marveled over her good luck. For an ordinary person—"a small cluck," as she put it—like herself, working with the great and gifted Elmer Rice just left her "trembling all the time." She did most of the writing, and when they weren't working on *Close Harmony*, the married Rice wanted to have sex, a small price to pay. To friends she confided that Elmer was "the worst fuck I've ever had." (Because she had sampled so few men, her rating had no statistical significance.)

After a Wilmington tryout, *Close Harmony* was scheduled to open in New York on the first of December. From her experience as a critic, Dottie knew that launching a play during the Christmas season could be risky, but the producer pooh-poohed her worries. The play would run a year whenever it opened, Arthur Hopkins promised.

When Hopkins turned out to be right, and *Close Harmony* met with complete praise from the critics, Dottie wound up throwing herself a party at the Gonk. The second week of the run, she decided to visit the show on a Saturday afternoon and see how everything was going. What fresh hell was this? When she arrived at the theater with Woodrow Wilson on a leash, she found practically every seat empty. Clearly, Arthur Hopkins was not infallible after all, because those admiring reviews had not brought audiences to the box office. Did anybody think to tell her? Not at all. Afterward she sent a grim telegram to Bob Benchley: "CLOSE HARMONY DID A COOL NINETY DOLLARS AT THE MATINEE STOP ASK THE BOYS IN THE BACK ROOM WHAT THEY WILL HAVE." On Christmas Eve the play closed after twenty-four performances. Why did these things happen to her?

1925

*The umbrellas of Antibes: Gerald and Sara Murphy spend every
morning sunbathing on the beach.*

CHAPTER SIX

IN STAMFORD, Connecticut, Ruth Hale purchased an abandoned farm, ninety-seven acres and a lake, and proudly named it Sabine Farm in honor of Horace's estate in the Sabine Hills outside Rome. It was generally agreed, however, that Ruth was not in her right mind, because her Sabine Farm looked like the Roman poet's might have after being sacked by the Goths, Gauls, and Vandals. Max Perkins, invited to a cookout, described it to Scott as "a ruin of thickets, grass-grown roads, broken walls, and decaying orchards." Invited to visit, Dottie and Aleck shuddered at the sight of a stiff brown toothbrush hanging from a nail on the back porch.

"In God's name," Aleck said, "what do you suppose she does with that?"

"Rides it on Halloween," Dottie said.

Sitting in the parlor with Ruth and some of her friends one night, Dottie was listening to their usual conversation about sewage and sump pumps when a plump brown rat trotted by. Ruth did not notice, nor did she blink when another rat toddled by with a businesslike step. Just then a whole bevy of rats began scooting around as if they owned the premises, but nobody paid the slightest attention. As a native New Yorker, Dottie was unruffled by the sight of cockroaches, but rats were different. While these appeared none too bright, they were big, beefy creatures built like Jack Dempsey. Finally she couldn't stand it.

"Does anybody but myself see giant rats in this room?" she said.

Ruth had been planning to say, "What rats?," but one look at Dottie's face changed her mind, and she confessed to enticing the rodents with bread pellets.

"You sons of bitches!" Dottie wailed.

That year practically everyone talked about real estate. The Round Tablers moaned how they needed to get out of town on the weekends, how that was the whole trouble with their lives. Moving to the country meant privacy, Ruth declared, although her friends assumed Sabine Farm, with its wood-burning stove, was an excuse to escape the increasingly onerous duties of ministering to party guests on West Eighty-fifth Street. Aleck, dreaming of storage space, was thinking of buying an island in the middle of a remote lake in Vermont, because he had had his fill of living in a town that had no attics, and what was a home without an attic. That sounded ridiculous to Dottie, who owned nothing worth storing. Any place without sidewalks aroused her suspicions, but as luck would have it, she fell in love with a man who lived in Stamford, not far from Sabine Farm.

Deems Taylor was an accomplished composer of several operettas and an orchestral suite. He also was music editor of the *New York World*, in fact the country's leading music critic. Small and blond, with

a receding hairline and a crinkly grin, he looked like a cheerful schoolboy, although he was forty. Dottie had known him ten years, ever
since, as a fledgling poet, she began submitting light verse to F.P.A.'s
column, and Deems, signing himself "SMEED," was Frank's most
gifted contributor. The days when Deems and his cat shared a bachelor apartment with Marc Connelly were long past, however. Married
twice, he was separated from the actress Mary Kennedy.

After Dottie's Boston terrier died, Deems went out of his way to be
comforting. As it happened, he was abandoning criticism for full-time
composition because the Metropolitan Opera had commissioned him
to write an opera. His example encouraged her to make changes in her
own professional life, which she considered a failure. Angrily summa-
rizing her writing career in "Song of Perfect Propriety," she enumerated
the lines of work for which she was, temperamentally, qualified: buc-
caneer, highway robber, anarchist, looter, spy, extortionist, strangler,
freelance hangman. And yet she was writing poetry, "as little ladies do."

Her mistake was obvious, she supposed. For years she had been pot-
tering along with hors d'oeuvres when she should have been cooking an
entrée. What she needed to write was a novel. Without giving up her
rooms at the Algonquin, she moved to Fairfield County to live with
Deems and began writing. The story was about a wealthy New York
family who lives on the Upper West Side, in a brownstone with twelve-
foot ceilings and a dark mahogany parlor, and plucks its Irish laun-
dresses right off the boat at Ellis Island. It was about children looking
after their widowed father, a millstone selfishly indifferent to the misery he inflicts. It was about Dottie's life—the years from fourteen to
twenty, when she did nothing but care for Henry Rothschild—but also
about her brother Harry, a drunkard unable to keep a job who finally
runs off and is never seen again.

Considering her finicky attention to details (writing five words and
erasing seven, she joked), progress on the novel was frustratingly slow.
Aside from the book, she continued to write humorous pieces for magazines. When some of her friends started a publication, she agreed to

help out with donations of verse and criticism. It was strictly a favor. Asking payment from a harebrained stunt that would not last more than a few weeks never occurred to her.

PEOPLE WERE CONSTANTLY rushing in and out of Jane and Harold's house in Hell's Kitchen. After five years they were finally about to launch the first issue of a weekly humor magazine about New York, written not for old ladies in Iowa but for New Yorkers. Through Ross's association with the Thanatopsis Literary and Inside Straight Club, one of the players had generously put up twenty-five thousand dollars. (He was Raoul Fleischmann, whose family money came from baking goods.) All that remained now was to find the right name.

Manhattan? Truth? Our Town?

At the Round Table one day, a press agent who ate there regularly looked up from his plate.

What was the big fuss? said John Peter Toohey. Wasn't the magazine about New York? So call it *The New Yorker.*

The New Yorker's angel, bored with the baking business, was pleased to be involved with "these amusing and interesting people." Harold Ross impressed Raoul Fleischmann as "an enthusiastic wild sort of player" who was "something to see in action" at the poker table (and presumably just as dynamic in business). Unable to do enough for Ross, Raoul offered him free office space in a building he owned on West Forty-fifth, but much of the editing and proofing took place in Hell's Kitchen. Several days before the first issue reached the newsstands, Frank Adams stopped by the house. *The New Yorker* stank, he said, an opinion he repeated a few days later in the Conning Tower. "Sunday February 15. To H. Ross's, and he shewed me a copy of The New Yorker, which is to be issued on Tuesday, but most of it seemed too frothy for my liking," he wrote, before going on to relate how he found himself in a restaurant without his wallet and had to borrow money for the check, a matter of greater importance.

That Frank himself had written some of those frothy sketches did not alter the fact that he was right. The magazine looked amateurish. Its humor was sophomoric. In short, it turned out an unqualified mess. Raoul Fleischmann, embarrassed, wished he had never laid eyes on Harold Ross.

ON WINTER EVENINGS, as she walked home from her job at the *Times,* Jane checked newsstands to see how the magazine was selling. Judging by the stacks, it wasn't. "It is difficult to describe my despair," she later recalled. In the following weeks, as circulation kept sliding, the smell of defeat "hung all around us."

At the outset Harold received help from some of his Round Table friends—Ferber, Broun, Parker, Woollcott, Connelly, Kaufman—all of whom lent creditability to the project by allowing him to use their names on his editorial board, but it was nothing more than window dressing. Edna, for example, sniffing failure, would not allow him to publish any of her writing and withdrew her name. The one who did the most was Dottie, who for the first several issues contributed humor, verse, and theater reviews under the byline "Last Night." Harold was happy to get her. In trying to develop an editorial mood for the book, one that might duplicate the Round Table wit—sharp, funny, and bad—he came up with the idea of a staple department he called "Talk of the Town," which he wanted to read like sophisticated, amusing dinner-table conversation. There were few people whose ordinary table talk effortlessly got more laughs than Dottie's. (Bunny had compiled a guest list for an ideal party and put her name near the top.) As Harold knew, she could not only talk it but write it, good New York vernacular prose that sounded easy, articulate, and terrifically funny. To be sure, whatever she gave him was a throwaway, tossed off in a spare moment, but since she was not being paid, he could hardly complain.

At a poker game one night, at the apartment of Herbert Swope, Harold won a few dollars. As he and Jane were pulling on their coats, another player began to taunt him for leaving when he was ahead and for allowing "a skirt" to push him around. To Harold those were fighting words. Without thinking, he took off his coat and returned to the table, and Jane went home by herself.

Next morning she noticed him weaving drunkenly across Forty-seventh Street, looking "more bent than usual." After he'd fallen into bed, she fished from his pockets IOUs that totaled thirty thousand dollars, more than their personal investment in the magazine. She felt sick and "disgraced," but what could she say to a man for whom everything was a personal tragedy anyway? Once he sobered up, she suggested there was "nothing left for us to do but commit suicide."

Actually, there were those who wanted to kill him. One of them must have been Raoul Fleischmann, whose twenty-five-thousand-dollar investment was gone.

WHEN DOTTIE and Frank Adams came by to pick up Edna on Sunday morning, they were planning to drive out into the country and lunch at an inn. There was no way Dottie was going to be happy spending the day in an automobile with Edna, but she agreed to the outing for Frank's sake. It had been an unpleasant year for him: Minna filed for a New York divorce, after the standard adultery charade in a hotel room, and he had promised to pay a monstrous amount of alimony. His bachelorhood was short-lived, however; he and Esther Root were going to be married in six weeks.

At the Prasada, Dottie expected to find Edna dressed and ready to go. But when she crept out of her bedroom in pajamas and slippers, it was plain she had changed her mind. Over her nightclothes was draped a bed jacket bedecked in pink feathers. What kind of getup was that? Dottie wondered. The last time she saw anything like it was on the stage of the Winter Garden pasted to the backside of a Follies girl.

They would have to go on without her, Edna said, because she was sick and going straight back to bed.

As soon as she and Frank made their exit, Dottie began marveling over the sight of the feathers and poking fun at Edna. What a disappointment. But how simply divine Ferber looked in spite of feeling unwell. Oh yes indeed. And what about that swooshy lingerie. "Pink marabou flowing like water," she went on, until she emptied her arsenal. Frank started cackling. Despite his affection for Edna, after all the wonderful meals she had fed him, he could not resist repeating the gibes at Ferber's feathers in the Conning Tower.

Dottie, increasingly impatient with phonies and snobs, found it hard to censor herself around people who put on airs. Among the guests at one of her cocktail parties was a well-known name-dropper. No sooner had the hoity-toity woman left than embarrassed friends attempted to defend her. "She's such a nice girl," one of them said to Dottie. "She wouldn't hurt a fly."

Dottie smiled politely. "Not if it was buttoned up," she said.

Dottie's feelings toward Edna were summed up when she penciled a cartoon showing her with head and eyes rolled back and nostrils flared, a dramatic pose that made her look like a ferret in orgasm. She sent it to Harold Ross. "Ah, look, Harold. Isn't it cute?" But her animosity was mainly based on the suspicion that Edna was abnormal. As far as Dottie could tell, Ferber was satisfied with her life. (She was "happier than her happiest stories," Bill White once said.) Certainly every time Dottie saw her, she was boiling over with sunshine, the sort of writer who whistled at her typewriter, she bet. Probably she had never once thought about suicide. All that enthusiasm was absolutely poisonous.

Even more disgusting was her success. She was a writing cash register who regularly manufactured bestselling potboilers notable for flowery prose and gooey indigestible endings. Dottie had no tolerance for overwriting or happy endings, which she believed to be synonymous with dishonesty. As she was fond of pointing out, in all of history, with its billions of human beings, "not a single one ever had a happy ending." In all likelihood, Edna had never noticed.

EDNA HAD NOTICED. Not just about happy endings but about the Round Table. She knew that trusting any of them could be as dangerous as turning her back on a family of hungry grizzly bears. To celebrate a rare total eclipse of the sun in January, she gave a dinner party, lavish as always. Her guests were Aleck, Harpo Marx, and Neysa McMein and her husband, Jack Baragwanath. During the course of the evening one of them spilled red wine on her rug and overturned a soup plate, and another kicked a foot through a nest of Chinese lacquer tables. Glasses shattered; an oxblood vase crashed. As if ruining her immaculate apartment weren't enough, the knuckle-dragging apes ran out and left her with the wreckage.

That spring Edna was concerned with more important things than the disgusting behavior of the Round Table. During the winter she had done extensive reading until she knew practically everything to be known about side-wheelers, stern-wheelers, and keelboats. In April, fired up, she eagerly returned to live and work on board the James Adams Floating Palace Theatre in North Carolina. She attended rehearsals, sold tickets, talked with the audiences, even played a walk-on, anything that would give her what she needed to re-create show-business life on the Mississippi in the final years of the nineteenth century.

This time her muse was a boat, which she named the *Cotton Blossom*. Once she had the setting, the story line fell into place rather easily, since so much of it was autobiographical. Portraying various members of the Ferber family had by this time become her well-disguised, standard plot. In *So Big*, Selina Peake and her weak blob of a husband (killed off as soon as possible) are a replay of her parents' marriage. Now, in *Show Boat*, the heroine has a domineering, puritanical mother modeled on Julia Ferber. Magnolia Hawks, a captain's daughter in love with a dashing cardsharp, is of course Edna herself transformed into the woman she could have been if only she had been born tall and beautiful.

In the summer, vacationing in a Basque village on the Bay of Biscay, Edna got to work but discovered the writing refused to flow. As it turned out, the manuscript would still be incomplete a full year later, by which time she was calling the book *Slow Poke*.

. . .

IN THE REAL-ESTATE SECTION of the Sunday *New York Times,* Vincent noticed an ad for a dairy farm near Austerlitz, New York, close to the Massachusetts border. She was unfamiliar with the area, but the property—seven hundred acres of wooded farmland on the western slopes of the Berkshires—sounded interesting. Gene agreed they should go take a look.

Since returning to New York the previous fall, Vincent had grown increasingly unhappy at "8¾" Bedford Street, as she jokingly called her house, no longer so cute after all. She had never felt truly comfortable living in the city—Bunny noticed that venturing across streets petrified her—and by this time her disaffection with crowds and tall buildings had grown intense. Feeling sluggish, disinclined to write, she was convinced that the din of the city was partly responsible for her malaise. Maybe she needed to be in the country, cut off from the world, where she could reduce life to its essentials: no intruders, no noise, "a nice gentlemanly mortgage" instead of rent.

Reaching the Berkshires took five hours by car, with the road winding through the rolling pastures of Dutchess County before sweeping up into the mountains. At Chatham, the town closest to the farm, they checked into a hotel and waited for the broker to arrive.

Columbia County turned out to be wild and mountainous. Near the sleepy hamlet Austerlitz they reached a fork and began twisting their way up a steep dirt road through the woods. After three bumpy miles and a sharp turn, the ride suddenly ended at a cluster of wooden buildings. At the time of the Civil War it must have been a fine working farm with guest house and barn, but this was the Twenties. The two-story main house was a typical period New England farmhouse with tiny rooms and a dark narrow kitchen, a rural version of 75½ Bedford Street. Although cheap, and certainly not as run-down as Ruth's Sabine Farm, the premises needed thousands of dollars in improvements to make them livable. Of course there was no plumbing, electricity, or running water. Buying the place would require tearing down walls to enlarge the rooms and installing a septic system, a furnace, and a generator for electric current. The absence of telephone lines did not concern Vincent, who did not want a phone in her house.

With no neighbors for miles around, the spot had an air of extreme seclusion. The idea that nobody would visit unless invited pleased Vincent enormously. Even in the sepia light of late winter, when the slopes looked slate gray and barren except for patches of snow, it was easy to imagine vistas of dramatic beauty. In summer, she was told, the pastures would be gorgeously brightened by the tall rose-colored shrubs known as steeplebush.

For Gene, moving to the Berkshires would mean giving up his importing business, and even though he had talked of such a move, he had not actually done anything about it. But Vincie's career was more important than his, he said. If a poetic citadel was what she needed, he would give up selling coffee and become a farmer.

On May 21, they were deeded the farm for nine thousand dollars. Euphoric, Vincent could only express her excitement to Cora by means of baby talk. She was "nearly daft in the bean—kidney bean, lima bean, string-bean, butter-bean—you dow whad I bean—ha! ha! ha!"

No. 14, RUE DE TILSITT, on the corner of Avenue Wagram, a good address in a proper bourgeois neighborhood, was a white wedding-cake building iced with gargoyle rosettes and fussy wrought-iron balconies. The brasserie on the ground floor got noisy, however, and the absence of an elevator meant climbing five flights. The flat was "swell," Scott insisted. To Zelda it smelled musty, like an old church. The red plush furniture, sat on by countless transients, was "genuine Louis XV from the Galeries Lafayette," she joked, and whoever installed the exotic wallpaper, purple and gold, must have had a peculiar sense of humor. But who cared? The flat was cheap, spacious enough to accommodate a writer, child, and nanny, and it was in Paris.

By this time Zelda had come to feel at home in France. After a mis-

erable winter, ill with colitis and an ovarian inflammation, she had recovered sufficiently to enjoy a beautiful spring. Horse chestnuts were
blooming in the Luxembourg; the air was cold and crisp, but café ter-
races were cozily heated. *The Great Gatsby* was to be published on the
tenth of April, and both Scott and Zelda felt confident they'd hit the
jackpot, critically as well as commercially. Happily juggling figures,
Scott was counting on sales of seventy-five thousand copies, but even
as few as twenty thousand would easily wipe out his debt to Scribner's.

Zelda, meanwhile, concerned herself with mundane matters. Their
wretched Renault, nothing but trouble from the first, was sitting three
hundred miles away in a Lyon garage. While in Naples boarding a ship
for Marseille, the car was damaged, and its roof had to be removed,
turning it into a convertible. Halfway between Marseille and Paris, it
rained so hard they were forced to abandon the rolling bathtub and
make the rest of their journey by train, a disagreeable undertaking with
a small child and a nanny and everything they owned.

Getting the car back would not be easy, Zelda knew, because Scott
kept procrastinating. But one day he came home and announced it was
all arranged. He was leaving for Lyon in the morning with a friend
of his.

In the Dingo bar weeks ago, Scott had met an American newspaperman, Ernest Hemingway, whose short stories he'd admired in the
Transatlantic Review. Ordering a bottle of champagne, Scott was quick
to tell Hemingway that he was a genius. Flattery continued to gush out
of him as from an open tap, and even though his remarks were completely sincere, the torrent of compliments embarrassed Hemingway:
"It was all about my writing and how great it was." Eventually Scott
tired of extolling his talent and moved on to other subjects that made
Hemingway feel even more uncomfortable.

Did Ernest sleep with his wife before their marriage? he asked.

Ernest could scarcely believe his ears.

Over a second bottle, Scott's upper lip broke into beads of perspira-
tion, and the color drained from his face. Alarmed, Ernest wondered if
he was going to pass out, possibly even die, on the spot.

Their next meeting, at La Closerie des Lilas, went better. *In Our Time*, Ernest's first collection of short stories, had been issued the previous fall by a small Parisian press and was now scheduled to be released by a major American house. Scott considered Boni & Liveright inferior to the white-collar Scribner's and did not hesitate to say so. Three years older than Ernest and assuming the role of the seasoned professional with a journeyman, he was happy to retail insider gossip about the business and elucidate the fine points of getting well published. He also felt sorry for Ernest, who lived poorly with his wife over a sawmill on rue Notre-Dame-des-Champs in a flat with no running water, toilet, or electricity. Their bed was a mattress on the floor. Hearing that, Scott offered to lend him a copy of *The Great Gatsby*.

It was at their second meeting that Scott proposed traveling to Lyon on the express train and driving home the Renault, a quick, enjoyable jaunt to Burgundy. Learning that Scott would pay all the expenses, Ernest eagerly agreed.

Zelda had never heard of Ernest Hemingway. For all she knew, he was just a bum Scott picked up in a bar. But she was happy about the Renault.

A T THE GARE DE LYON, Ernest waited for Scott to arrive with the tickets. When Scott failed to show up, Ernest purchased a ticket and went ahead alone, winding up hundreds of miles from home, having spent money he could ill afford on train fare, and trying to figure out what had gone wrong. In desperation, he called rue de Tilsitt and talked to a servant who said that Mr. Fitzgerald had gone to Lyon and Mrs. Fitzgerald was too ill to come to the phone. The next morning an apologetic (and obviously drunk) Scott appeared at Ernest's hotel.

He missed the train, he said.

Ernest had never heard of a grown man missing a train, but he let it go. On the way home, rain once again forced the topless Renault off the road, leading to another night at a hotel. Scott, drenched and positive that he had caught pneumonia, insisted Ernest find him a thermometer.

Afterward, in a burst of fake enthusiasm, Ernest wrote his new editor, Max Perkins, that it was a "great trip." In reality, it was a terrible trip, during which he sowed lifelong seeds of contempt for Scott, whose maddening behavior he considered both infantile and unmanly in the extreme. Being around him for even a short time could make a person weep with frustration.

Shortly after the jaunt to Lyon, Scott invited Ernest and his wife, Hadley, for lunch at rue de Tilsitt. Zelda, aware that Ernest and his war experiences—he had been wounded in Italy—made an impression on Scott, who regretted missing action, found her husband's new friend disappointing. He was attractive, a strapping six-footer with brown hair and thick full lips. But compared with Scott, in his natty collegiate suits and buttoned-down collars and with his gentleman's walking cane, Ernest looked like a roughneck. He had the chesty confidence of a small boy, with the bluster and social graces to match. Even though she looked down on Scott for being pathetically fearful, Ernest, exactly the opposite, was just as hard to take. He talked too much about who was tough and who was not, until his two-fisted bragging got to be silly. After all, the war was over.

Ernest's wife was overweight. Eight years older than her husband, she had evidently let herself go after the birth of their son, John. But what put off Zelda about Hadley Hemingway was her passivity. From what she could gather, Hadley did whatever Ernest wanted her to do. Didn't she ever stand up to her husband?

During lunch Ernest was busy inspecting Zelda. Anybody could see she was mighty spoiled, he told himself, but her skin was grand, and he liked her legs and the color of her hair. Her conversation was disturbing, though. It seemed to him that she was jealous of Scott—not only of their excursion to Lyon but also of her husband's work. He saw lots of women like her—competitive, obstructive, undermining, the most dangerous kind of wife for a writer.

The next time Zelda ran into Ernest, he told her something funny about the day of the luncheon. That very night, he confided, he had a wet dream about her.

Despite his uneasiness with both of the Fitzgeralds, Ernest was eager to introduce them to another American writer living in Paris, a wealthy woman who, like Scott, had taken an affectionate personal interest in his career. He wrote to Gertrude Stein that he was bringing the Fitzgeralds to her apartment on Friday afternoon. Scott's wife was "worth seeing."

Scott was thrilled at the prospect of meeting a celebrity like Stein, who with her older brother collected Cubist art and who had written *Three Lives*. That book was a little masterpiece, clean and lucid. But Gertrude, interested in experimentation, used an unconventional prose style in her new book, *The Making of Americans,* which relied heavily on repetition and often sounded like gibberish, at which she became so proficient that people ceased to read her. Before the visit Scott sent the fifty-one-year-old writer an adoring note, calling her "very handsome, very gallant, very kind," precisely the sort of soft soap she appreciated.

At 27 rue de Fleurus, paintings—a remarkable treasury of Picassos, Cézannes, Matisses—covered the walls from floor to ceiling, and the food was bountiful. Gertrude, authoritative and commanding, looking very much like the Picasso portrait of her on the wall, sat enthroned in a large chair at the center of the studio, and guests crowded around to hear her talk. While this event was taking place center stage, her companion Alice Toklas occupied a separate limelight. Using a manner normally reserved for children, Alice smoothly herded the wives into a corner, where they were served tea and expected to behave themselves with polite small talk. Gertrude and Alice made a strange-looking couple—Stein, a peasantlike figure in brown corduroy caftans and sandals, and Toklas, in lacy dresses, dark and hairy with a mustache that would have looked splendid on a grenadier.

From her vantage point in the ladies' ghetto, Zelda found it all a little offensive. Of course Gertrude and Alice were eccentrics—and lesbians—but that was beside the point. What made her indignant was how they treated women. She had never cared for the role of wallflower.

O N A SATURDAY afternoon in early May, two years after their meeting at Vincent's apartment, Frank Adams and Esther Root were married. All other obstacles finally overcome, the only remaining restriction was the law forbidding Frank to remarry in the state of New York for five years. For that reason, the wedding was taking place at the home of friends whose Greenwich property conveniently straddled the state line between Connecticut and New York, making it possible to hold the ceremony in their orchard, the reception on the lawn of their house.

Assembled for the marquee wedding was the cream of New York's publishing and theatrical communities: the Swopes and Lardners, Fleischmanns and Pulitzers, Boissevains and Benéts, and of course the leading citizenry of the Algonquin Round Table village. Beneath the apple trees stretched a white satin ribbon marking the state line. As throngs of notables squeezed into the garden, the couple marched slowly out of the house and down to the ribbon. The bride wore a frilly white gown and carried a bouquet of lilies of the valley. "I never saw her look so pretty," Vincent reported to her mother. "And I never saw Frank look so well, either, very serious and quite pale."

At the reception no expense had been spared on caterers and bootleggers, and guests began lapping up "rafts of caviar and oceans of champagne," Vincent would recall. In the crowd, wearing hangdog expressions, were Jane and Harold. Even when *The New Yorker*'s pressrun had dropped from fifteen thousand to eight thousand, the size of the book to twenty-four pages, Jane continued to believe in her husband, whom she knew to be a first-rate editor. People said that entrusting a manuscript to Harold was like "putting your car in the hands of a skilled mechanic, not an automotive engineer, with a bachelor of science degree, but a guy who knows what makes a motor go." But publishing a

magazine was another matter, and just the previous day Raoul Fleischmann and other backers made the decision to pull out. Under the apple trees in Greenwich, however, swigging champagne, Harold and
Raoul began to rehash the decision to cease publication. By the afternoon's end Raoul had been persuaded to offer a last-minute reprieve
enabling Harold to go on publishing throughout the summer.

Late Saturday afternoon the party began to break up. The newly-
weds hurried back to the city so that Frank could attend his regular Saturday poker game, an absurd detour, but he insisted on sitting in for
what he promised would be only a few hands. At the Fleischmann
home on East Seventy-fourth Street, Esther helped scramble eggs for
the Thanatopsis players before settling quietly on a stool behind her
husband's chair. Before she knew it, Frank had played more than a few
hands and their honeymoon money was gone. In order to take their European trip, he had to borrow from George Kaufman.

Dottie and Deems, meanwhile, who had come to the wedding together, left separately after a tiff. She went home with a close friend,
Elinor Wylie. A poet often compared with Edna St. Vincent Millay, Elinor had an insane ex-husband, a son she had not seen for years, several
suicidal siblings, and a nutty pathological obsession with a dead poet.
(Rebecca West once described her fixation on Percy Bysshe Shelley as
"not just crazy but dotty.") She was tall and skeletally thin, from constant dieting, and had slender wrists and ankles—a "fragile china deer,"
in the eyes of her worshipful poet-editor husband, William Rose Benét.
However, other men found her demeanor—it could be hard and icy at
times—a trifle intimidating. "I just couldn't imagine how it would be
possible to become intimate with Elinor," Arthur Ficke admitted in
later years. "She frightened me a little."

A year earlier Elinor talked Bill Benét into leaving their New York
apartment for an old-fashioned cottage in New Canaan. Even though
the move would mean an hour's commute to his job at the *Saturday Review of Literature*, it would offer healthy surroundings for his three children, and solitude for her writing. But having uprooted the family, she
soon grew sick of Connecticut and dealing with such trivia of home

ownership as temperamental furnaces. When Elinor lived in New York, Dottie had got into the habit of turning up on her doorstep to wring her hands and recount the endless indignities of her everyday life. So when Elinor insisted she spend the night in New Canaan, Dottie quickly piled into the taxi. Possibly she was unaware that Elinor had also invited Vincent and her husband and their closest friends, Arthur and Gladys Ficke. After an ugly fight with the cabdriver, who demanded a larger fare than agreed upon, the group settled into the Benét dining room for dinner and drinks. Conversation was dominated by Vincent and Gene, who had driven down from a farm in the Berkshires and could talk of nothing else.

Out of boredom or timidity, more likely anger because Vincent was a friend of Deems and his wife, Dottie had little to contribute. As the New Canaan dinner progressed, she found even less to say to Vincent, who in person turned out to be unamusing. The coolness was mutual as Vincent stared through Dottie as if she were invisible. (When she wrote her mother about visiting the Benéts, she failed to mention Dottie's presence.)

After the guests filed upstairs to bed, Elinor and Dottie stayed up drinking in the drawing room. They were joined by Arthur, who began pontificating on "life and death and the nature of man." Possibly to put a stop to his gas, Elinor asked Dottie to recite some of her poetry, which prompted a lecture from Art on how she might improve her work. Furious at his presumption, she said good night, only to be awakened some time later by noises that turned out to be Elinor and Art tiptoeing around the room.

Did she really cut her wrists? Art said. He was dying to see her scars. Dottie burst into tears.

Next morning everybody was suffering from hangovers that were "perfectly terrible," Art remembered, making them "a little on edge, everybody trying to conceal his own ediness. Sometime about noon the party broke up, with love and kisses."

Among the shoulders Dottie had cried on at Frank's wedding was Ring Lardner's. She had been having an "unfortunate affair," Ring reported to Scott, "and for some reason or other, I thought a visit to us would cheer her up." What she needed to feel better was plenty of fresh air and a quiet place to write.

But Dottie ignored Ring's invitation and continued to shuttle between Deems's farm and the city, which that June had never looked prettier. Fifth Avenue flappers were wearing clothes so artistic they should have been hanging in art museums: dresses, in lush reds and pinks, garnished with cheerful pansies; chintz dresses glazed in wallpaper prints; big floppy hats; flaring coats trimmed with wispy fur hems. No stockings either, just bare legs that made everyone look cool and trashy. But then a heat wave pushed the temperatures close to one hundred, and Dottie decided a week in Great Neck might not be a bad idea after all.

It would have been difficult to find a house less conducive to creative work than the Lardners'. At East Shore Drive they usually entertained a procession of visitors, with traffic so heavy that Ellis Lardner was known to complain of scarcely having time to change the sheets between guests. Moreover, Ellis and Ring had four boys under the age of twelve. Most disconcerting was Ring himself, who insisted on calling Dottie "Spark Plug"; he had completed eight weeks' worth of syndicated columns and was "constantly cock-eyed, drinking all night and sleeping all day and never working," he admitted. He was also horny; even though he was known as a faithful husband, Dottie later told friends that he was "after her all hours of the day and night."

At the end of July, despite the heat, she returned to Deems's farm full of determination to develop a more positive attitude. She was going to be a little more cheerful, a little less clingy, a generally more entertaining person. It was too late, however. When her back was turned, Deems had decided to patch up relations with Mary Kennedy. They were giving their marriage a second chance, he informed her.

IT WAS JULY 28, a month after their arrival at Steepletop. Vincent was sitting in her farmhouse writing letters while watching for Gene to come home from Albany, where he had gone to sell a crate of huckleberries. He promised to bring back presents—paintbrushes and loaves of good bread. Vincent had never been more content. She and Gene were going to love each other "forever," she wrote to a Vassar friend. They planned to live year-round at Steepletop, except in winter, when they would occasionally travel to the city for music or theater, and they were going to raise sheep, eventually five hundred and maybe a thousand on "these green hills."

As city folks, they hardly knew where to begin in running a farm, although they did manage to purchase every kind of garden tool sold in Great Barrington, including a twenty-foot pruning fork. They also received help on the gardens from Gene's nephew Freddie, a professional landscaper. Hiring crews of workers, they sunk thousands of dollars into remodeling, and within a few weeks the kitchen plumbing was connected, and three handsome chimneys installed. "Our home is now beginning to be comfortable," Gene told Art and Gladys. With plenty of hot water, and the final touch of a marvelous bathroom, "all we lack is a maid." On a hillside among the pines he rigged up a small shed for Vincent's desk and books, a sanctuary that could be heated by a wood-stove in winter. Next he was planning to add a guest wing to the main house.

Unfortunately, these projects kept them broke. The expenses of country life had turned out to be staggering, and, on top of everything else, they had to buy a third car, a Maxwell coupe, because the open Mercer was obviously impractical for a farm.

Now that Vincent had everything she ever wanted, she had a tendency to brag a little to her family: she spotted a rose-breasted grosbeak, she owned a German police dog named Altair and a cat named Smoky, she discovered the rhubarb and asparagus and an abundant variety of berries—the strawberries were gone, but she still had blueberries, currants, and cultivated raspberries. All this she described in rapturous detail.

What didn't she have? "Very little gin left." But the local applejack was supposed to be excellent.

One of the first visitors to the farm was Deems Taylor, whom Vincent knew from Paris. While he and Mary Kennedy were on their honeymoon, the three of them spent numerous convivial evenings together, and the Taylors were fond of Vincent. When Deems received his commission from the Metropolitan Opera and needed a librettist, it occurred to Mary that the ideal collaborator would be Edna St. Vincent Millay, who was not just an extraordinary writer but also a person with some musical training. If anyone was smart enough to find the ideal subject for an American opera, it would be Millay.

Without ado, Vincent suggested dramatizing an old Grimm brothers fairy tale about a beautiful maiden whose jealous stepmother is not satisfied to be less than the fairest in the land—and who arranges for the little girl's death. The choice of Snow White was a bit curious—certainly there was nothing American about it—but nonetheless it was agreed by all concerned that the story would make a compelling opera. Before moving to the country, Vincent completed the first act of *The Casket of Glass*, at which point it became evident that the material, at least as she conceived it, was not really suitable for an opera. Some of her stage directions made little sense.

Wouldn't it be difficult for Snow White to sing with a cloth covering her face?

Maybe, but that could be easily remedied.

Discouraged, she gave up Snow White and promised to find Deems another story.

During Deems's visit to the farm, they spent the afternoon splashing in the brook, but she had nothing to give him in replacement for the Snow White libretto. As for her own work, she had not published a book of poetry in two years. Once she had established herself as a literary star, certainly after winning the Pulitzer, her fame seemed to steam along on its own. In June she was awarded an honorary doctor of literature degree from Tufts College. Almost every day she received requests for readings, autographs, advice on how to become a poet, so much correspondence that she was sick of seeing self-addressed envelopes. How on earth could she pay attention to such matters when there were "six workmen and a swarm of bees" in her house?

But not everything at Steepletop, needless to say, was faultless. The flies were awful. In a place miles from the nearest neighbors, it was hard to keep household servants, which could have accounted for the behavior of "the big nigger Julia who went crazy last night" because she feared being lynched, Vincent told her mother. Julia had to be escorted to the train, and Joseph was also fired because he "pissed in the berries."

One other thing: ever since moving to Steepletop, she had a headache.

S COTT SWORE he was going to quit writing. No more novels. He couldn't live like this. Instead, he would go to Hollywood and learn the movie business.

A few days after publication of *The Great Gatsby*, Max Perkins cabled that the initial reviews were excellent but sales looked "doubtful." Several days later he wrote Scott praising the novel as "extraordinary" and saying it was of course far too early to judge sales.

As it turned out, Perkins's cautionary forecast had proved all too accurate: Scott's novel was selling poorly. Scribner's first printed 20,870 copies, and a second printing in the summer added another 3,000 copies, but 24,000 was a far cry from the 75,000 of Scott's dreams. Although his name remained well known to the public, as a pop celebrity if nothing else, five years had elapsed since *This Side of Paradise* and three since *The Beautiful and Damned*. That year the bestselling books were *The Green Hat* by Michael Arlen and another Sinclair Lewis novel, *Arrowsmith*. *Gatsby* did not reach the bestseller list; in fact, it would earn a total of $6,889 from 1925 to 1931, a sum less than half of the royalties for each of his two previous books.

"I'm not depressed," Scott assured his agent, although he was utterly devastated. But to Bunny he wrote angrily and truthfully: not one reviewer, not even the most enthusiastic, had the slightest idea what the book was about.

To be sure, writers who mattered—Edith Wharton, Gertrude

Stein—had been quick to recognize the novel's quality, and T. S. Eliot believed it was the biggest advance in American fiction since Henry James. Still, Scott could not help sorting through the wreckage. What did he do wrong? Was it because he killed off his central character? If only he had a better title; if only he had described the affair between Daisy and Gatsby after their reunion. The female characters should have been stronger, because everyone knew woman readers dominated fiction sales. While watching the rearview mirror in disbelief, he worked on a story ("The Rich Boy") and hounded Harold Ober to advance him money and to get Erich von Stroheim to direct the film. So far no studio was taking an interest, however.

Gatsby was widely reviewed, but despite Max's early reports the notices fell well short of "excellent." "A Dud," read the *World*'s headline, while the *Times* called it "a long short story," and the *Herald Tribune* sniffed, "Uncurbed melodrama." Attacks by the Round Table writers infuriated Scott. Frank Adams of the *World* massacred *Gatsby* as a "dull tayle" about the high jinks of the rich, famous, and juiced up. "And Lord! How much drinking is done by his characters!" Ruth Hale, who considered Scott a perennial juvenile, wrote in the *Brooklyn Daily Eagle* that "the boy is simply puttering around." At a party she told Max Perkins that the "new book by your *enfant terrible* is really *terrible*."

When summer arrived, the social scene in Paris turned into one big sleep-away camp, with more than forty thousand American tourists taking advantage of a fantastic exchange rate of twenty-four francs to the dollar. At home, people bought houses in which they lived only a few days a year and clothing they never wore at all. For their holidays, herds of them flocked onto luxury liners bound for France, where they stayed, for pennies, in hotels so elite they never had to speak the language or meet the natives. The summer was a blur of "1000 parties and no work," Scott wrote in his ledger. As Zelda observed, "There were Americans at night, and day Americans, and we all had Americans in the bank to buy things with." Usually the Fitzgeralds had nothing in the bank, even though Scott would earn more than eighteen thousand dollars, mainly from magazine sales, that year, about the same as in 1920.

Drenched in Coty's Chypre and
armed with a verbal switchblade:
Dorothy Parker in 1921.

Edna St. Vincent Millay
under the magnolia blossoms,
Mamaroneck, New York, 1914.

Edna Ferber with editor William Allen
White, covering the Republican National
Convention, Chicago, 1912.

By 1920, Edna had become a successful writer of commercial fiction, but she craved a literary prize.

Edna in Native American costume at a vacation spot in Colorado Springs.

Zelda Sayre at a dance recital in
Montgomery, Alabama, 1915.

Zelda Sayre in Montgomery a few
months before her marriage to
F. Scott Fitzgerald.

Zelda Fitzgerald wearing men's
knickers during a motor trip in 1920.
People were shocked.

Jane Grant before her marriage, in France, c. 1918.

After his discharge from the army, Edmund "Bunny" Wilson found a job at *Vanity Fair*.

Ruth Hale, a.k.a. Mrs. Heywood Broun.

Franklin Pierce Adams, or "F.P.A.," New York's most popular newspaper columnist.

Zelda, two months pregnant, visiting Montgomery with Scott, 1921.

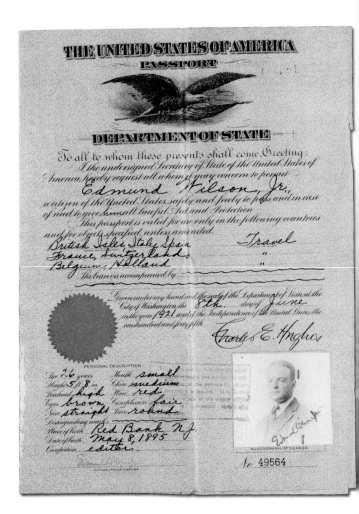

Bunny Wilson, shown in his 1921 passport photo, arrived in Paris and eagerly looked up Vincent.

Zelda and Scott with the baby on the lawn of their house in Great Neck, New York, 1922.

Vincent and her sisters, Norma and Kathleen, visiting their mother in Maine.

To 42 Commerce Street, New York City.
Paris,   29 Oct. 1924.

Darlings. Here we are in Paris, at last. We had so hoped to
find you still here.
        Our glorious and wonderful journey came to an unpleasant end
ar Delhi. Vincent got sick and I got sick and spent a week in
a hospital in Bombay. She with dyssentary and I with
(illegible) fever. We left the hospital too soon, to catch the
boat to Marseilles and on the boat I got flebitus. I had to be
taken from the boat to the train in a stretcher and ambulance
and the same way in Paris from the train to the hotel. Edna
arranged everything wonderfully, although she was still very
weak. We are now 14 days in this hotel. I have not moved and
must lie perfectly quiet on my back. Vincent does everything
for me, which is a lot. The doctor thinks I am doing fine and
we hope that I may get up in a few days and will be able to
leave for Holland in a few days and then for New York, where
ith the help og God we hope to be in your arms before the end
of November, about 14 days after this letter reaches you.
                (No signature)

Dear old Artie and Gladys--
                Isn't it the limit?-- (I sharpened this pencil
with a fruit-knife.) We shall see you soon and tell you all our
troubles-- never mind, we've had a lot of things besides
troubles since we set forth-- and it's been worth it.-- So
much love, dear friends
                        Vincent.

(Enclosure.)

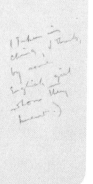

ABOVE: Vincent and Eugen Boissevain on a honeymoon voyage to the Far East, 1924.

LEFT: Letter home: Vincent mails Arthur and Gladys Ficke snapshots taken in China.

An abortion and a nasty breakup do not prevent Charles MacArthur and Dottie (seated together) from keeping up with the Long Island cocktail crowd. Other guests are *Harper's Bazaar* editor Arthur Samuels, a wigless Harpo Marx, and Aleck Woollcott.

On the Riviera: The Fitzgeralds with Scottie and her nanny, Lillian Maddock, in their secondhand Renault.

As hope of a commercial success slowly faded, Scott and Zelda climbed into their Renault and headed to the beach umbrellas of the Cap d'Antibes for a month's holiday with friends.

NOT LONG AFTER arriving in France in 1924, Zelda and Scott had made the acquaintance of a well-to-do American couple. In the accidental way these things happen, a Great Neck friend suggested they look up her brother and sister-in-law, who had left the country to live permanently in France. While not conspicuously wealthy, Sara and Gerald Murphy were sufficiently comfortable to do as they pleased without the inconvenience of having to work for a living. Gerald's family owned a store on Fifth Avenue in New York that sold luxury goods—pigskin luggage, Scottish golf clubs, thermos bottles—and Sara's father was an ink manufacturer. After settling first in a Paris apartment, they purchased a lush seven-acre spread in Antibes and began to transform its rather ordinary chalet and outbuildings into a fourteen-room villa, a pair of guest cottages, and a studio Gerald used for painting. They called the compound Villa America.

Sara had a tendency to worry, about her children, about her garden, about illnesses and bacteria and germs. Two cows supplied her family fresh milk because she distrusted local dairies. Coins were scrubbed before being handled by her tots, and railway compartments were draped in Lysol-laundered sheets. Sara did not believe in taking risks.

Before noon, arriving at the sandy cove called La Garoupe, she swam and sunbathed next to the crystal blue water of the Mediterranean with her swimsuit pulled off the shoulders. She wore a rope of pearls and let the pearls stream down her tanned back because, she said, pearls needed the salt and the sun. On a rug under a striped umbrella, she leaned on one elbow and observed her family while scribbling lists of things to do in a little book lying on the sand. Her children, two cuddly little boys and a girl, all sweet-faced cherubs, looked as if they might have been rented. Her husband, wearing a knit cap and a striped bathing suit, led Patrick, Baoth, and Honoria in calisthenics before spending the rest of the morning raking the beach of seaweed and stones. After refreshments, cold dry sherry and crackers, they collected their paraphernalia and went home for lunch.

Scott had always been infatuated with the rich, so it was natural he should be attracted to the Murphys, who not only knew how to live well but also were kind and intelligent. What made Gerald and Sara so exceptional was an unlimited capacity for fantasy, the fact that they had managed to create a special kingdom for themselves. In their grand conception, life could be art. Like painters approaching a blank canvas, they imagined the good life as a picture-perfect creation that can be willed into existence, then treated as if the fantastic creation actually existed. At Villa America, after all the messiness of living had been airbrushed away, what remained was not only niceness but improbable order and harmony. When Gerald mixed a Bailey cocktail (Booth's House of Lords gin and grapefruit juice), he used fresh lime juice and only a single sprig of mint, torn by hand. Whether it involved the correct preparation of a cocktail or the right table linen or the hundreds of dollars in subscriptions to the best American magazines, Gerald was the ultimate perfectionist.

But regardless of his romantic philosophy, he remained the consummate executive. Although he had turned his back on shop keeping and the leather business, Villa America operated with the efficiency of the Mark Cross Company in Manhattan, Zelda observed. In contrast to the sloppiness of her own household, priorities at Villa America tended toward perfection in every last detail. It made her wonder if the Murphys didn't talk a bit *too* compulsively about love, if their judicious standards weren't a little *too* painstaking, because every occasion seemed relentlessly rehearsed.

During August, Zelda and Scott lived at the Hôtel du Cap and dined almost every evening by candlelight under the linden tree on the Villa America terrace. In an unpublished novel Zelda described the fictionalized Murphys eating "remarkable things with champagne" and tasting "the night-bitterness of the garden until ten o'clock." Before dinner Gerald served his guests two—and only two—cocktails, although dictating alcohol consumption to Scott and Zelda was impractical. While Scott enjoyed himself in Antibes, Zelda often felt ill and had to take barbiturates in order to sleep. One night when she swallowed too much, Scott became sufficiently frightened to walk up to Villa America and pound on the Murphys' door for help. Sara and Gerald could not have been nicer about being awoken. At the hotel they helped him walk Zelda up and down, but when Sara wanted to dose her with olive oil to induce vomiting, Zelda rejected it.

"If you drink too much oil you turn into a Jew," she said.

From Antibes, Scott sent Max Perkins a brief summary of his next novel, *Our Type*, about a violent son who kills his possessive mother. The story was reminiscent of the Leopold-Loeb murder, he said, but it was also about "Zelda and me." No writing was actually being done, however.

In early September, outwardly pictures of health, the Fitzgeralds left behind the Renault for an overhaul by the Murphys' chauffeur and went back to Paris by train. Seeing them go made Gerald sad. "We were happy when we were with you," he wrote them. "My God!? How rare it is. How rare." And he signed the letter with the name his children used. "Thank God for you both. dow dow."

WHEN DOTTIE RETURNED to the Algonquin, in September, she put Deems and the failed romance behind her. Out of habit, she fell into her former routines and made nightly rounds of the clubs, sometimes alone, sometimes with Bunny, who had recently separated from his wife. Invariably, she would insist on stopping at Tony's, because she had to see Mr. Benchley—he was in the dumps, and she worried about him. After two years he was still in love with his showgirl, who, tired of wearing bananas on her head (and tired of Bob), had begun auditioning for serious plays. As Dottie explained to Bunny, Carol Goodner did not have the decency to be faithful even when Bob had gone into debt for her. But what else could you expect of a floozy?

Bob was not the only one in the doldrums. A casualty of the breakup with Deems was Dottie's novel, which she subsequently published as a short story in *Pictorial Review* under the title "The Wonderful Old Gentleman: A Story Proving That No One Can Hate Like a Close Relative." But she felt like more of a failure than ever.

"What are you having?" a bartender asked her one night.

"Not much fun," she said.

It wasn't for lack of trying. For lunch, every day, she went downstairs to the Rose Room and sat at the Round Table and listened to Aleck and the regulars boast about their stocks. At cocktail time, people dropping up to her suite for drinks boasted about their stocks. Later, at Tony's, people boasting about their stocks tried to cheer her up by saying she looked marvelous. "Oh, Dorothy," cried a bar buddy. "How nice to see you looking so well."

Looking? Where in hell was he looking? Anybody could see she looked dreadful.

At the Round Table or at parties, one person she could be sure of running into was Harold Ross, whose half-baked magazine was struggling to survive. Dottie considered Harold "almost illiterate," a classic ignoramus who "never read anything and didn't know anything." So it was hard to imagine that *The New Yorker* would amount to much. Editing his own magazine had turned him into a pest, always hustling his friends and trying to get something for nothing.

"I thought you were coming into the office to write a piece last week," he said to her.

Oh, did she say that?

"What happened?"

"Somebody was using the pencil."

This was not a joke. Since his office could afford only a single typewriter, writers were obliged to take turns. Actually, unable to afford the writers themselves, Harold shamelessly nickeled-and-dimed some of them and compensated others, like Dottie, with pocket change or worthless company stock. His nervousness around women notwithstanding, he was fond of Dottie, and she liked him, possibly because they shared a common view of the world: the suspicion, deeply held, that everybody was out to get them. He, too, imagined that the rules of existence had been written specifically to wear him down. In conversation, the two malcontents made quite a pair, she scarcely able to utter a sentence without using the word "shit," as noun, adjective, or verb, and he cringing at profanity but invariably beginning or ending his sentences with "goddamn it."

Despite *The New Yorker*'s miserable pay, Dottie gave Harold a poem in which she imagined herself comfy in a marble urn watching "the worms slip by." Maybe taking it for a joke, surely in desperate need of contributions, he published "Epitaph." To Frank Adams at the *World* she sent "Story of Mrs. W——," an old-fashioned postcard from beyond the grave picturing how good it is to be dead. Her other poems written at this time contained references to shrouds and coffins. That her favorite subject had become death failed to alarm any of her best pals, however.

But when misery "crushed her as if she were between great smooth stones," as she wrote in an autobiographical story, she became frightened enough to seek psychological help. She consulted Alvan Barach, the Round Table's house shrink whose patients included Herbert Bayard Swope, Heywood Broun, George Gershwin, and Aleck Woollcott. A pulmonary specialist, Dr. Barach had no particular qualifications for practicing psychotherapy. He charged fees of twenty-five dollars an hour and dispensed treatment that he labeled "psychosomatic medicine." Exactly what the term meant remained a mystery, but at least his commonsense advice—warning Aleck to lose weight—did no harm.

As Dr. Barach explained to Dottie, she had "a lot of tender expectancies that weren't adequately fulfilled." Like the rest of her Round Table friends, she had failed to develop the serious side of her personality. Distrust of sentiment, a rigid insistence on irreverence—Dottie's constantly searching for the punch line—was causing all of them to miss out on a great deal. Not that anything was wrong with having a good sense of humor, but she should also acknowledge the gravity of life. Embracing the idea of earnestness would enable her to create purpose in her life, he said.

Dottie, pretending to listen to his spiel, guessed that he was right. Keeping company with barkeeps and "cheap people" was pathetic. But wait, didn't she spend the better part of a year trying to change her life by writing a novel? Despite the best intentions, she failed.

Dr. Barach made clear that she had a severe alcohol disorder. Her dependence was a major problem, he said; she must make an effort to sober up. On this point Dottie begged to differ. Although she had made a hash of her life, alcohol was not to blame. Drinkers such as Eddie— sloppy, blacking-out, falling-down, puking-in-the-street, peeing-on-the-floor drunkards—were alcoholics. She was a social drinker, always wearing a nice dress and hat, careful to get back to the hotel before she passed out.

In the end, her sessions with Barach, and his preaching, became meaningless because she already had determined a course of action, which had been in the back of her mind for a long time. In New York State, sleeping powders could be obtained only with a doctor's prescription. Not so in New Jersey. For several weeks she made regular trips to Hoboken and tramped from pharmacy to pharmacy buying Veronal. To avoid suspicion, she always purchased a comb or a wash towel, and eventually, like a squirrel storing acorns for a long winter, she accumulated a sizable cache of powders.

One day she went into her bathroom and crammed every one of the Hoboken sleeping powders down her throat. It was not a matter of waking that morning and deciding that was the day. It was an absence of options, not a plan.

And that was just the problem, no planning. There was no question that killing yourself required organization, but for a second time she failed to do it right. With no idea, really, about the number of powders constituting a deadly dose, she had made no attempt to find out.

Next day she was in the Presbyterian Hospital, naked under a white gown, without her scotch. Dr. Barach was severe. She must stay there until she dried out, he told her. Every afternoon, however, Heywood Broun came to visit and brought with him a movable cocktail hour in his gin-filled hip flask. When Dr. Barach found out, he read the riot act to both of them.

Worse than being a failed suicide was being a twice-failed suicide and having to face a double barrage of reproaches and questions. One attempt apparently was reasonable to most people, but two demanded fancy explanations. The only person she could stand to be around was Mr. Benchley.

"If you don't stop this sort of thing," he said cheerily, "you'll make yourself sick."

1926

Vincent and Gene name their farm Steepletop after a Berkshires shrub.

CHAPTER SEVEN

VINCENT WAS WORRIED. The headache did not go away, and recently she'd developed spots before her eyes. Dosing herself with Carter's Little Liver Pills and Lydia Pinkham's Vegetable Compound brought no relief. The pain, she was sure, must be nervous exhaustion owing to the strain of moving. She had been working hard and needed to unwind. But lying perfectly quiet had no effect; in fact, she got worse. Probably it was "nothing serious at all," she explained to her mother, in that there were no other symptoms, no fever or joint pain. A physical by a good doctor down in Great Barrington ruled out the possibility of heart, liver, lung, or kidney disease. Nothing turned up on an

eye examination either. Could it be her tonsils? Her teeth? With no reprieve in sight, she took to her bed.

Cora came down from Camden to nurse her. As a general rule, her
solution for practically any ailment was a regular bowel movement, and
she immediately began to administer homegrown Down East remedies:
bran once a day, three quarts of water, no enemas. In a very short time,
however, Gene had had enough of both Cora's bran and the local horse
doctors and decided they must seek the advice of New York specialists.
It was discouraging therefore to learn that the best doctors in the city
could offer no organic cause for Vincent's persistent pain. Falling back
on standard remedies, they advised seclusion and bed rest, meaning no
activities whatsoever, not even reading or writing.

At the Chelsea Hotel in Atlantic City, Vincent sat in front of a wide-
open window facing the breakers, bundled in blankets with hot-water
bottles at her feet, a nurse in attendance. As awful as she felt, she did
not appear ill. A quilted dressing gown, peacock blue crepe de Chine
with white fur collar and cuffs, and newly shingled hair made her look
younger than thirty-three. Twice a day Gene pushed her in a chair along
the boardwalk. More than most men, he felt comfortable in the role of
caretaker and nurse. Even so, Vincent could tell he was getting heartily
sick of her illness.

To Arthur Ficke, who had moved to New Mexico after being diagnosed with tuberculosis, Gene began voicing his sentiments in a stream
of complaints. "What is the good of the house, the scenery, the beauty,
the apples and pears and ripening tomatoes, if Vincie is feeling rotten?"
He was "way down in the mouth," lower than a sick hippo, he told Artie
and Gladdie. He wouldn't be surprised if the reason for Vincie's crippling headaches was Deems and his stupid opera. The exertion must
have given her a nervous breakdown. Because alcohol was forbidden to
Vincent, Gene more or less stopped drinking, too. But he was counting
the days until he could get "roaringly, indecently, hilariously, indis-
creetly, and indiscriminatingly drunk."

In December a new set of specialists saw her and reversed Vincent's
treatment. The best cure after all might be fresh air and exercise. By

Christmas they had returned to Steepletop, where they remained more or less snowed in for the winter.

All of a sudden their lives revolved entirely around Vincent's headaches. A chiropractor walked from Austerlitz—five miles on snow-shoes—to work on her spine. To the Fickes in Santa Fe, Gene issued regular medical bulletins about the condition of "my sick poet": her strict diet (linseed oil and two enemas a day), her headaches, the "curse," as he called her menstrual periods (for which she had to drink anti-curse gin until she got tight). Sometimes Vincent added her own comments to the letters. Eating enough bran to choke a horse, she said, resulted in "a m. of the b. each A.M." Her mother also released dis-patches informing Kathleen that her sister "is gaining strength and weight, eats very well, and sleeps very well." Despite everything, Vin-cent's head was still pounding in March. She told Frank Crowninshield that she had consulted a thousand doctors but continued to see the world through a curtain of dancing black spots.

Constant pain did not prevent Vincent from returning to Deems's opera. She had come up with another idea, a more-adult theme than Snow White and her herd of dwarfs. This time it was a real event from *Gesta regum Anglorum* (*The History of the English Kings*)—one of the great histories of England written by the twelfth-century chronicler William of Malmesbury. The English monk was a skillful entertainer who doted on the private affairs of royalty and never missed a chance to slyly weave in sex, lies, and corruption, the juicier the better. In Malmesbury's titillating account of a tenth-century Saxon king seeking a bride, Vincent detected definite dramatic possibilities. King Eadger, a widower, decides to remarry. Hearing about a beautiful noblewoman in Devon, he dispatches a trusted henchman, actually his friend and fos-ter brother, on a special scouting mission to see if the stories are true. Aethelwold, however, falls in love with Aelfrida. He sends back word to the king that the girl is not pretty enough, and marries her himself, with predictably messy complications.

In the mornings when the thermometer read zero, Vincent tramped through the snow to her hut, where Gene had lit a scorching fire in the stove. She began fashioning out of Malmesbury's tale the libretto that would become *The King's Henchman*. In the spring she felt up to sending Deems the poem scene by scene, and soon they were discussing set designers.

DOTTIE WAS PREDISPOSED to like Ernest Hemingway before she met him. After reading *In Our Time*, she decided he must be the best short-story writer in America. Aware of the form's limitations, she was constantly struggling for the discipline to trim fat from her own fiction. Here was a great stylist who, with an "unerring sense of selection," understood how expert pruning could be used to discard details with "magnificent lavishness." So when Hemingway suddenly appeared in town in February, she couldn't wait to make his acquaintance.

As she listened to him describe his table at La Closerie des Lilas—his pencils, his notebooks, the lucky rabbit's foot in his right pocket, how he finished the first draft of his novel in the café—she had no trouble envisioning the scene. She valued his views on writing but also found mesmerizing his tales that skipped from the Left Bank to ski towns in Austria, where he had left his wife and son, to charging bulls and matadors who confronted death in Pamplona. For Dottie, her hometown would always be the center of the universe, but meeting Ernest made her realize a world might exist beyond Times Square.

For several months she had been discussing a book project with Horace Liveright, the adventuresome hustler and high roller who published all the important writers—Anderson, Dreiser, Crane, O'Neill—along with talked-about books such as Anita Loos's *Gentlemen Prefer Blondes*. Aside from having spectacular success, Boni & Liveright threw splashy, boozy parties at its offices in an old brownstone on Forty-eighth Street, the publishing equivalent of Jay Gatsby's free-for-alls. Horace ran an extremely loose ship: authors were permitted to wander in and cadge free liquor; mailroom clerks read manuscripts; editors napped after lunch; and Horace's private office was furnished with a shower, grand piano, and bed (not solely for naps either, because the handsome Horace was a legendary ladies' man).

To Dottie the opportunity to hook up with a showman like Horace seemed to be a dream come true. He was smart, he was fun, and his offices were conveniently located around the corner from Tony's. As he assured her, his firm had made a nice profit on other collections of light verse and could do the same with hers. After signing a contract for *Sobbing in the Conning Tower*, and collecting a modest advance, she was left with the job of making selections from her published work. Facing a dreary winter in the city, she wondered if she could not accomplish the same task just as easily while living in a romantic place like Paris.

With the haste of a short-order cook, Dottie reorganized her life. She booked passage on the same vessel Ernest was taking home, threw clothes into a steamer trunk, and arranged for her bootlegger to deliver a week's supply of scotch to the ship. At the last minute Bob Benchley offered to accompany her, although it was not easy to convince Mrs. Benchley that Dottie needed to be squired across the Atlantic. In the middle of a blizzard the *President Roosevelt* sailed from Hoboken on February 20 just after midnight. As the ship slipped down the Hudson, she and Bob ventured onto the icy deck for a glimpse of the skyline. To a person whose family nightmare was the sinking of the *Titanic,* the weather was not reassuring. "God, what a night to go out in the storm," Bob said. "And I wouldn't mind if the crew wasn't yellow!" He made so many awful jokes about icebergs and throwing the children's life preservers overboard that she could not stop laughing. The next morning she woke up to a tragedy infinitely worse than a shipwreck. Her stash of scotch had been stolen, a catastrophe she blamed on the bon-voyage revelers, most likely her Rothschild and Droste relatives.

Once under way, Dottie brightened up. "She is quite all right now that she is relieved of the stress and there hasn't been a fight yet," Bob wrote his wife. After a few days, however, Bob had plenty of his own troubles. "He said it was funny," Ernest wrote a friend, "but he felt just like the time he had crabs and the 6th day out he *had* crabs." During the crossing Dottie got better acquainted with Ernest. Over afternoon bridge he spoke of his novel, set mainly at the fiesta of San Fermín in Pamplona, and she confided how much she had loved Charlie Mac-Arthur and how it just about killed her to abort their child.

Actually, Dottie's impatience to leave New York involved more than just literature. For many struggling writers, like Ernest, Europe offered the opportunity to live cheaply but relatively well. Dottie, however, didn't have to live on her small advance from Liveright; indeed, for once she wasn't counting pennies at all. That was because she had a new man, an eligible bachelor of twenty-six (six years her junior), funny and lovable and eager to please. Soon after latching on to her at a downtown club, where she was partying with her sister, Seward Collins developed a terrific crush. In the space of a few days Sewie, bless his heart, endeared himself with a diamond-studded watch from Cartier's. This presented Dottie with a moral dilemma: Sewie clearly had considerable means, but this was never an attractive quality to anyone suspicious of nearly all rich people on principle. Still, the watch was too divine. In short, she had no choice but to accept.

Heir to a national chain of tobacco shops, the young prince was an earnest romantic who considered poetry to be "the *only* thing in life." A Princetonian and a friend of Bunny's, he was fairly well known in publishing circles, but not for literary achievements. He happened to be a passionate collector, reputedly a world-class collector, of pornography. Whenever he purchased a new piece of erotica, guests were invited to his book-lined apartment on Fifty-seventh Street or to his New Canaan estate, where he formally exhibited his acquisition just as if it were an old master. Aside from collecting pornography, Sewie aspired to publish a literary magazine and to write a biography of the English psychologist Havelock Ellis.

From the start Sewie was eager to advance Dottie's career. Pigeonholed by some of his friends as a severely bored dilettante who "leaped around like a flea from one intellectual fad to another," he fluttered in midair before landing on Dottie's case and treating her like the full-time office job he had never held. Before she knew it, she had acquired a manager with an organizational chart for her life who was willing to engage in endless analysis of the special blocks that prevented her from doing a novel like everybody else. (Sewie had been psychoanalyzed.) If she wasn't managing her professional life correctly, he had the solutions.

Six weeks after leaving New York, she and Sewie were in Barcelona watching a bullfight from the expensive shady seats. As the horns of a charging bull disappeared into the belly of a picador's horse, intestines began spurting into the sand. Dottie jumped out of her seat and ran for the exit, with Sewie at her heels. What was the matter? he kept asking. Wasn't she having a good time?

Didn't he remember anything she had said about mistreatment of defenseless animals?

Of course, but he didn't think it applied to horses or bulls. Wasn't she being "extremely sensitive"? Besides, those poor bulls sometimes killed the matadors.

She hoped to God they did!

ZELDA READ the manuscript of Ernest's novel, rewritten, cut, and shipped home to Max Perkins. It was unbelievable, she thought. There could be little doubt about who wrote *The Sun Also Rises*, because the author sounded exactly like a man obsessed with hunting and fishing—and killing bulls. Ernest's tough-guy act was a fake, in her opinion, because nobody could be "as male as all that."

In Juan-les-Pins, the town next to Antibes, she and Scott were living in Villa St. Louis, a beachfront house not a hundred yards from the casino. A friend of hers from Montgomery was visiting that summer.

What is the Hemingway novel about? Sara Mayfield asked.

"Bullfighting, bullslinging, and bull——"

"Zelda!" Scott chimed in. "Don't say things like that." He hated hearing her talk dirty.

"Why shouldn't I?"

"Say anything you please, but lay off Ernest."

"Try and make me!" she said. Ernest borrowed money from them and gossiped about her behind her back. "He's phony as a rubber check and you know it." Since Scott considered Ernest his best friend, any criticism was bound to annoy, especially when she called him "a pansy with hair on his chest."

Once she discovered Ernest to be a humorless lug, she took pleasure in pulling his leg at every opportunity. A few weeks earlier, attending a champagne-and-caviar party at the casino, she leaned into his ear as if to share an important secret.

"Ernest," she whispered, "don't you think Al Jolson is greater than Jesus?" Ernest didn't seem to understand she was baiting him.

Scott was doing precious little writing. The wind knocked out of him, he continued to talk about giving up fiction. For months and months he had fed on the fantasy of a life transformed by Jay Gatsby, dreaming of bestseller lists in moldy villas and fleabag flats. But one year after publication *The Great Gatsby* had sold a total of thirty thousand copies, causing his happy ending to recede like the green light on Daisy's dock. Fortunately, Harold Ober had finally succeeded in selling both dramatic and movie rights, which netted Scott about twenty thousand dollars. If not for this subsidiary money, their financial situation that year would have been dire, because Scott earned only six thousand dollars from magazine sales and book royalties.

They decided to rent a villa near Antibes to be close to Sara and Gerald Murphy, who the previous summer had offered them an intimate, almost homey retreat. This summer, however, was anything but private. Villa America saw a constant flow of visitors: Archibald MacLeish (the former lawyer turned full-time poet) and his wife, Ada; the newly married Don Stewart and his Santa Barbara debutante; the whole Hemingway family; and John Dos Passos, now the critics' first pick for literary use of collage and Cubism in his experimental novel, *Manhattan Transfer.*

For all these typewriter jockeys Gerald happily transformed his kingdom into an artists' colony offering practical services such as loans, doctors, apartments, matrimonial Band-Aids, and limitless advice and comfort. But mostly he gave the writers a creative haven and sweet memories. For the rest of his life John Dos Passos would get emotional about Villa America, where to his mind the air smelled purer than else-where, the food tasted more sublime. In the vegetable garden just be-low the terrace, Sara's Italian gardener had planted sweet corn, which turned up in some of her favorite dishes. Sara did not just toss corn into boiling water. When she served poached eggs, they were sprinkled with paprika and reposing on a bed of golden-bantam corn. On the side she served the finest tomatoes sautéed in garlic and olive oil. Zelda, ob-serving Sara and her husband with a cooler eye than Dos's, continued to marvel at how they could totally ignore "the great unhappiness of the world." Even though "a dread of implacable doom" hung over the Mur-phys, they successfully hid their fears under a smoke screen of triviali-ties—the real estate, the sloops, the domestic gadgets, all the trappings of the well-heeled.

In the early part of the summer Zelda returned briefly to Paris, where she underwent surgery at the American Hospital after inflam-mation of her right ovary caused near peritonitis. (Doctors wound up removing her appendix instead of the ovary.) Also absent were Sara and Gerald, who took a holiday in Spain with Ernest and Hadley and one of Hadley's girlfriends. It was after they returned from the bullfighting fes-tival in Pamplona that the summer turned into comic opera. Pauline Pfeiffer, a wealthy woman from St. Louis, was Hadley's friend but be-came Ernest's mistress when Hadley's back was turned. She had a boy-ish figure—flat front, sharp hipbones—and dressed smartly, as befitted an assistant to the editor of French *Vogue*. Since the winter she and Ernest had been sleeping together, but Pauline was not content with sex alone. As Ernest later complained, she was a conniving predator who led him by the nose into adultery by using "the oldest trick" in the book—befriending a married woman in order to steal her husband. In August, Ernest let it be known that he was planning to leave Hadley and marry Pauline. Switching women was made easier when Gerald, who encouraged him to leave Hadley for Pauline, a woman more to his taste, loaned him four hundred dollars and his Paris studio on rue Froidevaux.

In her own marriage, Zelda felt quite as abandoned as poor bewildered Hadley. Villa St. Louis was always full of guests, people in a stupor whom she didn't know or didn't care about, people she would find sleeping off their hangovers when she came downstairs in the morning. But Scott chose to spend his time elsewhere whenever possible. Clearly his drinking was getting out of hand. Hooking up with rowdy Americans like Charlie MacArthur, he scribbled obscene words on the walls of an opera singer's villa and kicked over the tray of a woman selling trinkets outside the casino. Zelda, still recuperating from her operation, went to the beach with Scottie at Juan-les-Pins. When she asked Scott to join them, he usually said no, he had to go over to La Garoupe and see Sara and Gerald and Archie and Ada. Zelda was beginning to feel practically invisible.

Her unhappiness was obvious and led to several odd incidents during that summer. Late one night at the Juan-les-Pins casino, Gerald noticed with some surprise that Zelda had stepped onto the dance floor alone. Suddenly he froze when he noticed her whirling by, almost in a trance, with her dress lifted above her waist to reveal lace ruffles. Another time, she was lunching with Sara when a man came up to their table and introduced himself. With her fine Southern manners, Zelda shook his hand warmly. Then Sara heard her murmur under her breath, "I hope you die in the marble ring." (The reference to a schoolyard marbles game was not really appropriate for a social occasion.)

One evening Zelda and Scott got together with the Murphys to visit a restaurant up in the hills above Antibes, in a tiny village of steep streets named Saint-Paul-de-Vence. La Colombe d'Or, Gerald said, was frequented by artists such as Picasso because of its fine cuisine. On the stone terrace they were just finishing dinner when Gerald called their attention to a fat middle-aged woman in a purple dress seated at the next table. Did they know who that was? None other than Isadora Duncan. At once Scott bounded over to introduce himself. Duncan, amused when he dropped to his knees, ran her fingers through his hair and called him her centurion, which led to toasts with lukewarm champagne. Throughout the horseplay Zelda sat in silence. With all eyes on Scott and Duncan, she got to her feet and jumped over the parapet wall into the darkness. After a minute or two she reappeared with bloody knees and dress. As they were leaving La Colombe d'Or, she signed the guest book. In her purse was a pair of salt and pepper shakers, glass automobiles, that she had pocketed when nobody was looking.

A FTER LUNCH Vincent wrote her sister a letter, even though she had nothing to say. "July 21, 1926. Dearest Kathleen: It is 92 degrees in the shade." She was sitting on the lawn under a maple, she reported. Mother was typing in her room; Gene was haying with Stanley, the hired man; Norma was hoeing beans—bush beans, pole beans, lima beans—in the kitchen garden. Once she had exhausted the subject of beans, she moved along to her peas ("including the little French ones"), then to her corn, potatoes, cabbage, beets, lettuce, endive, cauliflower, brussels sprouts, broccoli, pumpkins, cucumbers, turnips, celery, peppers, and tomatoes. After running out of vegetables, Vincent shifted gears and began to list the contents of her flower garden, and then gave a detailed description of Norma's gardening clothes and Cora's special pink lemonade with wild strawberries.

The rest of the letter offered an account of their social life: they'd invited a bunch of weekend guests from the city, and, what with the electricity from their own little power house, it was "a very gay time." Vincent certainly did not wish to give Kay the impression that she and Gene, with their brussels sprouts and such, had turned into fuddy-duddies. However, Norma, that very same week, pictured Steepletop to Kay as a place where "everyone gets up from the dining table with a yawn and after looking over the headlines of the paper mounts the stairs to bed."

Vincent's midsummer letter was an elegy on country living, designed to beguile and inform. But she neglected an important event: Kay's first novel, a story loosely based on their mother's life, was being published in the fall. After her own failure with *Hardigut*—the five hundred dollars she never returned to Boni & Liveright—discussing the particulars of her sister's fiction debut failed to interest Vincent.

Finally, having somehow managed to cover five sheets of paper, Vincent ran out of light conversation. "Ugin is going to the post office," she ended the letter. "So I'll send this just as is. Lots of love to you & Howard. Vincent."

Five years earlier, when Vincent was living in Europe, there was an unfortunate incident involving the loss of one of Kay's watercolors. Vincent honestly had no idea why her sister got upset. But Kay had kept telling people that Vincent purposely discarded the art and ruined her career as a painter. That was not true, actually. Throwing away the package was an accident ("terribly sorry . . . I do hope it was something . . . which can be replaced"). It was quite sad—but hardly her fault—that she was important and Kay was not. Was she to blame that Kay married a deadbeat? A lot of things in life were not fair.

How could Dottie complain? She was living in a ritzy hotel in Saint-Germain-des-Prés with a prince of a man who treated her like a Fabergé egg. He was always telling her how wonderful she was, how madly he loved his little Dottie, and how much he wanted to take care of her.

At the Hôtel Lutetia there were no worries. Sewie, a portable piggy bank, was turning out to be a double godsend. He couldn't have been sweeter in handling her correspondence with Boni & Liveright as its editors searched in a half-dozen places for poems that she had never bothered to keep copies of. Whenever Tom Smith ran into problems, he consulted Sewie. "I hate to bother you about these matters but—" While Smith was tracking down her missing work, Dottie reread what she did have. Much of it displeased her, and so she began writing substitutes.

Shortly before leaving home, she gave Frank Adams a poem called

"Résumé," a cheerful field guide for aspiring suicides and a list of re-
minders why she herself might as well live:

Razors: sharp

Rivers: wet

Acid: messy

Drugs: stomach cramps

Firearms: illegal

Nooses: unreliable

Gas: smelly

At the Hôtel Lutetia, using a typewriter borrowed from Ernest Hemingway before buying her own, she continued in a similar vein to "Résumé," striving for verses that were cynical, biting, sometimes vulgar,
always self-deprecating. Death and dying, neither of them laughing
matters, remained her favorite subjects, but a fresh literary theme—
1920s mating—began to emerge, one that would become a staple of her
verse and fiction. Dottie took fiendish pleasure in boring into picture-
perfect relationships to show how they were actually rotting from
within. When a woman and a man swear their passion to be undying,
she wrote in "Unfortunate Coincidence," the woman should keep in
mind that "one of you is lying." In "Indian Summer" she admitted that
she used to break her neck to please men, but now it was take it or
leave it. "To hell, my love, with you!"

In the end, the collection was uneven. There was a lot of A. E.
Housman and a little of Edna St. Vincent Millay. But the verses were
fun to read and perfectly suited to the mood of 1926. As a civic watchdog on behalf of her own sex, a Twenties everywoman, she was concerned in particular about encouraging her sisters to give men the
finger whenever possible. Among the verses she decided to republish
was, for example, a nine-word epigram that had originally appeared in
the Conning Tower. It merely pointed out the obvious: the typical male
could seldom manage to get aroused over the sight of a woman wearing

glasses. She tossed in "News Item" as an afterthought, never imagining that it would become her most famous poem. (This was probably the greatest indignity of her life.)

Dottie wanted to title her book *Enough Rope*, a reference to the colloquial expression "enough rope to hang yourself." But her editor at Boni & Liveright hated it.

"Tell her not to be crazy," Tom Smith wrote Sewie. It was a "very bad" title for a volume of poetry. "What was the one she gave me with the word sesame in it? Let us have that one." Two months later he caved in. "Everyone seems to be against me."

While Dottie was busy working, Sewie tended to his own affairs. He was obsessed with Havelock Ellis, from whom he'd sought permission to write an authorized biography. Earlier he had slyly extended a carrot to Ellis by inviting him to be his guest on the Riviera. Ellis, too smart to fall for that ploy, replied that he never accepted hospitality from friends, to which Sewie replied that he was not really a friend, to which Ellis replied he'd already selected a biographer. Undeterred, Sewie went on courting him, but he also kept busy with his hobby of collecting erotica.

For once, Dottie enjoyed boundless energy. In addition to writing the new verses, she did in fairly short order three stories for *The New Yorker* and a bunch of articles for *Life*. There was also time for play, and Sewie took her on holiday to the south of France. At Monte Carlo the casino objected to her bare legs and refused to admit her, "so I went and found my stockings and then came back and lost my shirt." Actually, it was Sewie's shirt, but an exchange rate of thirty-six francs to the dollar made it seem like play money anyway.

Any number of times, Sewie promised to give her whatever she wanted. At one point he bought her a Scottish terrier, named Daisy by her previous owner. While Daisy was not the name Dottie would have chosen, she realized that Daisy would not bother answering no matter what anybody called her. Never mind, she was still the smartest dog in the world. "Why, that dog is practically a Phi Beta Kappa." Daisy could sit up and beg, "and she can give her paw—I don't say she will, but she can." With a dog to baby, Dottie felt as if she and Sewie had practically become a family.

The rest of the summer passed pleasantly. On August 22, she turned thirty-three, a scary number that made her feel as old as the hills ("Time doth flit. / Oh, shit!"). But living with Sewie and Daisy, drinking moderately, working productively, even gaining a few pounds, all that made her feel like a normal person. "My Sewie," she called him, and "dearest," and "the loveliest" person in the world. For the first time since separating from Eddie, she considered getting a divorce, a subject that had never come up, because neither of them had plans to remarry. Now it was different, and she wrote to suggest that Eddie file for divorce in Connecticut.

"Understand now about you and S.," he replied. "Congratulations and best wishes to you both. Don't you think Paris divorce best plan."

A FTER A YEAR of brutal work Edna finished *Show Boat* and treated herself to a European vacation, the tonic that "counteracts all the acid." Although she packed her typewriter out of habit, she had no plans to use it. That year she and her mother visited Saint-Jean-de-Luz, in Basque country south of Biarritz, and stayed at the charming Golf Hôtel. Golf being the rage that summer, she took lessons and "drove some awfully good balls." Some days she and Julia went shopping in Biarritz, happily buying antiques and ordering custom-made brassieres, or they rented a chauffeur and car for an excursion to Lourdes. From Biarritz they moved on to Carcassonne and Avignon before traveling to Switzerland, which impressed her as gorgeous but stupid, "the show girl of Europe," with "no more soul than a birthday cake," despite the pretty "pink whatnots" on her hotel balcony.

As the picture-perfect days slipped by, however, she found herself getting bored to death. Writing to Aleck, who was traveling in Europe with Charlie MacArthur, she admitted having "got out the old Corona" with the thought of writing a story. *Slow Poke*, she was delighted to report, had advance sales of "almost 100,%000 (that's one hundred thousand but I can't seem to make the Corona write it")." It was a gaudy number, quite unbelievable, but of course all the doing of her publisher. Aleck ought to abandon those "roshers" at Dutton for a really first-class house such as her own. She could not praise the Doubledays enough. They were "simply delightful to deal with, and they sell a lot of books."

By the time *Show Boat* was published in mid-August, some 135,000 copies had been shipped to bookstores across the country. Two weeks later Doubleday, Page was threatened with a $100,000 libel suit. The complainant was Thomas Taggart, former mayor of Indianapolis, former U.S. senator, former Democratic National Committee chairman, but a public figure best known as the developer of a resort in French Lick, Indiana, a town notorious for its plush gambling casinos. On page 303 one of Edna's characters says, "In the evening we can take a whirl at Tom Taggart's layout." Taggart, who always denied any connection with the casinos across the street from his resort, contended that this reference damaged his reputation.

Almost immediately Doubleday panicked. Without consulting Edna—supposedly not a single person from the company contacted her—Effendi's son Nelson lost no time in announcing that he had stopped the presses. While nothing could be done about books already shipped, future editions would eliminate all references to the politician. A fictional name with the same number of letters would be substituted. Doubleday was "only too glad" to make the alteration, and "Miss Ferber is likewise agreeable." Real names in fiction were "bad stuff," added Nelson Doubleday.

Edna sprang into battle—against her publisher. The libel suit did not upset her half as much as the actions of Doubleday, which had approved the references to Taggart along with a number of other living celebrities (Aleck Woollcott, Alfred Lunt, and Lynn Fontanne), so many in fact that one critic suggested the book needed footnotes. As an expert in the fiction business, Edna would never have used real names without consultation. In a seething letter she reminded Nelson Doubleday of their correspondence on this very point, how she specifically asked him if she should omit Heywood Broun's name and "your answer was negative." Furthermore, she went on, "you had the manuscript of *Show Boat* in your office six months before the date of publication." If he opposed the use of real names, "why didn't you say so at the time?" She was kicking herself for being "a sentimental old fool" who took for granted that she and Doubleday were partners, when they were nothing of the kind.

"Tom Taggart" was changed to "Sam Maddock," but the fuss did not end. Publicly and privately Edna continued to denounce Doubleday for incompetence, insufficient advertising, and especially gross disloyalty. A more spineless publisher would be hard to imagine, she believed.

After the Tom Taggart episode, another complaint came from the Catholic Church when George Cardinal Mundelein threatened suit over what he perceived as a sexual innuendo, on page 327, against the Chicago archdiocese. This time Edna refused to change a word. "Sue and be damned!" she said.

What heartened her—and it was no small satisfaction—was the book's success. Aside from a handful of critics who thought it a mistake to end with Magnolia's daughter and her career as a Broadway actress in the Twenties, most critics hailed the novel as Mark Twain revisited: unforgettable story and characters, gorgeous river settings, thrilling descriptions of a lost chapter of American history. Not that the reviews, good or bad, mattered, because *Show Boat* scored a hit at the bookstores.

Despite its romantic story, the novel contained two unusual ideas. Magnolia's charming gambler is an abusive spouse who pawns her wedding ring, gambles away her inheritance, and finally leaves her six hundred dollars with a letter saying he'll be away a few weeks. "She never saw him again." More shocking than a villainous leading man was Edna's particularly sensitive portrayal of interracial marriage and her opposition to antimiscegenation laws. Julie, the showboat's leading actress, secretly half black, is illegally married to a white actor. As the Mississippi sheriff approaches for an arrest, Steve pulls out a knife, slashes Julie's arm, and swallows her blood. In this way he turns himself into a person with more than a drop of black blood, the two of them now a black couple.

Show Boat was the first popular American novel to treat sympathetically the forbidden subject of miscegenation. But in the age of Jim Crow, these controversial themes of racial prejudice remained unacceptable. Reviewers and readers alike simply ignored them and concentrated on the love story.

With *Show Boat*, Edna had another bestseller. That fall, as her rage toward Doubleday slowly receded, she became preoccupied with more important decisions. For instance, to which movie company should she sell the film rights? Edna was becoming an exceedingly rich author.

"OH KING," Gene wrote in a telegram to Art and Gladys Ficke, "we accept your royal invitation with servile brow in the dust but elated legs in the air. Oh Queen, let your royal horses kick our plebeian posterior that we may know if we are really awake." The Fickes had invited him and Vincent to New Mexico, all expenses paid. The minute he got a haircut, he said, they would hop the next train.

Once Gene sold his importing company, the family businesses had become poetry and agriculture, neither of which was exactly booming. Meanwhile, Artie was rolling in money after amassing $200,000 ($2 million in today's currency) in Wall Street. He and his wife had made a comfortable life for themselves in Santa Fe, although of course it was an invalid's existence. Gladys painted and kept a horse named Loraine. For Artie's hobby—photographing landscapes, flowers, and nude models—they rigged up a darkroom.

The arrival of the "Darling Kids," their first visit together in a year, turned out to be a bright spot in Art's dull routine. "Were there ever four such happy, darling gods as we are?" Gene wondered. Art could think of nobody "who more sincerely and creatively worshiped the act of being alive" than Gene Boissevain.

During their almost two-month visit, Vincent made an expedition to the Grand Canyon and shopped for souvenirs and beads. At a place called Zuni she watched a "thrilling" Hopi Indian dance, she wrote her mother, and loaded up on trinkets. Once they paid a call on Artie's friend Witter Bynner, the infamous prankster who had left her waiting at the church and who now lived nearby with his companion. Otherwise, everybody was content to stay home on Canyon Road, snapping pictures of each other in the garden, dining on the delicious meals prepared by the cook, Mercedes, and guzzling Artie's special "pinkey-pink cocktails." His usual attire was pajamas and dressing gown, and sometimes Vincent slipped into the same.

In an article titled "Wooing the Muse in a Santa Fe Garden," the *New York Times* printed a snapshot of her and Artie in robes and slippers and reported that Vincent was completing the libretto of a new opera. The fact was that the Metropolitan Opera had already begun rehearsing *The King's Henchman,* whose premiere was scheduled for February. To coincide with the opening, Vincent's publisher planned to release a reading version that would be considerably longer and slightly different from the libretto. Now she continued to make final revisions, and when Artie offered suggestions for changes, she frequently accepted them. He was one of the very few people from whom she would tolerate correction.

In Santa Fe a favorite pastime of theirs was posing for nude pictures in the garden. All his life Artie had disliked his penis, which was circumcised and "too long," but he felt no embarrassment around the Boissevains because they knew each other so well. One day, while standing between Vincent and Gladys, he was alarmed to see an erection and ran inside, "to the amusement of the girls." When he returned to the garden, they were still laughing, and the frolicking resumed. "I took some pictures of the two of them having intercourse," a sight he found amusing because Gladys "would never pose with me for that kind of picture," he wrote later. Vincent having sex with his wife failed to bother him. Suffice it to say, he considered Vincent a person who simply acted on her "normal, natural attractions," something that few people had the "courage" to do. The photographs, in any case, were extremely artistic.

Undoubtedly, the holiday distracted Vincent from her headache, now in its second year and increasingly the subject of rumors. Even in faraway Santa Fe, Art heard malicious gossip about the source of her trouble: tuberculosis or syphilis contracted from Gene. Such notions were "utterly ridiculous," he thought, but even so sometimes he could not help wondering if her health problems were not as much emotional as physical. Might psychoanalysis be worth a try? But Vincent absolutely rejected such an idea.

At this time Arthur certainly remained under Vincent's spell. Had anyone asked him to describe her, he would have said "impossible, utterly impossible." She may have been "a genius, a bitch," but he felt privileged to know "this strange, bold, beautiful spirit." It was also true that his feelings about her and her poetry were beginning to change.

W HEN VINCENT and Gene left for Santa Fe, Cora returned home after having spent a year at Steepletop, and she could hardly wait to get out of there. Kay, driving her back to Camden (where the sisters had chipped in on a cottage), knew enough to keep quiet and let her rant. "I have calmed her down little by little," Kay reported to Howard, "and not let her cuss Gene too much, but mostly let her get it off her chest." During the months on the farm Cora had a chance to get acquainted with her son-in-law, who everyone said could charm the birds out of the trees. But if Gene's quirks supplied some of the pleasures of a good vaudeville act, they failed to amuse Cora.

In the mornings he would appear at her bedroom door with coffee and a slice of rye toast, a poor breakfast to her way of thinking. To her face he was polite and respectful. Behind her back, however, he made plenty of jokes at her expense because Cora, as high-strung as her daughters, only shut up when asleep. "Pray for Ugin who has not murdered his mother-in-law as yet," he wrote Artie. One time he joked about locking Mother Millay alone in the house and shutting off the plumbing. "Having Mother Millay with us all the time" cramped his style and made privacy impossible. How could he snap nude photos of

Vincie when they couldn't run around the house "naked and abandoned"?

In her diary Cora began mentioning "unpleasant wrangles" over, for example, religion. Evidently Gene, who had never set foot in a church in his life, delighted in signing letters blasphemously—"We love you and Jesus"—and he also regularly took the Lord's name in vain: "Good God, and good Devil, please send [U.S.] Steel Common up to the boiling point." After one nasty quarrel she got angry enough to leave and stay with Norma for a week. All this aggravation grated on Vincent's nerves, and she had to ask for meals in her room.

Cora naturally never blamed Vincent. The problem, she later told Kay, was the three of them "being together for so long," a mistake she did not intend to repeat. The truth was, she thought Gene was the problem.

Mindful of posterity, Cora every now and then liked to muse about how she planned to bequeath this or that of her belongings "to my first grandchile and failing that to my first great grandchild," as she told Kay. However, living at the farm made her realize the unlikelihood of Vincent's having children with Gene, who behaved like a mother with a young child. Come bedtime, he would bundle her off to bed while he retired to a separate room. For that matter, neither Howard nor Charlie had any interest in siring children, which suited Kay and Norma just fine. (Kay's marriage to Howard seems to have been virtually sexless, while Norma, a lesbian, had coupled with a man said to be asexual or, most likely, homosexual.)

T HE WEATHER in Paris had grown chilly. It was clear to Dottie that her relationship with Sewie was also cooling, a turn of events that she was reluctant to face. There came a day in November, however, when a showdown could no longer be avoided. Of course she was "the swellest person" he'd ever known, Sewie told her.

Didn't he love her?

"Very much."

In their sitting room at the Hôtel Lutetia, Sewie was busy throwing on the brakes and making a U-turn.

Didn't he want to marry her?

No, he said, how could he know she wanted to get married. No, the reason was that he couldn't make her happy. It had nothing to do with how well they got on. And no, this was not a recent decision. When they first met, he took her for a tough cookie. As a matter of fact, he remembered actually saying to himself that "this is the safest thing in the world." He would be "a temporary anodyne" for a writer he'd always venerated.

A tough cookie?

Now he understood how "helpless" she really was. What she needed was somebody, such as her sister, to protect her from herself.

But he loved her.

Yes, he did, but he was not right for her. If he had given her false hopes, he was sorry.

Dottie went over to open a window: did she plan to jump? From her wrist she slipped off the Cartier watch and flipped it into the Boulevard Raspail. Without a backward glance she walked away from the window. The whole thing took a second. Sewie, once he'd realized what she had done, became hysterical. No woman he'd ever heard of threw away a Cartier as carelessly as a banana peel. She was a maniac. To try to save the watch, he ran down to the street and picked it out of the gutter. When he came back upstairs, he handed her the watch. It was still running.

Dottie was on her way home before the week was out. Among the friends helping her make a quick getaway was Ernest Hemingway, who thoughtfully presented her with a stack of books for the trip. In a thank-you note she expressed appreciation for both the reading material and his "sweetness and sympathy." As for Ernest, unknown to Dottie, he had written a poem about her, "To a Tragic Poetess—Nothing in Her Life Became Her Like Her Almost Leaving of It." One night at

Archibald MacLeish's apartment, with the intention of entertaining, he read it aloud to the MacLeishes and Don and Beatrice Stewart. "Oh thou who with a safety razor."

As it happened, Ernest had converted Dottie's confidences into verse. There was the Charlie lover who had left her pregnant, the fetus's little hands, the razor blades and sleeping powders she "always vomited in time and bound your wrists," the men in Spain who "pinched the Jewish cheeks of your plump ass." Safely in Paris, her "ass intact," she sat in the Hôtel Lutetia writing shallow poetry for *The New Yorker* and talking about how much she loved doggies.

Ernest's poem failed to get any laughs. It was "viciously unfair and unfunny," said Don Stewart, who would never speak to him again.

Whenever Dottie thought of Sewie, who had remained in Paris, she felt ashamed of herself. Of course the split was all her fault. Expecting marriage from a man who said he loved you was bad judgment. He had always been exceedingly kind to her, always a gentleman, and now he probably would never want to see her again. Eager to apologize, and ask for his forgiveness, she cabled, "Don't hate me." Never would she forget the "loveliness" he had brought to her life. "Helen has watch for you." If only she hadn't made a scene about the damned watch.

I T WAS A LOVELY TIME, Dottie said. After ten months, happy to see old friends, she paid a surprise call on Frank Adams at his *World* office. What was the news of Paris? he asked. How old is this Hemingway fellow?

How would she know. "All writers are either twenty-nine or Thomas Hardy."

At Tony's, with her Scottie in tow, she tossed off one-liners left and right and managed to keep everyone in stitches.

How was the crossing?

"Rough," she said. "The only thing I could keep on my stomach was the first mate."

All week long she managed to stay busy celebrating her homecoming. Several evenings she hung out at Tony's with Bunny, who, quick to notice details, thought she looked "bloated" and her ragged bob stringy. She accompanied Thornton Wilder to a concert of English ballads and made herself the life of the party at Ruth and Heywood's house. On the spur of the moment she composed an entertaining ditty that she titled "Despair in Chelsea":

> Osbert Sitwell
> Couldn't shit well.
> His brother, Sacheverell
> Doubts if he ever'll.

Everything was fine until the weekend, when her ability to make wisecracks dried up, just like that. She could feel herself slipping. Before previous suicide episodes she had not revealed her state of mind to anybody. This time, however, she did. On Sunday morning she got dressed and went downtown to the Village. There was only one person who might listen—without exhibiting horror or disbelief—and that was Elinor Wylie. (In Elinor's family, a brother, sister, and ex-husband had taken their own lives.) Outside 36 West Ninth Street, Dottie pressed the bell for Benét/Wylie. From the second floor Elinor came down to see who could be ringing at that early hour. Dottie announced quickly the reason for her visit: She was tired. Her life was meaningless.

In the face of that admission, Elinor went straight into action and telephoned Bill, who had gone to his office. Notwithstanding the urgency of the situation, and his promise to rush home, he did not show up until three, by which time Elinor had grown nervous. They first yelled at Dottie, then resorted to begging, reasoning, scolding, and kidding. At the end of the afternoon, feeling better, she agreed to do nothing for the present and went home. ("I suppose she thinks we are experts on the subject!" Elinor complained to her mother.)

Dottie soon forgot about killing herself, because the most astonishing thing happened a couple of weeks later. In bookshop windows in time for Christmas appeared *Enough Rope*, perky in a yellow-and-gray dust jacket, and the critics were already praising her to the skies: In *The New Republic*, Bunny saluted—some said overrated—her as a "distinguished" poet whose "flatly brutal" wit reflected her "particular time and place." No less enthusiastic were the *Herald Tribune* ("whisky straight") and *The Bookman*, whose review described her as "a giantess of American letters" writing "poetry like an angel and criticism like a fiend." At a party at the Algonquin, having nothing to complain about for once, Dottie showed up wearing her prettiest red dress. The Cartier watch sparkled on her wrist.

Becoming successful didn't mean she wanted to keep writing verse. Not for a minute did she believe herself to be a poet; she was just showing off. It was in fiction—short or long—that she believed she might be able to develop whatever skills she had. But suddenly she found herself in an extremely awkward position. She was receiving fan letters addressed to "Mrs. Dorothy Parker, The Algonquin Hotel," as if she were Santa Claus at the North Pole. How could she quit writing poetry? She was too famous.

THE HOLLYWOOD DEAL was too good for Scott to pass up: $3,500 advance and $12,500 on acceptance of a scenario. A couple of weeks and eight or ten thousand words amounted to easy pickings, and they would be back East before they knew it. Scott had promised Zelda a house.

After Christmas they moved into the Ambassador on Wilshire Boulevard, a palatial, ten-dollar-a-night hotel whose management provided a fruit basket and accommodations in one of the exclusive bungalows on the hotel's vast grounds. John Barrymore lived next door, Zelda wrote Scottie, who had stayed behind with Nanny and Scott's parents in Washington. All around her were movie stars, white roses floating on a trellis outside the window, a swimming pool rippling like aquamarine gelatin, a red-and-blue parrot perched all day long on the terrace being rude to guests. Zelda was wild about California.

Succumbing to the lure of Hollywood, desperate to replenish his

Edouard Jozan, the French naval pilot
whom Zelda met in Saint-Raphaël.

Edna returning to New York after
a summer abroad, 1924.

Ernest Hemingway outside his Paris
apartment, just about the time he
met Zelda and Scott.

The Fitzgeralds in Paris, with all
their eggs in one basket. But *The
Great Gatsby* was not destined for
success in 1925.

Jane Grant and Harold Ross, after
Jane cut her hair like a man's.

Frank Adams and Esther Root's wedding, Greenwich, Connecticut, May 1925. Literary celebrities included (at right of the bridal couple) Arthur Ficke, Vincent, Elinor Wylie and husband William Rose Benét, Gladys Ficke, and Gene holding glass. Seated on the ground (far right) is Dottie.

Frank and Esther depart on their honeymoon, with money borrowed from George S. Kaufman.

Scott would dedicate *Tender Is the Night* to the classiest of the American expatriates in France: "Gerald and Sara Many Fetes."

The terrace of Villa America, the Murphys' Shangri-la in the south of France.

Zelda and a kittenish Scott being photographed by their new friend
Sara Murphy, Antibes, c. 1925.

Gerald and Sara with Honoria, Baoth, and Patrick on a visit to the United States, 1925.

Paul Robeson in the 1936 film *Show Boat,* based on Edna's bestselling novel. The Hammerstein-Kern stage production became a landmark in the history of American musical theater.

Vincent and Gene reunited with Arthur Ficke (left) in Santa Fe, 1926.

Cora Millay's visits to Steepletop became burdensome. "Oh! Jesus!— Oh! Christ!" Gene wrote afterward. "She's gone!"

Edna and her collaborator George S. Kaufman after the opening of their hit comedy *The Royal Family*, 1927.

Frank and Esther's son Anthony greeting guests: Vincent and Gene, Gladys and Arthur Ficke, Lyons Plain, Connecticut, 1928.

George Dillon, twenty-one and romantically good-looking. His love affair with Vincent inspired some of her best sonnets.

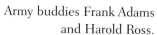

Army buddies Frank Adams and Harold Ross.

Midmorning rituals at La Garoupe beach: Gerald Murphy (center) dispensing chilled sherry to Dottie, summer 1929.

Dottie at the tuberculosis sanatorium,
Montana-Vermala, Switzerland, 1930.

Zelda's room at Les Rives de Prangins,
a prison without bars on Lake Geneva.

bank account, Scott contracted with United Artists to write an original screenplay for Constance Talmadge, a comedienne and one of the biggest stars in the business. He proposed a *College Humor*–formula story about Princeton boys and their prom girls, a tired flapper theme but not so passé that UA didn't bite. Since several of Scott's stories had been filmed, he saw no reason why he couldn't crank out a scenario for big bucks like other writers who took the money and ran. Didn't the movie people come to novelists such as himself because they were desperate for good stories? One night he and Zelda amused themselves by seeing the film version of *The Great Gatsby* but walked out before it was over because it was so dreadful.

With Scott at the studio all day, Zelda occupied herself as best she could. She was interested in costume design, and, having got her feet wet fashioning paper dolls with exquisite wardrobes for Scottie, she began to design and sew dresses for herself. Otherwise, she wrote cheerful letters to Scottie describing poinsettias tall as trees. After only two weeks, however, she had had her fill of the movie capital. If you took away Hollywood's flowers and sunshine, there would be nothing left, she thought.

Despite Zelda's grumbling, Hollywood royalty rolled out the welcome mat. At a party they met a fetching young actress who started gushing over Scott and claiming he was her favorite writer. Lois Moran was a cuddly pink-cheeked blonde who could act, dance, and sing and whose seventeen years had been carefully orchestrated by an ambitious stage mother. Born in Pittsburgh, Lois had lived in France, where she appeared in French films and danced with the Paris Opéra, and made her Hollywood debut the previous year in Samuel Goldwyn's excellent *Stella Dallas*. The child reeked of good health and sexuality. ("Her body hovered delicately on the last edge of childhood—she was almost eighteen, nearly complete, but the dew still on her," as Scott would describe Rosemary Hoyt in *Tender Is the Night*.)

At first Zelda saw no need to pay any attention to Lois Moran, whom she thought of as "breakfast food." Scott, however, was very much taken with her. When Lois insisted he was handsome enough to be in films, and proposed the daffy idea of taking a screen test for a role in her next movie, Zelda said he'd better do it. They could use the money.

It wasn't long before the girl began giving her fits, however. For one thing, Scott could not stop praising her: She was talented, independent, and serious about her career and knew how to bake devil's food cake. Lois was doing something with her life.

"Everybody here is very clever," Zelda wrote Scottie, which made her feel stupid. And ugly.

Zelda was still slender and attractive but no longer the belle of the ball, and she was painfully aware of how much her appearance had changed. Her buttercup tresses had darkened, her blue eyes looked lifeless, the rose-and-ivory complexion that Scott described in *This Side of Paradise* as "unimpeachable" had a tendency to break out. (She made the blemishes worse by picking at them and also developed a nervous habit of biting the inside of her mouth until it bled.) Her premature aging into a rather ordinary young woman horrified her. Without beauty, what did she have?

When Scott began taking Lois out for the evening and leaving Zelda at the hotel, she got mad. What was the fuss about? he said. He and the girl were friends. Of course it was hard to believe they could be anything else, she told herself. Lois was a virgin with a watchdog mother, Scott a thirty-year-old with a paunch. Nevertheless, his "flagrantly sentimental" behavior with a child was unseemly as well as irresponsible. Alone in the bungalow one evening, when Scott was dining with Lois and her mother, Zelda dumped into the bathtub all the dresses she had recently sewn for herself and set them on fire. But Scott failed to take her destruction of the clothing any more seriously than he did the creation of it. She should stop being so childish, he told her.

The three-week job at United Artists lengthened into eight before *Lipstick* was finally completed. By the time they boarded the train for Washington, Zelda had become sick with longing for Scottie. She was going to go straight from the train to Scottie's hotel, she said, and "eat you up—yum, yum, yum!" Every bit as exciting was the idea of soon having a home of her own, with a garden full of lilac trees and perhaps a Japanese room with a ducky little tea table and a screen painted with pink cherry blossoms.

On the train, as they were traveling east, Scott told Zelda that he'd invited Lois Moran and her mother to visit just as soon as they got settled in a house. Without thinking, she pulled off her platinum-and-diamond watch, the courtship watch engraved on the back FROM SCOTT TO ZELDA—the watch that cost Scott six hundred dollars—and tossed it out the train window.

1927

*Dottie walks with John Dos Passos in Boston while singing "The Internationale"
and protesting the execution of the convicted anarchists
Sacco and Vanzetti. Minutes later she is arrested.*

CHAPTER EIGHT

IN THE WEEK BEFORE Vincent's opera had its first performance at the
Met, her mother went on a rampage and roared into the *New Yorker*
office, demanding to see the editor. It was hard to say who was more
upset, Cora or Harold Ross.

Learning that an angry female, waving a banner of motherhood and
family honor, was breathing hard in the reception room, Ross refused
to poke his head out. Damned near all the women in the world were

militants out to get him. As if this weren't enough, the one outside was threatening to sue. Somebody had to get rid of her.

Tears, fistfights, loud voices—any sort of confrontation—put a strain on Ross's nervous system. The person he chose to go out and pacify the intruder, one of the few females on his staff, was his literary editor, Katharine Sergeant Angell (later Katharine White), a Bryn Mawr graduate, a person of taste and fearsome demeanor. But if Katharine Angell was capable of scaring Ross, she failed to intimidate Cora Millay, who got straight to the point: *The New Yorker* had published lies about herself, her daughter, and a number of innocent bystanders.

In the February 12 issue, the magazine carried a personality piece on Edna St. Vincent Millay. To Ross, who had edited the "Vincent" profile with his usual fussiness, it appeared to be a straightforward account of the poet and the imminent arrival of *The King's Henchman* at the Metropolitan Opera. The writing was grammatical. The information was fresh. Personal foibles included a tendency toward arrogance. ("She has been known to tremble when she meets a person whose literary reputation exceeds her own.") A smattering of gossip (her chronic headaches) added a bit of spice. Although Ross liked to call reporters a bunch of goddamned sissies and pinheads, this particular writer was no worse than most. Griffin Barry was a reputable journalist, specializing in foreign affairs, who appeared to have a good grasp of Millay's years in Europe. Ross never suspected that Barry might be one of Millay's former lovers, much less a hostile one.

Katharine Angell listened patiently to Cora's grievances. As it turned out, this was less about false statements regarding her daughter, which were difficult to prove one way or another, than about a slew of misinformation about herself and her ex-husband. Mr. Millay, for example, never worked as a stevedore. She, Cora, never sang with an opera company, only in church choirs and "oratorio clubs." Why, she wondered, did nobody bother to verify the facts?

Katharine Angell had no answer.

Even though it appeared Cora might have been overstating her case, the errors called for correction, and the fact remained that she was furious. To defuse the situation, Mrs. Angell suggested she go home and put everything in a letter, which would be printed on the letters page under the head "We Stand Corrected."

Cora's little melodrama embarrassed Ross. Next to misuse of punctuation and grammar, misinformation was an unforgivable sin in his eyes. To make certain he would never again be assaulted by a deranged mother, and of course because he was a perfectionist, he resolved to establish procedures for checking facts. Six weeks after Cora's visit, a memo ordered that the magazine be cleansed of all errors, typographical and factual. "A SPECIAL EFFORT SHOULD BE MADE TO AVOID MISTAKES," he warned in capital letters.

When Vincent's opera opened a few days later, *The New Yorker* proclaimed *The King's Henchman* to be the "greatest" American opera ever written. This was not an effort to atone. Hardly anyone else disagreed.

I N RED SLIPPERS and a Florentine brocade gown of crimson and rusty gold, Vincent swept back and forth in front of the curtains, trying not to trip on a train that was too long. Deems Taylor, in evening clothes and boutonniere, scampered barefoot behind the unruly train. He appeared shell-shocked. (He was not wearing socks.)

That Thursday night in February, when *The King's Henchman* had its world premiere at the Metropolitan Opera House, the audience packed the orchestra floor and the two tiers of boxes and the four balconies. Along the sides and at the back of the house, standees were clogged five and six deep. On hand was Vincent's family—or most of it—Cora down from Maine, Norma, and Charlie, as well as Esther and Frank Adams and Gladys Ficke alone because Artie was not up to the trip from Santa Fe. Since Vincent had been unable to obtain complimentary tickets, Kay and Howard were seeing the show at a later time, when the price of seats had returned to normal. Gladdie's seats, way over on the side, were so awful she had trouble hearing most of the singers.

As the curtain fell on the henchman's suicide, waves of applause surged through the opera house and continued without letup for twenty minutes, through seventeen curtain calls. Even after the orchestra had left the pit, hundreds of people kept clapping crazily and calling, "Speech! Speech!" Finally, giggling with pleasure, Vincent hurried forward and spread out her hands triumphantly while Deems followed. (According to Gladys, "She was quite fussed and acted rather baby-girlish.")

"All I can say is that I love you all," Vincent called out.

"I was just going to say the same thing," Deems added.

Greeting them in the wings were Gene and Mary Taylor. "No one sleeps tonight," Vincent said triumphantly. "It is our New Year's."

In the crush of reporters and photographers backstage, she was asked how she felt. "Oh, just wonderful." She loved every minute of it, especially all those curtain calls. "Looking down into all those faces I seemed to be riding on a cloud. Oh yes, I could have kept going on forever."

In the middle of that fairy-tale day, however, Vincent had been obliged to deal with an unexpected complication. When she and Gene had business in the city, they often used as a pied-à-terre the Fifth Avenue apartment of Florence Mixter, a friend of theirs and the Fickes'. Gladys, arriving early in New York for the opening, had hand-carried a box full of the erotic photographs shot during the Boissevains' visit to Santa Fe the previous fall, pictures too scandalous to be mailed. She dropped off the package at Florence Mixter's home, with instructions that it be turned over to Vincent and Gene upon their arrival. Never did she imagine that the parcel might be opened. On the afternoon of the premiere, however, chest heaving with moral indignation, Florence confronted Vincent about the "disgusting" pictures.

Vincent lost her temper. Why did she open a box that was "obviously private"? Why did she look at the pictures?

Florence refused to acknowledge any wrongdoing. She couldn't have such lascivious things in her house, she said. What if the servants had seen them?

Her behavior, Vincent said, was "beneath contempt." Their friendship was over. Never would she step foot in her house as long as she lived.

Wasn't she going to sit in her box at the opera? Florence asked.

Absolutely not. She would stand.

Vincent and Gene quickly packed their suitcases and left for the Vanderbilt. Later that day many—but certainly not all—of the snapshots were burned in Kay's fireplace. Still tremendously upset, Vincent called Florence a "nasty-minded thing" who had kept the photographs two days in order to drool over the titillating images.

Fortunately, the electricity surrounding the premiere—and next morning's reviews—drove the ugly scene straight out of Vincent's head. *The King's Henchman* had been extravagantly advertised as a landmark in the history of opera. Luckily, it lived up to the promotion. Despite a few quibbles about English being an inferior language for singing, there were unanimous accolades for Deems's music ("startlingly original," "a masterpiece of orchestration"), Vincent's book ("truly remarkable"), and the splendid cast headed by the young baritone Lawrence Tibbett playing the king. Reviewers repeatedly mentioned the influence of Wagner, and one went so far as to salute the libretto as possibly "without equal among opera texts since Wagner."

For that whole weekend Vincent fairly burst with smiles. When Bunny arrived at the Vanderbilt to dine with her and Gene on Saturday night, she still felt keyed up and began rehashing her night of glory. She showed him a souvenir she had smuggled out of the opera house, a red, white, and blue wreath with *The King's Henchman* in gilt letters. The wreath represented everything she had worked for her whole life, every sugarplum out of reach for a poor girl who never expected to leave Camden.

But it was only a lobby decoration, Gene teased. And he doubted if the Met would be happy to find it missing. Soon afterward he picked up a book (*Wine, Women, and War: A Diary of Disillusionment*) and withdrew to the bedroom so that she and Bunny could be alone to talk.

Her cheeks fiery with happiness, Vincent told Bunny that she was madly in love with the beauty of life, every single minute of it. She loved sitting next to him, she loved the sound of his voice, she loved the drumming of the sleet on the windowpane. Actually, she was having a hard time showing real interest in some of Bunny's comments. He kept using odd lingo ("pushover," "all wet," "the sticks") and bringing up unfamiliar names, undoubtedly talking about a trendy crowd that she suspected were not famous, not rich, probably not even intelligent. How on earth was she expected to know of such people?

No, she admitted, she had never heard of Hart Crane.

He lifted his eyebrows. Never heard of Hart Crane!

He made it sound as if she had lost touch. "I'm not a pathetic figure," she said, annoyed. "I'm not!"

"Whoever said you were?"

At 10:15, Gene emerged from the bedroom to announce her bedtime, just as he always did, and Bunny said it was time he went home.

Once the Met season ended, *The King's Henchman* was scheduled for a road tour of thirty cities. To Vincent's surprise, the libretto turned out to be a huge publishing success that went through three printings practically overnight. In fact, in early March she was excited to see a front-page story in the *New York World* reporting sales of ten thousand copies. Only the nosy Florence Mixter and the distressing profile in *The New Yorker* spoiled her pleasure. Damn Griffin Barry, but Cora's pointless defense only made it worse. Of course it was an outrage, she told her mother, but the magazine was not that important. Better forget it. (The correction, printed in April, called new attention to the original article.)

For the rest of the winter Cora was content to remain in the city with Norma and Charlie, but in May, passing north on her way home, she stopped briefly at Steepletop. Gene, who had to watch his step, dreaded her visit.

"Oh! Jesus!—Oh! Christ!" he wrote afterward to the Fickes. "She's gone!" At last he could be himself again. He and Vincent went straight for the applejack and began drinking like hell. "We are lovely drunk," Vincent added.

"I am cocktailly," Gene scribbled in a postscript. "Very cocktailly."

Cora's visit, short as it was, also placed a strain on Vincent, whose headaches had been exacerbated lately by an accident. One snowy evening in March a horse-drawn sleigh in which she was riding swerved off the road into the trees. A branch whipping across her left eye scratched the cornea, causing incredible agony, and soon she could not open either eye. Until the injury healed weeks later, she was more short-tempered than usual with her mother, who was nervous over the publication of Kay's first volume of verse (*The Evergreen Tree*). "Won't you please R E L A X?" Vincent snapped. Cora was taking everything too seriously. Kay was "not a baby" and could look after herself.

ZELDA WAS TIRED of open suitcases. Her latest fantasy was an ordinary life in which each week would have a Sunday and a Monday "different from each other." But most of all she was determined to settle in a real house where they could have old-fashioned Christmases and Scottie could invite friends over. It would be a fresh start.

In March, Scott signed a two-year lease on a very grand house outside Wilmington, Delaware, in the small town Edgemoor. When Zelda first saw the three-story white mansion on the banks of the Delaware River, she was crazy about its majestic Doric columns, the great lawn, the chestnut trees, the white pine "bending as graciously as a Japanese brush drawing." Ellerslie whispered to her of tranquillity. The house, built in the 1840s, was occupied at one time by managers of the nearby Edgemoor Iron Works before becoming the residence of several wealthy Wilmington families. In every respect, the place was elaborate, with a circular staircase and more than thirty rooms, including a drawing room nearly a hundred feet long.

Moving into a house after seven years of hotels and furnished quarters was hard because the Fitzgeralds owned hardly a stick of furniture. Furnishing a mansion full of enormous rooms was even harder: Zelda had to order custom-built oversize sofas and chairs, and for the dozens of windows she tried her hand at sewing curtains with the assistance of Lillian Maddock. Full of energy, she threw herself into organizing a proper household by hiring a cook and a maid and adopting from the pound two dogs, which they named Ezra Pound and Bouillabaisse.

By spring, after six weeks of manic labor, Ellerslie had become gorgeous. But the house that she hoped might open the door to a new life failed to improve her marriage. Scott, emotionally withdrawn, kept his distance, and they had virtually no physical contact, although it wasn't just a matter of sex. He made frequent trips to New York by himself. From these jaunts he would return with a suitcase full of bootleg liquor and a hangover, which meant little writing would get done. Their battles lasted for days.

For the second time in three years she considered separation, but this step would clearly have raised more problems than it solved. They had "never been very happy," she thought, but nonetheless she was "awfully" used to living with him. If she left, the question was where might she go. If only they could find a way to "reverse time," return to the distant country of their courtship, and begin again, but that was a fairy-tale solution.

A short while after getting settled at Ellerslie, Zelda turned to writing magazine articles. Having done nothing of consequence for three years, she quickly produced several pieces good enough to be purchased for three hundred dollars apiece and published under a joint byline. For *Harper's Bazaar* she wrote an essay about white-gloved Park Avenue, describing the elegant parade of nannies and their charges clutching imported dolls, a scene that reminded her of the Bois de Boulogne. *College Humor*, one of Scott's regular second-string markets, accepted an essay on the meaning of success to the postwar generation and another that examined love after the age of thirty.

Behind Zelda's writing binge lay economics, not boredom or personal ambition. It was the old story, need of money. The Hollywood trip turned out to be a complete loss. After United Artists rejected *Lipstick*, no other buyers could be found. The expense of living two months beyond their means at the Ambassador Hotel had eaten up the entire thirty-five-hundred-dollar advance. Living in the baronial splendor of Ellerslie now looked like another expensive mistake.

No matter how much Scott earned, the money continued to slip away somehow. In 1926 his income was a little over twenty-five thousand dollars, far more than the average person's, but three-quarters of it came from film and play adaptations of *The Great Gatsby* and only a small portion from book royalties and magazine sales. So far that year, he had done no serious writing and constantly, often once a week, wired Harold Ober for advances.

Financial troubles aside, the Fitzgeralds began hosting house parties as soon as the weather turned warm. The episode of the diamond watch notwithstanding, Lois Moran and her mother were among the first guests to be entertained. Zelda was determined to play the role of gracious wife, but she could not help examining Lois at close quarters—and passing judgment. She noticed how the girl went down to the river and walked self-consciously in the moonlight, all smiles, as if the cameras were rolling. She was lush as a milkmaid, slightly hysterical, and overly romantic, Zelda thought, but also just plain empty-headed. During the weekend, the same weekend that Charles Lindbergh flew his plane across the Atlantic and landed it in Paris, Scott was the life of the party and Zelda the dutiful hostess. Before long, though, all pretense of hospitality began to dissipate. When Scott's amorous attention to Lois proved too much to bear, Zelda drank heavily. Ugly scenes transformed the party into "such a mess" that afterward she felt it necessary to send another guest (the novelist Carl Van Vechten) a sheepish note apologizing for her "putrid drunkenness." Increasingly, even moderate amounts of alcohol made her feel sick. (On one such occasion, after a hellish bout of drinking and arguing, she became hysterical, and a doctor had to be summoned from Wilmington to administer morphine.) In the snapshots Scott pasted into their album, Lois and the houseguests are seen posing in front of the white columns, but Zelda is nowhere in sight.

Beyond the crisis of the house party, Lois Moran could not help appearing as a depressing apparition who served to heighten Zelda's sense of failure. Zelda was brought up to regard men—preferably older, richer, wiser, smarter—as the route to personal success. Beauty was supposed to serve as a lifetime ticket for a free ride, exempting a woman from ever needing to be anything other than decorative. Now she saw girls younger than herself achieving positions of prominence and came to realize how completely outdated—"wrong and twisted," in her words—her notions had become. More than anything else, "the greatest humiliation of my life" was inability to support herself, she believed. It was not butterflies but women with marketable skills—women such as Lois—who were admired.

If only she could do something. But she had no profession, no talents that would earn money. Without typing skills, she was ill equipped for even a secretarial job. It looked hopeless.

EDNA WAS ATTENDING a literary tea.

"You're handsome, yes," she said to a softly good-looking lad. "But you're stupid."

The remark just popped out of her mouth, and of course she immediately apologized.

He wasn't offended, was he? She didn't mean to insult him.

No, ma'am, he replied. Her candor was refreshing.

Afterward, however, the kid whispered to another guest that Miss Ferber scared him. (Later *The Bookman* published the exchange verbatim.)

More and more, she found herself growing testy with certain types of men, usually lumps that she thought of, or actually addressed, as Sonny or Bub. But even men she knew and respected were not necessarily immune. Take Harold Ross, for example, an old friend, a good friend, but a fantastic chicken, she was sorry to say. He was deathly afraid of real women, halfway smart females such as his wife, Jane, who, Edna figured, must have reminded him of his mother, or his grade-school teachers. The only women he wanted were "girlies who have just emerged, dripping, from Earl Carroll's bathtub." (Earl Carroll produced frothy Broadway revues.)

But she didn't really blame Harold. Were she a man, she once told him, she, too, might prefer the company of sexy chorus girls. "I'd never look at anything except beautiful defectives."

Forty-one and in her prime, Edna appeared to have everything she needed to be happy: an elegant apartment, a live-in cook whipping up biscuits for breakfast, vacations abroad, a Pulitzer Prize, and two best-sellers. Just about the one thing she did not have was a husband.

Since society still viewed spinsterhood and bachelorhood as per-fectly acceptable if somewhat Victorian ways to live, most people took Edna's marital status in stride. To Marc Connelly, a bachelor whose mother often accompanied him to Europe, Edna's single life seemed unremarkable. She was "a maiden lady who traveled with her mother," he said. What of it? To the children of other friends, however, Edna was not a role model. The daughters of George Kaufman and Irving Berlin both regarded her as a manless old maid, and Mary Ellin Berlin would look back in later years and say emphatically, "Nobody wanted to be like her."

Literary spinsters were indeed part of an honorable tradition that extended back to Alcott and Dickinson, Brontë and Austen. Edna fi-nessed inquiries regarding the reason she had remained single. Cer-tainly, there were men she wanted to marry, she said, and men who wished to marry her. Alas, they were never the same. But the true ex-planation was even less complicated. She knew who she was. Tem-peramentally unsuited to be a man's shadow, unwilling to make the necessary compromises, she was accustomed to relying on herself. In truth, she had no desire whatsoever to be anybody's wife.

Spurning marriage was not the same as celibacy, of course, and Edna had yet to experience physical love, despite plenty of opportunities. In her twenties, spunky and adorable, she had caught the attention of var-ious men, such as Bill White. Bill, meeting her at the Republican Na-tional Convention in Chicago in the summer of 1912, would remember the "good lines" of a "sturdy body" still shedding its sweet adolescent plumpness. She looked as fresh as a peppermint drop: clean, healthy skin; glowing cheeks; and her "great mop of dark hair, blue-black, wavy, fine," just the kind "one is tempted to tousle." He loved treating her like an adorable pettable puppy, "teasing her, helping her, tripping her, rolling her over, loving her to death."

Of course Bill was older—but in his mid-forties not that old—and married, and so the puppy was careful to keep her distance. Still, he remained the most important man in her life. Had he not been married, she might—or might not—have been content as his wife.

There was never a shortage of men as pals, escorts, or collaborators, however. Ever since *Minick*, she and George Kaufman had been searching for another subject. He in the meantime had written two successful shows (*The Butter and Egg Man* and a Marx Brothers musical, *The Cocoanuts*), while Edna was occupied with *Show Boat*, now being adapted as a stage musical by Oscar Hammerstein and Jerome Kern. Primary among the various ideas she and George explored—and discarded—was a show about Herbert Bayard Swope, editor of the *New York World*, until Edna one day had a brainstorm: show business, life in the theater, the follies of egocentric actors and actresses. Why not lump into one family all the lunatics they knew personally? What could be more glamorous than a backstage romp with a famous acting clan? For Edna, with her passion for the stage and her fictional trademark of generational sagas, a valentine to show business, a kind of *Show Boat* on dry land, sounded like an ideal subject.

Afterward she and George would deny the play was a roman à clef about the Drews and Barrymores. Of course nobody believed them. The only theatrical dynasty in the country was Mrs. John Drew, her grandchildren John, Lionel, and Ethel Barrymore, and the rest of their clan. When Edna's Emma McChesney stories had been adapted for the stage in 1915, Ethel Barrymore starred in the leading role. Edna adored the actress, whom she regarded as a friend. For ten years she was a regular guest at Ethel's dinners and parties. Surely the regal Ethel would not be able to resist the delectable joke of playing herself in what Edna and George had begun to call *The Royal Family*.

The idea was slow to coalesce. For almost eight months they struggled with the main character, Julie Cavendish. She is Broadway's leading actress and must worry about all manner of family crises: her ingenue daughter; the determination of her sick mother, Fanny, to go on tour; her movie-star brother Tony and his breach-of-promise suit. The writing usually took place at Edna's apartment, but they also rented a hotel suite in midtown, convenient to George's *Times* office. Sometimes they would check in at noon and work until after midnight, behavior that eventually attracted the suspicion of management.

When the phone rang late one night, Edna answered and heard the room clerk stammering, "I've got to ask you this, Miss Ferber. Is there a gentleman in your suite?"

"Wait a minute," she said. "I'll ask him."

With a first act cobbled together, their next step was finding the right producer. Both of them wanted Jed Harris, Broadway's "new Wonder Boy." George, slightly acquainted with Harris, offered to make the approach.

The first time Edna met Jed Harris was the day he came to lunch at the Prasada. He was reputed to be a genius—and also a snob, a sadist, and a womanizer. "He'd fuck anything," said a rival Broadway producer who despised him. "If you got hold of a snake, he'd fuck it."

Nevertheless, Edna was looking forward to the lunch, not only to clinch the deal but to show Jed she was a lady. He was likewise intrigued, if only because his friend Alfred Lunt forewarned him that Edna had had a nose job. He was prepared to see "a magnificent Byzantine ruin."

With her mother conveniently out of the house and her cook, Rebecca, beating up special sauces in the kitchen, Edna put herself out to show the boy wonder she was a person of consequence. There was an awkward moment when he admitted never having read any of her books—an oversight, he assured her. His taste in literature ran to the classics, and what with perusing the *Iliad* and the *Odyssey*, he seldom had time for popular fiction. When Edna tried to find out what he thought of the play, he volunteered as little as possible. ("Like a true disciple of Laotzu, the Chinese philosopher, I tried to assert nonassertion," he recalled.) Finally he mentioned a speech in the first act, when the fortyish star is being wooed by an old flame promising moonlit

nights floating down the Nile, better yet the Arabian desert and a cara-
van of sensual tents.

Surely not tents, Jed told Edna. Surely not sand. "I should think
peace and quiet and security would be a far more romantic prospect."

It was plain that Jed, at twenty-seven, didn't know the first thing
about the erotic fantasies of middle-aged women. But Edna pretended
to mull it over. Finally she said, "You're absolutely right."

Not long after their lunch, Jed agreed to produce *The Royal Family*
and became part of Edna's life. Thereafter, when he began telephoning
her at ungodly hours, even at four in the morning, she didn't dare of-
fend him. Jed was a chronic insomniac. Anybody else she would have
verbally skinned alive before hanging up.

Very shortly, however, the excitement of those intimate after-
midnight calls became irresistible. Groggy, she found herself drawn into
the kind of slumber-party confidences that led to jokes—George always
"smelled of dried apples," cracked Jed—and then to private gossip
about individuals. Didn't Jed understand that Aleck was a freak with
"clotted glands"? Oh, it was impossible to hurt George's feelings because he only cared about cards and the *Times*. Did Jed know that
George and Beatrice never had sex, at least not with each other? This
last revelation turned out to be a dangerous indiscretion, because Jed
would store it until a future time when, in a fit of anger, he called
George "a withered cuckold of a husband" and his wife "a fat Jewish
whore."

Young Jed, born Jacob Horowitz in an Austrian village, was the picture of sexual sin: dark, thin as a grasshopper, often unshaven, with a
purring voice and foxy hooded eyes. In short, he was just the type of
rogue Edna might have invented. In fact, she had already done so, because Jed could have stepped out of the pages of *Show Boat*. Her
novel's hero, Gaylord Ravenal, was a sexy bastard like Jed.

If Jed's name was invented, and his official biography half fake, his
ability to pick winners was nonetheless genuine. In the previous season
he had mounted a bang-up hit (*Broadway*), and currently in the pipeline
was *Coquette* with Helen Hayes, which would turn out to be another

success. It was said, first by Jed himself, then by Broadway gossip, that he simply could not fail.

Edna's fascination with the self-made mogul had its limits, though. Right away she caught on to his trick of turning on the charm—and flipping it off just as quickly. What she had been slower to recognize was Jed the shark, a cunning businessman who had made a monkey of her, the world's toughest negotiator, by smoothly maneuvering her into a rotten contract.

Otherwise, everything was proceeding in an orderly manner. Edna left for Europe in June with the expectation that Jed would take over. During her absence he would cast *The Royal Family*, with Ethel Barrymore undoubtedly, rehearsals would get under way, a tryout would be set for Atlantic City, and in late September the show would arrive on Broadway.

But when she saw Jed next, Edna was astonished to learn the play had yet to go into rehearsals, indeed was not even fully cast. Due to circumstances beyond his control, no star had been signed for the Barrymore role either. In disbelief, she accepted an invitation to weekend with Lucy and Winthrop Ames and went off to Providence, where she indulged in a bit of—for her—"serious" boozing. She reported to her family that she drank "a great deal" (her mother didn't approve), and proceeded to tick off the rounds of "highballs, cocktails, champagne, and gin fizzes" she had consumed. Little had she imagined that Ethel Barrymore could be such a royal bitch.

ZELDA HAD ALWAYS loved dancing. From the age of six, she had studied with Montgomery's best teachers and took her first steps onstage at the Grand Theater when she was seventeen. Ballet was, of course, the province of children, eight-year-olds with soft bones and undeveloped muscles whose feet can be slowly forced into ballet positions, thighs rotated to achieve the all-important turnout. Although Zelda understood that a person like herself, a woman in her mid-twenties, was too old to start over and become a professional ballerina, she still enjoyed dancing. Two years earlier she had even taken a few lessons in Paris. It was Gerald Murphy who had recommended his daughter's dance school, run by a former principal from the Maryinsky Theater of St. Petersburg.

With so much time on her hands at Ellerslie, Zelda decided to enroll herself and five-year-old Scottie in ballet classes that fall. Inquiries had produced the name of a teacher said to be reasonably good, for an American. Catherine Littlefield, trained first by her mother, who operated a local school, had made her Broadway debut when she was fifteen. Afterward she studied in Paris with Lubov Egorova, coincidentally the same teacher Gerald had suggested to Zelda in 1925. Zelda admired Catherine Littlefield, who was no withered danseuse but a twenty-two-year-old beauty, only five years younger than herself. With leotards packed into a small suitcase, she and Scottie began catching the train to Philadelphia once a week.

At home the lessons went almost unnoticed at first. Scott dismissed her dancing, like her writing and painting, as just another whim of a semi-talented amateur ("a third-rate writer and a third-rate ballet dancer," he called her). For that matter, everybody pretty much ignored her classes, and if the subject did come up, she would shrug and say that she wanted to see how far she could go.

Since dancing was such strenuous work—the hardest she had ever done—Zelda began drinking more coffee and smoking more cigarettes. The classes, declared her heroine in *Save Me the Waltz*, were agonizing. Like Alabama Beggs, Zelda was always stiff, with "blue bruises inside above the knee where the muscles were torn." At bedtime, too exhausted to move, she rubbed her legs with Elizabeth Arden oil.

Once, in Philadelphia, she came across an enormous gilt mirror in a shop. Its decoration was so outrageously trashy—cherubs, scrolls, and fanciful Victorian wreaths—that it ought to be hanging in a brothel, she thought. Tickled with her find, she had the mirror delivered to Ellerslie and installed in one of the parlors. From that day on, her life took an unexpected turn. With the purchase of the mirror, so essential to correcting her movements, and with a ballet barre and gramophone, she was able to rig up a makeshift studio and practice several hours a day, always to the same recording, "The March of the Toy Soldiers." Sweating and straining, stopping only for water, she lost track of time. Before long, Scott, who had laughed about the "whorehouse mirror," was getting fed up. As the music—the same music—kept playing feverishly, he felt as if he were going mad. It was like living in a dance studio, he said, but she didn't care.

When she began going to Philadelphia three times a week, taking as many as four lessons a day, Scott lost patience and started to raise hell. After seven years of what he considered her willful interruptions of his work, she no longer bothered him—because she was never home. Who was going to supervise the household? Every time he saw her she was either consulting a train schedule or flying out the door. What about Scottie? (Lillian Maddock had returned to Europe.) What about the cost of these lessons? Furthermore, did Zelda really fancy herself a professional dancer?

She supposed not, she shot back, but there was only one way to find out.

IT WAS AUGUST and beastly hot as Dottie marched up and down Beacon Street, counting the minutes until she would be arrested. In an embroidered dress with matching scarf, Hattie Carnegie cloche, and charming little white gloves, she followed behind a beet-faced John Dos Passos and sang "The Internationale." In front of the Massachusetts State House, a picket line resembled a gathering of a Communist Party social club as the New Masses and Daily Worker crowd chanted and waved homemade signs. With Boston under martial law, about a hundred locals were standing around and sucking on pop bottles, expressing their feelings: "Bolshevik." "New York nut." "Guinea lover."

Two police officers grabbed Dottie by the arms. She refused to get into the paddy wagon and insisted on setting off on foot to the Joy Street Station, three blocks distant, an ill-advised decision given her ankle-strap high heels. At the jail a matron with gold teeth took away her cigarettes and put her behind bars. When Sewie and Ruth arrived later to post bail, Dottie teetered outside but took her time about leaving. To a group of newspaper reporters she began heatedly denouncing the police as a bunch of big shits.

A pair of Italian-American anarchists, Nicola Sacco and Bartolomeo Vanzetti, had been found guilty in 1920 of the robbery and murders of a paymaster and a guard. What began as an obscure local crime had developed into an international cause célèbre. As Bunny wrote John Bishop, he was too far away in France to appreciate why the case mattered: it challenged fundamental principles of the American political and social system. Dottie had never exactly been interested in politics—she'd never voted—nor had she concerned herself with issues of social justice. But like many others, she did believe in the innocence of the fish peddler and shoemaker, sentenced to die in the electric chair on August 23. For the two weeks following her arrest, she worked at the Sacco-Vanzetti defense headquarters on Hanover Street. A last-minute influx of celebrity glamour girls—Edna St. Vincent Millay, Katherine Anne Porter—arrived to picket the statehouse, and John Dos Passos managed to get arrested a second time. He jumped into a paddy wagon with Vincent (a "passable poet" who "intoxicated every man who saw her," he once wrote).

On the night of the execution Dottie waited out the deathwatch vigil from the pressroom inside Charlestown Prison. Afterward she joined other defense workers at the Hanover Street office, where the telephone kept ringing but none could bring himself to answer. Unlike many of the writers who had come to Boston, she would never write anything about the deaths of Sacco and Vanzetti, and she seldom ever discussed her doings there with family or friends. There was nothing about her comfortable upbringing that suggested she might become a radical. Still, the executions had a powerful influence on her thinking.

When she headed home to New York at the end of August, she could easily have spun out of control. That didn't happen, though. Instead, she fell in love with a man whose views were the antithesis of everything she held dear. John Wiley Garrett II was a Waspish investment

banker in a Brooks Brothers suit whose memberships included the
Leash and Downtown Association and the American Legion. No civil
libertarian, he was hopelessly right-wing, even reputed to be something
of a parlor fascist, and of course he hadn't a drop of sympathy for the
Sacco and Vanzetti business. She was a socialist "heart and soul," she
told her Wall Street boyfriend, but he remained unmoved. After her experience with Edwin Pond Parker II, she knew better than to fool
around with downtown types like John Wiley Garrett II. Still, he had a
voice "as intimate as the rustle of sheets."

The weeks in Boston left her a different person, but those experiences gradually were pushed aside. There remained her real life, that
"coarse and reeking business" of being a professional writer. She had so
much work she could barely keep her desk clean for a change. *McCall's*
asked for a monthly column, and Horace Liveright was eager to bring
out a second collection of verse. As a popular author, she found herself
besieged by invitations: literary luncheons in hotel ballrooms crowded
with ratty people "who looked as if they had been scraped out of
drains," and publishers' teas promoting new books with vats of Fish
House punch.

Most curious of all, she had established a special relationship with
The New Yorker, where Harold Ross was turning into an unofficial fairy
godfather willing to publish anything she wished to write—poetry, fiction, criticism, it made no difference—without rejections or rewrites.
Publication was guaranteed, bless his heart. "Any chance of more
verses?" he asked. "Please, please, please. Your old admirer, H. W.
Ross."

The bunch of verses she sent him were accompanied by a warning.
They were all "lousy," she said, except the one titled "Healed." But "because I think it's good, it's probably—probably hell certainly—lousier
than any of them. Love Dorothy."

"God Bless Me!" Harold replied. "If I never do anything else I can
say I ran a magazine that printed some of your stuff. Tearful thanks."

Association with Ross's magazine was no cause for embarrassment, as it had been in the beginning. In its third year, *The New Yorker* was more than an undergraduate weekly. Witty, impeccably styled, it was recruiting decent writers and even a few talented editors, among them Katharine Angell, E. B. White, and Wolcott Gibbs. Ross was fond of stories he called "casuals," light, brief fiction or humorous essays, almost any piece of writing whose tone was offhand, chatty, informal. Since Dottie's writing epitomized Ross's "casual," he was constantly pursuing her. "Please do a lot of things for us—please do some prose pieces and more verses." The trouble was, he paid poorly, two dollars a line for poetry, twelve cents a word for prose. So she was surprised when he suddenly enticed her with one hundred dollars a week to take over the magazine's book column.

Expecting Dottie to contribute anything on a regular basis was unrealistic. Nevertheless, Reading and Writing by the pseudonymous "Constant Reader" made its debut in October. One of the first books to be eviscerated was a memoir by Nan Britton, mistress of the late President Harding and mother of his illegitimate child. Britton claimed that efforts had been made to suppress the book and that policemen had tried to seize plates from the printing plant. "Lady," Constant Reader explained, "those weren't policemen; they were critics of literature dressed up."

Although serious books (Hemingway's *Men Without Women,* for example) were certainly not ignored, Dottie could never resist memoirs like Britton's, trivial first novels, how-to books, any work that might supply grist for her mill. *Crude,* the title of a new first novel, "is also a criticism of it," she chortled, and Margot Asquith's new book had "all the depth and glitter of a worn dime." *Happiness,* by a Yale professor, was the next-best thing to a rubber ducky, because readers soaking in their tubs could balance it against the faucets and complete it before the water cooled. "And if it slips down the drain pipe, all right, it slips down the drain pipe."

Deadlines presented headaches. Each week copy was due on Fridays, but it was usually Sunday before she heard from an editor. Did she by any chance have her column ready? Wolcott Gibbs wanted to know. Of course she did, except for the last paragraph. She needed a better ending. Would he mind waiting an hour or two?

But an hour or two later Gibbs got the same answer. With new hires, Ross was firm about editor-author relations. "I don't give a damn what else you do," he warned Gibbs, "but for God's sake don't fuck the contributors." There was no prohibition on homicide, though, a thought that occurred toward midnight, when the magazine had to go to press without Constant Reader and Gibbs became frantic. "I'm so sorry," Dottie would finally apologize. "But it was just awful and I tore it up." The column was in fact not written. It was not even started.

Dottie was the opposite of Bob Benchley, whose antics were deliberately aimed at driving Ross bughouse. Bob turned in single-spaced copy that left no room to edit between the lines. Dottie, never one to let work get in the way of drinking, was more often than not battling a hangover on Sunday morning. For that matter, any time of day (on any day of the week), an ordinary phone call—even the doorbell—made her so jittery that she automatically began to prepare for the worst. "What fresh hell is this?" she would wonder aloud.

Actually, Ross didn't appear to care one way or another about the missed deadlines. He was simply "grateful to the point of tears" for her columns. By the way, did she have any "unused verses"? Did she need fiction ideas? What about a conversation, in a hotel room, between a married man and a single woman thrown together for the sole purpose of the man obtaining grounds for a divorce? (Adultery was the only ground in New York State.) Women had begun doing such things to earn pin money, Ross had heard. (He and Jane had come to a parting of the ways. "I never had one damned meal at home" without a lecture on feminism, he would say.) Dottie passed on his hotel-room suggestion.

Despite the racy adultery idea, Ross was prudish and would permit nothing off-color in the magazine. Once or twice he caught Dottie trying to slip double entendres into her copy. After failing to notice a slang expression ("like shot through a goose"), which sounded like bathroom stuff to him, he alerted the copy editors to be extra vigilant.

Among Ross's editors was a young man from Ohio who owned a Scottish terrier named Jeannie. Immediately Dottie became friendly with Jim Thurber, who was funny and loved dogs as madly as she did. One night at a party of hers, his impersonation of the cartoonish Ross, complete with Harold's usual brays of "Done and done" and "Well, God Bless you, goddam it!," had people falling off their chairs. Next morning he was summoned into Ross's office.

"I heard you were imitating me last night, Thurber," he said. What the hell was there to imitate? "Go ahead and show me." But Thurber could not.

Because Ross knew nothing about fiction—and started out publishing none—Dottie sold her stories to magazines such as *Harper's Bazaar*. But after Katharine Angell, an outstanding fiction editor, joined the staff, *The New Yorker* became an important market, especially for the type of urban story that forever would be associated with the magazine. Dottie's strength was observation. She wrote down what people said and how they said it. Adept at reproducing speech with perfect pitch, she made readers feel as if they were eavesdropping on conversations they never expected to hear. Her characters—the young man in the chocolate brown suit, the girl with the artificial camellia, the socialite worried about her manicure in a time of horror, despair, and world change—could easily have escaped from Schrafft's or last night's Park Avenue cocktail party.

Stylistically, she had always preferred tight construction, but meeting Ernest Hemingway made her fanatic about stripping sentences to the bone. She agreed with Scott, who, writing about *In Our Time* for *The Bookman*, described Ernest's stories as snapshots developing before your eyes. "When the picture is complete," he wrote, "a light seems to snap out, the story is over. There is no tail." After returning from the Sacco-Vanzetti executions, Dottie gave Ross a story with neither tail nor head: At a cocktail party a bleached blonde with pink velvet poppies entwined in her hair gushes over a famous black singer. As she shakes his hand, she professes her admiration and makes a point of addressing him as "mister." It was clear that Dottie based the character Walter Williams on Paul Robeson, but beyond that Ross probably did not fully understand "Arrangement in Black and White." No revolutionary, just as bigoted as anybody else in 1927, he was not interested in race relations or in admitting soapbox issues into his humor magazine. What he did want was anything he could get from "Dottie, my heart."

IN JED HARRIS'S OFFICE Edna sat silently and let the effusive blonde do the talking. Ann Andrews said she was from the Coast, where she had attended drama school. Until the age of twenty-two, she'd never been inside a Broadway theater but had made up for lost time in recent years by playing any number of leading roles. She was deeply devoted to her cats, all twelve of them.

Edna knew full well of Jed's doubts about Andrews and her ability to carry a show. At least, Edna told him, she did look the part. Jed thought Ann had the "artificial manners of a stock-company leading lady." Be that as it may, the situation called for desperate measures, and Edna promised to meet her before any contract was offered.

Ann attempted to ingratiate herself with dramatic flourishes. So sorry about the play, she had the nerve to say. And what a pity it was so "uncommercial." Those misguided remarks got Edna's back up; she clamped her mouth shut. The actress began to regale them with an uninhibited discussion of her medical history, specifically "the deplorable condition of what she called her *cunetta*," Harris recalled. Edna, rendered speechless by Ann's references to her never you mind, stared at her as if she had escaped from a psycho ward. With the conversation taking this alarming turn toward the clinical, Edna arranged her face and waited for Jed to steer the interview back to business. Eventually the actress took her leave.

"Well!" Edna said to Jed.

"Oh, yes, absolutely."

As it happened, Ann Andrews's gynecological woes were insignificant compared with the calamities facing *The Royal Family*, now on the brink of collapsing before it could open. It was all the fault of Edna's wonderful friend Ethel Barrymore, who, failing to appreciate Julia Cavendish, was calling *The Royal Family* a deliberate and vicious insult to her family. As the first lady of American theater, the forty-eight-year-old actress was being honored with a Broadway theater bearing her name. Associating herself in any capacity with a play making fun of the Barrymores was out of the question. What's more, she was going to consult a criminal lawyer about halting production. (Edna found her name struck from Ethel's guest list.) Luckily nothing came of Barrymore's legal threats, but their effect on casting was chilling. Either out of deference to Ethel or from reluctance to play a middle-aged woman, no other actress of Ethel's caliber would touch the leading role. What Jed said about Ann Andrews being a pedestrian actress was true, but with his back to the wall he had little choice. Without her there would be no show; even with her the production could not be opened until the end of the year.

Jangled nerves made Edna sick to her stomach. Hoping to ward off an ulcer, she took to her bed for three weeks of complete rest. In her notebook she complained how much she hated the life she had been leading—the waking early and "doing setting-up exercises and sitting in front of a typewriter and putting words down on paper." In future "I'm going to buy a black lace nightgown and never get up." She was back on her feet, however, as soon as boredom overcame depression.

All during the fall, almost every day, she bounced between the Plymouth on Forty-fourth, where *The Royal Family* was in rehearsals, and the New Amsterdam on Forty-second, where *Show Boat* was rehearsing. In the case of *Show Boat*, she had no official business except to sit in the empty house and observe. It was no longer her property; it was Oscar Hammerstein's. Adapted for the musical stage, her work had been gutted, stuffed with songs and production numbers, and neatly tied up with a sentimental ending. Still, she was crazy about the music, such songs as "Ol' Man River" and "Make Believe." And it thrilled her to watch the chorus in bathing suits and shorts run through the various numbers like "Life upon the Wicked Stage" and to listen as Jerry Kern pounded the piano and Flo Ziegfeld yelled at the sweating dancers to get moving because, he swore, they looked like corpses. Every minute the New Amsterdam vibrated like a noisy factory, feverish, chaotic, but under tight control.

The situation was precisely the opposite at the Plymouth, where there was no heat. At eleven the *Royal Family* cast began rehearsing with the stage manager. At five, unshaved and surly, having just woken up, Jed Harris would finally appear. Take it from the top, he ordered nonchalantly. On the ninth day of rehearsals he fired the company without warning and paid everybody two weeks' salary. The boy wonder claimed it was a nervous breakdown; he would need to be hospitalized very likely. When his panic attack subsided two days later, the cast was rehired. But by mid-December, when the play finally opened in Atlantic City, it was Edna who was having the breakdown. She was overheard predicting that "both plays will probably fail."

Behind the orchestra seats she stood next to a coolheaded Jed Harris and studied the latecomers straggling in. Pay no attention, he told her. All those people—the coughers, the belchers, the sleepers—were only retired clerks and letter carriers. "Can you imagine an intelligent person living here in the winter?"

George Kaufman rushed up to them at intermission. Did Jed hear what he heard, "that tremendous fart in the lobby just as the curtain was going up"?

Yes, Jed replied, of course he heard it. Wasn't it considerate of the fellow to relieve himself before taking his seat? Nothing, evidently, fazed the boy wonder.

On the Tuesday after Christmas, at the brand-new Ziegfeld Theater, *Show Boat* opened to unanimous praise, indeed the sort of fanfare that guaranteed not only a long run but also milestone status in the history of musical theater.

It was followed the very next evening by *The Royal Family*, which drew equally unanimous raves. Even Aleck, Edna's biggest critic, wrote in the *World* that he would always remember that amazing first night as "one of the happiest evenings ever I spent in the theatre."

On the opening night of *The Royal Family*, Edna stayed home and ate dinner on a tray, or so she said in her autobiography a dozen years later. That she would forgo the pleasure of attending one of the most memorable events of her life might sound puzzling, she supposed. Whether this was due to some peculiar "psychological quirk"—possibly another tummy ache?—she simply could not, or would not, say.

At least that would be her recollection of Wednesday, December 28. According to Jed Harris, however, something more complicated took place. Edna, he claimed, stopped off at his apartment on her way to the theater with a bad case of opening-night jitters. She looked quite the femme fatale, dressed to the nines in a peach-colored gown and a fur coat with scarlet lining.

As he poured champagne, Jed plied her with extravagant compliments. There was no reason to worry because the evening would go "like a house on fire." *The Royal Family* was certain to become one of the biggest hits of the decade. For himself, it would mean his third success in fifteen months, but she of course would be the toast of the town: two of the most impressive shows in Broadway memory, both in one week. Two hits back-to-back. Wasn't that a writer's fantasy? Surely 1927–1928 would go down in theater history as "the Ferber season." Jed knew how to pile it on.

According to Jed, some time later—how much is unclear—Edna stopped mid-sentence and looked at her watch. It was ten-thirty, she cried. She had missed her opening night.

"Without a word," Jed was to write in his memoir, "I swung the little clock on my bedside table around. She stared at it and murmured, 'Oh, dear, I'm so upset.' "

In her autobiography Edna omitted any mention of visiting Jed's apartment on opening night, let alone climbing into his bed. Even if something did take place, she probably wanted to obliterate the memory. As she found out a few days later, Jed really was a cruel man who enjoyed terrifying people. During a chatty phone conversation with

George toward the end of the week, Jed paused and said, without warning, "I'm going to close the play."

Close? He wanted to close *The Royal Family*? George had suspected Jed was a mental case, but now he was sure. "But why, for God's sake!" he answered. They'd got raves.

Exactly, Jed said. But it wasn't performing at the box office.

Well, it was Christmas, for God's sake. The show just needed a chance to build, George said.

Sure, but they weren't selling out. A play that gets rave reviews but doesn't sell out *ought* to close.

"Listen to me," George finally said. He was coming over to Jed's apartment. If Jed insisted on closing *The Royal Family*, well and good. But George would have no choice but to kill him.

The Royal Family did close, but not until December 1928, after a run of 345 performances.

1928

Ferocious ambition: Zelda's determination to become a professional ballerina disturbs her husband.

CHAPTER NINE

THE HAPPIEST PLACES in New York City were speakeasies, especially Tony's, where Dottie dropped in faithfully on most evenings. As everybody knew, even a tiny swallow of bad bootleg liquor could cause pains in the back of the head, but Tony Soma's customers felt confident of getting superior stuff. She must have downed thousands of drinks there and never regretted a single one. Chain-smoking Herbert Tareytons, mooching Luckies or Camels if she ran out, forgetting to eat, or ordering a steak sandwich if she thought of it, she considered Tony's joint her own private club.

Nothing was more fun than drinking. After finding out the hard way that she had no better friend than scotch whiskey—Haig & Haig if she could get it, or "White Hearse"—she refused to touch any drink with a name: no planter's punches, mint juleps, Tom Collinses, not even Manhattans, although occasionally she would accept a sidecar. It made no sense to waste time on those syrupy things that had been invented for the sole purpose of disguising bad alcohol. Few pleasures were as cheap and joyous as a bottle of scotch.

She made no secret of the fact she got tight a lot. But that did not make a person an alcoholic. Even supposing she did drink too much now and then, it was no more than anybody else—drinking was a normal part of civilized life, and New York was a hard-drinking town. Besides, she could stop anytime she wanted. One time when she teased Marc Connelly that she was thinking of going on the wagon, he grimaced like a Park Avenue specialist with a hypochondriac. Don't be foolish, her old friend advised. He knew somebody who'd stopped and it didn't make a bit of difference.

She thought he should be the last person to offer advice on drinking. Without his noticing, she told him, three owls had roosted in his mouth. They were tiny, of course, not really objectionable, but wait until they tried to bring home a houseguest.

Occasionally, she would test her willpower by refusing a drink. A few minutes later, however, she'd change her mind in the manner of a guest unwilling to disappoint her host. Well, she would say, maybe a little one. So frequently did she request "just a little one"—it became a joke among her friends—that she wound up writing a story for *The New Yorker* with that very title. Usually it was more efficient to water her drinks. "Make it awfully weak," she whispered, in a voice suggesting she might be doing everyone a favor. "Just cambric scotch." Thank God, nobody took her seriously. Certainly not Mr. Benchley, her bosom drinking companion who no longer managed to attend all the plays he reviewed for *Life*. Alcohol had taken its toll on not only his professional duties but also his physique, which bore no resemblance to the trim boyish editor she'd known at *Vanity Fair.*

To her indignation, silly stories about their drinking were rife. It was rumored that they once staggered out of Tony's on a spring night, only to discover the air had suddenly turned wintry and West Forty-ninth Street lay under a soft white blanket. Padding toward them through the powdery snow, without making a sound, came a procession of ele-phants, each holding the tail of the animal ahead.

"That does it," Bob cried. "From now on I'm on the wagon." Where-upon, the story went, they ducked inside for another round to steady their nerves.

That was a downright lie. All along she knew those were circus ele-phants on their way to the Garden. If anybody was going to peddle pink-elephant jokes about Dorothy Parker, it ought to be Dorothy Parker. Her *New Yorker* column, which might have been called "Read-ing and Writing and Nursing Hangovers," was frequently used for per-sonal confessions about, for example, her bouts with "the rams." That was when she felt afraid to turn around abruptly for fear of seeing "a Little Mean Man about eighteen inches tall, wearing a yellow slicker and roller-skates." She was well acquainted with the rams, as well as the less virulent strain known as the German rams, but happily the con-dition was never terminal. Usually it could be traced to a stalk of bad celery at dinner. Of course, she could not deny that a severe case of the rams was like something out of Gounod's *Faust.* Those rams qualified to be preserved "in the Smithsonian under glass."

JOHN WILEY GARRETT II had little going for him besides his looks. In his case, that might have been sufficient, because he was a strik-ingly handsome fellow in his mid-thirties, athletic, with long legs and dark brown hair, who knew how to wear expensively tailored suits. His passions were war, sports, and business. Dottie might've expected an Ivy League graduate to pick up a book occasionally. But no. Practically illiterate, he had the gall to complain that her column never mentioned books that ordinary people read, so she reviewed something he did read, the tabloid comics.

The main trouble with John was that they had nothing in common, a fact she preferred to ignore. Most of the time "we were both pretty fairly tight," she realized later. Another problem with John: he slept with other women, she discovered.

Not true, he insisted.

Then why was his apartment full of monogrammed dressing gowns? And what about all those expensive cigarette cases?

She hated sitting in his Murray Hill apartment and listening to the telephone ring and ring, as it always did, with calls from women eager to make dates. "You damned *stallion*!" lashes out a character in her short story "Dusk before Fireworks." Why does she work herself up over nothing, the man replies. She knows damn well that she comes first with him.

Obviously John was a liar. On the other hand, he stayed with her, didn't he? He was thirty-five and would have to settle down sometime.

Could life get any worse? Very likely, because suddenly she had to be rushed to the Presbyterian Hospital, a place she ordinarily patronized for overdoses and abortions. But this time it was a respectable ailment, abdominal pain, which turned out to be not the bad scotch she had self-diagnosed but appendicitis. After the operation she retired to her new apartment (above a piano store on Fifth Avenue) for a month's convalescence. It would be nice to have indoor entertainment, she thought, something exciting like an electric train. "Hell, while I'm up, I wish I had a couple of professional hockey teams." Worst of all, the doctors banned drinking, although her cooperation was far from religious. As a result of this sudden shift in her normal schedule, without cocktail parties and midnight forays to Tony's—without even giving it much thought—she began writing a short story. Once it got under way, the project moved surprisingly fast, as if the Presbyterian doctors had quietly removed her writer's block during the appendectomy.

"Big Blonde" is the story of a wholesale dress model who is married to an alcoholic. Once he leaves her, and Hazel Morse must fend for

herself, she becomes a hard-drinking, good-sport party girl who enter-
tains—and is kept by—a series of Seventh Avenue buyers from cities
such as Des Moines and Houston. Eventually she is derailed by life,
age, and loneliness. Hazel goes into the bathroom and begins to swallow sleeping powders with water until the "splintering misery" suddenly
oozes away and she feels as excited as a child about to receive an "unan-
ticipated gift." The next day she is found unconscious by her maid, who
pokes, shakes, and finally calls for help.

For months Dottie kept tinkering with the story, still obsessive about
putting in commas and pulling them out. It was the longest piece of fiction she had ever undertaken, almost a novella, nearly three times the
length of her usual work. Judging the story too long, and certainly too
depressing, for *The New Yorker*, she gave it to *The Bookman*, the highly
respected literary journal that Sewie's father had recently purchased for
him. Published in February 1929, "Big Blonde" was pure Parker. The
story won the prestigious O. Henry Award as the Best American Short
Story of 1929. Ironically, it also drew a complaint from the New York Society for the Suppression of Vice, not on the grounds of obscenity but
for giving readers explicit instructions on how to procure illegal drugs.

Nobody could say that drinking interfered with her writing. She was
in top form, and the proof of her control over drinking—for the last
time, she was not an alcoholic—was that she could write "Big Blonde,"
a story about a drunk who could not control her drinking. On top of
that, she managed to produce a second collection of verse, *Sunset Gun*,
which turned out to be another excellent seller. That year her royalties
amounted to the incredible sum of $5,708.95, not bad for someone as
poor as a parish mouse. If this kept on, she might wind up filthy rich
like everybody else she knew and require the services of an accountant.

Confident of her ability to handle just about anything, she decided
to give Hollywood a try. Not that she was carried away by the idea of
screenwriting. Quite the opposite, she couldn't stand motion pictures—stepping into a theater prompted hellish visions of "an enlarged
and a magnificently decorated lethal chamber"—especially the new
talking pictures. She always felt like shouting at the screen, "Oh, for

heaven's sake, shut up!" Mercifully, interest in film proved unnecessary. By this time the smell of money had wafted across the continent to the nostrils of New York writers. "Millions to be grabbed out here," Herman Mankiewicz wired Ben Hecht, "and your only competition is idiots. Don't let this get around." An idiot she wasn't. From MGM, Dottie obtained the sweetest deal, a three-month contract for three hundred dollars a week (three thousand dollars in current dollars). Subletting her apartment, she departed for the Coast in November.

M ADAME EGOROVA wanted to know why.
It was the same question everybody asked Zelda, but Lubov Egorova expected an answer. Why did she wait until now?

Zelda's standard reply was that she had studied dancing as a child, that probably the idea had been at the back of her mind ever since, but in truth she hardly knew the reason herself. The distractions of living, she finally said. She was busy.

And she was no longer busy? The woman looking at her coldly, a former principal ballerina at St. Petersburg's Maryinsky Theater, was middle-aged with a dramatic white face and eyes full of anguish. She shrugged aside Zelda's excuses and continued to stare. You are too old, she said.

Clutching her valise, Zelda stammered that she found Russian ballet thrilling.

What had she seen?

La Chatte. (La Chatte was a work choreographed by George Balanchine.) She would give anything to dance La Chatte someday. There was no emotion on the Russian's face. Don't get your hopes up, Madame said, and sent her off to change clothes.

In April, Zelda and Scott had decided to close Ellerslie and spend a few months in Paris, where they rented a flat in a nondescript building across from the Luxembourg Gardens and hired a Mlle Delplangue to look after six-year-old Scottie.

That summer marked the true beginning of Zelda's training in classical ballet. Each morning she rose long before Scott and braced herself with coffee and cigarettes before heading off to class. The Egorova ballet school was located on the top floor of the Olympia Music Hall over on Boulevard des Capucines. To reach the studio, she had to make her way to the stage entrance of the music hall, around the corner on rue Caumartin, and walk through the wings of the theater, along the concrete walls, up seven flights of stairs to a large bare room of blue walls and scrubbed floors. Under the skylight the room was redolent of female flesh and sweat and "reeked of hard work," she wrote.

From the start Zelda found herself powerfully drawn to Lubov Egorova. Born in St. Petersburg, a graduate of the Imperial School of Ballet, Madame Egorova was considered a brilliant exponent of Russian classical ballet. During her career at the Maryinsky Theater, where she was known for her daring pirouettes and beautiful legs, she danced all the big leading roles: Aurora in *Sleeping Beauty* and Odette in *Swan Lake*. After retiring and opening her own school, it was to her that Serge Diaghilev's dancers would come for coaching.

At forty-seven, Madame Egorova was one of the best teachers in Paris. Her private students were divided into two groups: sober-faced young dancers in modest circumstances; and the offspring of the wealthy or famous being pushed into lessons, children such as Sara and Gerald's daughter, Honoria, and James and Nora Joyce's daughter, Lucia. In this setting Zelda stood out as a misfit, not just because of her age, or her position as a rich foreigner and wife of a famous writer, but because of the way she treated Madame. In the morning she arrived at the studio carrying a bouquet from the flower stalls near La Madeleine, lilacs and tulips, lemony carnations "perfumed with the taste of hard candy," garden roses "purple as raspberry puddings," the most glorious combination of blooms that she could pluck. To the ritual of the daily flowers were added invitations to tea at Rumplemeyer's, dinner at Hôtel George V, and concert tickets for Madame and her husband. Such largesse from pupils was not expected, but not rejected either. Dance instruction was a cash business, at least in the case of students such as Zelda, who paid three hundred dollars a month in fees.

Throughout the summer Zelda was struggling to discipline her body. After group classes in the mornings and private instruction with Madame in the afternoons, she would spend four hours a day practicing at home when she was not browsing secondhand shops poring over ballet books, paying as much as forty dollars for something special. At night she felt too tired to move.

Convinced that living the life of Mrs. Scott Fitzgerald had delayed her dance career, Zelda went to the opposite extreme and deliberately swept out everything but her work. Living for Madame's praise, she told herself that all it took to become a first-class dancer was practice and hard work, and she began to imagine herself dancing with a top ballet company. These ambitions were strongly opposed by Scott, who not only hated the Egorova dance school but felt exploited. The exorbitant tuition, twice the monthly rent on Ellerslie, the flowers, and the dinners were all for nothing because Zelda was no good at dancing, and never would be. She was turning into a phantom that lived at the Olympia Music Hall and only came home to wash her tights. Why was he forced to pay the bills for "this desolate ménage," which consisted of a lousy apartment with lousy servants? Zelda paid no attention. If the apartment didn't suit him, she replied, he should make more money. She didn't like Mlle Delplangue either, but if the governess truly bothered him, he should send Scottie away to school.

With Scott, who on good days managed to rise by lunchtime, the example of Zelda's self-discipline, a freakish energy without apparent bounds, did not sit well. Neither did the loneliness of an apartment empty except for Scottie and her governess. ("Unbearable," he said. "Literally, eternally" inebriated, she said.) Wine, he insisted, had become necessary to tolerate her monologues about ballet technique—the obsessive concern with her legs—which put him into narcoleptic trances.

. . .

ZELDA WAS EATING lunch with her Montgomery friend Sara May-field at Pruniers, a seafood restaurant near La Madeleine. Bolting down several martinis, she picked at her shrimp and *salade niçoise*. When Sara complimented her on her appearance—thin and stylish in a blue Patou frock—she brushed it aside. Lately she had been sleeping poorly and to her dismay again developed asthma, which had not bothered her for several years. "I look like hell, feel like hell, and act like hell." Pulling a mirror out of her bag, she bent over the glass to study her face. Look at those bags under her eyes, she said, and the lines around her mouth, and she was twenty-eight.

It had been a hideous summer, she told Sara. Most of her time had been passed at Madame's sweating and drinking water to stave off dehydration. Practically every waking minute of Scott's had been spent, as usual, getting plastered and landing in trouble. At the moment they were not speaking, not even to say, "Pass the butter, please."

Scott with a snoot full became insanely reckless. While visiting friends who lived in a sixth-floor apartment, he teetered along their balcony railing, yelling, "I'm Voltaire. I'm Rousseau." Nobody laughed. And another evening when they were invited to the home of Sylvia Beach (a bookshop proprietor who published James Joyce's *Ulysses*), he turned the dinner into a sideshow by groveling at Joyce's feet and threatening to jump out the window. The Irish writer and his wife, Nora, impressed Zelda as superannuated at best, an old-fashioned couple who addressed everyone as Mister or Missus, but Scott's antics were mortifying.

Scott was twice arrested for disorderly conduct that summer, which did not prevent him from pumping out the staples of his trade, the short fiction for the *Saturday Evening Post* that paid thirty-five hundred dollars each. The previous year he managed to coast by on earnings that amounted to a healthy thirty thousand dollars, but he was running a bit behind that figure. Most of his income came from a series of *Post* stories about the misadventures of a teenage Midwestern boy name Basil Duke Lee. Apart from the seven Basil stories, and contrary to his hearty assurances to Max Perkins, and the fifty-seven hundred dollars squeezed out of Scribner's as an advance on the new novel, he was completely blocked. He had come to think of the book as "a dream" receding slowly into the distance.

They returned to America in October, accompanied by Scottie's nanny and a second servant, whom Scott had acquired over the summer to be a combination chauffeur, valet, companion, and general dogsbody. Zelda was not pleased about Philippe, a taxi driver and ex-boxer who behaved like a thug. On the trip home she could not help grieving for Madame Egorova, whom she missed far more than she had expected. How deeply she loved her, how dull life in Delaware would be without her. Madame, she thought sadly, was a good woman who worked hard her whole life with nothing to show for it. Suddenly the intensity of her feelings had begun to worry her, and she asked Scott if he thought feeling attraction to Madame was abnormal.

What did she mean by abnormal?

She wasn't sure.

Abnormal like a lesbian? That was nonsense, he replied.

VINCENT INVITED Bunny to Austerlitz for the weekend. When Bunny arrived, Gene was planting pansies but immediately lost all interest in gardening and declared it cocktail time. ("But what isn't cocktail time?!!!" he'd say.) On this first visit to Steepletop, Bunny was enthused by the tapestry of scenic views and told Vincent of passing a dandelion-speckled lawn that made him think of "grated egg on spinach." As Mr. Hospitality, Gene laid down the welcome mat with Cockney song and uncorked bottles of homemade vintage from their private cellar—Château Steepletop—in addition to plying Bunny with several varieties of local apple brandies and wines. Vincent, who had taken up the piano again, attempted a Beethoven sonata but became impatient with what she considered a miserable performance. Finally she dug out a batch of her newest poems, and they all settled down to an afternoon of sipping applejack. On a soggy May weekend there was little else to do but drink.

The pedestal on which Bunny had placed her, some eight years before, remained solid. The previous year, extolling the virtues of "perhaps one of the most important of our poets," he elevated her to a headliner in his "All-Star Literary Vaudeville," along with T. S. Eliot, Edwin Arlington Robinson, Elinor Wylie, and Léonie Adams. Some people would pounce on his obstinate overrating of Millay (along with Parker and Fitzgerald) as hairline cracks in the literary judgment of an otherwise-shrewd critic, but Bunny never wavered in his enthusiasm for Vincent. At one of their meetings that winter, the two of them were debating some of James Joyce's poems when she attempted to express her appreciation for his loyalty. For the first time she wished to put into words what he meant to her, but one look at his pale face warned her it was best left unsaid.

Bunny could always be relied on for editing and admiration, but less attractive qualities were also developing. At thirty-three, he was physically a ghost of the worshipful boy she had met in 1920. His body was going to seed, and he had taken to slicking back his thinning and receding hair. Otherwise, he suffered from depression, fits of hysteria, and anger that sometimes burst into violence, and his evolution into an alcoholic was well under way. More disturbing was a growing tendency to become crotchety, even irrationally argumentative. In the winter, when she and Gene were in town celebrating her birthday, they invited him to the hotel one night. With the proofs of a new poem about to be published in *The Delineator,* she suddenly felt uncertain and needed his advice. To her disappointment, Bunny showed little interest in "The Bobolink," a poem about a bedraggled little bird that derived more from its mood than from ideas. Noting his indifference, she could not help feeling annoyed. "You mean it sounds like Mary Carolyn Davies!" If she thought that were true, she'd tear it up. Certainly she was not going to give *The Delineator* anything that brought to mind Mary Carolyn Davies. (Davies was a third-rate poet, the poor man's Sara Teasdale.)

Throughout the evening Bunny continued to be grumpy. He insisted on reminding her of the pressure she had been under when she published *Second April,* in 1921. Had she forgotten how anxious she was? he asked pointedly. Did she recall that some critics said the collection wasn't literature at all? She could not deny that those poems were written in a panic, to prove beyond reasonable doubt that she was a poet, and to prove it in a hurry.

"Yes," she snapped. "And I still want to knock 'em cold!"

When a young woman, in Camden and at Vassar, she had hungered for fame, not art. Right after the war *A Few Figs from Thistles* and *Second April* turned out to be exactly the raw thrills that readers, especially women, especially provincials, desired. No doubt it was partly the idea of liberation: to be an adventuress, to ride around New York Harbor all night with a lover, to buy newspapers she would never read, and to give away everything in her pocket but subway fare. All she knew was that upon these patented images of her exploits in the Village, quite unlike anything experienced by her readers in the hinterland, was her following built. (And would continue to rest.) But at thirty-six, she needed to prove other things beyond a reasonable doubt.

Gene had taken no part in the acrimonious exchange between Vincent and Bunny. Invigorating intellectual conversations were healthy for her, he believed, but he didn't care for the way this one was going and slammed on the brakes at last. Certainly Vincent's recent work, he reminded Bunny, was more objective than *Second April.* Then he changed the subject to Kathleen's first volume of poetry, which some reviewers had called glib. What did Bunny think of *The Evergreen Tree?* Maybe Kay wasn't cut out to be a poet?

Vincent was able to relax around Bunny more than with most people. It was to him she confided that settling at Steepletop had probably been a mistake, because the woods and mountains walled her in like a cage. Still, their intimacy had limits. She somehow managed to conceal her plans to publish a new collection of verses, the first in five years; he hid from her the news that he was writing a novel, in which a central character was coincidentally an impoverished Village poet. Nor did he mention the California woman he had decided to marry. And of course he did not tell Vincent, or anyone else, about his secret mistress, a waitress from the Seventy-second and Broadway Childs.

It had been five years since Vincent left Mitchell Kennerley for a distinguished mainstream publisher, Harper & Brothers, which had brought out the Pulitzer Prize–winning *The Harp-Weaver and Other Poems.* Her editor was Eugene Saxton, a quiet man in his mid-forties clad in checked vests and sporting a gold watch chain, leaving the impression of being a refined Edwardian gentleman. Cut from the same cloth as Max Perkins at Scribner's, Saxton was a first-rate editor with a knack for working with temperamental woman poets. (He had been Elinor Wylie's editor at George Doran.) In Vincent's case, where no editing was permitted, not even so much as moving a comma, he stood aside and oversaw production details. Saxton, a clubbable fellow who owned a country home in the Berkshires, and his wife, Martha, enjoyed dropping in for cocktails with the Boissevains.

Saxton understood instinctively how to handle royalty, but some of his colleagues resisted conferring special treatment. Interoffice memos referred to Vincent as "the one and only Edna." One editor loved taunting Vincent by addressing letters to "Madame Vincent" and referring to Gene as "Prince Eugen." This was only partly in jest, because the high-handed Edna tended to treat the staff as her subjects.

Vincent's main nemesis was Arthur Rushmore, head of book production. Ever since *The Harp-Weaver,* when Vincent made Harper's reset the entire book (with each poem on a separate page), the two of them had butted heads. As a result, Gene Saxton received any number of complaints about "your Mr. Rushmore," who pretended to listen but did as he pleased. Evidently in love with his printing presses, he was so busy fussing about Lutetia italics and mold-made papers that he forgot they were making a book of poetry, not widgets. Vincent was aghast to see Rushmore slapping dedications on copyright pages and omitting "The End" in favor of a note describing the typeface. As practically the house's poet laureate, she could not believe that anybody at Harper & Brothers would disregard her wishes. But Rushmore did not consider coddling authors part of his job.

All personal contact between Vincent and her publisher was filtered through Gene. In his management of her business, he operated under a simple rule: If Edna St. Vincent Millay was not entitled to the best seat in the house, who was? Which was why his letters could get a bit growly. *Miss Millay has asked me to inform you . . . Miss Millay is unable to attend to her correspondence . . . Miss Millay is extremely dissatisfied with Harper's behavior . . .*

After *The Harp-Weaver* she did not release another book but went on publishing in various literary periodicals. Her habit was to hold back a poem, sometimes for as long as two years, working on it "again and again, whenever I get a new point of view," she said, and she also liked to store verse until it was "cold, as if it weren't mine at all." In April, finally, having accumulated an adequate number that pleased her, she signed a contract for a collection to be titled *The Buck in the Snow and Other Poems.* Harper's agreed to pay five hundred dollars on delivery of a completed manuscript and five hundred dollars on publication, against a royalty of 15 percent.

IT HAD RAINED steadily all summer, almost every day since the beginning of April. The sunless Berkshires weather was exasperating, depressing, and finally cruel. With so few dry days Gene could only spray the potatoes twice, and his twelve acres of oats threatened to rot. Inside the house, conditions were hardly better. Servants were sneaking off without giving notice. And in the city Harper's was nagging Vincent in the most unpleasant way. Dissatisfied with her speed in returning proofs, they claimed she was wrecking their production schedule. Saxton, bristly, postponed her publication date by a week. The last straw was his announcement of a publication party (nothing too "fussy," he said). Would she please supply a guest list? Miss Millay, Gene informed him, was not in a party mood, maybe another time.

The Buck in the Snow, published on September 27, was not what Vincent's fans had been expecting. Gone was her usual urban landscape, the ferries and narrow streets, the pretty lads and sex-addled maidens. Reflecting her new pastoral life was the title poem about the death of a deer in her woods (a common sight during hunting season), while others celebrated nature and wildlife outside her door. Bucks and bobolinks apart, there was a group of five poems that recalled the Sacco and Vanzetti executions, including "Justice Denied in Massachusetts" and "Hangman's Oak"; a handful whose exotic locales seemed memories of her travels in Europe and the Far East; and tributes to Art Ficke and Bunny. Perhaps the most eloquent is the opening lyric, "Moriturus," which could almost have been "Renascence: The Sequel," the same subjects of claustrophobia and death seen by a grown-up who wishes to bolt her door against death "with a bureau and a table." Ending the volume was "On Hearing a Symphony of Beethoven," an exceptional sonnet that undertakes the difficult task of exploring in words the power of music, "the tranquil blossom on the tortured stem."

Ever since the publication of "Renascence," one of her trademark themes had been the affirmation of life over death. Her other frequent theme was sex, but the erotic Edna St. Vincent Millay with her burning candle was absent from the new book. There were no love poems, not a one in fact that might have been a tribute to her husband. Had her marriage not inspired a single passionate poem? Or was theirs, as tittle-tattle claimed, a marriage of convenience? In *The Buck in the Snow* she seemed to be more a forest ranger than the sultry vamp of the West Village.

Prepared to "knock 'em cold," Vincent sat back to receive accolades for her long-awaited book. Gene's former housemate Max Eastman detected new maturity in her work and called the title poem "one of the most perfect lyrics in our language, a painting of life and death unexcelled, indeed, anywhere." But Max's review was not typical. The difficulty, said *The New Republic*, was that "the poet has already said so perfectly all that she had to say," so the collection could not help sounding redundant. Words used by other critics were "not good enough," "no retrogression and no advance," "the frontier of sentimentality," and "lack of intellectual force."

As a romanticist who relied on traditional forms, Vincent made no effort to sound like modern American English. Her poems, she said proudly, were written "in old-fashioned form, in the very musical tradition that people have always known and loved." That's why people appreciated her work. They could understand it, memorize it, quote it.

The painful fact was that just as she was establishing herself, a new generation of poets had come along: first the so-called imagism movement of Ezra Pound, Hilda Doolittle, William Carlos Williams, and other unromantic outlaws whose experimental work used concrete images and spare language. And it was followed shortly by the razzle-dazzle innovations of T. S. Eliot with "The Love Song of J. Alfred Prufrock" and "The Waste Land," the latter a poem complete with seven pages of scholarly notes, published in *The Dial* the year before Vincent won her Pulitzer. According to the modernists, poetry ought to be realistic and sound like conversation, the colloquial speech of real people talking to each other, and anything else was phony. One of those disparaging Vincent was Archibald MacLeish, who said that the English language she used wasn't even speech. "It is poems," he said, work that he scorned as "prettiness conscious of its own prettiness." When Louis Untermeyer defended Vincent as a poet who "touched greatness," MacLeish wisecracked back, "With what does she?" Because if she did, that made him "a cracked thermometer."

Defiantly skeptical of the new poetry, Vincent could not admit that a generation of excellent poets might be passing her by. The writer whose photograph she kept in her study—"a fine poet and a great man," she said—was the nature poet Robinson Jeffers. T. S. Eliot to her was ridiculous.

The Buck in the Snow's negative reviews distressed Vincent. As for Gene, he was outraged by criticism of his wife's work and suspected Harper's was to blame. When, in later years, he suggested the publisher recruit "friendly people" to write reviews, Saxton replied that publications customarily select their own writers. Efforts to influence critics usually backfire, he added firmly.

By this time Vincent had come to believe she had proved beyond a reasonable doubt that she was a poet, as well as a household name. Not only did she care fiercely about her writing, but her work had been honored with a Pulitzer, and her popularity among the reading public verged on the mythic, which made the criticism all the more puzzling.

Despite poor reviews, advance sales pointed to a commercial triumph. In early November, as Vincent prepared to set out for Chicago on the first leg of a reading tour, *The Buck in the Snow* was doing extremely well and by Christmas had sold forty thousand copies.

MADAME EGOROVA and the Olympia Music Hall had become a lost world. In their place was Ellerslie, with a new cast of characters and a makeshift household that Zelda felt no part of. Neither she nor Scott, not even Scottie, really liked Mlle Delplangue, a nervous woman who smelled of too much sachet. If she was a mistake, the insolent Philippe was a bigger one, because the governess fell in love with him. Philippe, however, did not reciprocate and spent more time catting around the neighborhood than chauffeuring. The household was in a state of constant upheaval. Through it all, Scottie played by herself. As lonely and woebegone as her weeping governess, she knocked a croquet ball around the house and cried because her Du Pont and Wanamaker playmates had more money.

In Philadelphia, Zelda found a new ballet teacher, a Russian who had trained at the Imperial School of Ballet and danced with Diaghilev's Ballets Russes in prewar Paris (*Les Sylphides*). Alexandre Gavrilov had also understudied Nijinsky and liked to describe himself as a protégé of the great artist. Although Gavrilov made a favorable impression, he could be intimidating. One afternoon after lunching together, he invited Zelda to his apartment on Chestnut Street. Looking around, she noticed that the place was practically empty of furnishings, stark and cold except for a white spitz dog and a stunning collection of ballet sketches by Léon Bakst. It soon became clear that Gavrilov had more on his mind than displaying his artworks. As soon as possible, she excused herself and ran terrified through the streets. Still, she could not say the months with Gavrilov were wasted. He was a capable instructor, and she worked diligently, both in class and at home. The result was steady, unmistakable growth as a dancer.

Sometimes Zelda went out to eat with other students, socializing that made Scott furious. Mostly he paid little attention to her activities, but when he did, it could precipitate a crisis. While Zelda's sister and brother-in-law were visiting earlier that year, Scott came home unexpectedly from a trip to Princeton and immediately flew into a rage. In front of Rosalind and Newman Smith, he accused Zelda of breaking into his liquor closet. Then he became angry because he thought she called his father an Irish cop.

She said no such thing, she replied, but trying to reason with Scott when he had been drinking was a waste of time. The next thing she knew he hurled her favorite blue vase into the fireplace.

Go to bed, he ordered.

When she refused, he punched her in the nose. ("You had a nosebleed," he said later. Besides, she was behaving badly, throwing herself into her brother-in-law's arms, "making dives and he was pretending to catch you.")

Scott's behavior outraged Rosalind. She would never permit a man to strike her, not that Newman ever would, but the idea was unthinkable.

"No matter what a woman does," Newman warned Scott, "you ought never to lose your temper with her."

Zelda should divorce Scott, Rosalind urged. From the beginning, Scott made the Sayre family uneasy. Judge Sayre spotted the Yankee soldier for a lush at once, and Rosalind could never stand him.

No, she was not going to leave Scott, Zelda told her sister. And do what? Be Zelda Sayre, in a three-cornered bedroom on Pleasant Avenue, sitting on the porch swing with Mama? How could she go back to Montgomery? Besides, she really did love Scott. Of course he was a fright, but he didn't drink all the time.

Rosalind and Newman slipped away from Ellerslie in the middle of the night.

In the fall, right after the election in which Herbert Hoover defeated Al Smith, Ernest and Pauline Hemingway visited Ellerslie. Zelda's feelings about Ernest had not changed, and his dislike of her had intensified. A few weeks before the reunion, responding to a remark of Max Perkins's about Zelda's sharp mind ("so able and intelligent"), he hurried to set the editor straight. The person responsible for Scott's failures as a novelist, he replied, was Zelda. Married to another woman, the poor guy would have been the "best writer" around.

After two years of not seeing Ernest, who now lived in Key West, Florida, Scott was excited at the prospect of entertaining his old friend. They arranged to meet in Princeton for the Yale game before returning to Ellerslie for the rest of the weekend. The trip was a treat for Zelda, who had pleasant memories of the campus, with its worn parade grounds and old brick buildings. In high spirits after undefeated Princeton's 12–2 victory, the two couples and Scott's college friend Mike Strater boarded the Pennsy at Princeton Junction late that afternoon. Tippling from his flask, Scott roamed up and down the aisle annoying woman passengers. Even though the train was packed with celebrating football fans none too sober themselves, Scott's misbehavior went too far, and Ernest and Mike tried to make him return to his seat. He whipped a medical book out of a passenger's hands. "I've found a clap doctor," he announced to the entire car. "You are a clap doctor, aren't you?" The man did not reply. "Physician, heal thyself." Like a lepidopterist spotting an endangered species, he began chanting, "A clap doctor, a clap doctor."

At dinner Scott was lavish with the wine, uncorking six bottles of Burgundy exclusively for Ernest while he served the others Moselle. Around the table everybody was chatting happily until Scott began yelling at the maid.

"Aren't you the best piece of tail I ever had?" he said. "Tell Mr. Hemingway." Whenever Marie bustled past him with a dish—by which time everybody was sitting stiff as boards—Scott started up once more. "Tell him what a grand piece of pussy you are." ("He must have said it to her ten times," Hemingway recalled.) Suddenly all business again, Scott forgot the maid and took off on the subject of Gertrude Stein.

Sunday morning, in white flannels and blue blazer, Scott tried to organize a game of croquet, but the Hemingways were impatient to make their getaway. They arrived at the station long before the train was due, anything to avoid spending another minute at Ellerslie. (Mike Strater, who left first thing, thought both Scott and Ernest were "really awful" and hoped never to see either of them again.) From the train Ernest wrote, "We had a grand time." Ellerslie was the "most cock-eyed beautiful" place he had ever seen, and Pauline sent her love.

With one successful novel and the first draft of his second completed, Ernest felt superior to Scott, who was obviously washed up, thanks to a sabotaging wife and the debasement of his talent by chronic whoring, his compulsion to "poop himself away on those lousy Post stories." Only Zelda's death or the loss of his liver would make a writer of him again, Ernest believed.

Shortly before Ernest's visit, Scott managed to mail two chapters of his novel to Scribner's. It was about eighteen thousand words, he told Max Perkins, an estimated quarter of the book, and the remaining chapters would be coming in batches. They were "excellent," Max replied, some of the best writing he had ever done. Could they get the book out in the spring?

His trouble with the novel could be traced to the summer of 1925, which he spent complaining about book reviewers and hoping for a quick movie sale. Still, there was no cause for worry, he believed, because his next book, inspired by the recent Leopold-Loeb murder case, was already worked out in his head. It was going to be about a Hollywood film technician named Francis (Scott's own first name) Melarky, a nice, unspoiled lad who falls in with a bad crowd of Americans on the Riviera and ends by killing his mother in a fit of rage.

Periodically Scott would dispatch reports to Max: "The novel has begun. I'd rather tell you nothing about it quite yet." "My book is *wonderful.*" "The novel goes fine. I think it's quite wonderful." But after three years of starting and stopping, exaggerating and lying, changing the story, characters, and titles (*Our Type, The World's Fair, The Melarky*

Case, and one suggested by Zelda, *The Boy Who Killed His Mother*), he was stuck. There was nothing workable down on paper.

That winter at Ellerslie, Scott fell into a routine. For a week or two he would stop drinking hard liquor and confine himself to wine and black coffee until he had completed a story. During the periods of semi-abstinence he felt rotten and complained of listlessness and dark circles under his eyes. Mostly he was asleep at the wheel.

At Christmas their maid, Marie, danced barefoot around the tree on broken ornaments. Scottie wrote to Santa and asked for a set of Lionel trains and a doctor's kit, but if she wasn't "nice enough to have both," she chose the train. Scott read Oswald Spengler's *The Decline of the West*. And Zelda dreamed of spring, when their two-year lease on Ellerslie would end and they could go back to Paris.

T HE BOY showed up at the reading and stood over Vincent, bending down to shake hands and say his name was George Dillon and he would be doing her introduction. Twenty-one, he looked much like the scores of students waiting to hear her perform that Friday night in November. He was sweet, she thought, reluctant to release his hand.

Vincent was backstage at the school auditorium of the University of Chicago, her first stop on a tour that promised to be difficult even with Gene's company. The reading was being sponsored by *Poetry*, the magazine that was founded in Chicago before the war by a socially connected aspiring poet and was among the first to publish Vincent's earliest work. Now seventy, Harriet Monroe relied more and more on younger staff to help run *Poetry*, among them the terribly nice boy George Dillon.

Vincent's reading was followed by the usual reception organized to honor visiting poets, the type of social event that she always found unpleasant, loud, and crowded with people she had no desire to meet. It was Gene's job to brush off long-winded admirers before hustling her away as soon as possible by pleading exhaustion on her behalf. This time, however, she did not want to be rescued. As George Dillon rose to declaim some of his own poems, Vincent kept her eyes on him. Such adorable lips he had, the kind of bee-stung mouth that would have looked good on a girl. His black hair was probably much too wavy to be fashionably slicked back.

Wasn't George gifted? someone said.

She agreed.

Wasn't his work remarkable for someone so young?

Remarkable for anyone, she said.

A Southerner, an only child born in Florida, George had recently graduated from the university. Known as something of a prodigy, he had published his first book of verse while still an undergraduate and found himself taken under the wing of Harriet Monroe. Nevertheless, he remained a baby chick, barely out of the nest. He was working at his first job, copywriter for an advertising agency, and lived at home with his parents in an apartment overlooking Lake Michigan. The love of his life, the person for whom he wrote poems, was his mother.

Unable to pull her eyes away, Vincent felt hypnotized by an "enchanted sickness." All she could think of was that she must see him again. Before leaving the reception, she slipped him a note, inviting him to lunch the next day. In her hotel room she used a pencil and the back of a telegram to quickly compose a sonnet in which she confessed her hunger ("this love, this longing") and her inability to think straight. That she was seized by feelings more animal than human must have been obvious to everyone at the party, she feared. The sonnet's message was frank: she wanted to sleep with him. Probably she was "two fools," not only wanting him so badly but also telling him about it. Had she doubted his response, she might have hesitated, but the expression on his face told her he was dying to be seduced.

The next day at lunch she handed him the scribbled poem.

No SOONER HAD Vincent and Gene left Chicago on November 9 than she began writing letters to her young man. She could think of nothing else but him, she said. She was going to love him "always."

If George doubted her, she simply would not be able to bear it. And he mustn't worry about the future either, because she would "never let you go out of my life."

For the next five weeks, like a traveling carnival, she slogged her way back east, from Chicago to wintry Syracuse to Boston and finally to New York, where she would do her last booking before returning to Steepletop for Christmas. In a dressing room at the Brooklyn Academy of Music, while changing into a trailing silk gown the texture of heavy cream, she overheard people outside the door talking about Elinor Wylie. Wasn't it awful? Such a shock. What a way to get word of Elinor's stroke. Feeling shaky, Vincent walked onstage and came down to the front, where she began speaking directly to the audience. She was devastated, she said. A greater poet than she had just died, not only a finer writer but her beloved friend, and she didn't see how she could read in the circumstances. Instead, she was going to recite, from memory, the poems of her friend Elinor Wylie.

When she arrived the next morning at the Benét apartment in the Village, the house was packed with mourners, and Elinor was laid out in a coffin wearing her favorite silver Poiret gown. Placing a sprig of laurel in Elinor's hands, Vincent recited a poem that Elinor had written for her ("Musa of the Sea-Blue Eyes").

Despite Elinor's death, Christmas was particularly festive that year. Art Ficke's improved health had permitted him to leave Santa Fe and return east. To be close to the Boissevains, the Fickes purchased property in nearby Hillsdale and built a house they called Hardhack (another name for the steepletop flowers). To entertain the Boissevains, they planned a special two-day gala with period costumes. Gladdie painted an elaborate invitation: "Lord and Lady of Hardhack require the honorable company of Lord and Lady of Steepletop at Christmas revels." The program promised a chess tournament, prizes for best costume, and "light liquid refreshments in the Bar Room every two hours!"

. . .

"TELL HIM it is a matter of life and death," Vincent urged George. "Him" was George's boss at the advertising agency. In January she was going to Europe, and she had to see George before she left. He must come to Steepletop for the weekend of January 4 to 7, or the whole week if he wished. If he left Chicago on Friday, he would arrive Saturday in Albany, where they would meet his train, and if he really had to return quickly, they could motor him back to Albany on Sunday evening.

George answered immediately. He couldn't.

Of course he could, she replied.

Did she want him to lose his job? he said.

Naturally she would not want him to "mess things up for yourself." But what was the matter with that company of his? Surely it could be reasonable, under the circumstances. He ought to know that her mind was made up. She was going to see him. Next, Gene tried to convince George. Listen, he said, just pack your gayest tie, some evening clothes, and a clean shirt, and hop on the train. They would "drink wine and laugh together."

In Vincent's next letter she was losing patience. Why wouldn't George do what she asked? All she wanted was to kiss him, to sit on the edge of his bed and be "incredibly happy, be like children." She was not going to leave the country until she saw him, and that was final.

1929

Edna snuggles up to Noël Coward (far right) during a misbegotten summer vacation in the Basque country. Others are the novelist Louis Bromfield, Edna's mother, Julia, and Noël's scenic designer, Gladys Calthrop.

CHAPTER TEN

GEORGE DILLON did not come to Steepletop. Gene canceled their steamship passage for January 19 and booked a March 11 sailing on the *Rotterdam*. It made no difference. Vincent's lover still failed to show.

By this time Gene had become aware of the whole business, because concealing such a state of affairs would have been impossible. If he felt troubled by the intrusion of a boy young enough to be his son, he chose not to show it. When Vincent needed George at Steepletop, he, too, had penned encouraging notes. "I'm going to make you love me," he wrote cheerfully, "and you must make me love you," an idea that may have struck young George as a bit peculiar.

From the first, Vincent spelled out the geography of the relationship to George. Three of them were involved, she warned. In the sonnet she slipped to him under the table at their first lunch, she cautioned that any intimacy was sure to act as a knife between her and "my troubled lord." To make absolutely sure he understood, she said pointedly, "I am devoted to my husband." And while it was true that her "lovely thing" occupied her thoughts "all day and half the night," that in no way changed her affection for Gene.

Wives torturing husbands ran in Vincent's family. Cora's mother was married to a man named Eben Buzzell, but she didn't give a damn about abandoning him for another man, regardless of six children. For Cora, caring for the dying and weaving hairpieces were better than putting up with Henry. Eben Buzzell and Henry Millay met similar fates. But Vincent never deluded herself: she intended to stick with Gene.

In January, Vincent spent a considerable amount of her time writing George long letters ranging in mood from the childish to the ecstatic. Something about the youth brought back her own childhood, baby-talking with her sisters, calling herself Sniggybus, playing dress-up in Mumbles's curtains. But while she always meant to treat kindly her adorable "Scramdoodle," she could turn on a dime too, and then her moods became possessive.

How come George stayed in Chicago when she needed him?

Were they never to be together?

Did he have a girlfriend? she demanded.

Did he hate her?

"Perhaps I wanted to hurt you," she said, realizing how wounding she must sound. "I don't know."

In the meantime, the snow had come, and plenty of days Steepletop was half-buried, which meant they could usually get out but never felt confident of getting back up the hill. After a path to her shed was shoveled and a blazing fire stoked in the stove, Vincent lit a cigarette and hunkered down to write sonnets. Just hours after meeting George, she had written one that began "This beast that rends me in the sight of all," and now she went on struggling to put desire into fourteen lines. Usually the speaker was herself, but in a sonnet that began "Oh, sleep forever in the Latmian cave," she reprised the myth of the goddess Selene and the youthful Endymion.

Never in her life could she remember working so hard. "Night and day I concentrated," she remembered. The sonnets never seemed to leave her mind, not when she was working outside or talking to people, not when she woke in the middle of the night and found herself "writing in bed furiously until dawn." At her bedside she kept a notebook and a pencil. To her poet friend Stephen Vincent Benét, whom she'd known in France, she called herself "a non-union" poet who was slaving twenty-two hours a day "on her own stuff," although she offered no information about the subject. The presence of a lover—her muse—was known only to her husband.

As the weeks passed, the sheer physical effort aggravated her headaches, ever present even on good days. It had been four years—she never imagined they would last—and creative work, without fail, worsened the pain. Owing to the extreme concentration that went into each of her poems, the act of writing generated "a nervous intensity" that ended predictably in exhaustion and agony. By and by, the pitiless throbbing in her head had become part of her life, an "occupational disease," she called it. In an attempt to forget, she made light of the "ungracious guest" who didn't know when to say good night. "And must I then, indeed, Pain, live with you," she wrote sardonically. In the back of her mind lay the awful suspicion that the only escape would be death.

IN JANUARY, Gene brought home a parcel from the Austerlitz post office. It was the manuscript of Bunny's first novel, *I Thought of Daisy*, which had been accepted by Max Perkins at Scribner's. He wanted Vincent's opinion, Bunny said, adding that he certainly hoped she would not be offended.

It did not take long to figure out the reason for his nervousness. The story took place in New York, when the city was still battered from the dislocations of the Great War. The protagonist, a writer living in downtown bohemia, is torn between the traditional and the modern, high art versus down-and-dirty popular culture. He also can't decide between two women: Daisy, the vivacious but somewhat vulgar chorus girl, and Rita, the suffering artist embracing a life of hardship for the sake of truth and beauty. A bohemian prone to reckless behavior, Rita Cavanagh values independence above husband, children, even simple friendships, "all the natural bonds and understandings which make up the greater part of human life." "Well, don't you think that *my* life makes me bitter?" she says. (Rita dramatizes just about every impulse.) "Don't you think *I* hate the way I've been living?" Not at all, because poetry is her religion. Proud of her choices, she regards adversity with fatalistic acceptance as the path a genuine artist must be prepared to walk. It is the oafish narrator, the Bunny character, who fails to appreciate the superior sensibilities of an artistic person such as herself.

On two points Vincent felt quite certain: the Rita Cavanagh character was based on herself—certainly Rita's attitude toward art was more or less her own—and the novel was badly written. Obviously Bunny was expecting her reaction, but it was a delicate situation. She began scribbling notes for revisions, some of them general suggestions for polishing, others commentary on various characters. Gearing up to full throttle, she then proceeded to rewrite all the Rita Cavanagh speeches.

No, she finally wrote Bunny, she was not offended. But honestly the book was not ready. While she liked much of it, the rest was "very uneven." Publication would do nothing to enhance his reputation. "It really isn't good enough, yet, Bunny, I swear it." Hearing this would probably make him "mad as hell," but she couldn't help it.

At the end of the week she posted her revisions. She would be in town for a few days, to take in shows and attend parties, she wrote. There was a batch of new sonnets to show him, and of course she was keen to talk about his manuscript. She promised a bottle of the best red wine he ever tasted, made by her own French chef, Pierre. Was he free for dinner on Tuesday? He should call the Vanderbilt that afternoon before five and leave a message.

At the hotel waited no word from Bunny, rather oddly. No phone call, no reply to her letters, which was not like him at all. "Whamming" his book, she thought, was harsh, and maybe she should have minded her own business, but what she said was for his own good.

Some time later, her letters turned up at the Austerlitz post office stamped "Return to Sender": no such person as Edmund Wilson lived at the address, nor at the forwarding address either. Evidently it was the sort of mix-up that happened all the time in New York. She wondered about it for a while, and then she and Gene went abroad. By the time they returned in May, she had forgotten.

ELIZABETH, Rahway, Perth Amboy, South Amboy, Matawan, the coast train rattled down the ragged rim of the North Jersey shore. Almost every week it was Bunny's routine to leave the city and dutifully visit his daughter, Rosalind. At the rail station in Red Bank, met by his mother's car and chauffeur, he would be driven to her house in Vista Place, where he had a comfortable book-filled room of his own. On his way to Red Bank that particular weekend in January, however, he got no farther than the backseat of a taxi in the West Village, when he began to tremble uncontrollably. Knowing he was not himself, "I could not go down to my mother's." Alarmed, he hurried to consult a doctor and learned there was nothing to worry about. He'd simply been drinking too much, that was all. Admitted to a hospital and put to sleep with a shot of morphine, he was relieved to see the agitation clear up.

Since returning from the Coast at Christmas, Bunny had been living opposite a taxi garage on West Thirteenth Street, not far from his job at *The New Republic*. It was "a narrow, stale-smelling little hole," without a toilet, which meant he had to walk down one flight to a scabby-looking communal bathroom. In these boom times, when everybody seemed to have money to spare, he had little beyond his salary from the magazine. Still, he figured the squalor of the room could easily be ignored because it was cheap and he was never there on the weekends.

Bunny knew he drank too much. Difficulties concentrating had already interfered with a work he was calling *Axel's Castle*, a critical study tracing the influence of the French symbolists on modern writers such as Joyce and Eliot. Then one night after seeing the new Noël Coward revue, he lapsed into a musical delirium in which fragments of tunes circled persistently in his head. Shortly afterward the shaking and shuddering started.

Several days after his discharge from the hospital, the shivers returned. Now he wondered if he might be going crazy. Two or three times a week he began visiting "sort of a nerve doctor" about feeling overwhelmed by panic attacks that descended without warning and left him flattened. He described a fantasy in which a pencil seemed to be "writing for him all by itself." He also sensed that he was being followed. Bunny felt especially vulnerable because insanity seemed to run in his family: his favorite cousin was confined in a state mental hospital after a schizophrenic breakdown, and his father, too, had suffered serious psychological problems. In addition to anxiety, Bunny thought of suicide. Yet whenever he mentioned these violent feelings, his doctor turned Pollyannaish and kept correcting him. Certainly he felt like killing himself, the doctor agreed, but the impulse was bound to pass. Think of it as a bad headache. And besides, he was still holding down a job, wasn't he?

Eventually the psychiatrist acknowledged his fears and arranged admission to a private mental hospital in upstate New York. Clifton Springs Sanatorium and Clinic offered a full menu of psychiatric services: electrical stimulation, cold sheet packs, massages, medications, everything its clientele could want, except alcohol. Bunny sweet-talked an attendant into giving him a double dose of paraldehyde, a drug to which he eventually became addicted.

For all the complaints of boredom, his concentration began to return. On good days he was able to rewrite the opening of *Axel's Castle*:

A *Study in the Imaginative Literature of 1870–1930.* The title referred to a drama by Philippe-Auguste Villiers de L'Isle-Adam, whose Count Axel of Auersburg is the lord of an ancient castle in the depths of the Black Forest. Axel, convinced that life is vulgar and futile, withdraws from the wretchedness of the world and its "dens of loathsome creatures" by shutting himself away in his citadel, the private realm of his imagination. In addition to working on *Axel's Castle,* Bunny reviewed the proofs of *I Thought of Daisy.* To his disappointment Vincent never acknowledged receipt of the manuscript. He guessed she must be furious at this portrait of her younger self, before she became a prosperous married woman.

In between massages and shock treatments, Bunny kept busy writing lengthy letters, whose tone suggested a happy-go-lucky person away on holiday. He wrote Seward Collins that he was "enjoying a brief nervous breakdown up here" but planned to see him shortly. After three weeks at Clifton Springs, whose attendants "couldn't quite make it in a Turkish bath," he was convinced that the sanatorium was a racket.

The publication of *I Thought of Daisy* that fall elicited no comment from Vincent. The book got bad reviews and sold poorly.

BACK IN PARIS, Zelda became absorbed in her ballet studies again. She was determined to succeed if it killed her. Nobody, neither Scott nor anyone else, could make her "put out her light till she got good and ready," she thought. It was her turn now.

In the mornings she would arrive at Lubov Egorova's unheated studio and eat a pretzel (the dancers' regular breakfast) before warming up for her first class. By noon the dressing room had begun to smell of wet wool and glue from the toe shoes and to thrum with the laughter, gossip, and endless jealous bickering of the women. Zelda was reluctant to leave at the end of the day. She clung to her classmates, drinking coffee, gobbling soggy Russian rolls bursting with poppy seeds, and comparing stories of bleeding feet and infected corns. Often she brought Madame gardenias, or a champagne glass full of daisies, or cold lemonade, because she loved her "more than anything else in the world." It saddened her that a great artist should be reduced to wearing cheap dresses and carrying her lunch—cheese, apple, thermos of cold tea— in a small suitcase. To reciprocate, Madame once invited her and Scott for supper, a humiliating experience because he flirted in the most disrespectful way. (Worse still, she appeared to enjoy it.) After dinner he passed out.

On this trip Zelda and Scott were living near Saint-Sulpice in a handsome, old stone building. Their apartment had a panoramic view of the cathedral dome and drawing-room furniture upholstered in yellow brocade. It was clean and bright and would have been their nicest Paris flat if not for the bells that seemed to be constantly tolling for services or funerals. The few weeks of sweetness when they first arrived had ended abruptly when Scott was arrested for disturbing the peace, a reminder that nothing had changed. Zelda's complaints about his drinking brought sly taunts. Look who was talking, he said, because she, too, was drugged—drunk on dance. Evenings when they went out together, Zelda would sit silently without even trying to keep up her end of conversations. None of their friends exhibited interest in her work, except to express curiosity about her motives, or acknowledged her abilities. ("Dreadfully grotesque," thought Gerald Murphy after seeing her dance. "Her legs looked muscular and ugly. It was really terrible.") Frankly, Scott told her, she had turned into a bore. "She no longer read or thought, or knew anything or liked anyone except dancers and their cheap satellites." Often he announced it was her bedtime and sent her home in a taxi.

One day, without warning, Scott walked into the dance school and said he wanted to watch a class. He immediately lit up a cigarette, a complete taboo. Zelda angrily reprimanded the dancer who had admitted him. To make matters worse, he brought with him friends who were as naive as he was about dance training and who failed to understand that ballet is as strenuous as any sport. The sight of sweating bodies laboring like plow horses, the spittle trickling from the dancers' mouths, made them snicker. (Zelda's "extraordinary sweating" was repulsive, Scott thought.)

As the months passed since her first lessons with Catherine Little-field, physical misery almost ceased to bother Zelda. All dancers suffered. Pain, a constant companion, was as much a part of dancing as the music. Sometimes, depleted, she felt like "a gored horse in the bull ring, dragging its entrails." Groans of fatigue evoked no sympathy from Madame Egorova, who believed that Americans sleep too much. Four hours was enough. Sore feet and lost toenails? Grow harder ones. While Madame withheld compliments—seldom, in fact, said much of anything—she did occasionally remark that Zelda was doing good work. Even if Zelda herself was never satisfied, there was no question she had done wonders in only a few years.

The dance company Zelda admired above all others was the Ballets Russes, with its daring ballets (*Le Spectre de la rose*), its sublime dancers (Nijinksy and Massine) and composers (Stravinsky) and choreographers (Balanchine and Fokine). One day people supposedly from the Diaghilev troupe came to Egorova's studio to observe her work. But later she learned they were Folies Bergère scouts wondering if she could be transformed into another American act like Josephine Baker and her popular banana dance. Hearing this made Scott laugh. Her training was not totally useless after all, he said. Apparently she was qualified for a music hall.

ONE NIGHT as Zelda and Scott were returning home from the theater, a man and a woman waited in the doorway of their building.

"I'm Morley Callaghan," the man said, "and this is Loretto." Max Perkins said it would be safe to look them up without phoning first. A Canadian writer who had published his first novel with Scribner's, Morley was carrying with him some new writing, on which he wanted Scott's opinion. Such visitors were a pain in the neck. It was hard to know what to say, except that they were tired and please leave the manuscript. After that, however, the two couples met occasionally for dinner. They were at a restaurant in Montparnasse, a place favored by James Joyce, when Zelda told Morley that she, too, was a writer.

Was that so? The idea appeared to startle him.

His voice was stiff with disbelief. He imagined she was, he finally replied. ("The boldness of her insistence that she too be regarded as a talent . . . was surprising," he thought.)

Despite all-consuming classes, Zelda had just completed four short stories in as many months. The editor at *College Humor* proposed a series of sketches focusing on different types of women—debutante, club girl, movie actress, Southern belle—an insider's look at the world inhabited by the fast set. No philosophical discussions, he cautioned, because the stories had to go down like a glass of champagne. Each woman should have a name, and the narrative should describe her personality and behavior. Depending on length, he would pay four or five hundred dollars.

At that particular time Zelda had utterly no literary ambitions. What she did have was the need for money to pay for her lessons. Before leaving Ellerslie, she had already begun working on these "girl" stories. She approached each of her heroines economically, from the viewpoint of a nameless observer, a sort of female Nick Carraway. All the young women were beautiful and worldly but, despite their intelligence and ambition, corseted by straitjackets, powerless to achieve happiness, or a professional career, that was independent of a man. (Unlike Zelda, no character had a husband who continually belittled her artistic ambitions.) The sympathetic portraits were essentially vignettes—she had not yet learned the mechanics of dialogue or character development—but with plenty of atmosphere.

In "The Original Follies Girl" a blond clotheshorse, owner of the only French telephone in New York, is so "sick with spiritual boredom" that she packs her trunk with three thousand dollars' worth of "georgette crepe cobwebs" and goes to live in Paris, where she eventually dies in childbirth. Both Helena ("The Girl the Prince Liked") and Lou ("The Girl with Talent"), one the mistress of presumably the Prince of

Wales, the other a cabaret performer, abandon husband and children in their struggle to be somebody. The best of the series was "A Millionaire's Girl," in which Zelda's gift for creating mood resulted in a collage of New York and Hollywood and their fashionable beauties just after the war. "In front of the Lorraine and the St. Regis, and swarming about the mad-hatter doorman under the warm orange lights of the Biltmore façade, were hundreds of girls with marcel waves, with colored shoes and orchids, girls with pretty faces, dangling powder boxes and bracelets and lank young men from their wrists—all on their way to tea." Her protagonist is pretty, ambitious, and extravagant, but can a gold digger affix herself to the Social Register and live happily ever after? If she's smart, she can, Zelda decided.

Each of the *College Humor* stories contains clues that point to her mature style in *Save Me the Waltz*—a style that would have the feel of an opium dream exploding with color, smell, and texture. Her work was already moving in that direction, but she still felt insecure about using too theatrical a form for a lowbrow magazine such as *College Humor*.

Zelda wrote in longhand, using a pencil and editing herself as she went along, because she had never learned to type. Although Scott helped her to work out the construction of the stories, he took no part in the actual composition. Generally, his only contribution was a superficial polish before adding a title and byline, "By F. Scott and Zelda Fitzgerald," and giving it to a typist. He naturally put his own name first. There was nothing to gain by making a fuss, she knew. A Zelda Fitzgerald story would bring $250, the double byline $500 or more.

In Scott's opinion, the six girl sketches (he refused to call them fiction) had a nice satiric point of view. Someday, he thought, they might be published in a book. Otherwise, he was dismissive of Zelda's skills and told her she could write "in the sense that all non-professionals who have a gift for words, can write." Her nonfiction might not be first-rate, although it was good enough for magazines such as *The New Yorker*. The fiction was another matter, because her descriptive powers could be virtuosic—"an extraordinary talent for metaphor and simile," he had to admit. (Max Perkins praised her "astonishing power of ex-

pression.") Still, fiction wasn't a potluck supper of metaphors and sim-
iles, as any fool knew. Beyond experiences to report, she basically had
nothing to say.

Apart from the quality of Zelda's writing, Scott seemed most to resent
the speed with which she produced it. While he, who styled himself "the
highest paid short story writer in the world," was forced to sweat over
every paragraph, she slapped together an entire story between lunch and
dinner, as if she were making sausages. "Just automatic writing," he
sniffed. The truth was, her automatic writing contributed exactly
twenty-seven hundred dollars to their thirty-two-thousand dollar income
that year.

That summer they went to Cannes and rented another villa, this one
called Fleur des Bois. They bought a blue Renault touring car. Every afternoon Zelda worked on technique with the ballet master at the Nice
Opéra, and for the first time she danced professionally in brief local engagements. In July she celebrated a quiet twenty-ninth birthday.

Something had changed in their close friendship with the Murphys,
some subtle strain. Villa America, as usual, glowed with visiting literary
lights: Don and Bea Stewart, Philip and Ellen Barry, and Bob Benchley
with his family. Dottie Parker, a newcomer to the villa, was writing a
novel in the Murphys' guest house. Ernest was busy correcting proofs
of his forthcoming book. But for some reason, the Fitzgeralds weren't
invited to as many dinners this year. Zelda paid no attention, but Scott
felt left out. Sara and Gerald seemed standoffish, he thought. They
claimed to be busy and unable to see him every day. In a stern note,
quite unlike her, Sara scolded him for asking unpleasant personal questions, what she termed constant, unfriendly "analysis and subanalysis
and criticism." In another disapproving note she condemned his ab-
solute lack of consideration for other people's feelings. He had no idea
"what Zelda or Scottie are like—in spite of your love for them."

In September, a few days before the season ended and they were
supposed to leave for Paris, Zelda received a letter from the director of
the San Carlo Opera Ballet in Naples. Julia Sedova extended an invitation to join the troupe and make her debut in Giuseppe Verdi's *Aïda*. It

would be a small start (presumably she would be cast in act 2, scene 2, the ballet during the famous triumphal march), but she would have the chance to perform in additional productions during the season. Madame Sedova, who had trained with Egorova at the Imperial School of Ballet, was clearly basing her offer on Egorova's recommendation. The San Carlo, the oldest opera house in Europe, older than La Scala or La Fenice, boasted a distinguished history and a ballet school that dated back to 1812. Verdi's tale of doomed love was among the greatest of nineteenth-century operas, and its ballet, an ensemble effort of three or four minutes, was brief but pleasing. Altogether, it was an attractive opportunity for a newcomer.

When Zelda failed to respond immediately, Julia Sedova dispatched a second letter. Not only was their opera house "magnificent," she wrote, but Zelda would be glad to know that food and lodging in Naples were reasonable and comfortable pensions available for thirty lire a day.

How could Zelda refuse? Turning down the offer, she realized, might jeopardize ever receiving another. And what of the work—the punishing miles of pas de bourrée—that had brought her to that moment? She had gone through hell. Was it all a waste of time? She could not imagine living in a cramped pension room, unable to speak the language, alone but for the hours at the theater. Of course Scott would never agree to accompany her, certainly not to Naples, which he always ridiculed as a postcard-perfect nightmare.

A position with the San Carlo Opera Ballet was the last thing Scott ever expected to happen. Immediately he forbade her to take it, as Zelda later told Rosalind. That was one reason she could not bring herself to accept. The other was her health. Lately she had felt increasingly jittery, "nervous and half-sick but I didn't know what was the matter."

THEY DROVE BACK to Paris. With the nice fall weather and the swirling leaves it was a pleasant trip spent looking for good food and friendly lodging, stopping at ruins to take silly snapshots of each other with Scottie and their new terrier, Adage. At Arles they slept in a room that had once been a chapel. Traveling through the Cévennes valley, they found an inn—Zelda remembered its sausage but not its name—with sawdust floors and fluffy featherbeds. The three of them appeared to be a normal family, everyday tourists with their dog on a leash.

It was odd therefore that Zelda suddenly, for no reason, clutched the steering wheel on a steep mountain road and tried to make Scott drive off a precipice. Or so he would say afterward. What she remembered was grabbing the side of the Renault as it began to fly mysteriously toward "oblivion," as if to say the machine had a mind of its own. She genuinely had no explanation for the near mishap, just as she could not account for other things either. Once she had looked from the window of Egorova's studio and seen people below scrambling about like ants in a bottle.

For the winter they settled down in rue Pergolèse, in a gloomy apartment in an expensive neighborhood. "The Fitzgeralds are here again," noted one of their friends, Richard Myers. As always, they became the subject of gossip among the American expatriates. "Scott cannot seem to finish his book," Dick reported to Stephen and Rosemary Benét. "Poor Scott, if only he wouldn't finish so many bottles of Scotch." Morley Callaghan felt sorry for Scott. Zelda must be competing with him again, he figured. (God forbid that his wife would "jockey with me publicly for attention.") When, in the spring, Ernest had first heard of their return to France, he broke out with the "horrors." Please, he wrote Max Perkins, don't give Scott his address, because he "pee-ed on the front porch" of his building and got him kicked out. Should something similar happen again, he would have to "beat him up," even "kill him."

IN THE SPRING of 1929, Viking Press offered Dottie an advance to write a novel. It was an alluring idea, admittedly based on lots of scotch, as so often happened, and the premise that anybody who could write short stories could also write a book. After all, shouldn't she be doing something worthy of her talent? In bookshops, customers picked up short stories and said, "Oh, what's this? Just a lot of those short things." Even an outstanding volume of stories such as Ernest's *In Our Time* created about as much stir "as an incompleted dog fight on upper Riverside Drive."

Unlike Boni & Liveright and its list of bestselling titans, Viking was a small house, with an undistinguished track record, founded only a few years earlier by two enterprising twenty-five-year-olds. Harold Guinzburg, who inherited a fortune from the family dress-goods business, was a quiet intellectual with an amusing wife, Alice. His partner, George Oppenheimer (family money from pearl jewelry), who had a West End Avenue nasal accent, was said to have come into the world with a single idea on his mind: social climbing. By purchasing the firm of B. W. Huebsch, Harold and George had acquired a backlist of excellent titles (all the works of James Joyce except *Ulysses* and nine books by Sherwood Anderson, for example), but they had yet to develop a decent front list and brought out only a handful of new titles each year. They could not have been more enthusiastic about signing a writer of Dottie's stature and began talking bestsellers and spring 1930 catalogs. How were they to know that a more realistic publication date, taking into consideration her normal writing pace, would have been spring 1940?

Dottie was fond of Harold and Alice but barely managed to stomach "Georgie Opp," whose hysterical "Dotty Darlings" made him a perfect butt for countless jokes. A loud crash? "Pay no attention," she said quickly. "It's only George Oppenheimer dropping a name." Behind his back she served him up to friends as "a shit," even though he could not have been kinder. Her deal with Viking was based on goodwill, an imaginative title, *Sonnets in Suicide; or, The Life of John Knox*, and an oral description of the story. (No records survive to indicate the plot.)

With her Viking advance, she sailed for Europe in search of a place where she could not only live cheaply but also avoid John Garrett, a romance that had disintegrated into an orgy of self-inflicted humiliation. The only way to avoid further wreckage, she believed, was to leave the country. During a brief stopover in England she purchased a Dandie Dinmont terrier, fourteen months old, beautifully housebroken. Practically as soon as she and Timothy landed in Paris, she got so sick that it became necessary to consult a French doctor, who diagnosed an enlarged liver and attributed the cause to excessive alcohol. Ordered to stop drinking, she killed time with shopping binges and stocked up on nightgowns and slips with matching panties. Among her more costly mistakes was a cream-colored summer fur coat of unborn lamb, durable as toilet paper but much less useful. After four wearings, she shipped it home to her sister. Her spending spree came to a blessed halt, though, when Bob Benchley and his family passed through Paris, on their way to Antibes, to visit the Murphys. Although Dottie had never met Sara and Gerald, she decided to tag along.

O N THE TROPICAL GROUNDS of Villa America, a confusion of lemon and tangerine orchards and terraced vegetable gardens, stood a stone cottage that the Murphys called the *bastide*. It was a cozy guest bungalow, cunningly decorated to resemble a Provençal farmhouse, that had been specially created to ensure writers the privacy to work without interruptions. In short, the *bastide* provided the very sort of seclusion that normally sent Dottie shrieking up to Tony's in search of company. However, that was New York. The medicine she needed now was solitude.

Shortly after taking occupancy of the *bastide*, she was told that the fat purple blobs on the trees outside her windows were figs. Ah, yes. Figs! How exciting. She never knew figs grew on trees. Secretly she "hated figs in any form." Never mind, because Villa America was, as she reported to her sister, "the loveliest place in the world," and her dandy little house was fully equipped with "plumbing and electricity, exquisitely furnished."

The weather was glorious, and Dottie swam two kilometers at La Garoupe beach every morning. Feeling "disgustingly well and strong," she spent her days writing in the *bastide* and soon had produced an immense stack of paper. Always her own worst critic, she began wondering how much of it was "rotten." At least some of the pages must be good, she thought. Just in case, she decided that a request for divine intervention couldn't hurt. "Dear God, please make me stop writing like a woman. For Jesus Christ's sake, amen."

It surprised her to feel such bliss living thousands of miles offshore of the Algonquin Hotel, a guest in the home of rich people, almost like poor Ewing Klipspringer freeloading grandly on Jay Gatsby. She always despised people who had it easy. And yet it was unaccountable how much and how quickly she came to like Sara and Gerald, even to think of them as her best friends. Yes, they were rich, maybe even elitist snobs famously enamored of blue-blood writers, as some people said. But to her they were regular folks—dog people, like herself—who just happened to be wealthy. At Villa America lived an adorable pair of Sealyhams, Judy and Johnny, and two Pekingese, "but they don't count," all of whom got treated like royalty. In Dottie's opinion, anybody who remembered, let alone celebrated, their canines' birthdays had to be good eggs.

While Villa America was almost too perfect, the rest of the Riviera scene turned out to be terrible. The local watering holes were crackling with gold diggers and sugar daddies, the worst crowd of tripes this side of Times Square. ("The rocks at busy cocktail hour," Bob Benchley wrote Harold Ross, "resemble Tony's, so familiar and bloated are the faces.") Homesick for the sight of a friend, Dottie was delighted to run into Scott and Zelda, who were renting a house in Cannes for the summer. The fact that she had a book contract interested Scott, but he didn't think much of Viking Press. Why didn't she take her novel—novelette, she corrected, wanting to minimize the whole thing—to a good editor such as Max Perkins? Shrewd advice no doubt, but she wasn't convinced that she was important enough for an editor like Perkins.

A check of her funds at summer's end revealed a mere forty dollars. Luckily, Harold Guinzburg was due to arrive in Paris soon. There was no choice but to go there and pester him for more money, which meant of course showing what she had accomplished so far. On close inspection, the pile of completed manuscript seemed to have shrunk when she wasn't looking. She scrambled to fatten it up, stuffing in carbons, letters, every sheet of paper she could lay her hands on, and she prayed Harold would not want to read it.

In the end, there was nothing to worry about. Of course she must stay in France and finish the book, Harold said. Without asking for explanations or sample pages, he even offered more money to tide her over. Relieved by the last-minute rescue, she now intended to speed back to Antibes and dig in her heels, although more and more she tended to think of *Sonnets in Suicide* as "that Goddamn book." Secretly, she was almost ready to admit that she was a better title writer than novelist. What she wished for was somebody else to come along and write the book, because she was getting sick to death of the thing. And continuing to sponge off the Murphys also felt a bit humiliating. However, with nine servants in their establishment, the presence of a lodger appeared to make no difference. ("Mother loved having her around," recalled Honoria Murphy. "Dottie was very affectionate.") Knowing that she must regain some momentum, Dottie planned to avoid people and remain quietly holed up in the *bastide* with her dog, restricting her entertainment to reading about murders and dismemberments in the local papers.

As luck would have it, though, events entirely beyond her control delayed getting to work. First came her birthday, the thirty-sixth. After that, Harold Ross assigned her to interview Ernest Hemingway, whose *A Farewell to Arms* had just been published, which meant going all the way back to Paris. The meeting was a disaster. Ernest grew prickly and unreasonable and forbade her using any personal information. She had no choice but to turn in a disappointing piece, "The Artist's Reward," which read like a shameless piece of fluff.

At Villa America the atmosphere had completely changed during her absence. The Murphys' eight-year-old son, Patrick, had taken sick with a persistent fever and cough thought to be bronchitis. By early October, however, it had become clear that this was no ordinary cough. He was diagnosed with tuberculosis; one of his lungs was severely compromised. Any hope of survival—cold air and a rich diet could prolong life, but no cure was known—depended on pneumothorax treatments. Less than a week later Gerald whisked Patrick to a health resort near Sierre in the Swiss Alps, a thousand meters above sea level, while Sara began dismantling the villa and organizing the removal of their household to Switzerland.

Watching her friends struck down by such improbable misfortune frightened Dottie. It was an instance of bad luck that she could remember encountering only once before, when her uncle Martin Rothschild went down on an unsinkable ship. In a few short weeks the Murphys' dream life had abruptly vaporized: the every-day-a-fiesta atmosphere was replaced by overwhelming anxiety about sanatoriums and treatments. Sara and Gerald blamed the contagion on a coughing, most likely tubercular, chauffeur they had employed during a recent trip to Los Angeles. Others—such as Ernest—secretly wondered if this evil could be some type of horrific divine justice they had inadvertently courted.

As Dottie was packing to go home, Sara unexpectedly begged her to accompany them to Montana-Vermala, where they would be living for the next two years. Taken aback, Dottie replied that she would have to think about it. In truth, it sounded like a crazy idea, but Sara was serious. The last place on earth Dottie wanted to go was Switzerland. All her life she had got the Swiss and the Swedish mixed up, and she figured "it was too late for me to change now." And quite frankly, mountains always made her "a little yippy" because she was terrified by heights.

Dubious, she cabled Bob Benchley for counsel before making a decision, but the "big shit" never answered. She could guess his advice, though. With her "best friends in bad trouble," she would be a "fine louse" if she let them down.

And so at the end of October, as the last inhabitant of Villa America, Dottie closed up the house and assembled everything that was left behind, the five dogs and the eleven trunks and the seventeen hand pieces, the remainder of the family baggage. In bringing up the rear, she was responsible for dragging this cortege of animals (two of them in heat) and household goods through three changes of trains and customs at Geneva. The last leg of the journey was a harrowing ascent from Sierre to the small Alpine station of Crans, a mile from Montana-Vermala. There she boarded the funicular, a cable car winding vertically up the side of a mountain for "as long as it takes to get to Stamford."

In her bag was a letter from Harold Guinzburg hoping *Sonnets* was coming well. "When the manuscript is done," he wrote, "put a special delivery stamp on it and include about six words explaining where you are, where you will be, and any other vital statistics." Viking Press was looking forward to its first bestseller.

O VER THE CENTER BEAM in Vincent's library was tacked a sign, in large red letters, that warned, SILENCE. When a visitor once inquired about how she managed her household, she reacted with surprise. Household? She had nothing to do with the household, she answered. Giving orders to the servants was her husband's department. He hired and trained the staff, planned the menus, purchased the supplies. If something displeased her, she just took her complaint to him. (Servants were not really human, she wrote in her diary. It was hard to say whether she hated anybody more than cooks, maids, and laundry girls.)

In the mornings Gene would come down to the kitchen and personally prepare her regular breakfast tray of orange juice, toast, and a pot of tea. When she appeared later, she liked strolling around her garden before beginning work. Writing did not leave time to spare for fretting about laundry and meals. The last thing on her mind was what she was going to eat. At the end of the day she wanted to walk into her dining room "as if it were a restaurant, and say, 'What a charming dinner!'" On evenings when company appeared, she changed into a trailing silk gown. Cocktails would be accompanied by a Stilton cheese wrapped in a pure white cloth, for Gene was fond of theatrical flourishes. After a leisurely dinner, served as late as ten, she silently slipped away. The poetess tired easily, Gene would tell the guests, and so he had put her to bed.

Gene looked after everything. It wasn't just the breakfast tray. He also picked her clothes and shoes, wrote letters, scheduled appointments, administered medicine, and notified friends when she was ill or having "the curse." As he once wrote Gene Saxton, Miss Millay wanted him to know she had tonsillitis—all she had kept down for three days was "weak tea and morphine."

Morphine, Vincent had discovered two summers earlier, was a wonderful drug. While she was hospitalized at Mount Sinai for a dilation and curettage, the doctors gave her all she desired. Ever since then, tea and morphine had allowed her to happily withdraw into her bedroom, with as little regret as Alice dropping down the rabbit hole.

O NE DAY THAT SUMMER, while visiting friends in Hillsdale, Bunny decided to call on the Boissevains. Since a number of others had stopped in, too, no opportunity arose for private conversation. As always, Gene was bare-chested and jovial, and the local gentry talked about dogs and horses and home renovations. Glancing around the long living room, its windows hung with chintz curtains, Bunny took in the pianos, the comfortable sofas, the bust of Sappho on a marble pedestal. As it began to get dark, before the lamps were lit, the room blurred into half shadows. He glanced at Vincent, sitting quietly in the corner near the window, buried in her favorite chair, immobile. She reminded him of a tiny boat that had paddled into port after being buffeted by rough seas, now safely docked in her own private harbor.

Bunny, standing to one side, noticed for the first time the exact geometry of Vincent and Gene's marriage, the nursery scene with the protective parent quietly watching and managing the child. What had happened to his first love, the joyous string bean with her bright green eyes bounding down Macdougal Street, her red-gold hair swinging? Would she end up being meekly led off to bed in her woodland fortress?

When Bunny drove away that night, he was not to see Vincent and Gene for nineteen years. In the summer of 1948 he and his fourth wife happened to be visiting the Berkshire Music Festival at Tanglewood when he realized the proximity of Austerlitz and made up his mind to pay a call. He found the couple exactly as he had left them in 1929, he would write, together in their artificial paradise, a pair of "deteriorated ghosts" haunting an old farmhouse castle that was sealed off from the world.

IT WAS AN AUTUMN of great bounties after a summer of flawless weather. From her window Vincent saw teams of horses hauling immense loads down from the dusty oat fields. Her kitchen garden was still ripening into picture-book pumpkins and tomatoes that took her breath away. The damned chickens, which used to drop manure all over the lawn, were fenced inside a yard now. The old crumbling barns had been torn down, and the boards stacked in a tidy woodpile. Every building glowed with fresh paint.

Their financial situation had never been better. (In the second half of 1928, she earned royalties of $15,000, $156,000 in current dollars.) She was dying to redo the floor of her front hall with the same kind of gray-and-rose slate she had admired in Deems and Mary Taylor's drawing room. And Gene talked about converting the stone foundation of a barn into a pool, where they could swim naked. These days everybody she knew was living a good life.

Upstairs in the library, where she kept her Petrarch and Dante, she continued to work on the George sonnets at a mahogany writing desk. She had completed the first draft, fueled by that initial rush of inspiration. Now came the harder work of sharpening each one, picking it to pieces. "This is awful," she'd think. Or "that's not so bad." She played the piano several hours a day and also liked to pick up the latest bestsellers, most recently a powerful war novel, *All Quiet on the Western Front.*

The only shadow across her life was George, whom she had not seen for months. In emotional letters, raging and crying, she threatened to "lie on the floor and kick and howl" because she needed him. Alternating, she bossed, scorned, praised. Remorseful, she apologized. Scolding him was wrong of her, she knew—probably he figured she was crazy—and she told herself that she must be more patient. In the grip of her love, George felt as if she were sinking her teeth into him, he told a friend.

If the sonnets of the winter radiated fever and euphoria, the autumn poems began to reflect the precise state of her illusions, punctured, released, spilling every which way, leaving her deflated. Mind you, she had not given up. Sooner or later she would bring him to heel.

THE CITY COOLED, the leaves began to drop, the chestnut men advanced over the Queensboro Bridge and fired up their stoves on Fifth Avenue. Edna sat by herself in a new East Side penthouse, thinking of the lawless Oklahoma Territory with its land runs and oil millionaires, a man named Yancey and a woman named Sabra, who is elected to Congress. In the home stretch of a new novel, she kept the characters curled up in her head as they went about their business.

From her terrace, on the nineteenth floor of the Lombardy, could be seen a silver-and-pale-gold landscape: the dome of Grand Central Station, and beyond that loomed up the mighty ribs of the tallest buildings in the world, the almost-completed shaft of the Chrysler Automobile Company, topped by a sublime stainless-steel spire, and still farther downtown just starting construction a colossus of concrete and steel that would tower 102 stories over the biscuit-box office buildings on Thirty-fourth Street. But these days Edna had no time to admire the skyline. Her book was going to end in the town of Bowlegs, a "one-street wooden shanty town, like the towns of the old Territory days, but more sordid," with Yancey, a rumpled drunk dying in Sabra's arms, quoting Peer Gynt's last speech to Solveig. Was Ibsen a touch overblown? Perhaps she would have to change the last scene. Even better than knowing how a book would end was knowing when. Having hit her stride, she just might be done in a month, perhaps as early as November 10 if she could keep her nose in the typewriter. Then she absolutely had to do something about her mink. This year they were wearing furs short—long coats looked so sloppy—and she feared appearing frumpy. Her furrier promised to see what could be done. He also agreed to make a collar for her red suit.

Each day she watched nervously as news of the stock market dominated the front pages. After the Dow Jones Industrial Average hit a record 381 in early September, the headlines became extremely confusing. One day professional optimists were predicting "Stock Prices Will Stay at High Level for Years to Come," the next pessimists were warning the opposite, calling the market a "Creeping Bear" and talking in measured tones of recessions and crashes, slumps and readjustments. Even in the best of times, the market had always been a mystery to Edna. But at tiny moments something made her feel particularly suspicious, and she wasn't sure why. Maybe it was when the fool of an elevator boy in her building began talking market tips as they ascended to the penthouse.

Time had passed, almost two years since *The Royal Family* and *Show Boat* opened on Broadway. Not only was Edna wealthy, but she'd proved it was possible to be both a hugely successful writer of commercial and literary fiction and a decent dramatist. But after fighting her way to the top, she had no work. What about the rest of her life?

With nothing to do except recuperate from success, she spent months busying herself with her home. After six years on Central Park West she transported her lemon chintz curtains and her grand piano to an apartment on East Fifty-sixth next door to her friend Richard Rodgers; in fact, she and Dicky shared the spacious terrace. The new place, with its grand views and wood-burning fireplace, was splendid, but she could not twiddle her thumbs indefinitely. In the spring of 1928 she had left town and drifted out west, to visit Bill and Sallie White in Kansas. Each day began when she and Bill strolled down Emporia's Commercial Street to the *Gazette*, where the office brought back memories of her first job on the *Appleton Daily Crescent*. Sitting in the Whites' big front room every night, she was able to drop all pretenses. No, she said sourly, she never went by to see how her shows were doing. They were ancient history, stale as old bread crusts.

Bill and Sallie were full of enthusiasm about a motor trip they had taken to Oklahoma. The place had turned out to be fascinating, they said, and its history could not be stranger. Edna listened politely. Oklahoma was somewhere south of Kansas, she believed, but that was the extent of her knowledge about the state. The Whites could not stop talking about the settlement of the territory, the famous land runs of the 1880s and 1890s, when thousands lined up to take ownership of free property. They told stories about Indians penned like cattle on reservations, which turned out to be the richest oil land in America, and about these very same Indians in blankets later riding around in Pierce-Arrows.

How very dramatic, Edna agreed.

For heaven's sake, Bill said, there might be a good book in all of it.

Oh, a novel about Oklahoma sounded like a fine idea, she said. But she didn't believe she could write it. Wasn't it a man's story? Anyway, she was through with family sagas and river epics. From here on she was going to write little plebeian stories about "two people in a telephone booth."

On Edna's next visit to Emporia, however, Bill persuaded her to visit Oklahoma. He even ferried her to Tulsa, where he more or less dumped her out before heading home to Kansas. Once he had gone, finding herself an "unwilling prisoner" in a high-rise luxury hotel, she went around talking to old-timers who had made the 1889 run. With her notepad, she sat on front porches and asked questions just as she had done in her reporter days. She sifted reminiscences for the telling details: the red clay, the rattlesnakes, the sturdy brick brothel next door to shanties, the oil millionaires in mansions the size of Versailles.

Oklahoma in summer was hot, windy, and maddening. She was not crazy about the miserable weather, and she certainly did not appreciate the swaggering arrogance of the Oklahoma men either. In the one-horse town of Bartlesville, at a dinner party, local encyclopedists attempted to ram down her throat a condensed course in state history. Arms folded across their chests, the pontificators wanted to make sure she got her facts straight, although they mainly held forth to show off their knowledge. One particular eminence droned on sonorously until Edna could barely control her irritation. Having too many facts could be a nuisance, she told him. Her business was writing fiction, meaning she imagined events and created characters as she saw fit.

Madam, the man replied, if she wished to appear ridiculous in the eyes of the world, that was her affair. But she would do well to heed people who knew a thing or two. His name was well respected in the state of Oklahoma.

His name? Listen, bub, she said angrily, people would be reading her novel long after his name was forgotten.

She wasted no more time in Oklahoma than absolutely necessary: only a few days in Tulsa with scrapbooks of old newspaper clippings and a few more in Oklahoma City, where the state library agreed to sell her a set of historical pamphlets containing original diaries and letters. It was a thin reporting job, one she could not have got away with in her days on the *Daily Crescent,* but she decided not to worry about hard facts. Realizing she had collected all she required in two weeks came as a tremendous relief to her. She hauled her research materials to the Broadmoor Hotel in the clear, brisk air of Colorado Springs, where she proceeded to renew herself in a luxury suite with a sleeping porch. There she began organizing her notes.

By the time she got home, the skeleton of a heavyweight novel, with big themes and gigantic characters, had begun to emerge. Its subject dealt with greed and corruption, and its dark tone evoked materialism triumphing over righteousness—in other words, some of the same ground she covered in *So Big.* The characters were typically Ferber: women with steely backbones (whom life transforms from sweet ado-lescents to tough grandmothers), puny-souled men (who die or run off and never come back), and anemic sons. In 1889 an adventurer by the name of Yancey Cravat sets out for the Oklahoma Territory with his wife, four-year-old son, and a printing press. Despite primitive condi-tions in the town of Osage, the Cravats and their children prosper un-til the day Yancey runs off to another land giveaway, leaving behind

Sabra to run the *Oklahoma Wigwam* and fend for herself. Edna was calling the novel *Cimarron*.

That summer she was dragooned into renting a house next door to Louis and Mary Bromfield in Socoa, France. Nestled on a cliff overlooking the ocean, the property had its own private beach. A Spanish cook and a housemaid were engaged for the cozy bookish paradise, in which she and Louis wrote from early morning to noon. For the remainder of the day they indulged themselves in overeating baby langouste and wild strawberries, washed down with bottles of golden Vouvray. The summer might have been quite pleasant were it not for an individual who cropped up in her diary as "dear Mary" or "that Bromfield woman," more often the latter. Even though Edna made a specialty of creating stalwart fictional women, strong-willed types based on herself and her mother, she seemed fated to live among jellyfish and frankly did not bargain for three months in the Basque country with "dear Mary" and her odious scenes. Only a surprise visit from Noël Coward brightened her mood. Unable to keep her mind on *Cimarron*, she made irritable entries in her diary—little work done, frightful headaches, damnable quarrels.

Dominating her New York social life were friendships with a number of married couples: not just the Bromfields but also the Ameses (Winthrop and Lucy), the Kaufmans (Georgie and Bea), the Kerns (Jerry and Eva), and the Lunts (Alfred and Lynn). With most of these couples, it was a case of attraction to the gifted husbands and bare toleration of wives who were largely Alice-sit-by-the-fires, although Edna would never admit it.

In New York, after Labor Day, the weather continued sultry. Out on her sunny terrace Edna lined up pairs of shoes in rows. Honestly, some of them looked as bad as old Ziegfeld dancers, she was annoyed to notice. She needed a few good things and scheduled fittings for a sport suit, a blouse, and a corset. And her mind was made up on the red-velvet evening coat. It definitely needed a band of fur attached to the bottom. Once *Cimarron* was finished, she planned to get out of the market and invest in "good old United States government bonds and live happily ever after." A firm believer in fiscal prudence, Edna operated by three simple rules: never buy on credit, never borrow or lend, always save for a rainy day. But like everybody else's, her rainy-day money was in the market.

At the New York Stock Exchange, Wednesday, October 23, began quietly. By early afternoon, however, a sharp sell-off of automobile stocks had suddenly sent the market into a tailspin, and during the final hour of trading an outlandish 2.6 million shares changed hands. When the gong sounded, the Stock Exchange had lost $4 billion, the Dow Jones Industrial Average had tumbled twenty points (the biggest loss in history), and the overwhelmed clerks were unable to clear the transactions until 5 a.m.

Of course the next day was bedlam. At ten on Thursday, October 24, hell broke loose as the market took off like a bolt of lightning, a stampede to unload that would end in a 12.9-million-share sell-off. Friday and Saturday saw investors dazed or frightened, or both. Since nobody easily understood what the bloodbath was all about, there was the hope that it would simply disappear. But the scene was like one of those hallucinatory massacres from bygone days, when there is no time to count the bodies. Over the weekend, though, people started to grasp the extent of the carnage. By the morning of Monday, October 28, almost everybody had become hysterical. Some who'd been wild to buy stocks priced at 349 only a few weeks ago had to sell at 23.

The Dow Jones would keep on sliding until it bottomed at 198 on November 13, a drop of 39 percent since October 23. During this period after Black Thursday, Edna lost more than half of her savings. "This should have depressed me," she wrote in her autobiography. "It didn't. I wasn't disturbed for a moment—or for very little more than a moment, at least. Money lost is money lost." That was that.

Before Christmas there was an unseasonably mild week when just about everybody came down with laryngitis or colds and had to drink hot whiskey with lemon and sugar. By this time plenty of investors had come to believe they had figured out the trouble: the economy had suffered what amounted to a flat tire. It just needed to be fixed, that's all. Somebody would know how to do it—change the currency, remodel the banking system—somebody would fix the flat. Remember what President Hoover said: the system is sound.

1930

La Bruyère, the Murphys' Alpine chalet where Dottie spends much of the year until she becomes nearly unhinged by "loneliness and discouragement."

CHAPTER ELEVEN

AGAINST HER BETTER judgment, Edna fired off a threatening letter to the rich kid running *The Bookman.* "Dear Editor," she wrote Seward Collins. After twenty years as a writer she understood that "yammering" over a bad review was a waste of time. But what in the name of God could he be thinking.

After getting wind of a *Bookman* review of *Cimarron,* Edna was seething. The review was not only extremely impertinent; it was also patronizing, as if she were a rather inept first novelist. Who was this person named Edward Donahoe, anyway? To satisfy her curiosity, she snooped around and learned that his only qualification for reviewing her book was his birth in Oklahoma as the son of a man who had participated in the first land run; and further investigation revealed this Donahoe to have no connection whatsoever with publishing. In fact, he was employed by an East Side antiques shop, of all things. She decided to call this travesty to the attention of Seward Collins.

Wasn't she entitled to a review by a peer or a recognized critic? If she recalled correctly, *The Bookman* did not commission the nonentity son of a traveling Kansas evangelist to review *Elmer Gantry*, nor did the magazine assign *Death Comes for the Archbishop* to the son of a Mexican priest. "This fellow is not a critic; he is not a writer; he is not a lecturer or teacher. He is an interior decorator and, incidentally, a rather nasty little cad." What kind of an idiot editor would publish such a review?

Were she a man, she would go over to Ronsard, Inc., and "punch Mr. Edward Donahoe's silly head." What she would do to Mr. Seward Collins's head, were she a man, was left unsaid. (Sewie replaced the offensive review with a complimentary one describing *Cimarron* as "Edna Ferber at her best.")

When *Cimarron* was published in March, Edna laboriously spelled out her intentions in a foreword: "There is no attempt to set down a literal history of Oklahoma," she warned. No town of Osage actually existed. There was never, ever a real man such as Yancey, no woman like Sabra. Everything and everybody was imaginary. As it happened, she could have saved her breath. The *Saturday Review of Literature*, for example, ignored the disclaimer and accused her of falsifying "dates, places, and historical events," misrepresentations that suggested a writer "unaware of the real historical background." Willa Cather, another literary carpetbagger, needled the *Review*, had given a better performance with *My Ántonia*. Judged as fantasy, however, *Cimarron* was good entertainment. Another magazine called the book a romantic Western—"a crude picture rather than a work of art"—written with a movie sale in mind.

Cimarron, Edna knew, was no more a historical romance than *Show*

Boat was a seafaring saga. Just as the public had resisted her criticism of antimiscegenation laws, it now ignored her harsh depiction of the birth of Oklahoma: unbridled greed, materialism triumphant, exploitation of women.

Literary critics who pounced on *Cimarron* were gentle compared with the immensely offended Oklahomans. Writing a novel about showboats was fairly safe, since practically nobody knew more about the subject than Edna did. But a novel about the state of Oklahoma was another matter. What upset people like the interior decorator Edward Donahoe was not the Cravat family that achieves, grows up, suffers, and dies but the dark view she offered of their native state. One local newspaper editorial denounced her as "an extremely offensive personality," best known for egotism and hair dye. During her brief visit to the state, she had waved a highball glass and "proved herself to be as ignorant as she was ill mannered. 'Say, Big Boy,' she blatted in that tone children of the Ghetto are apt to use after the third shot of Oklahoma corn, 'I know my business.'" The outcry over *Cimarron* proved, if nothing else, that there were a lot more literate, book-buying Sooners than anybody could possibly have imagined.

Still, she had to remind herself about displaying her anger publicly, for fear of sounding deranged. *Cimarron* did, after all, turn out to be her third bestseller, with 200,000 copies in print. Her attorney did, after all, sell the film rights to RKO Pictures for "a telephone number." Every actress in Hollywood was panting for the plum role of the year—Irene Dunne got it—and the movie, another travesty in Edna's mind, would turn out to be a tremendous success. So she did not want to appear a sore winner.

In April the market rallied just as the optimists had predicted. The Dow hit 294.07, a high for the year, and some stocks climbed above their 1928 prices. For all her losses, Edna had managed to complete *Cimarron* on schedule and turn it over to *Woman's Home Companion* for serial publication. With money rolling in once more, nobody in her family was reduced to eating beans at the Automat, least of all Julia Ferber, who splurged on a broadtail coat with sable collar. Edna herself continued to attend lavish parties, most memorably a midnight soiree thrown by the Lunts, featuring a five-piece Hungarian orchestra and the most glorious blini with caviar and sour cream in the whole world.

Her own parties were small formal affairs, limited to a select guest list of eight or ten. Every detail was planned weeks in advance, not only the perfect combination of guests but also a lavish menu. Edna had utterly no use for people watching their weight. Diet on your own time, she would huff. A typical dinner assembled by her cook might start with an assortment of appetizers (caviar and egg, water chestnuts encased in bacon), followed by miniature cheese soufflés, succulent leg of lamb, vegetables, salad, and Brie, ending with finger bowls and crème brûlée. At Edna's dinners the butter was always curled, and the entertainment always prime. On one memorable evening some of the guests wound up playing for their suppers. Edna could not help gloating to her sister Fannie that Jerry (Kern), Noël (Coward), and Dicky (Rodgers) all took turns at the piano and nobody left until four.

In Edna's circle, people were trying to make the best of hard times. They still spent money, and East Side dinner parties continued to be sumptuous, but some of her friends were in a mess. Poor Frank Adams took a thumping in the market. Aleck Woollcott lost $200,000, and his friend Groucho Marx $240,000. (Groucho said he would have lost more but it was everything he had.) Edna felt desperately sorry for Herbert and Pearl Swope, who lost $16 million, practically every penny they had, supposedly. Would Pearl stop sending her chauffeur to the Upper West Side for those irresistible salted almonds?

"ARE PEOPLE NICER NOW that they are poorer?" asked Dottie, who was dying to hear the latest dirt. So who got wiped out? In the Paris papers she read that Hoover saw no reason to be pessimistic. Ah, jeez, that was reassuring.

At the New Weston Hotel her suite was crowded with reporters. Dottie was sipping Hennessy and getting more laughs than Laurel and Hardy. Who was her favorite poet? Edgar Guest (Christmas card verse).

Favorite novelist? Myrtle Reed (*Lavender and Old Lace*). What accounted for the "deep despair" in her work? "Nobody's business." She came home, she said, for professional reasons and because she was awfully homesick for New York, but planned to stay only a month. Her book was to be published in the summer, she guessed.

To tell the truth, after two months in the goddamned mountains she couldn't take it any longer. When she first arrived at Montana-Vermala, and realized the Palace Hotel was a death house, she reminded herself that Switzerland was still preferable to Hollywood, where she had been incarcerated for three months the previous year. But it took only a few weeks, until Thanksgiving Day to be exact, when the Palace served veal for dinner, as it did every night, before she changed her mind about Switzerland. She had always considered Switzerland "the home of horseshit" and saw no reason to revise her opinion. Of what use was a country that had no history except William Tell, no culture but cuckoo clocks? No, Switzerland was far worse than Hollywood.

Attempts to cheer up Sara and Gerald were unrealistic, because parents overwhelmed by worry had no energy for merriment. The brutal treatments to stop the spread of Patrick's disease involved injection of gas into the pleura through a thick, hollow needle inserted between his ribs. Gerald scarcely left the boy's side, and Dottie would catch a glimpse of him in the hall carrying a chamber pot in one hand and a thermometer in the other. There was nothing she could do to help, no matter how much she longed to.

At the Palace Hotel the chief topic of conversation among the patients was death. For Dottie, a person who had always professed to find humor in dying, it was like finding herself a tap dancer on death row. Sometimes in the middle of the night she would overhear people expiring next door and their rooms being fumigated and prepared for a new arrival. Unable to listen, she went outside to her balcony and screamed at the Alps. Sex was the obvious solution, or else stiff liquor and plenty of it. Alas and alack, she had become an involuntary celibate and teetotaler, because the elevation ruled out drinking, except for a little wine. So she retired to her freezing hospital room and went to bed at nine, sober. Since mornings no longer had to be spent bleary-eyed and battling hangovers, that left the whole day for the "slow, even heebs" over more important matters.

An average day in the sanatorium offered plenty of solitude to ponder the meaning of life, but it did not inspire decent prose. "I'd like to finish that Goddamn book," she wrote her sister, "but I find it terribly hard to work here." As her discipline slowly blurred, her stupid typewriter went on the blink and began jamming the lines together, and there was not a single typewriter-repair shop in Montana-Vermala. She wrote less and less, then not at all. A single-spaced seven-page letter to Benchley bristled with typos and frustration. "Write novels, write novels, write novels—that's all they can say. Oh, I do get so sick and tired, sometimes." Better to clean out ferryboats for a living. Better to be a Broadway chorus boy. If only she had taken up some rewarding career, such as interior decorating. When asked once why she wrote, she said, "Need of money, dear."

In New York that winter Frank Adams declared he loved her "mighty much" on the opposite editorial page of the *New York World*. She was "the only limited-edition girl I know, by which I mean there is nobody like her, nor ever was." The limited-edition girl visited her old haunts (Tony's, "21," Horace Liveright's brownstone) and some new ones as well. Along the East River, Aleck had a ritzy new apartment that she promptly christened "Wit's End," and Bob Benchley forsook the Gonk for a classically ratty apartment across the street at the Royalton. This enabled him to spend even less time with his family in Scarsdale and more with his three mistresses. In the offices of *The Bookman* over on Fourth Avenue she found Sewie half asleep at his desk, her former white knight looking uncannily corpse-like.

Wherever she went, the subject of her book came up every ten minutes. Naturally she lied, always referring to *Sonnets in Suicide* as something alive and thriving, a sort of stockpot bubbling away on the back burner. Even thinking about it made her sick, because she could not bring herself to admit the truth. How could she face Harold and Georgie Opp? On the other hand, why did she ever listen to those people in the first place? How foolish to imagine she was capable of writing a novel. Still, it was stinking to take their money, keep them in the dark, and tell God knows how many cockeyed lies. Now, why did these horrible things happen to her?

There appeared to be only a single exit out of this hopeless situation. Unfortunately she lacked easy access to guns, knives, rope, drugs, rivers, or gas (the most obvious, tall buildings, she apparently ruled out), and creating a mess in the New Weston's lovely bathroom would be ill-mannered. In the end, with precious little choice available, she employed the means at her disposal and drank a bottle of shoe polish. Of course it didn't work. All the foolish gesture accomplished was to make her extremely ill and cause a commotion requiring the hotel doctor and an ambulance.

Since there were no recorded deaths from drinking shoe polish (lye, yes), her attempted suicide was not taken too seriously. On the other hand, the gesture did happen to be a novel, admittedly extreme, means of breaking a book contract without returning the advance. Seen in light of the shoe polish, her message to Viking was clear: no Dorothy Parker novel would head their list that season. The publishers remained optimistic about an eventual delivery, however. (Viking got nothing, ever.)

In June, after she had left the hospital, Harold and Georgie Opp were satisfied to collect thirteen of her stories, including some of her best ("Big Blonde," "Arrangement in Black and White") and a few of the worst ("New York to Detroit"), and publish her first book of short stories. It was titled *Laments for the Living*. By that time she had returned to Switzerland and was living among the bacilli.

"Dotty Darling," exclaimed Georgie Opp, *too* distraught with missing her, "I can't even go near '21' without shedding tears."

Dotty Darling decided that she might as well live. What else could she do?

. . .

ZELDA, on the other hand, had just decided she was at the end of her rope. Arriving home after class one afternoon, she found Scott drinking with Michael Arlen, the English novelist who had written the immensely popular *The Green Hat*. To Arlen she began describing her highly nervous state. Some days she felt as if she were losing her mind. She had no idea why. There were places specializing in nervous exhaustion, said Arlen, trying to be helpful. Why didn't she go to a clinic? The idea was not appealing, but afterward she began giving it some thought. She felt her life was a "real mess." For example, she felt unable to walk on the street unless she'd been to her classes. Any kind of shopping, even to buy Scottie an Easter present, became impossible without the company of the housekeeper. It was Scott's theory that the whole business was due to overwork or some physical cause like autointoxication.

On April 23, she medicated herself with several drinks before checking herself into the Sanitarium de la Malmaison, a psychiatric hospital about six miles from Paris. Unable to sit still, she picked at her fingers, paced the room, even regressed to an adolescent Southern belle and flirted with the doctors. She appeared to be slightly intoxicated and acutely anxious, according to the medical history that was taken. The attending physician, a Professor Claude, duly noted what he interpreted as an attempt at seduction.

Her biggest fear was that her condition might prevent her from dancing. "It's horrible," she told Professor Claude. "What's going to become of me? I must work and I no longer can." She also worried about disappointing Madame Egorova, who "has given me the greatest joy in the world." Over the next several days she listed a variety of physical complaints: dizziness, headaches, and optical illusions.

No, she could not sleep.

Yes, she supposed that she did go days without eating. (Looking skeletal was practically a job requirement.)

Sometimes she heard voices and buzzing noises, and behind her forehead fluttered the sound of music. When she requested her husband's help, he locked himself in the bathroom and began singing, "Ah's mama's li'l Alabama coon . . ."

News of her hospitalization, meanwhile, had spread through expatriate Paris. Some of their friends could not help raising their eyebrows knowingly. Dick Myers told Scott to his face that "you can't expect anybody to live on the edge of a crater all their lives without having some kind of nervous reaction." He didn't blame Zelda for wanting to escape from Scott.

After ten days Zelda was disgusted with Malmaison. Going there had been a ridiculous waste of time and money. Its main clientele was Americans recovering from DTs and drug overdoses. Her problem was, the doctors said finally, "exhaustion from work in an environment of professional dancers." In other words, overwork. Since this provided no constructive guidance whatsoever, she immediately checked out and went home. Besides, she was impatient to return to class.

At rue Pergolèse the household was in a state of wild upheaval. Scott was busy with preparations for the wedding of the brother of his Princeton friend Ludlow Fowler. With celebrations in full swing, the apartment was overrun by a crowd of aging Princeton boys bent on holding the first great beer party of the decade. The amount of liquor consumed—"a gigantic cocktail in a nightmare"—awed even Scott.

The respite at Malmaison was calming, but Zelda found it impossible to resume a normal routine and within a week or two felt worse than ever. In urgent need of a private conversation with Madame Egorova, she invited her to rue Pergolèse for tea. Poor Egorova now had problems of her own, mourning ever since the previous summer, when Serge Diaghilev died. The ballet company whose dancers had often come to her for coaching, and that Zelda had secretly hoped to join, was no more. They had finished tea in the parlor when Zelda walked over and stood above her teacher. She went down on her knees, quivering in a heap at Egorova's feet like a scrambled egg.

Madame carefully rose. She must leave now, she said.

. . .

AFTER TWO WEEKS of "enormous pressure" from Scott, Zelda agreed to visit a hospital in Switzerland. He promised she would have opportunities to dance again, perhaps even in New York, but she needed to get her health back first. Without wanting to, she agreed to go away, mostly because she could not think of an alternate solution. They left Scottie with her governess and set out for Glion-sur-Territet, near Montreux. Following a four-hundred-mile trip from Paris, they reached Valmont Clinic only to discover that the hospital specialized in gastrointestinal conditions, not psychiatry. Nevertheless, it was a reputable institution, and so Zelda was admitted as a patient on May 22. She was not sick, she insisted. Her husband had forced her to come. But her protests were ignored.

As part of the examination, the Valmont doctors quizzed her on symptoms of mental disturbance. Any family history of psychiatric problems?

Yes, she said. Two of her sisters had always been depressed, possibly suffering nervous breakdowns, but she could not say for certain. A third sister had some sort of problem with her neck, which the hospital recorded as "a nervous affliction of the neck." Her brother, Anthony, also had dangerously weak nerves. (He would leap to his death from a hospital window in 1933.) Family members who had taken their own lives included Zelda's grandmother and great-aunt. It was a grisly recital, unfortunately providing support for Scott's dim view of her relatives. (He once said the only resemblance among the five children of Anthony and Minnie Sayre was that all of them were "unstable.")

Zelda continued by describing her most recent symptoms. During the winter, she said, she had bronchitis and fever but went to her lessons just the same. After a trip to North Africa, where everyone had strange eyes, she returned home only to notice that people were spying on her, whispering behind her back. Sometimes she felt herself spinning out of control, and it became necessary to take morphine. Most humiliating was when she had been forced to quit her dance lessons after years of work. Success in ballet depended heavily on nerves, but hers evidently couldn't take it, and now the single thing in the world she ever wanted was gone. "I want to die."

When asked about her daughter, she shrugged. She had no idea about Scottie. "That is done now. I want to do something else."

Of more relevance was the man who'd brought her to Valmont. He was a fairy, she told the doctors. He was in love with another man, an American he had met in Paris five years ago. Hearing this talk of fairies startled Scott. (He disliked homosexuals, whom he referred to as "fairies.")

It was untrue, he snapped. The man was just a friend.

That's how it seemed to her, Zelda replied. This lover was a writer, too, a hairy-chested he-man novelist, a complete phony of course, but he had become quite successful.

She was a liar, insisted Scott, growing very angry.

Two weeks later, despite constant pleas for release, she was still at Valmont awaiting results of the testing. Her illness, the hospital finally determined, did not involve any physical disease, and so it would be necessary to summon an outside authority on nervous disorders for an opinion on whether psychiatric treatment was indicated. On June 3, Zelda was examined by Dr. Oscar Forel. A tall man in his late thirties, well dressed and cultured, Dr. Forel was at ease conversing about literature, art, and music. He even played the violin. He explained that he was the director of a new clinic near Geneva, one of the best-appointed facilities in Europe, where she might have superior treatment in tasteful surroundings. There were no barred windows, and she would not be closely confined. (That was not exactly true.) Should she agree to come of her own free will, and if her husband promised to stay away, he was inclined to believe she could recover. Zelda, favorably impressed, as much by Forel's manner of presentation as anything else, agreed it sounded like a sensible plan.

That was Tuesday evening. The following morning she woke up in a panic and said she had changed her mind and wished to return to Paris. What appeared to be perfectly reasonable the night before seemed a very dangerous decision after all. She knew that her life had fallen apart. But how could she be mad, as everybody was implying? Her sanity had never been questioned; indeed, anybody in the world could tell that Scott was the insane one. Now he was in a great hurry to put her away in a madhouse.

Her brother-in-law hurried to Montreux from Brussels, where he worked for the Guaranty Trust Company. Throughout Wednesday and early Thursday, Newman Smith and Scott both tried to sway her. They warned her to be sensible and transfer to Oscar Forel's sanatorium. Surely she could understand that she had no choice—caring for herself was no longer possible. With the proper treatment she could sort out her life and get well. While she did not disbelieve this, she did not believe it either, but she became tired of struggling. On Thursday afternoon the three of them finally departed for Nyon, some fifty miles away.

O N THE LAKESHORE south of Geneva, the elegantly appointed Rives de Prangins, whose château once belonged to Joseph Bonaparte, turned out to be more a five-star resort than a mental institution. There were a half-dozen villas and hundreds of acres of grounds at Prangins, a manicured oasis catering to rich foreigners suffering nervous breakdowns. Zelda's sunny corner room on the second floor of the main building had a private bath, Oriental rugs, and windows overlooking the lake. Nevertheless, it wasn't long before she sized up the clinic as a "nut farm" and wanted to leave, despite the gentlemanly Oscar Forel.

Forel was born and raised at the renowned Burghölzli Mental Hospital in Zurich, where his father was the director. By virtue of his background and training, he belonged to the elite inner circle of Swiss psychiatry, the small group of physicians, including Eugen Bleuler and Carl Jung, who were associated with the Burghölzli.

From the outset it seemed clear to him that Zelda's case was complicated; that is, she was a patient likely to improve but never be cured. On his initial examination at Valmont, he diagnosed her as a schizophrenic. Some years later, however, he would become less certain and describe her as "a constitutional, emotionally unbalanced psychopath." In his view, she was neither a pure neurotic nor a real psychotic.

Schizophrenia ("split mind"), once known as dementia praecox, had been relabeled by Eugen Bleuler in 1911. By any name, it was the most severe and complex of psychotic illnesses, because, unlike depression, it did not respond to treatment. Nineteenth-century physicians such as Emil Kraepelin held the psychosis to be incurable and degenerative, essentially a death sentence delayed. In 1930 this gloomy view—and the stigma attached to it—continued to prevail, and those afflicted could probably expect to be incarcerated in mental institutions. In later years schizophrenia would come to be considered a syndrome—not one disease but a group of related disorders—of genetic origin. But while heredity was thought to be a predisposing factor, environment could also play a role, along with vulnerability to psychological stresses. Generally the psychosis was believed to be triggered not by any single trauma but by a string of damaging events that accumulate over time.

Of all her talents, Zelda's ability with speech, her use of language in grand theatrical manner, was probably the most dramatic. When Bunny met her for the first time at the Biltmore, where she was dressed in Southern-belle flounces and getting stewed on orange blossoms, he immediately noticed her unconventional use of non sequiturs and free association. Her conversation just overflowed with spontaneous color and wit, almost in the same way her writing did, and her ideas tended to ricochet around so wildly that you could "never follow up anything," he remembered. There seemed nothing abnormal about it to him. On the contrary, her illogic offered proof of her originality, her palette of lush expressions deriving freshness from reluctance to copy "readymade phrases."

This type of impaired thought process, however, is also a common symptom of schizophrenia. Others include episodes of hallucinations, delusions (voices, false beliefs), and bizarre thoughts. There is gradual deterioration in the person's ability to perform ordinary daily activities and to distinguish the real from the unreal. In the months prior to her arrival at Prangins, Zelda seemed to be suffering from many such abnormalities. Was Forel's diagnosis correct? At the time it certainly seemed justified by her mental symptoms. (Seventy-five years later, some thought that she may have been misdiagnosed as a schizophrenic when she actually suffered from severe depression, in which case aggressive treatments such as insulin and electroshock could only have been detrimental.)

Schizophrenics appear mostly normal during childhood because the disorder typically does not manifest itself until young adulthood, in women usually the twenties or early thirties. In Zelda's case, the onset of the illness could have come several years before she was ever hospitalized. Scott, in the fall of 1928, had made a cryptic entry in his ledger: "Dirt eating in hotel." (The psychiatric term is "stool smearing" or "stool eating.") This incident must have happened on their return to New York, during a brief stopover before they went south to Ellerslie, and presumably nobody knew of it but Scott. Whatever he saw was so disturbing that he tried to block it from his mind.

During the course of that summer at Prangins, the details of Forel's diagnosis were of little interest to Zelda. She was growing increasingly sick.

HARPER'S AND THEIR annoying Mr. Rushmore had been nagging Vincent for weeks. It was not a bit urgent either, only a new limited edition of her complete works, and yet he persisted in inundating her with rush requests. That summer, with so much on her mind, Vincent had no patience for Arthur Rushmore.

Even at Steepletop, semi-isolated among the hamlets and small farms of the Berkshires, Vincent and Gene were not insulated from ominous events in the rest of the world. In Gene's opinion, prospects for an early economic recovery looked dim. He sent a thousand dollars to Cora, along with a warning to be extra careful and make the money last as long as possible. Don't go haywire and buy any Rolls-Royces on the installment plan, he joked. But he and Vincent made no attempt to cut back on their spending. In June they began making plans for an old-fashioned house party in grand style to honor Art and Gladys Ficke. Actually, during the past two years Art had decided he did not care for the Berkshires, he did not care for his "silly life" partying with Gene (who just discovered a new cocktail, gin and bitters), and he did not care much for Vincent anymore either.

Apart from Gene's tedious rhapsodies on bitters (available in any drugstore, he insisted), a far more serious problem was "Little Wince," who mightily tried Art's patience. It had become increasingly hard for him to make a distinction between the former "flawless goddess"—the "greatest woman poet who ever lived"—and the present Vincent, who, plainly put, tended to be a disagreeable drunk. She had changed drastically. After psychoanalysis with Dr. Karl Menninger in the late Thirties, he wanted to write a "very cruel" novel called *The Mirror of the Huntress* about a great genius who becomes "poisoned to the core by the worst Narcissus complex I have ever known" and who ruins her life from an "inability to love anybody or anything but the secret guarded image of herself." At Hardhack, "frightfully bored," Artie passed his time guzzling gin.

The house party for Artie and Gladdie was the high point of Vincent's summer. In early June she began mailing out personal invitations, invariably addressing her friends, whatever their ages, as "Dear Kids." From July 21 to 24, or longer than four days if the hosts and the liquor held out, she and Gene would be entertaining more than a dozen guests, and it was going to be "a hell of a lot of fun," she wrote. They expected Floyd Dell and his wife, B. Marie, from Croton; Deems and Mary Taylor and perhaps baby Joan from Stamford; and Max Eastman and his lovely Russian wife, Eliena, the painter. Among the local gentry were Bill Brann, once in advertising but now the owner of a horse farm and a breeder of racehorses, and George and Emla La Branche, a couple of "old darlings" living nearby at High Holt in summer and Florida in winter. George was a highly successful stockbroker who raised pheasants as a hobby and had written a book on fly-fishing. And those were just the houseguests, because another forty or fifty visitors were expected to appear for a show performed by the Jitney Players, perhaps something amusing such as a Gilbert operetta. Vincent promised plenty of entertainment, both conversational and theatrical.

To George Dillon in Chicago, Gene composed a special invitation, one that would be hard to refuse. (Apparently he did, though.) Steeple-top was going to be crawling with beautiful girls, but there might be a shortage of beautiful men, Gene teased. Would he please agree to come and stay a day, a week, or a year? "Love, Eugen," he signed himself.

Other than the house party, the subject on Vincent's mind that summer was George, as usual. After eighteen months—a year and a half of frequent letters and all-too-few meetings—their romance was slowly souring, not just because of the geographic distance separating them, not even owing to the difference in their ages. It was the old trouble: George, in memory, was a lover without fault; George, in reality, left her crackling with anger and desperation because he did not love her as much as she loved him. Pigheaded, absorbed by his own affairs, her beloved went skylarking around Chicago. She told him he was destroying her sanity; he wanted her to stop controlling him. Later that year, stricken to learn he had lost his job and was considering a move to California, she threatened to board the next train for Chicago if he did not come to Steepletop at once. He ignored her.

By no means had she given up on George, still the darling of her heart, but she was able to step back and see a panoramic view of the unfolding affair, from its first wild blossoming, to the wilting and yellowing middle, to what would most likely be a lingering death. The complete precarious story, soup to nuts, she would relate in fifty-two sonnets, because the affair, for all its pain, had plunged her into one of her most prolific writing periods. Publication of the sonnets was bound to expose her personal life, including piles of dirty laundry, in a most disagreeable fashion: her adultery, her husband's condonation, the boy plaything, altogether a spicy stew. On the other hand, she had been cautious to conceal the relationship not only from loose-tongued gossips but also from friends. When Esther Root, for one, later asked about the man in the sonnets, Vincent replied, "What makes you think that they're all about the same person?" Former lovers were not fooled for a minute. Bunny understood immediately this was not an imaginary liaison but a specific individual, although he was never able to identify the secret lover. (George Dillon never occurred to him, because in 1950 he suggested George as a possible biographer of Vincent.)

Overriding all other considerations was the need to publish some of her best work, and so Gene informed Harper's in May about the new poems. Miss Millay wanted him to say, he wrote to Eugene Saxton, that she will have a collection ready for publication in the spring of 1931. It was to be a major work comprising one long sequence of more than fifty love sonnets. Thirty were ready for publication and twenty more not quite finished.

Over the summer of the big house party Vincent began stewing about a title. Looking for a fitting line in one of the sonnets, she first considered A Garland for Your Living Hand and Love in the Open Hand, both of which were succeeded by Twice Required, which she also rejected. Her fussing soon got Gene's goat. He was tired of hearing about "the god damn title for Vincent's god damn book," he sputtered to Artie. (Eventually it would be called Fatal Interview.)

In the meantime, there was the pestering Mr. Rushmore. According to his letters, which Vincent had been trying to ignore throughout the party preparations, she alone was responsible for holding up his production schedule. Only someone as pathologically rigid as Mr. Rushmore could make such a fuss over nothing. Harper's, she finally told him, would simply have to make allowances for her personal situation. Of course she wished to make corrections to the new edition, but owing to circumstances beyond her control the house was "entirely upset" by workmen, and therefore supplying anything at that particular moment was out of the question. Surely he could appreciate her problem.

At last she must have made herself clear, because their Mr. Rushmore wrote back, acting offended but resigned. He would accept whatever cooperation he could get until such time as she was "freed of your building problems."

. . .

THE BODY that Zelda had tortured into an instrument of beauty was dribbling "into the beets in the clinic garden." Once she stopped exercising, the muscles began shrinking, and she felt stiff all over now. Her legs had become horribly flabby. Any prospects of joining Léonide Massine's company in New York that fall would be out of the question. The missing months could never be recovered.

All she had left were memories of the dancer who came to class in a Rolls-Royce, the one who performed for the President of France, the one who stank up the studio by leaving a half-eaten can of shrimp behind a mirror, the chanting "failli, cabriole, cabriole, failli." But most painful of all was the memory of Lubov Egorova. If ever she were to resume training, Madame would not want her back, Zelda believed. And yet, burning to know how Egorova rated her ability, she instructed Scott to write and ask how far she could develop "before it is too late." Madame's reply would be most honest if the question came from him, she told herself.

Other than a monthly visit to see Scottie in Paris, Scott was living in various hotels, in Geneva, Montreux, and Lausanne. He labored over stories for the *Saturday Evening Post*, his novel untouched for almost a year. (His previous seven books were bringing in royalties of roughly thirty dollars a year.)

Zelda's "rotten" letters got a bare glance before being filed under Z. Scott had yet to recover from "the horror of Valmont" and Zelda's "stinking" accusations about him and Ernest. He felt unable to lift his eyes to other men on the street. He tried to remember that she was "my own girl" whom he loved with all his heart despite everything.

The news of Zelda's confinement in an asylum was greeted with incredulity by Bunny, who immediately wrote Scott an encouraging letter. Don't let the neurologists depress him, he said, because they are a "funereal and unnerving" bunch. His own experience in Clifton Springs proved most people who break down generally recover. Less sympathetic was John Bishop, who felt Scott must surely be exaggerating about the severity of Zelda's illness. "He lies so that I could only make out her state is serious," John told the poet Allen Tate. His information was based on "Scott's drunken gossip and that depends upon whether he's trying to bolster himself up or make himself out a lowly Mid-Western worm." It was easy to lose patience with Scott.

After several weeks Madame Egorova replied to Scott's letter. Zelda, in her expert opinion, would never be exceptional, never a soloist of the first rank, because she had begun too late. By the same token, however, there was no doubt she had advanced beyond the corps de ballet. She promised to be a "good to very good" dancer performing important roles in companies such as Léonide Massine's.

In answering as she did, Egorova was mostly responding to Scott's strong implication that Zelda's doctors did not encourage further dancing, along with his detailed questions and his naming of specific ballerinas. Could Zelda, he wondered, ever be a Marie Danilova? (Comparing Zelda, almost thirty, with the greatest Russian dancer of the nineteenth century was ridiculous in the extreme.) Implied in Egorova's analysis was an important observation: had Zelda been mentally healthy, had she gone on to pursue a career, she might have danced professionally, as others did, for another ten years. In a discipline in which newcomers expect a period of apprenticeship while they prove themselves and rise in the ranks to become, one day if they are lucky, principals, a good many students would have been pleased by such an appraisal.

Zelda, however, felt shame. She chose to believe that she was not good enough after all, "the saddest thing in my life." Soon after she received Madame's reply, the skin on her face, neck, and shoulders broke into a red rash, and then erupted in pus-filled blisters. While this was not her first attack of eczema, the itchy lesions were far more unbearable and proved immune to the standard treatments of topical medications, sedatives, and morphine. Before long, the terrible oozing sores were accompanied by mental deterioration, and it became necessary to transfer her to Villa Eglantine, a locked, barred residence for troubled patients. For five weeks she lay slathered in grease, a "living agonizing sore," as Scott would imagine when he described a patient in *Tender Is the Night*. Zelda considered herself a "half human-being" imprisoned in bandages, and her only desire was to die. Finally Dr. Forel tried hypnosis, and she was able to find relief from the lesions. She slept for thirteen hours. When she awoke, most of the eczema had disappeared, and she was moved back to her bed in the main building.

For weeks afterward her room continued to smell of antiseptic. She soon regained enough strength to complain, to keep begging for her release, and even to make jokes. When Rosalind spoke of sending medicated soap, she replied that her eczema was not the type to be cured by Cuticura. If Rosalind really wanted to help, she should send the Brussels fire department.

F OR A TIME Zelda's condition improved. She read through Spengler's *The Decline of the West* and studied books on playwriting, even dipped into James Joyce ("a nightmare in my present condition"). She also wrote a lot: resentful, bitter letters to Scott and a short story, "Miss Bessie," that would be published in *Scribner's Magazine.* But eventually her mental state began to unravel again, and after another outbreak of eczema she was returned to Villa Eglantine and its locked doors. This setback so greatly discouraged Scott that he demanded a second opinion of both her diagnosis and her treatment in November. The two men he considered to perform the evaluation, those said to be the most highly regarded in the field, were Eugen Bleuler and Carl Jung. In the end it was not Jung who traveled from Zurich to Geneva—he no longer treated psychotics—but his former mentor at the Burghölzli, Eugen Bleuler.

Bleuler was seventy-three, an ascetic man, slight, bearded, self-contained. His sister happened to be a catatonic schizophrenic, and other family members also suffered variants of the same condition. His belief that schizophrenia could be treated, or at least stopped from progressing, led to unorthodox methods of therapy. A legend at Burghölzli told how he presented an ax to an ax murderer and took him to the woods to chop trees. Ax or not, Zelda still took an immediate dislike to the old gentleman.

After he had finished examining her, Bleuler remained for several hours at Prangins discussing his findings with Oscar Forel and Scott. Predictably, he confirmed Forel's diagnosis. After treating hundreds, if not several thousands, of schizophrenics, he found nothing the least unusual about Zelda's case. Her sexual attraction toward women, for example, was "a symptom of the illness and not constitutional," he explained, "just as Madame Egorova was the first lesbian passion after the onset of the illness." In general, he approved of Zelda's treatment but recommended fewer shopping trips to Geneva and more "rest and re-education." Her chances for recovery were excellent, he said. In cases such as hers, odds were that three out of four patients would be discharged—one completely cured, two remaining "slightly eccentric" throughout life—and the fourth would degenerate into total insanity. Still, for a person of her particular temperament, he predicted a favorable outcome. Of course, he added, a definitive judgment might require another year of treatment.

That last remark alarmed Scott. Another year? They were planning to go home soon, he protested. (And besides, Zelda's care at Prangins was costing him a fortune, although the thousand dollars a month he mentioned to Bunny was an exaggeration.) But Bleuler remained adamant. Absolutely no traveling, he warned, not even with day and night nurses, not even in the royal suite on the *Bremen*. Mrs. Fitzgerald was too unstable. For the foreseeable future, discharge was out of the question.

Bleuler's words infuriated Zelda. He was "a great imbecile," she burst out. She refused to stay at Prangins one minute longer, she wrote Scott. She was thirty years old and would take full responsibility for herself. What happened to her gramophone? Where were her clothes, her jewelry, her ballet library, the crocheted quilt her mother had given them? Was nothing left? She could not keep living like an infant, spied on and stripped of every possession.

Nobody had a legal right to detain her. As she had already made clear, she wanted a divorce. Their marriage had gone to hell, and she could not think of a single reason to continue "except your good looks," and those were nothing special, because she now realized her hairdresser was every bit as handsome. What she had not said before was her determination to leave Prangins whether he liked it or not. She would ask Newman to make arrangements so that she could return to Montgomery. Should Scott try to stop her, if he fought her in court, he would be sorry. Rest assured, there were plenty of things she could say to displease him. And she would do it, too. He was not going to run her life, she repeated. And neither was that fool Bleuler.

"Baby's boat is the *Saturnia,*" Dottie cabled Bob Benchley. "Sailing from Cannes November 15 arriving New York so far as I can make out some time in early April." Please tell Helen and Sewie, "and will I be glad to see you dearest Fred." By this time she could scarcely remember the reasons she had come to Europe. Her extended sojourn with the Murphy family was a little like being the last guest at a party and not knowing how to say good night. She wondered if anybody at home had missed her. Probably they figured she was dead.

One morning at breakfast she watched Gerald reprimanding Baoth. When he slapped him with a slipper, she could no longer remain silent. Please, she said, don't be so hard on the boy. Gerald, often in a cross mood these days, told her to mind her business.

She was making it her business, she replied. By the looks of it, he was being horribly mean to his son, and she was telling him how she felt about it.

He didn't care how she felt.

Maybe she ought to leave, she said.

Maybe she should, he agreed.

Even though they patched up the silly quarrel, she understood it was time to go. For too long she had rented herself out to the rich. With her bank account overdrawn, she had to wire Harold Guinzburg for two thousand dollars so that she could pay her debts and book passage home. She was going mad with "loneliness and discouragement," she cabled Georgie Opp.

Shortly before 8 a.m. on Tuesday, November 25, the *Saturnia* edged up the Hudson, past the forests of giant towers, and docked at Pier 84. The shock of seeing her hometown again, the skyscrapers hanging heavily below a smudgy sky, the not-quite-believable chaos of steel and neon, left her speechless. Cradling her new dog, a dachshund named Robinson, she struggled not to cry as she stepped into a flock of friends who were gathered at the pier. The reporters and photographers covering her arrival kept fishing for wisecracks, but for once she remained very quiet. "I'm tired," she said gruffly. "Maybe it was Switzerland." The press failed to pry loose any entertaining remarks from a person never known to hide her wit under a bushel. This was why, that evening, the *New York Telegram* captioned its picture of her with the single word "Sparkless" and headlined the story "Dorothy Parker Returns, Silent."

Not for long, though. It was the week of Thanksgiving, her favorite holiday. The city was cold with snow flurries, a new Barney Google balloon made its debut in the Macy's parade, and the police were busy searching for a missing head to match the torso found floating in the North River. A man plunging from a Times Square window managed the precision maneuver of killing himself and seriously injuring a pedestrian. It was Hieronymus Bosch on the Hudson. But when was it ever otherwise?

The welcome-home parties began promptly. The first was hosted by Georgie Opp and Harold, then Dottie threw herself a huge celebration and invited just about every soul she'd ever known, even those she didn't much like. "So to Miss Edna Ferber's," wrote Frank Adams in the *World*, "and caught her up with us, and we all set down at a great and merry party that Dorothy Parker gave." Among her most important items of business was to present Harold Ross with a new Constant Reader column, her first in almost two years. "Maybe you think I was just out in the ladies' room all this time," she began cheerfully. Not true. She was in Switzerland trying to forget. But "when the day comes that you have to tie a string around your finger to remind yourself of what it was you were forgetting, it is time for you to go back home."

Again she settled at the Algonquin, a hotel that never seemed to

change. But there was much else about the city that had. In her absence, some imbecile richer than God bought the leases on three
blocks of Manhattan real estate, not a cow pasture in far-off Staten Island, but the very blocks in midtown that were home to Tony's and all
the best speakeasies. Hundreds of buildings were going to be dyna-
mited beginning in the spring. And why? This millionaire with a steam
shovel had the idea of putting up a city within a city. Honestly, she did
not know one living soul who didn't think it was insane. Didn't this
Rockefeller *live* in New York? Didn't the old fool know New York *was* a
city? What would happen to Tony's? And Jack and Charlie's "21"? What
would become of Horace Liveright when his brownstone was gone?

While she was away, the exclusive Algonquin Round Table had expired. No formal burial marked its demise, but when nobody showed
up for lunch, the hotel began seating other guests at the big table in the
Rose Room, out-of-towners who wanted to eat at the famous table of
the wits. On a happier note, publishers' "teas" were serving stronger
booze. Around the lethal punch bowls the main subject was the peculiar choice of Sinclair Lewis for the Nobel Prize in literature, the first
American writer to be honored. Some people thought it was disgraceful. Dottie said the prize should have gone to Edith Wharton. After all,
since when did Sinclair Lewis write literature?

December was a month of nervous breakdowns, creative suicides,
and tumbling stock prices. To Dottie, whose bank account looked "photographic" and whose only assets were *New Yorker* stocks Harold Ross
had given her in lieu of money, the Crash did not seem worth any tears.
Actually, the fate of rich bankers did not matter to her one bit. So what
if four hundred houses were for rent in Greenwich? She could work up
no sympathy at all for poor dumb bastards forced to give up their butlers. To be fair, she did feel sorry for certain of her friends. Some of
them, she heard, were going to be evicted from their penthouses. Her
only advice for investors was never to trust a round garter or a Wall
Street man.

Despite a grim December, New Year's Eve turned out to be one of
the best in memory. Never had there been so many parties, and nobody

blinked at receiving a half-dozen invitations. Even before sundown on that Wednesday, midtown Manhattan began rocking. At the Yale Club, on Vanderbilt Avenue, a member jumped to his death during the afternoon. In Times Square dozens of Prohibition agents descended without warning and began raiding restaurants, a highly futile operation if ever there was one. By the time darkness fell, taxis carrying revelers in black tuxedos and pastel silks had begun chasing from building to building in search of friendly parties. Without a second thought, people would burst into smoky living rooms where they had not been invited. They upset drinks and dumped cigarette butts into the empty punch bowls of perfect strangers. And everywhere everybody seemed to be talking his head off. Watch for the rebound in April. Industrials would be the first to recover, then rails. Wait'll next spring.

W/HERE DID THE TIME GO?
    In his office downtown at the *New York World,* Frank Adams spent the afternoon of December 31 writing his final column of the year. Looking to the future, he dutifully made a New Year's resolution—"to do better." (It was the same one he made every year.) That evening he and Esther were going to a party at the home of his boss, Herbert Bayard Swope. By the time they rode the Long Island Rail Road to Port Washington out on the North Shore, and by the time dinner was finally served at ten, Frank was starving. "I so happy with the dinner that I. Berlin and I to the pianoforte and I sang a dozen songs or so to his accompaniment and the delight of a majority of the listeners." At the Swopes' house, only a few minutes from Great Neck Estates, where Scott not so long ago had invented Jay Gatsby, Frank and Irving Berlin and the rest of their friends merrily rang in the decade with music and remembrances.

    Still, certain sights and sounds were already becoming harder and harder to conjure up. In a Swiss hotel, a few weeks later, Scott sought to bear witness to his lost world. There were times, he said in an article for *Scribner's Magazine,* when he could almost hear "a ghostly rumble among the drums, an asthmatic whisper in the trombones that swings me back into the early twenties when we drank wood alcohol and every day in every way grew better and better . . . and it all seems rosy and romantic to us who were young then, because we will never feel quite so intensely about our surroundings any more." His words—a message in a bottle to distant generations—failed to rouse much nostalgia in 1931.

The endless party was over, and eventually even the ghostly whispers died out. For Dottie and Vincent and Edna and Zelda, and all those they loved, the Twenties would shortly roll into memory and myth, merely a stepping-stone on the way to the rest of their lifetimes.

No speakeasy was ever to replace Tony's in DOROTHY PARKER's af-
fections, although it was not for lack of searching. In the 1930s she and
her second husband, Alan Campbell, became a highly paid screenwriting team and won an Academy Award for *A Star Is Born.* Membership
in the Communist Party resulted in her being blacklisted in the 1950s.
At her death in 1967, an estate of twenty thousand dollars was be-
queathed to the Reverend Martin Luther King Jr.

In 1931, the same year she published *Fatal Interview,* a national poll
named EDNA ST. VINCENT MILLAY one of the ten most famous
people in America. Over the next two decades she went on writing poetry despite chronic pain, alcoholism, a debilitating morphine addiction, and a career in decline. In October 1950 her body was found at the
bottom of a staircase at Steepletop. She died of a broken neck.

The motion picture based on EDNA FERBER's *Cimarron* won an
Academy Award for Best Picture of 1931. During an extraordinary career
of a half century, she published twelve novels, two autobiographies,
nine plays, and twelve collections of short stories. Her novels lent
themselves to Hollywood epics, most notably *Giant,* which starred
James Dean. She died, of cancer at age eighty-three, as she lived—a
loner. Her grandniece called her "an ardent feminist, a precursor of all
the Friedans and Steinems."

Despite her determination to leave Prangins and divorce her husband, ZELDA FITZGERALD did neither. Released from the clinic in late 1931, she returned to America, where she continued to write and paint. *Save Me the Waltz*, published a year later, would be one of the finest ballet novels ever written. After a series of hospitalizations, she burned to death at Highland Hospital, in Asheville, North Carolina, at age forty-seven.

RUTH HALE in 1933 divorced HEYWOOD BROUN, "saying she must resume her career, but she made no effort to do so," said their son, Woodie. A year later she died suddenly (from "generalized visceral congestion," said the death certificate); some of her friends suspected that she deliberately starved herself. Obituaries identified her as "Ruth Hale, the wife of Heywood Broun."

The New Yorker became one of the outstanding publishing successes of the twentieth century. JANE GRANT and HAROLD ROSS divorced in 1929. With her second husband, Jane was to establish the renowned Connecticut nursery White Flower Farm. Harold remained the editor of *The New Yorker* until his death from throat cancer in 1951.

In 1938 EDMUND WILSON got married for the third time, to a young writer named Mary McCarthy, and moved to the area of Cape Cod where the Millay family summered in 1920. He bought a home in the village of Wellfleet, adjoining Truro on the south side, where he would live, mostly, for the rest of his life. By his death in 1972, he had established himself as the finest literary and social critic in American letters.

In the bar of the "21" Club, on West Fifty-second Street, hangs a plaque dedicated to ROBERT BENCHLEY. It simply says, "Robert Benchley—His Corner." Beginning a new career in the 1930s, he acted in some forty motion pictures before dying of cirrhosis of the liver in 1945.

The stage and screen career of Robert Benchley's protégée CAROL GOODNER spanned a half century in England and the United States and included leading roles in such memorable productions as *The Man Who Came to Dinner* (1939) and *A Man for All Seasons* (1961). She died in 2001, at the age of ninety-seven.

CHARLES MACARTHUR married the actress Helen Hayes. His Broadway hit, *The Front Page* (written with Ben Hecht), was followed by a successful career as a Hollywood screenwriter.

When ARTHUR DAVISON FICKE died of cancer in 1945, Edna St. Vincent Millay recited at his funeral one of the sonnets she had written for him ("And You As Well Must Die, Beloved Dust").

The Shangri-la created by SARA and GERALD MURPHY at Villa America fell victim to economic depression and world war. When the family returned home in 1932, Gerald took over the operation of the Mark Cross Company. Their son Patrick lost his battle against tuberculosis in 1937, at age sixteen. He was preceded by his brother, Baoth, who died two years earlier after contracting spinal meningitis.

The novel that F. SCOTT FITZGERALD had so much difficulty completing was finally published, in 1934, as *Tender Is the Night*. A loyal husband and father, he continued to look after Zelda and to supervise the upbringing of their daughter. When he died of a heart attack at the age of forty-four, he was working in Hollywood as a screenwriter and living with the gossip columnist Sheilah Graham. *The Great Gatsby* went on to become a classic. The American paperback alone now sells a half-million copies a year.

SCOTTIE FITZGERALD had two broken marriages and four children. Alcoholism and mental illness went on stalking her family. Her son Tim, after serving in Vietnam, shot himself in the heart.

In addition to two novels (*Wayfarer* and *Against the Wall*), KATHLEEN "KAY" MILLAY published three volumes of poetry. Abandoned by her husband, she ended her days in destitution struggling against alcoholism and mental illness, begging in vain for help from her sisters before dying at the age of forty-six.

The 1954 Nobel Prize in literature was awarded to ERNEST HEMINGWAY. Following a long period of depression and psychiatric treatment, he died of a self-inflicted gunshot wound at his Idaho home in 1961. His memoir of Paris in the 1920s, *A Moveable Feast*, contains portraits of Zelda and Scott.

Four years after meeting Zelda, EDOUARD JOZAN married the granddaughter of a marshal of France, General Joseph Gallieni (the national hero who in 1914 saved Paris by turning back the invading Germans), and sired four sons and a daughter during a fifty-year marriage. In the Resistance during World War II, he was captured and spent two years in a concentration camp. After the war he commanded French naval forces in Morocco and then Indochina in the 1950s. In 1959 he retired as a five-star admiral and died in Cannes at the age of eighty-two. He was "afraid of nothing," said his daughter, Martine.

With the demise of the *New York World* and the *New York Tribune*, FRANKLIN PIERCE ADAMS became a regular on the popular radio quiz show *Information Please*. He and Esther Root had three sons and a daughter, Persephone, whose name was chosen by Edna St. Vincent Millay, "unfortunately, because it was a hell of a moniker, and a terrible handicap her whole life," said her brother Anthony. Frank and Esther eventually divorced. The severe mental deterioration of his final years was due to arteriosclerosis.

In 1939 George S. Kaufman and Moss Hart wrote a hit comedy, *The Man Who Came to Dinner*, about ALEXANDER WOOLLCOTT at his most poisonous. A popular radio personality, Woollcott collapsed and died in 1943 after suffering a heart attack and cerebral hemorrhage during a CBS panel discussion titled "Is Germany Incurable?"

Edna Ferber collaborated with GEORGE S. KAUFMAN on two more successful plays, *Dinner at Eight* and *Stage Door*. In the 1930s his collaboration with Moss Hart won a Pulitzer for the musical *You Can't Take It with You*. His forty years in the theater resulted in forty-five plays, half of them hits.

With the death of EUGEN BOISSEVAIN, of lung cancer and a cerebral hemorrhage in 1949, Edna St. Vincent Millay collapsed and had to be hospitalized. In his absence she survived for about a year.

Both of Dorothy Parker's husbands took their own lives, EDWIN POND PARKER II in 1934 and ALAN CAMPBELL in 1963. Her investment-banker lover JOHN WILEY GARRETT II, who married finally in 1945, fired a gun into his mouth at the Martha's Vineyard airport in 1961.

Once *The Bookman* ceased publication, SEWARD COLLINS took over a monthly journal, *American Review*, in which he sought to present increasingly ultraconservative, pro-fascist views. In 1936 he married his assistant.

After living with Edna St. Vincent Millay in Paris during 1932, GEORGE DILLON became her collaborator on a translation of Baudelaire's *Flowers of Evil*, published in 1936. For many years the editor of *Poetry* magazine, he lived a reclusive life with his parents and never married.

The following abbreviations are used for frequently cited sources:

EB	Eugen Boissevain
EF	Edna Ferber
FSF	F. Scott Fitzgerald
ZSF	Zelda Sayre Fitzgerald
EM	Edna St. Vincent Millay
KM	Kathleen Millay
NM	Norma Millay
DP	Dorothy Parker
EW	Edmund Wilson

BEINECKE	Beinecke Rare Book and Manuscript Library, Yale University (Papers of Arthur Davison Ficke and Gladys Brown Ficke, Richard Myers, Seward Collins, and Edmund Wilson)
BERG	Berg Collection, Astor, Lenox, and Tilden Foundation, New York Public Library (Papers of Edna St. Vincent Millay, Kathleen Millay, Norma Millay, Cora Millay, and Henry Millay)
COLUMBIA	Columbia University Libraries Special Collections/ Oral History Collection, Columbia University
HOUGHTON	Houghton Library, Harvard University
LOC	Library of Congress (Edna St. Vincent Millay Papers)
MUGAR	Mugar Library, Boston University
NEW YORKER RECORDS	Rare Books and Manuscripts Division, New York Public Library
PUL	Department of Rare Books and Special Collections, Princeton University Libraries (Zelda and F. Scott Fitzgerald Papers)
TC/LC	Billy Rose Theatre Collection, Lincoln Center Library of the Performing Arts, New York Public Library

ONE: ᧡ 1920

5 "sometimes in the fresh body": *Casket,* July 1919.

5 "R. Benchley tells me": Franklin P. Adams, *The Diary of Our Own Samuel Pepys, 1911–1925* (New York: Simon and Schuster, 1935), 1:241.

6 "the greatest act of friendship": DP interview, *Writers at Work: The Paris Review Interviews,* 1st ser. (New York: Viking, 1958), 74.

7 "a brisk walk": *Vanity Fair,* Dec. 1919.

8 "thick ankles": Jeanne Ballot Winham interview.

8 "an inch smaller": DP interview, *Writers at Work,* 74.

9 "Oh, God": Edmund Wilson, *The Twenties* (New York: Farrar, Straus and Giroux, 1975), 48.

9 Edna St. Vincent Millay's nickname: To family and close friends she was known as Vincent. After 1920 she began calling herself Edna to some of her friends, as well as to the public. Her middle name derived from a New York City hospital in Greenwich Village. In a persistent family fable, St. Vincent's Hospital saved the life of her uncle, a stevedore loading cargo on the New Orleans docks who became trapped belowdecks of a ship bound for New York and miraculously survived ten days without food or water. (Charles Buzzell fell into the hold while drunk.)

9 "nothing I wouldn't do": Jim Lawyer to EM, quoted in Daniel Mark Epstein, *What Lips My Lips Have Kissed* (New York: Henry Holt, 2001), 142.

10 "going like hell": NM to KM, winter 1919, Berg.

10 "Ah, awful weight": EM, *Collected Poems* (New York: Harper & Row, 1956), 3.

10 Millay's college education: In her "Good Times Book" (Berg), Kathleen Millay recorded certain events that took place in the summer of 1912, at the Whitehall Inn, in Camden, Maine: "Some of the swells asked if they could have some singing . . . Vincent sang her 'Circus Rag,'" followed by a recitation of verse, including "Renascence." Asked to return, she performed the poem again the next evening. "They were just so crazy over her and talked of her all the time and again sent her home in a carriage," Kay wrote. They also gave her "three crisp new five dollar bills—wasn't that lovely?" Among the guests was Caroline B. Dow, head of the YWCA's National Training School, who arranged for Vincent to attend Vassar College.

11 "Oh, no, not you": KM to EM, c. 1941, draft possibly unsent, Berg.

11 Millay's Nancy Boyd stories: Between 1919 and 1923 she published in *Ainslee's* and *Vanity Fair* more than thirty short stories, satiric sketches, and playlets under the pseudonym Nancy Boyd. As her main source of income during desperately hard times, the stories were generally slapdash. In one letter to Kathleen, Norma described how Vincent stayed up most of the night writing a story, which she planned to deliver to *Ainslee's* before five in order to "get the check for it tomorrow" (NM to KM, winter 1919, Berg). At least one of the sto-

ries, "The Seventh Stair," seems to be a collaboration with Norma, who was not a writer. At best sprightly and witty, the pieces were most often silly potboilers, presumably the reason for the pen name. In a 1931 interview with *Pictorial Review*, however, Vincent insisted the stories had been carefully composed: "I know they sound as if they tripped off my typewriter, but I had such anguish of mind over them, so much preparation went into each one."

11 "I hope": Adams, *Diary*, 1:244.

12 "poor fish": EM to Millay family, Feb. 26, 1920, LOC.

12 "fiery handwriting": Wilson, *Twenties*, 52.

12 "and although I needed": Ibid., 33.

13 "genial": Geoffrey Hellman, "Frank Crowninshield," in *The Saturday Review Gallery* (New York: Simon and Schuster, 1959), 228.

13 "the manager": Llewelyn Powys, *The Verdict of Bridlegoose* (New York: Harcourt, Brace, 1926), 41.

14 "almost supernaturally": Edmund Wilson, *The Shores of Light: A Literary Chronicle of the Twenties and Thirties* (New York: Farrar, Straus and Young, 1952), 749.

15 "One of the most distinctive": *Vanity Fair*, July 1920, 45.

15 "so much work": Wilson, *Twenties*, 63.

16 "God—or something": ZSF to FSF, Feb. 1920, *Correspondence of F. Scott Fitzgerald* (New York: Random House, 1980), 50.

18 "he smelled": ZSF, *Save Me the Waltz*, in *The Collected Writings of Zelda Fitzgerald* (Tuscaloosa: University of Alabama Press, 1997), 39.

19 "This looks like a road company": Wilson, *Twenties*, 48.

19 "God! How I miss": FSF to EW, Jan. 1918, *A Life in Letters* (New York: Scribner's, 1994), 18.

20 "WERE YOU EVER": *New York Times*, Apr. 4, 1920.

20 "manic depressive insanity": FSF, "Early Success," in *The Crack-Up*, ed. Edmund Wilson (New York: New Directions, 1945), 88.

20 "queen of the campus": Marc Connelly interview. A playwright and member of the Algonquin Round Table, Connelly is best remembered for his 1930 Pulitzer Prize drama, *The Green Pastures*.

20 "The only excuse": FSF, *This Side of Paradise* (New York: Scribner's, 1920), 159.

21 "a garden party": ZSF, "Caesar's Things," PUL.

21 "No evening clothes": EF, *A Peculiar Treasure* (New York: Doubleday, Doran, 1939), 249. A period expression that meant entertainment. As Robert Benchley once put it, a writer could say practically anything in *Vanity Fair* "as long as he said it in evening clothes."

22 Newman Levy: Ferber's first theatrical collaborator, Levy was a pillar of the Players Club, known for revue sketches and satiric light verse, as well as a

distinguished lawyer who specialized in civil-liberties cases with his partner Morris Ernst.

22 "along the upper reaches": Edith Wharton, *The Custom of the Country* (New York: Scribner's, 1913), 18.

23 "ditch-digging": EF, *Peculiar Treasure*, 5.

23 "there was [not] a day": EF quoted in Julie Goldsmith Gilbert, *Ferber: A Biography* (Garden City, N.Y.: Doubleday, 1978), 431.

23 Scott Fitzgerald's scorn for Ferber: In *This Side of Paradise* the Tom D'Invilliers character singles out Edna Ferber, Zane Grey, and Fannie Hurst as writers whose novels would not be remembered in ten years, even if they did earn fifty thousand dollars a year. "They won't sit down and do one honest novel," Tom says (197–98).

24 "ugly": EF, "The Homely Heroine," classicreader.com.

24 "except mother": EF to Jay "Ding" Darling, c. 1912, University of Iowa Libraries Special Collections.

24 "the old stingy-guts": EF, *Peculiar Treasure*, 159.

24 "I hate New York": EF to William Allen White, quoted in Gilbert, *Ferber*, 402.

24 "Stop it": Ibid.

25 "There are heaps": EF to Paul Reynolds, Oct. 21, 1913, Columbia.

25 "three pages": EF, *Peculiar Treasure*, 224.

26 Flappers: H. L. Mencken originated the term in 1915 to describe certain unconventional post-Victorian women who sought equality with men. Mencken's liberated women drove cars, played golf, and appeared to be unshockable and unflappable. However, the word did not come into general use until the Twenties, when it was popularized by F. Scott Fitzgerald and the illustrator John Held Jr. to embody the spirit of the times.

27 "You'll recognize": FSF to Maxwell Perkins, c. Feb. 21, 1920, *Dear Scott/Dear Max: The Fitzgerald-Perkins Correspondence* (New York: Scribner's, 1971), 29.

27 "They filled the house": FSF, *The Beautiful and Damned* (New York: Modern Library, 2002), 197–98.

28 "I *cut* my *tail*": ZSF to Ludlow Fowler, Aug. 16, 1920, PUL.

28 "It's been a wild": Ibid.

28 "Without you": ZSF to FSF, c. summer 1920, PUL.

28 "I began to bawl": FSF, *Crack-Up*, 28.

29 "complacent": Heywood Broun, *New York Tribune*, April 11, 1920.

29 "sloppy and cocky": Adams, Conning Tower, *New York Tribune*, July 14, 1920.

29 "FPA is at it": FSF to Maxwell Perkins, July 17, 1920, *Dear Scott/Dear Max*, 62. Perkins, a memorable editor but inept when it came to copyediting and proofreading, had not noticed the mistakes.

29 "I married the heroine": FSF interview with *Shadowland* magazine, 1921, quoted in Nancy Milford, *Zelda* (New York: Harper & Row, 1970), 77.

30 "What would you like me": EM to EW, Aug. 3, 1920, Edmund Wilson, *Letters on Literature and Politics, 1912–1972* (New York: Farrar, Straus and Giroux, 1977), 96.

30 "Damn it": EM to John Bishop, c. June 1920, PUL.

31 Millay sisters' nicknames: Kathleen's pet name for Vincent was Titter Binnie. Sefe and Hunk were short for Josephus and Bohunkus, two brothers in a ditty sung by Cora. The derivation of Wump is unknown.

31 Wilson's description of Cora Millay: Wilson, *Shores of Light*, 760; Edmund Wilson, *The Forties* (New York: Farrar, Straus and Giroux, 1983), 224.

32 "That might be": Wilson, *Shores of Light*, 764.

32 "By the time": Wilson, *Forties*, 223.

32 "stopped defecating": John Bishop to EW, Aug. 1920, Beinecke.

33 "stupid, hot": KM to Howard Young, Aug. 7, 1920, Berg.

33 "who was the editor": KM to Ann Eckert, Jan. 24, 1938, Berg.

33 "Glory Be": KM, "The Good Times Book," 1912, Berg.

34 "the only worthwhile": Howard Young to KM, June 9, 1920, Berg.

34 "the Most Distinguished": *Vanity Fair*, Nov. 1920.

34 "very famous": EM to Witter Bynner, Oct. 29, 1920, *Letters of Edna St. Vincent Millay* (New York: Harper & Brothers, 1952), 102.

34 "some strange animal": EF, *Peculiar Treasure*, 263.

36 "the sweetest new evening gown": EM to Witter Bynner, Oct. 29, 1920, *Letters*, 102.

36 "sad so much": Ibid., 104.

36 "better settle": Cora Millay to KM, Sept. 1, 1920, Berg.

37 "some wretched child": Llewelyn Powys to EM, Dec. 16, 1920, quoted in Epstein, *What Lips*, 154.

37 "For God's sake": John Bishop to EM, Nov. 1920, quoted in Epstein, *What Lips*, 151.

37 "better share": Wilson, *Twenties*, 65.

37 "I gave it all up": KM to Howard Young, c. 1937, Berg.

37 "quite sick": EM to Cora Millay, Dec. 20, 1920, *Letters*, 105.

38 "fresh grass": Ibid.

38 "I'll be thirty": Wilson, *Shores of Light*, 766.

TWO: ∾ 1921

39 "tall, thin, greasy": EF to Alexander Woollcott, Feb. 4, 1921, Houghton.

40 "disagreeable": Edmund Wilson, *The Twenties* (New York: Farrar, Straus and Giroux, 1975), 45.

40 Woollcott's mumps: Woollcott's masculinity mystified his friends, who

agreed there was something wrong with him but insisted he was not a homosexual (Murdock Pemberton interview with James Gaines). The women on whom he had crushes included Neysa McMein and Beatrice Kaufman, whose husbands were Jack Baragwanath and George S. Kaufman.

40 "New Jersey Nero": Julie Goldsmith Gilbert, *Ferber: A Biography* (Garden City, N.Y.: Doubleday, 1978), 336.

41 "rude": EF to Alexander Woollcott, April 7, 1920, Houghton.

41 "harder and harder": EF to Alexander Woollcott, April 23, 1920, Houghton.

42 "breathlessly and ruthlessly": EM to Arthur Ficke, Jan. 24, 1922, Arthur Davison Ficke and Gladys Brown Ficke Papers, Beinecke.

42 "a great success": Henry Millay to EM, Jan. 1, 1921, Berg.

43 "go and not come back": EM to Esther Root, Aug. 24, 1923, *Letters of Edna St. Vincent Millay* (New York: Harper & Brothers, 1952), 176.

43 "hundred other false": EM to William L. Brann, c. 1935, Berg.

45 "throw bombs": EW to John Bishop, July 3, 1921, Edmund Wilson, *Letters on Literature and Politics, 1912–1972* (New York: Farrar, Straus and Giroux, 1977), 66.

45 "A little housework": Alex McKaig diary, quoted in Nancy Milford, *Zelda* (New York: Harper & Row, 1970), 78.

46 "Can you imagine": H. L. Mencken, *My Life as Author and Editor* (New York: Knopf, 1993), 329.

47 "the equal of any": FSF to Maxwell Perkins, July 30, 1921, *Dear Scott/Dear Max: The Fitzgerald-Perkins Correspondence* (New York: Scribner's, 1971), 40.

47 "highly original": FSF, *The Beautiful and Damned* (New York: Modern Library, 2002), 120.

47 "rather silly": EW to Stanley Dell, Feb. 19, 1921, Wilson, *Letters,* 55.

50 "I love you too much": George Slocombe to EM, July 29, 1921, quoted in Nancy Milford, *Savage Beauty: The Life of Edna St. Vincent Millay* (New York: Random House, 2001), 211.

50 "all shot to pieces": EM to KM, Aug. 1921, Berg.

51 "sweet": EM, "Keen," *Collected Poems* (New York: Harper & Row, 1956), 171.

51 "I cried": KM to EM, c. 1941, Berg.

51 Cora Millay's writings: Since the 1890s Vincent's mother had been composing novels, songs, verses, and melodramas, which she saved in a wooden box. Among Kathleen Millay's papers at the New York Public Library can be found, for example, Cora's research notes on the colonial economy; a seagoing novel, "The Star of the North," about a female ship captain; dialect songs about tough Irish women named Maggie Magill and Katie Kilroy (typed from memory by Kay in 1942); and notebooks describing the moon and her recipe for macaroni with white sauce.

One of the rejected stories from 1921 was "The Chore Boy," a homespun tale of sin, shame, and atonement that relied heavily on Cora's familiarity with New England farm life and included far more description of raspberry and blueberry picking than anyone needed to know. A city priest revisits the farm where, as a hired boy, he once seduced and abandoned a young woman. His objective is to tell his illegitimate daughter the truth about her paternity, but "something held and hurt his throat," and so he leaves without confessing his youthful indiscretion (Millay Papers, LOC).

52 "wonderful": Cora Millay to EM, Sept. 27, 1921, LOC.

52 "He's exceedingly handsome": EM to KM, Feb. 25, 1918, Berg.

53 Arthur Davison Ficke in fiction and nonfiction: Edmund Wilson considered Arthur Ficke a pathetic snob. An unpleasant character in "Glimpses of Wilbur Flick," one of the five stories in Wilson's *Memoirs of Hecate County*, is said to be a partial portrait. The nonfictional Ficke was an unhappy person, unable to forget a cruel childhood punishment in which his parents, departing on a trip to Mexico, tied him to a banister of their house and threatened to leave him. By his own account, he hated his last name ever since learning it meant "fuck" in German. During psychoanalysis later in life, he confided to Dr. Karl Menninger that his only lifelong interests had been alcohol and sex. In fact, he was a timid man who lacked confidence in his sexual ability. Chained to a wife who loathed sex and who had demanded his presence during childbirth, an experience that supposedly traumatized him, he became a "masturbating young Galahad" (Ficke, "Psychoanalytical Notes," c. 1939, Beinecke). One of his biggest worries was the size of his penis, which he considered too long.

53 "didn't matter": EM to Arthur Ficke, Aug. 1921, Beinecke.

53 "I don't know": Arthur Ficke to EM, Aug. 15, 1921, Beinecke.

53 "dirty little Gladys": Arthur Ficke to Gladys Brown, Aug. 8, 1921, Beinecke.

53 "never have, and never could": Arthur Ficke to Gladys Brown, Oct. 5, 1922, Beinecke.

54 "This place": Quoted in Joseph Bryan III, "Funny Man," *Saturday Evening Post*, Oct. 7, 1939.

55 "My husband": DP to Thomas Masson, c. 1922, George Horace Lorimer Papers, Historical Society of Pennsylvania, quoted in Marion Meade, *Dorothy Parker: What Fresh Hell Is This?* (New York: Villard, 1988), 89.

55 "it's really not so rotten": George Horace Lorimer to DP, June 14, 1921, Lorimer Papers.

55 "Why, Ednaaaa": Quoted in Gilbert, *Ferber*, 340.

56 "A story about old maids": EF, *The Girls* (Garden City, N.Y.: Doubleday, Page, 1921), 3.

56 Ferber and children: Edna considered child care as "exciting as a treadmill." She saw babies as "pink healthy lumps," potbellied creatures who needed

bottles stuffed into their mouths at intervals (*So Big* [New York: Perennial Classics, 2000], 216). Older children held little attraction either, although she would be an affectionate aunt to her sister's offspring.

56 "flashily written": *Dial*, Jan. 1922.

57 "I would like to hear": EF to Paul Reynolds, Dec. 23, 1921, Columbia. The agent representing Ferber's first novel, *Dawn O'Hara*, was Flora May Holly.

57 "Ten per cent": EF to Paul Reynolds, Dec. 26, 1921, Columbia.

57 "Whisk it": EF to Paul Reynolds, Dec. 29, 1921, Columbia.

57 "A great party": Franklin P. Adams, *The Diary of Our Own Samuel Pepys, 1911–1925* (New York: Simon and Schuster, 1935), 1:299.

58 "a most embarrassing position": Heywood Hale Broun, *Whose Little Boy Are You? A Memoir of the Broun Family* (New York: St. Martin's, 1983), 73.

58 "Why don't you two": Heywood Hale Broun interview.

59 "a nice quiet boy": Marc Connelly and Ruth Goodman Goetz interviews.

THREE: ᢆ 1922

60 "a shred of sunlight": EM to Arthur Ficke, Jan. 24, 1922, *Letters of Edna St. Vincent Millay* (New York: Harper & Brothers, 1952), 143.

61 Millay's finances: In 1921 *Vanity Fair* paid her eleven hundred dollars for the Nancy Boyd satires. The publication of *Second April* boosted her reputation but added nothing to her bank account, and Mitchell Kennerley, the mom-and-pop-type publisher who had also issued *Renascence and Other Poems* in 1917, was in financial difficulties. Doing business with his company became increasingly frustrating because authors could not get their phone calls returned.

61 *Hardigut*: Millay's idea puzzled Sinclair Lewis, who met her in Rome that fall. Why would anyone write a novel that might be suppressed? Edna, he reported to his publishers, "thinks very well of herself—sweet, pretty & loves Edna" (Sinclair Lewis to Alfred Harcourt and Donald Brace, Dec. 1, 1921, *From Main Street to Stockholm: Letters of Sinclair Lewis, 1919–1930* [New York: Harcourt, Brace, 1952], 89).

61 "No, dearest": Arthur Ficke to EM, Dec. 12, 1921, Beinecke.

62 "You will let me": EM to Witter Bynner, Dec. 23, 1922, *Letters*, 139.

62 "Yes": EM to Witter Bynner, Jan. 6, 1922, LOC.

62 "sort of engaged": EM to KM, Jan. 30, 1922, Berg.

63 "light": Arthur Ficke's gloss on his correspondence with EM, March 1922, Beinecke.

63 "nothing at all": EM to Arthur Ficke, Jan. 25, 1922, Beinecke.

63 "a coward": Witter Bynner to EM, Jan. 19, 1922, LOC.

63 "Oh, Lord": EM to Witter Bynner, Feb. 22, 1922, *Letters*, 146. The marriage hoax was not Ficke and Bynner's first prank. In 1916 they were responsible for a

literary spoof in which they invented an experimental school of poetry called Spectra. It was the kind of silliness they both enjoyed.

64 Father story: FSF, "The Baby Party," in *All the Sad Young Men* (New York: Scribner's, 1926), 209.

65 "matronly and rather fat": EW to Stanley Dell, March 25, 1922, Edmund Wilson, *Letters on Literature and Politics, 1912–1972* (New York: Farrar, Straus and Giroux, 1977), 78.

65 "blubberingly sentimental": *Bookman*, Feb. 1922.

65 "absolutely perfect": ZSF, "Friend Husband's Latest," *New York Tribune*, April 2, 1922.

66 "business methods": ZSF, "Eulogy on the Flapper," *Metropolitan*, June 1922.

67 "dirty panderer": Cora Millay, autobiographical fragment, quoted in Nancy Milford, *Savage Beauty: The Life of Edna St. Vincent Millay* (New York: Random House, 2001), 235–36.

67 "mummie": EM to NM, May 11, 1922, *Letters*, 152.

68 "almost an orgasm": Milford, *Savage Beauty*, 236.

68 "snake-headed fish": Ibid., 237.

69 "child-like": Ibid., 236.

69 "a bad time": Cora Millay to KM, July 1, 1922, Berg.

69 Vincent's abortion: Cora Millay's recipes for inducing abortion dated back to colonial America, when women gathered herbs from gardens or woods. Throughout the nineteenth century, abortion (before "quickening" in the fourth month) was common, inexpensive, and legal, with pills ordered by mail. By 1900 abortions had been outlawed except when a woman's life was in danger and in cases of rape, incest, or a deformed fetus, but illegal abortions continued. In the 1920s self-induced or knitting-needle abortions carried significant risks, but safe "therapeutic" abortions were easily available to middle- or upper-class white women who would request D & Cs or pills from their doctors.

70 Memories of Edwin Pond Parker: Marc Connelly and Ruth Goodman Goetz interviews.

71 "That would be the last": DP, "Such a Pretty Little Picture," *Smart Set*, Dec. 1922.

72 "What a perfect world": Ben Hecht, *A Child of the Century* (New York: Simon and Schuster, 1954), 365.

72 "God damn New Yorker": Ben Hecht, *Charlie: The Improbable Life and Times of Charles MacArthur* (New York: Harper & Brothers, 1957), 77.

73 "a machine-gun nest": Ibid., 99.

73 "tips of castles": ZSF, "The Changing Beauty of Park Avenue," *The Collected Writings of Zelda Fitzgerald* (Tuscaloosa: University of Alabama Press, 1997), 404.

74 "or whether they hired": John Dos Passos, *The Best Times* (New York: New American Library, 1966), 128.

74 "elongated squirrel": ZSF to C. O. Kalman, Oct. 1922, PUL.

75 "nobody's goddamn business": Dos Passos, *Best Times*, 128.

75 "embalmed": ZSF to Xandra Kalman, c. Nov. 1923, "Zelda: A Worksheet," *Paris Review* (Fall 1983), 217.

75 "out on his feet": Dos Passos, *Best Times*, 129.

76 "good looking hair": John Dos Passos interview with Nancy Milford, quoted in Milford, *Zelda* (New York: Harper & Row, 1970); 93. Six years before he died, Dos Passos told Milford that he had found Zelda's physical presence repellant and her conversation as frightening as peering into "a dark abyss." In his own autobiography he claimed that his first meeting with Zelda, particularly the Ferris wheel ride, convinced him of "a basic fissure in her mental processes."

76 "nifty little Babbit": ZSF to C. O. and Xandra Kalman, Oct. 13, 1922, PUL.

76 "more than people": Sinclair Lewis, *Babbitt* (New York: Penguin Signet Classic, 1991), 6.

76 "the wildest confusion": ZSF to C. O. and Xandra Kalman, Oct. 1922, *Paris Review*, 217.

77 "social sewer": Quoted in André Le Vot, *F. Scott Fitzgerald* (Garden City, N.Y.: Doubleday, 1983), 122.

77 "very drunken town": FSF to C. O. Kalman, c. Nov. 17, 1923, *Correspondence of F. Scott Fitzgerald* (New York: Random House, 1980), 135.

77 "rich forever": FSF to Maxwell Perkins, Aug. 12, 1922, *Dear Scott/Dear Max: The Fitzgerald-Perkins Correspondence* (New York: Scribner's, 1971), 62. Scott borrowed heavily against future earnings. On publication of *The Beautiful and Damned*, he owed Scribner's fifty-six hundred dollars, not an extraordinary amount for a company to advance a popular author, but the very fact of the debt was ominous, because it meant he could not live on his income. Turning Scribner's into his personal cash cow, he became a sort of literary con man with a clever shell game that allowed him to spend what he did have and then what he did not. Requesting money he would be earning a year or two hence meant, however, always producing a new book to wipe out the debt and never failing to deliver on time, a game liable to blow up in his face.

78 "a real home": EF to Fanny Butcher, quoted in Butcher, *Many Lives—One Love* (New York: Harper & Row, 1972), 343.

78 "this wonderful place": EF quoted in Julie Goldsmith Gilbert, *Ferber: A Biography* (Garden City, N.Y.: Doubleday, 1978), 390–91.

78 "fresh from the factory": Butcher, *Many Lives*, 342.

78 "my own darling place": Ibid., 343.

79 "soused": EF quoted in Gilbert, *Ferber*, 397.

79 "thick rich enamel": EF, *A Peculiar Treasure* (New York: Doubleday, Doran, 1939), 275.

79 "silk stockings": Ibid.

80 "but she had health": EF, *So Big* (Garden City, N.Y.: Doubleday, 1924), 166.

81 "jade and burgundy": Ibid.

81 "He wants a peanut": Heywood Hale Broun, *Whose Little Boy Are You? A Memoir of the Broun Family* (New York: St. Martin's, 1983), 22.

82 "they didn't drink": Allen Saalburg interview.

82 "Doctor Sunshine": Refers to a popular abortionist. However, there were many Doctor Sunshines.

82 "Judas": Marc Connelly interview.

82 Please cheer up: Marc Connelly and Allen Saalburg interviews.

83 "as tough as a muffin": Marc Connelly interview.

FOUR: ∾ 1923

85 "high bright gaiety": Franklin P. Adams, *The Diary of Our Own Samuel Pepys, 1911–1925* (New York: Simon and Schuster, 1935), 1:382.

85 "considerable recklessness": Edmund Wilson, *The Shores of Light: A Literary Chronicle of the Twenties and Thirties* (New York: Farrar, Straus and Young, 1952), 771.

85 Crohn's disease: Symptoms of the disorder, an abnormality of the immune system, include severe abdominal pain, diarrhea, and constipation from intestinal blockage.

85 "[b]eautifully": EM to Horace Liveright, Nov. 1922, *Letters of Edna St. Vincent Millay* (New York: Harper & Brothers, 1952), 167.

86 "a rich amiable": EW to John Bishop, June 20, 1923, Edmund Wilson, *Letters on Literature and Politics, 1912–1972* (New York: Farrar, Straus and Giroux, 1977), 106.

86 "It's nice here": Quoted in Sally Ashley, *F.P.A.: The Life and Times of Franklin Pierce Adams* (New York: Beaufort Books, 1986), 170. No source cited.

87 "You were so right": Arthur Ficke to EM, c. March 1923, unpostmarked letter addressed to 156 Waverly Place, quoted in Daniel Mark Epstein, *What Lips My Lips Have Kissed* (New York: Henry Holt, 2001), 134–35.

88 "I slashed my wrists": Jane Grant, *Ross, the New Yorker, and Me* (New York: Reynal, 1968), 120.

88 "setback": Ibid.

89 "a great deal of prodding": Ibid., 121.

89 "the homeliest man": Ibid., 21.

90 "Never mind the floss": Bennett Cerf interview, Columbia Oral History Collection.

91 "just like a boy": Grant, *Ross*, 183.

92 "it was apparent": Floyd Dell, *Homecoming: An Autobiography* (New York: Farrar & Rinehart, 1933), 308.

92 "opera-going": Max Eastman, *Enjoyment of Living* (New York: Harper, 1948), 324.

92 "How long": Inez Milholland memorial service notes, 1917, LOC.

92 "Shall I come with you": Eastman, *Enjoyment of Living*, 572.

93 Eugen Boissevain and Carl Jung: Max Eastman, in his autobiography *Enjoyment of Living*, states that Gene had been "psychoanalyzed by Dr. Jung in Zurich" (521). However, there is no record of any treatment with Jung, nor does Boissevain's name appear in the indexes of the Kristine Mann Library, C. G. Jung Center of New York.

93 "about everything": Max Eastman, *Great Companions: Critical Memoirs of Some Famous Friends* (New York: Farrar, Straus and Cudahy, 1959), 91.

94 "walking-stick": Arthur Ficke shopping list, summer 1923, Beinecke.

94 "Aren't you glad": Arthur Ficke to KM, June 12, 1923, Berg.

95 "I love him": EM to Cora Millay, May 30, 1923, *Letters*, 174.

95 "bully good husband": NM to Cora Millay, c. July 1923, LOC.

95 "our Ed St. Bincent": Ibid.

95 "I'm going to kill": Anita Loos, *Kiss Hollywood Good-by* (New York: Viking, 1974), 122.

96 "the heroine": "What a 'Flapper Novelist' Thinks of His Wife," *Louisville Courier-Journal*, Sept. 30, 1923.

98 "I'm not marrying": Quoted in Nancy Milford, *Savage Beauty: The Life of Edna St. Vincent Millay* (New York: Random House, 2001), 254.

98 "I shall be immortal": Quoted in Miriam Gurko, *Restless Spirit: The Life of Edna St. Vincent Millay* (New York: Crowell, 1962), 155. No source cited.

98 "cut holes": EM to KM, Aug. 8, 1923, Berg.

99 "bored to death": KM to Howard Young, Oct. 17, 1923, Berg.

99 "a lot of fun": KM to EB, c. 1941, Berg.

99 "a nice strong healthy man": Ibid.

101 "Five hundred dollars": Nathaniel Benchley, *Robert Benchley* (New York: McGraw-Hill, 1955), 159.

101 "Very inferior": Edmund Wilson, *The Twenties* (New York: Farrar, Straus and Giroux, 1975), 47.

101 "Thick ankles": Ibid., 345.

102 "For God's sake": FSF to Maxwell Perkins, Nov. 5, 1923, *Dear Scott/Dear Max: The Fitzgerald-Perkins Correspondence* (New York: Scribner's, 1971), 68.

103 Critical reaction to *The Vegetable*: "Drivel," wrote Ben Hecht reviewing the published play (*Chicago Literary Times*, June 1, 1923). A lack of talent for writing dialogue was not the problem. Instead of creating real characters, Scott

was more interested in devising rafts to float his ideas about the stupidity of politics. He believed any idiot could become President, a theme similar to one that George S. Kaufman and Morrie Ryskind—and the Gershwins—would turn into *Of Thee I Sing* eight years later.

103 "careless people": FSF, *The Great Gatsby* (New York: Simon and Schuster, 1995), 187.

103 "terribly disappointed": ZSF to Xandra Kalman, Nov. 1923, PUL.

104 "a complete flop": FSF to Harold Ober, c. Feb. 5, 1924, *As Ever, Scott Fitz—Letters between F. Scott Fitzgerald and His Literary Agent, Harold Ober, 1919–1940* (London: Woburn, 1973), 59.

104 "going out the door": John Bishop to EW, Nov. 10, 1929, quoted in Elizabeth Spindler, *John Peale Bishop: A Biography* (Morgantown: West Virginia University Library, 1980), 152.

105 "a swine": EM to EW, Jan. 8, 1924, *Letters*, 179.

105 "irresponsible": EW to John Bishop, Jan. 15, 1924, *Letters*, 118.

105 "a very nice honest fellow": Ibid.

106 "for which she longed": John Bishop to EW, c. 1924, Wilson Papers, Beinecke.

106 "popular and happy": EF to Fannie Ferber Fox, c. Dec. 1923, quoted in Julie Goldsmith Gilbert, *Ferber: A Biography* (Garden City, N.Y.: Doubleday, 1978), 396.

106 "as low hearted": Adams, *Diary*, 1:442.

106 "I am a confirmed admirer": Ibid., 444.

FIVE: ∾ 1924

109 "when I have none": Franklin P. Adams, *The Diary of Our Own Samuel Pepys, 1911–1925* (New York: Simon and Schuster, 1935), 1:450.

109 "genuflect in homage": *New York Tribune*, March 16, 1924.

109 "a novel to read": *New York Times*, Feb. 24, 1924.

110 "Call me up": EB to KM, Feb. 5, 1924, Berg.

110 "it comes up for air": EM to EB, Jan. 1924, *Letters of Edna St. Vincent Millay* (New York: Harper & Brothers, 1952), 181.

111 "Tell as many people": EB to KM, Feb. 5, 1924, Berg.

111 "lamb chops and money": EF to Aleck Woollcott, c. 1923, Houghton. Millay did not reciprocate Ferber's admiration. She belittled Ferber's writing and even joked about changing her name to avoid confusion (EM to Esther Root, May 1927, *Letters*, 219; EM to George Dillon, 1936, ibid., 275).

111 "with too little variation": Adams, *Diary*, 1:458.

112 "whistles around": KM to Howard Young, Nov. 4, 1924, Berg.

112 "of an entirely different nature": *Portland Sunday Telegram*, Nov. 21, 1924, Berg.

113 "Shoot her": Quoted in Marc Connelly, *Voices Offstage: A Book of Memoirs* (Chicago: Holt, Rinehart & Winston, 1968), 75.

113 "Charles Dickens": Quoted in Malcolm Goldstein, *George S. Kaufman: His Life, His Theater* (New York: Oxford University Press, 1979), 103.

114 "walk with me": Quoted in Marion Meade, *Dorothy Parker: What Fresh Hell Is This?* (New York: Villard, 1988), 85.

114 "I'm fond of her": George S. Kaufman to Marc Connelly, quoted in Julie Goldsmith Gilbert, *Ferber: A Biography* (Garden City, N.Y.: Doubleday, 1978), 103.

114 "Daddy and Edna": Anne Kaufman Schneider interview.

115 "GEORGIE KAUFMAN": EF, *A Peculiar Treasure* (New York: Doubleday, Doran, 1939), 312.

115 "trash": FSF to EW, summer 1924, FSF, *A Life in Letters* (New York: Scribner's, 1994), 76.

116 "incompetency": ZSF to EW, June 1924, Beinecke.

116 "wonderful": FSF to Thomas Boyd, May 1924, *Correspondence of F. Scott Fitzgerald* (New York: Random House, 1980), 141.

117 "had never really accepted": FSF, *The Great Gatsby* (New York: Simon and Schuster, 1995), 104.

117 "the best American novel": FSF to Maxwell Perkins, Aug. 27, 1924, FSF, *Life in Letters*, 80.

118 "quite alone": ZSF to EW, June 1924, Beinecke.

118 "bronze and smelled of the sand": ZSF, *Save Me the Waltz*, in *The Collected Writings of Zelda Fitzgerald* (Tuscaloosa: University of Alabama Press, 1997), 86. According to Edouard Jozan's daughter, Martine Jozan Work, he was five feet eight with light brown hair and brown eyes, "a very daring person who loved adventure and always pushed the limits." When various writers queried Jozan about the Fitzgeralds in the 1960s, he had mostly forgotten them. What he did remember was Zelda's intelligence and beauty and Scott's vulgarity and drinking. Other biographical information on Edouard Jozan was supplied by the Service Historique de la Marine and the Association pour la Recherche de Documentation sur l'Histoire de l'Aéronautique Navale. Chase pilots provide support for other aircraft during flight training or testing.

119 "make a pass": John Dos Passos, *The Best Times* (New York: New American Library, 1966), 130.

119 "sit around": Taped interview with Zelda and Scott Fitzgerald, May 28, 1933, by Dr. Thomas Rennie, Henry Phipps Psychiatric Clinic of Johns Hopkins University, F. Scott Fitzgerald Papers, PUL.

119 Scott's sexual problems: His weak libido probably had more to do with his drinking than with his penis size, because problems with erection, impotence, and premature ejaculation generally accompany alcohol abuse. The Paris brasserie

incident is recounted in Ernest Hemingway to Harvey Breit, Aug. 18, 1954, *Ernest Hemingway, Selected Letters, 1917–1961* (New York: Scribner, 1981), 834.

120 "I was locked": ZSF, autobiographical essay, summer 1930, quoted in Nancy Milford, *Zelda* (New York: Harper & Row, 1970), 174.

120 "Big Crisis": FSF, *F. Scott Fitzgerald's Ledger: A Facsimile*, ed. Matthew Bruccoli (Washington, D.C.: NCR/Microcard Editions, A Bruccoli Clark Book, 1972), 178.

120 "no one I liked": FSF to ZSF, summer 1930, *Dear Scott, Dearest Zelda: The Love Letters of F. Scott and Zelda Fitzgerald*, ed. Jackson R. Bryer and Cathy W. Barks (New York: St. Martin's, 2002), 62.

121 "getting brown": FSF, *Ledger*, July 1924, 178.

121 "Give me a cigarette": Gilbert Seldes interview with Nancy Milford, quoted in *Zelda*, 111.

121 "germs of bitterness": ZSF, *Save Me the Waltz*, in *Collected Writings*, 95.

122 "horribly sick": ZSF to FSF, summer/fall 1930, *Correspondence of F. Scott Fitzgerald*, 247.

122 "the year of Zelda's sickness": FSF, *Ledger*, 179.

122 "you took what you wanted": ZSF, *Save Me the Waltz*, in *Collected Writings*, 94.

122 "plodding along": EF interview, unidentified clipping, c. 1932, TC/LC.

123 "What's a show boat": EF, *Peculiar Treasure*, 288.

123 "vile": FSF to Maxwell Perkins, c. Aug. 25, 1924, *Dear Scott/Dear Max: The Fitzgerald-Perkins Correspondence* (New York: Scribner's, 1971), 76.

123 "the most popular": Maxwell Perkins to FSF, Sept. 10, 1924, ibid., 77.

123 *So Big* sales figures: *New York Times*, May 1, 1925. The novel was filmed three times: in 1924 with Colleen Moore in the role of Selina Peake, in 1932 with Barbara Stanwyck, and in 1953 with Jane Wyman.

123 Scott's disparaging remarks about Ferber's work: FSF to Maxwell Perkins, in *Dear Scott/Dear Max*, January 10, 1920, p. 25; August 25, 1924, p. 76; December 20, 1924, p. 89. FSF to Maxwell Perkins in *A Life in Letters*, June 1, 1925, p. 118–19.

124 "peter out": EF quoted in Gilbert, *Ferber*, 297.

124 "Effendi": The exotic nickname was coined by Rudyard Kipling, on the basis of Frank Nelson Doubleday's initials, F.N.D., and happened to suit his outsize personality. In the Middle East the word "effendi" is a title of respect for a man of property and authority.

124 "sing it": William Allen White to Frank N. Doubleday, Jan. 27, 1925, quoted in Gilbert, *Ferber*, 385.

125 "Angel Child": *Autobiography of William Allen White* (New York: Macmillan, 1946), 463.

125 Previous bestselling Pulitzer winners: *His Family* (1918) by Ernest Poole and *The Age of Innocence* (1921) by Edith Wharton.

126 "pleased": EF to Flora May Holly, May 5, 1925, University of Delaware, Flora May Holly Papers.

126 "after having had her nose straightened": *New York Times*, May 1, 1925. The literary establishment would continue to overlook Ferber. In *Exile's Return: A Literary Odyssey of the 1920s* (New York: Viking, 1951), the critic Malcolm Cowley omitted her from his account of important American writers. In the 1950s *The Paris Review* began conducting interviews for its *Writers at Work* series but apparently did not find her worthy of inclusion.

126 *Minick* reviews: *New York World*, Sept. 25, 1924; *New York Sun*, Sept. 25, 1924. Burns Mantle selected *Minick* for inclusion in *The Best Plays of 1923–24*. It was filmed three times: *Welcome Home* (1925), *The Expert* (1932), and *No Place to Go* (1939).

127 "My name is Edna": EF, *Peculiar Treasure*, 290.

128 "a small cluck": DP interview, Columbia Oral History Collection.

128 "the worst fuck": Ruth Goodman Goetz interview.

128 "CLOSE HARMONY DID A COOL": DP to Robert Benchley, quoted in Alexander Woollcott, *The Portable Woollcott* (New York: Viking, 1946), 186.

SIX: ∾ 1925

129 "a ruin of thickets": Maxwell Perkins to FSF, Aug. 8, 1924, *Dear Scott/Dear Max: The Fitzgerald-Perkins Correspondence* (New York: Scribner's, 1971), 75.

130 "In God's name": Alexander Woollcott, *The Portable Woollcott* (New York: Viking, 1946), 188.

130 "Does anybody but myself": Heywood Hale Broun, *Whose Little Boy Are You? A Memoir of the Broun Family* (New York: St. Martin's, 1983), 48.

131 "as little ladies do": DP, *The Portable Dorothy Parker* (New York: Penguin, 1976), 103.

132 "these amusing": Raoul Fleischmann, untitled reminiscence, *New Yorker* Records.

132 "Sunday February 15": Franklin P. Adams, *The Diary of Our Own Samuel Pepys, 1911–1925* (New York: Simon and Schuster, 1935), 1:505.

133 "It is difficult": Jane Grant, *Ross, the New Yorker, and Me* (New York: Reynal, 1968), 221.

133 "a skirt": Ibid., 187–88.

135 "Pink marabou": Adams, *Diary*, 1:516.

135 "She's such a nice girl": Alvan Barach interview with James Gaines.

135 "Ah, look, Harold": DP to Harold Ross, n.d., *New Yorker* Records.

135 "happier than her happiest": William Allen White, *World's Work*, June 1930.

135 "not a single one": Garson Kanin, *Hollywood* (New York: Viking, 1974), 284.

137 "a nice gentlemanly mortgage": EM to Cora Millay, June 22, 1925, *Letters of Edna St. Vincent Millay* (New York: Harper & Brothers, 1952), 195.

138 "nearly daft in the bean": Ibid.

138 "swell": FSF to EW, spring 1925, FSF, *The Crack-Up*, ed. Edmund Wilson (New York: New Directions, 1945), 271.

138 "genuine Louis XV": Sara Mayfield, *Exiles from Paradise* (New York: Delacorte, 1971), 110.

139 "It was all": Ernest Hemingway, *A Moveable Feast* (New York: Scribner, 1964), 148.

141 "great trip": Ernest Hemingway to Maxwell Perkins, June 9, 1925, *Ernest Hemingway, Selected Letters, 1917–1961* (New York: Scribner, 1981), 162.

141 Hemingway's recollections of the luncheon at 14, rue de Tilsitt: See *A Moveable Feast*, 177–84. He evidently wrote two versions of the occasion but discarded the more favorable one.

142 "worth seeing": Ernest Hemingway to Gertrude Stein and Alice Toklas, quoted in James Mellow, *Hemingway: A Life without Consequences* (Boston: Houghton Mifflin, 1992), 291.

142 "very handsome": FSF to Gertrude Stein, June 1925, FSF, *A Life in Letters* (New York: Scribner's, 1994), 115.

143 "I never saw her look": EM to Cora Millay, May 10, 1925, *Letters*, 192.

143 "rafts of caviar": Ibid.

143 "putting your car": James Thurber, *The Years with Ross* (Boston: Little, Brown, 1959), 69.

144 "not just crazy": Rebecca West interview with Stanley Olson, in Olson, *Elinor Wylie: A Life Apart: A Biography* (New York: Dial Press, 1979), 258.

144 "fragile china deer": William Rose Benét, "The Dust Which Is God," in ibid., 163.

144 "I just couldn't imagine": Arthur Ficke interview with Stanley Olson, in ibid., 251.

145 "life and death": Ibid.

145 "perfectly terrible": Ibid.

145 "unfortunate affair": Ring Lardner to FSF, Aug. 8, 1925, *Correspondence of F. Scott Fitzgerald* (New York: Random House, 1980), 176.

146 "constantly cock-eyed": Ibid.

146 "after her all hours": Ruth Goodman Goetz interview.

147 "forever": EM to Frances Shapli, July 1, 1925, Berg.

147 "Our home": EB to Arthur and Gladys Ficke, 1925, Beinecke.

147 "Very little gin": EM to Millay family, July 28, 1925, *Letters*, 195.

148 Snow White opera: An operatic version of the Snow White fairy tale, *Schneewittchen*, was completed by the Swiss musician Heinz Holliger in 1998.

148 "six workmen": EM to Cora Millay, Aug. 20, 1925, *Letters*, 100.

149 "the big nigger Julia": EM to Millay family, July 28, 1925, Berg; edited version in *Letters*, 195.

149 "doubtful": Maxwell Perkins to FSF, April 20, 1925, *Dear Scott/Dear Max*, 101.

149 "extraordinary": Maxwell Perkins to FSF, April 25, 1925, ibid., 102.

149 Notable novels of 1925: Dreiser's *An American Tragedy*, Woolf's *Mrs. Dalloway*, Glasgow's *Barren Ground*, Mann's *Death in Venice*, Loos's *Gentlemen Prefer Blondes*, Stein's *The Making of Americans*, Dos Passos's *Manhattan Transfer*.

149 "I'm not depressed": FSF to Harold Ober, May 28, 1925, *As Ever, Scott Fitz—Letters between F. Scott Fitzgerald and His Literary Agent, Harold Ober, 1919–1940* (London: Woburn, 1973), 78.

150 *Gatsby* reviews: *New York World*, April 13, 1925; *New York Times*, April 19, 1925; *New York Herald Tribune*, April 19, 1925; *Brooklyn Daily Eagle*, April 18, 1925.

150 "new book": Ruth Hale quoted in A. Scott Berg, *Max Perkins, Editor of Genius* (New York: E.P. Dutton, 1978), 106.

150 "1000 parties": FSF, *F. Scott Fitzgerald's Ledger: A Facsimile*, ed. Matthew Bruccoli (Washington, D.C.: NCR/Microcard Editions, A Bruccoli Clark Book, 1972), 179.

150 "There were Americans": ZSF, *Save Me the Waltz*, in *The Collected Writings of Zelda Fitzgerald* (Tuscaloosa: University of Alabama Press, 1997), 99.

152 "remarkable things": ZSF, "Caesar's Things," PUL.

153 "If you drink too much": ZSF quoted in Nancy Milford, *Zelda* (New York: Harper & Row, 1970), 111. Source is Calvin Tomkins's letter to Nancy Milford, Jan. 4, 1966. According to Gerald and Sara Murphy's belated recollections, twenty-five years later to Calvin Tomkins for a *New Yorker* article, this mishap took place in 1924. But the year was actually 1925, as dated by Zelda's own statement only five years later (ZSF to FSF, c. summer/fall 1930, Prangins), plus Scott's notation in his *Ledger* (p. 179) for August 1925 ("Zelda drugged"). Zelda identified the drug as Dial, but that brand of allobarbital was not manufactured until 1927; the product she took must have been similar, however. Some writers have interpreted the overdose as an attempted suicide, but there is no basis to see it as anything other than a simple accident, most likely caused by a cross-reaction between a powerful barbiturate and alcohol.

153 "Zelda and me": FSF to Maxwell Perkins, Aug. 28, 1925, *Dear Scott/Dear Max*, 119.

153 "We were happy": Gerald Murphy to FSF and ZSF, Sept. 19, 1925, Linda Patterson Miller, *Letters from the Lost Generation: Gerald and Sara Murphy and Friends* (New Brunswick, N.J.: Rutgers University Press, 1991), 14.

154 "What are you having": DP quoted in John Keats, *You Might As Well Live* (New York: Simon and Schuster, 1970), 85.

154 "Oh, Dorothy": Johnny Weaver, quoted in Peggy Wood interview with James Gaines.

154 "almost illiterate": *New York Herald Tribune*, Oct. 13, 1963.

154 "never read anything": *Esquire*, Sept. 1959.

154 "I thought": Thurber, *Years with Ross*, 17.

155 "the worms slip by": DP, "Epitaph," in *Portable Dorothy Parker*, 79.

155 "crushed her": DP, "Big Blonde," in ibid., 209.

155 "psychosomatic medicine": Alvan Barach interview with James Gaines.

155 "a lot of tender expectancies": Ibid.

156 "cheap people": DP to Seward Collins, March 22, 1927, Beinecke.

157 "If you don't stop": Robert Benchley quoted in James R. Gaines, *Wit's End: Days and Nights of the Algonquin Round Table* (New York: Harcourt Brace Jovanovich, 1977), 116.

SEVEN: ∞ 1926

158 "nothing serious at all": EM to Cora Millay, Aug. 20, 1925, *Letters of Edna St. Vincent Millay* (New York: Harper & Brothers, 1952), 200.

159 "What is the good": EB to Arthur and Gladys Ficke, n.d. 1925, Beinecke.

159 "way down in the mouth": EB to Arthur and Gladys Ficke, Dec. 30, 1925, Beinecke.

159 "roaringly, indecently": EB to Arthur and Gladys Ficke, Dec. 1925, Beinecke.

160 "my sick poet": EB to Arthur and Gladys Ficke, Nov. 4, 1925, Beinecke. Millay's headaches remained undiagnosed. Headaches may have dozens of causes, including food allergies, sinusitis, stress, constipation, anemia, brain disorders, hypertension, and bowel problems, but victims of chronic pain are also known to suffer from psychological problems and personality disorders.

160 "curse": EB to Arthur and Gladys Ficke, Dec. 30, 1925, Beinecke.

160 "a m. of the b.": EM to Arthur and Gladys Ficke, Jan. 2, 1926, Beinecke.

160 "is gaining strength": Cora Millay to KM, Feb. 4, 1926, Berg.

161 "unerring sense of selection": DP, *New Yorker*, Oct. 29, 1927.

162 "God, what a night": Edmund Wilson, *The Twenties* (New York: Farrar, Straus and Giroux, 1975), 346.

162 "She is quite all right": Robert Benchley to Gertrude Benchley, Feb. 1926, Mugar.

162 "He said it was funny": Ernest Hemingway to Louis and Mary Bromfield, March 8, 1926, *Ernest Hemingway, Selected Letters, 1917–1961* (New York: Scribner, 1981), 195.

163 "the *only* thing in life": Seward Collins, college essay, Feb. 1920, Seward Collins Papers, Beinecke.

163 "leaped around like a flea": Burton Rascoe, *We Were Interrupted* (Garden City, N.Y.: Doubleday, 1947), 160.

164 "extremely sensitive": Seward Collins to Havelock Ellis, 1926, Beinecke.

164 "Bullfighting, bullslinging": Sara Mayfield, *Exiles from Paradise* (New York: Delacorte, 1971), 114.

165 "Ernest, don't you think": Ernest Hemingway, *A Moveable Feast* (New York: Scribner, 1964), 184.

165 *Gatsby* the play: The dramatic adaptation of *The Great Gatsby* opened on Broadway on February 2, 1926, with James Rennie in the title role, and ran 112 performances.

166 Sara Murphy's corn: John Dos Passos, *The Best Times* (New York: New American Library, 1966), 149.

166 "the great unhappiness": ZSF, "Caesar's Things," PUL.

166 "the oldest trick": Hemingway, *Moveable Feast*, 207.

167 "I hope you die": Calvin Tomkins, *Living Well Is the Best Revenge* (New York: Viking, 1971), 121. Games like ringer were played in a ten-foot-diameter ring with thirteen marbles arranged in the center of a cross.

168 "July 21, 1926": EM to KM, July 21, 1926, Berg.

168 "everyone gets up": NM to KM, July 1926, Berg.

169 "terribly sorry": EM to KM, Sept. 5, 1921, Berg.

169 "I hate to bother you": Tom Smith to Seward Collins, June 17, 1926, Beinecke.

170 "one of you is lying": DP, "Unfortunate Coincidence," in *The Portable Dorothy Parker* (New York: Penguin, 1976), 96.

171 "Tell her": Tom Smith to Seward Collins, June 29, 1926, Beinecke.

171 "Everyone seems to be": Tom Smith to Seward Collins, Aug. 27, 1926, Beinecke.

171 "so I went": *New Yorker*, Sept. 8, 1927.

171 "Why, that dog": "Toward the Dog Days," *McCall's*, May 1928.

172 "Time doth flit": Allen Saalburg interview.

172 "My Sewie": DP to Seward Collins, various correspondence, 1926–1927, Beinecke.

172 "Understand now": Edwin Pond Parker to DP, Nov. 3, 1926, Beinecke.

172 "counteracts all the acid": EF to Aleck Woollcott, July 8, 1926, Houghton.

173 "In the evening": EF, *Show Boat* (Garden City, N.Y.: Doubleday, 1926), 303.

173 "only too glad": *New York Times*, Sept. 3 and 4, 1926.

174 "your answer was negative": EF to Nelson Doubleday, Sept. 1926, quoted in Julie Goldsmith Gilbert, *Ferber: A Biography* (Garden City, N.Y.: Doubleday, 1978), 378. Ferber continued to be a Doubleday author the rest of her life, but the relationship remained contentious. When the house wanted to sign an au-

thor who shared her last name, she went off the deep end. Her editor feared she might "disappear in smoke." With no way to calm her, Ken McCormick allowed the conflagration to subside naturally. He decided the screaming must have constituted "her sex life." Even by the standards of literary prima donnas, Edna's outbursts could be frightening (Columbia Oral History Collection).

174 "Sue and be damned": EF, *A Peculiar Treasure* (New York: Doubleday, Doran, 1939), 309.

174 "She never saw him again": EF, *Show Boat*, 364.

175 "Oh King": EB to Arthur and Gladys Ficke, Sept. 11, 1926, Beinecke.

175 "Were there ever": EB to Arthur Ficke, Jan. 1, 1927, Beinecke.

175 "who more sincerely": Arthur Ficke gloss on EB letter to Arthur and Gladys Ficke, Dec. 30, 1925, Beinecke.

176 "thrilling": EM to Cora Millay, Dec. 6, 1926, *Letters*, 211.

176 "pinkey-pink cocktails": EB to Arthur Ficke, November 1925, Beinecke.

176 "too long": Arthur Ficke, "Psychoanalytical Notes," c. 1939, Beinecke.

176 "I took some pictures": Ibid.

176 "normal, natural attractions": Arthur Ficke, "Journal Notes," Aug. 4, 1941, Beinecke.

177 "utterly ridiculous": Arthur Ficke gloss on letter from EB, Dec. 1925, Beinecke.

177 "impossible": Arthur Ficke biographical fragment about Millay, 1922, Beinecke.

177 "I have calmed her": KM to Howard Young, Oct. 7, 1926 (misdated Oct. 7, 1924), Berg.

177 "Pray for Ugin": EB to Arthur Ficke, Feb. 1, 1926, Beinecke.

178 "naked and abandoned": EB to Arthur Ficke, Aug. 9, 1926, Beinecke.

178 "We love you and Jesus": EB to Arthur and Gladys Ficke, Dec. 1925, Beinecke.

178 "Good God, and good Devil": EB to Arthur and Gladys Ficke, Nov. 1925, Beinecke.

178 "being together": KM to Howard Young, Oct. 7, 1926, Berg.

178 "to my first grandchile": Cora Millay to KM, Nov. 2, 1924, Berg.

178 "the swellest person": Seward Collins's account of the breakup is given in a letter to Parker's sister Helen Droste, Nov. 1926, Beinecke. Eventually the Cartier watch wound up with Helen and became a family heirloom.

179 "sweetness and sympathy": DP to Ernest Hemingway, Nov. 3, 1926, quoted in Michael Reynolds, *Hemingway: The Paris Years* (New York: Norton, 1999), 83.

180 "Oh thou": Ernest Hemingway, *88 Poems* (New York: Harcourt Brace Jovanovich, 1979), 87.

180 "viciously unfair": Donald Ogden Stewart, *By a Stroke of Luck!* (New York: Paddington Press, 1975), 157.

180 "Don't hate me": DP to Seward Collins, Nov. 19, 1926, Beinecke.

180 "All writers": Franklin P. Adams, *The Diary of Our Own Samuel Pepys, 1926–1934* (New York: Simon and Schuster, 1935), 2:675.

180 "Rough": Mildred Gilman Wohlforth interview.

181 "bloated": Wilson, *Twenties*, 344.

181 "Despair in Chelsea": Marc Connelly interview.

181 "I suppose she thinks": Elinor Wylie to Nancy Hoyt, Nov. 22, 1926, Berg.

182 *Enough Rope* reviews: *New Republic*, Jan. 19 and May 11, 1927; *New York Herald Tribune*, March 27, 1927; *Bookman*, March 1927.

183 *Gatsby* the movie: Film adaptations of *The Great Gatsby* were released in 1926 (Warner Baxter), 1949 (Alan Ladd), and 1974 (Robert Redford). A TV adaptation (Toby Stephens) was broadcast in 2001.

183 "Her body hovered": FSF, *Tender Is the Night* (New York: Scribner's, 1934), 4.

183 "breakfast food": Taped interview with Zelda and Scott Fitzgerald, May 28, 1933, by Dr. Thomas Rennie, Henry Phipps Psychiatric Clinic of Johns Hopkins University, F. Scott Fitzgerald Papers, PUL.

184 "Everybody here": ZSF to Scottie Fitzgerald, n.d. 1927, PUL.

184 "unimpeachable": FSF, *This Side of Paradise* (New York: Scribner's, 1920), 159.

184 "flagrantly sentimental": ZSF to FSF, summer/fall 1930, *Correspondence of F. Scott Fitzgerald* (New York: Random House, 1980), 247.

184 Bathtub fire: Five years later Scott recalled this incident for Zelda's doctor and called it "the first appearance of definitely irrational acts." He described the burned clothing as "old." FSF to Oscar Forel, Jan. 29, 1931, FSF, *A Life in Letters* (New York: Scribner's, 1994), 204.

184 "eat you up": ZSF to Scottie Fitzgerald, c. winter 1927, PUL.

EIGHT: ∾ 1927

187 "She has been known": *New Yorker*, Feb. 12, 1927.

187 Cora Millay's grievances: Katharine Angell White interview with Nancy Milford, quoted in Milford, *Savage Beauty: The Life of Edna St. Vincent Millay* (New York: Random House, 2001), 290.

187 "oratorio clubs": *New Yorker*, April 23, 1927.

188 "A SPECIAL EFFORT": Harold Ross to Raoul Fleischmann, March 21, 1927, quoted in Ben Yagoda, *About Town: The New Yorker and the World It Made* (New York: Scribner, 2000), 203.

188 "greatest": *New Yorker*, Feb. 26, 1927.

189 "She was quite fussed": Gladys Ficke to Arthur Ficke, Feb. 1927, Beinecke.

189 "All I can say": *New York Times*, Feb. 18, 1927.

189 "disgusting": Gladys Ficke to Arthur Ficke, Feb. 1927, Beinecke.

190 *The King's Henchman* reviews: *New York Times*, Feb. 18, 1927; *New York Post*, Feb. 18, 1927.

191 "I'm not a pathetic": Edmund Wilson, *The Twenties* (New York: Farrar, Straus and Giroux, 1975), 348.

191 *The King's Henchman* sales: In its eighteenth printing by year's end, *Henchman* would become Millay's best-selling work.

191 "Oh! Jesus": EB to Arthur and Gladys Ficke, May 19–20, 1927, Beinecke.

192 "Won't you please": EM to Cora Millay, May 25, 1927, *Letters of Edna St. Vincent Millay* (New York: Harper & Brothers, 1952), 220.

192 "different from each other": ZSF to FSF, Aug. 1930, *Dear Scott, Dearest Zelda: The Love Letters of F. Scott and Zelda Fitzgerald*, ed. Jackson R. Bryer and Cathy W. Barks (New York: St. Martin's, 2002), 89.

192 "bending as graciously": ZSF, "Show Mr. and Mrs. F. to Number ———," in *The Collected Writings of Zelda Fitzgerald* (Tuscaloosa: University of Alabama Press, 1997), 425.

193 "never been very happy": ZSF to FSF, fall 1930, "Zelda: A Worksheet," *Paris Review* (Fall 1983), 231. Scott later claimed that their sexual relations in 1927 were normal but infrequent.

193 "reverse time": ZSF to FSF, Aug. 1930, *Dear Scott, Dearest Zelda*, 93.

193 Zelda Fitzgerald's 1927 articles: "The Changing Beauty of Park Avenue" appeared in *Harper's Bazaar* in January 1928. *College Humor*, in its June and October 1928 issues, respectively, published "Looking Back Eight Years," accompanied by sketches of Zelda and Scott by the prominent illustrator James Montgomery Flagg, and "Who Can Fall in Love after Thirty?" A fourth joint article was "Editorial on Youth." Commissioned by *Photoplay* for five hundred dollars but never paid for, it appeared in *The Smart Set* as "Paint and Powder" in 1929.

194 Scott's income: He sold two stories ($3,375) in 1926. The following year he wrote little until the fall, when he sold five stories (including "Jacob's Ladder" and "Magnetism") to the *Saturday Evening Post*, earning almost thirty thousand dollars for the year. Included in that amount was $5,752.06 from Scribner's as an advance against his next novel.

194 "such a mess": ZSF to Carl Van Vechten, May 27, 1927, quoted in Andrew Turnbull, *Scott Fitzgerald* (New York: Scribner's, 1962), 178.

195 "wrong and twisted": Taped interview with Zelda and Scott Fitzgerald, May 28, 1933, by Dr. Thomas Rennie, Henry Phipps Psychiatric Clinic of Johns Hopkins University, F. Scott Fitzgerald Papers, PUL. Hereafter, Rennie transcript.

195 Zelda's lack of professional skills: In the unfinished autobiographical novel "Caesar's Things," Zelda's alter ego, Janno, claims she married the Yankee

Army lieutenant because few opportunities existed for small-town Southern girls. They could either marry or become stenographers. However, in Zelda's own family women worked at various jobs. On Judge Sayre's six-thousand-dollar-a-year salary, they were far from wealthy, unable even to afford home ownership. Before marriage, Zelda's sister Marjorie taught school, and Rosalind was a reporter and society columnist for a local paper. But the idea of keeping business hours never appealed to either Zelda or her heroine Janno.

195 "You're handsome": *Bookman*, Jan. 1926.

195 "girlies": EF to Harold Ross, Nov. 28, 1933, *New Yorker* Records.

196 "a maiden lady": Marc Connelly quoted in Julie Goldsmith Gilbert, *Ferber: A Biography* (Garden City, N.Y.: Doubleday, 1978), 382.

196 "Nobody wanted": Mary Ellin Berlin Barrett interview.

196 Ferber's rejection of marriage: There is nothing whatsoever to support the idea of Edna being a lesbian, repressed or otherwise. Although she found women in general to be "stronger in character, more ingenious, more perceptive" than men (Ferber, *A Kind of Magic* [Garden City, N.Y.: Doubleday, 1963], 283), she didn't very much like her own sex. Attracted to virile men, she repeatedly wrote novels that teem with good-looking, aggressive, supermasculine heroes generally up to no good. The prototypical Ferber hero would be epitomized in *Gone with the Wind*. No Ashley Wilkeses for Edna; she preferred the Rhett Butlers.

196 "good lines": *Autobiography of William Allen White* (New York: Macmillan, 1946), 462–63.

198 "I've got to ask": Quoted in Scott Meredith, *George S. Kaufman and His Friends* (Garden City, N.Y.: Doubleday, 1974), 235. No source cited.

198 "new Wonder Boy": EF, *A Peculiar Treasure* (New York: Doubleday, Doran, 1939), 313.

198 "He'd fuck anything": Lee Schubert quoted in Martin Gottfried, *Jed Harris: The Curse of Genius* (Boston: Little, Brown, 1984), 95.

198 "a magnificent Byzantine ruin": Jed Harris, *A Dance on the High Wire: Recollections of a Time and a Temperament* (New York: Crown, 1979), 93.

198 "Like a true disciple": Ibid., 94.

199 "smelled of dried apples" and other remarks: Harris, *Dance on the High Wire*, 103–4; Gottfried, *Jed Harris*, 100. In his autobiography Harris attributed the dried-apples remark to Edna.

200 "a great deal": EF to Fannie Fox, quoted in Gilbert, *Ferber*, 371–72.

201 "a third-rate writer": Rennie transcript.

201 "blue bruises": ZSF, *Save Me the Waltz*, in *Collected Writings*, 117.

202 "whorehouse mirror": John Biggs Jr. interview, quoted in Nancy Milford, *Zelda* (New York: Harper & Row, 1970), 143.

203 "passable poet": John Dos Passos, *The Best Times* (New York: New American Library, 1966), 173.

204 "heart and soul": *New Yorker*, Dec. 10, 1927.

204 "as intimate as the rustle": DP, "Dusk before Fireworks," in *The Portable Dorothy Parker* (New York: Penguin, 1976), 135.

204 "coarse and reeking": DP to unknown correspondent, c. 1962.

204 "who looked": *New Yorker*, Feb. 11, 1928.

204 "Any chance": Harold Ross to DP, Feb. 17, 1927, *New Yorker* Records.

204 "lousy": DP to Harold Ross, Feb. 1927, *New Yorker* Records.

204 "God Bless Me": Harold Ross to DP, Feb. 26, 1927, Harold Ross, *Letters from the Editor: The New Yorker's Harold Ross*, ed. Thomas Kunkel (New York: Modern Library, 2000), 29.

205 "Please do a lot": Harold Ross to DP, May 31, 1927, *New Yorker* Records.

205 "Lady": *New Yorker*, Oct. 15, 1927.

205 DP reviews: *New Yorker*, Oct. 22 and Nov. 5, 1927.

206 "I don't give": Wolcott Gibbs, *Season in the Sun (and Other Pleasures)* (New York: Random House, 1946), vii.

206 "I'm so sorry": Wolcott Gibbs to Nathaniel Benchley, n.d., Mugar.

206 "grateful to the point": Harold Ross to DP, Nov. 21, 1927, *New Yorker* Records.

206 "I never had one damned meal": Charles McGrath, "The Ross Years," *New Yorker*, Feb. 20 and 27, 1995.

207 "like shot": James Thurber, *The Years with Ross* (Boston: Little, Brown, 1959), 40.

207 "Done and done": Ibid., 4.

207 "When the picture": FSF, "How to Waste Material," *Bookman*, May 1926.

208 "artificial manners": Harris, *Dance on the High Wire*, 97–98.

209 "doing setting-up exercises": EF notebook, quoted in Gilbert, *Ferber*, 373–74.

210 "both plays": *Bookman*, March 1928.

210 "Can you imagine": Harris, *Dance on the High Wire*, 109.

210 Successes of *The Royal Family* and *Show Boat*: *The Royal Family* ran 345 performances, *Show Boat* 572. (In *Show Boat* the minor role of Windy was played by a handsome blond actor from Richmond named Alan Campbell, whom Dorothy Parker would marry—twice.)

211 *Royal Family* opening night: For Ferber's version, see EF, *Peculiar Treasure*, 318. For Jed Harris's version, see Harris, *Dance on the High Wire*, 112–13.

212 "I'm going to close": Quoted in Meredith, *George S. Kaufman and His Friends*, 246–47. No source cited.

NINE: ∾ 1928

214 "just a little one": DP, *The Portable Dorothy Parker* (New York: Penguin, 1976), 241.

214 "Make it awfully weak": Ibid.

215 "That does it": Gertrude Benchley to Hy Gardner, April 10, 1952, TC/LC.

215 "the rams": *New Yorker*, Jan. 28, 1928.

215 "in the Smithsonian": *New Yorker*, April 21, 1928.

216 "we were both": DP to Robert Benchley, Nov. 7, 1929, Columbia.

216 "You damned *stallion*": DP, "Dusk before Fireworks," *Harper's Bazaar*, Sept. 1932.

216 "Hell, while I'm up": *New Yorker*, Aug. 25, 1928.

217 "splintering misery": DP, *Portable Dorothy Parker*, 205.

217 "an enlarged": *New Yorker*, Nov. 26, 1927.

217 "Oh, for heaven's sake": *New Yorker*, Sept. 1, 1928.

218 "Millions to be grabbed": Ben Hecht, *A Child of the Century* (New York: Simon and Schuster, 1954), 435.

218 Lubov Egorova: Zelda described her introduction to Madame Egorova's ballet school in *Save Me the Waltz*, in *The Collected Writings of Zelda Fitzgerald* (Tuscaloosa: University of Alabama Press, 1997), 113–15.

219 "reeked of hard work": Ibid. A brief spell at the ballet school in 1925 had been terminated by an ovarian infection.

219 "perfumed with the taste": Sara Mayfield, *Exiles from Paradise* (New York: Delacorte, 1971), 131.

220 "this desolate ménage": FSF to ZSF, summer 1930, *Dear Scott, Dearest Zelda: The Love Letters of F. Scott and Zelda Fitzgerald*, ed. Jackson R. Bryer and Cathy W. Barks (New York: St. Martin's, 2002), 63. In response to Scott's accusations of extravagance, Zelda made an effort to pay for her classes by writing. *College Humor* paid two hundred dollars for "Who Can Fall in Love after Thirty?," published under a joint byline, even though she was the sole author.

220 "Unbearable": FSF to ZSF, summer 1930, *Dear Scott, Dearest Zelda*, 64.

220 "Literally, eternally": ZSF to FSF, summer/fall 1930, *Correspondence of F. Scott Fitzgerald* (New York: Random House, 1980), 248.

221 "I look like hell": Mayfield, *Exiles from Paradise*, 131.

221 "I'm Voltaire": Quoted in André Le Vot, *F. Scott Fitzgerald* (Garden City, N.Y.: Doubleday, 1983), 232.

222 "a dream": FSF to ZSF, summer 1930, *Dear Scott, Dearest Zelda*, 64.

222 Zelda's attraction to Egorova: Scott did not forget this conversation, which he mentioned to Zelda's psychiatrist Mildred Squires in 1932 as the first hint of lesbianism.

222 "But what isn't cocktail time": EB to Emla La Branche, n.d., TC/LC.

222 "grated egg": Edmund Wilson, *The Shores of Light: A Literary Chronicle of the Twenties and Thirties* (New York: Farrar, Straus and Young, 1952), 775.

223 "perhaps one of the most important": Ibid., 242.

223 "You mean it sounds": Edmund Wilson, *The Twenties* (New York: Farrar, Straus and Giroux, 1975), 438.

225 "the one and only Edna": Various interoffice memos to Arthur Rushmore, Columbia.

225 "your Mr. Rushmore": EM to Eugene Saxton, various correspondence, Berg.

226 Miss Millay has asked me: EB to Eugene Saxton, various correspondence, c. 1927–1945, Berg.

226 "again and again": Elizabeth Breuer, "Edna St. Vincent Millay," *Pictorial Review*, Nov. 1931.

226 "fussy": Eugene Saxton to EM, Aug. 16, 1928, Berg.

227 "with a bureau": EM, "Moriturus," in *Collected Poems* (New York: Harper & Row, 1956), 199.

227 "the tranquil blossom": EM, "On Hearing a Symphony of Beethoven," in *Collected Poems*, 629.

227 "one of the most perfect": *Nation*, Dec. 5, 1928.

227 Other *Buck in the Snow* reviews: *New Republic*, Nov. 7, 1928; *Outlook*, Oct. 31, 1928; *Christian Century*, Jan. 3, 1929; *Saturday Review of Literature*, Dec. 22, 1928; *New Statesman*, March 30, 1929.

228 "in old-fashioned form": *Pictorial Review*, Nov. 1931.

228 "It is poems": Archibald MacLeish to Louis Untermeyer, June 22, 1932, *Letters of Archibald MacLeish, 1907 to 1982* (Boston: Houghton Mifflin, 1983), 251.

228 "touched greatness": Archibald MacLeish to Louis Untermeyer, Oct. 4, 1929, ibid., 231.

228 "a fine poet": *Pictorial Review*, Nov. 1931.

228 "friendly people": EB to Eugene Saxton, Sept. 18, 1934, Berg.

230 "You had a nosebleed": Taped interview with Zelda and Scott Fitzgerald, May 28, 1933, by Dr. Thomas Rennie, Henry Phipps Psychiatric Clinic of Johns Hopkins University, F. Scott Fitzgerald Papers, PUL.

231 "so able and intelligent": Maxwell Perkins to Ernest Hemingway, Oct. 2, 1928, *The Only Thing That Counts: The Ernest Hemingway/Maxwell Perkins Correspondence, 1925–1947* (New York: Scribner, 1996), 81–82.

231 "best writer": Ernest Hemingway to Maxwell Perkins, Oct. 11, 1928, ibid., 82.

231 "I've found a clap doctor": Ernest Hemingway, "Une Soirée Chez Monsieur Fitz . . . ," unpublished fragment deleted from final draft of *A Moveable Feast*, JFK Library, item 720B, quoted in Scott Donaldson, *Hemingway vs. Fitzgerald: The Rise and Fall of a Literary Friendship* (Woodstock, N.Y.: Overlook Press, 1999), 120–21.

231 "Aren't you the best": A. E. Hotchner, *Papa Hemingway* (New York: Random House, 1966), 121.

232 "really awful": Quoted in James Mellow, *Invented Lives* (Boston: Houghton Mifflin, 1984), 328.

232 "We had a grand time": Ernest Hemingway to FSF and ZSF, Nov. 18, 1928, *Ernest Hemingway, Selected Letters, 1917–1961* (New York: Scribner, 1981), 290.

232 "poop himself": Ernest Hemingway to Maxwell Perkins, Oct. 11, 1928, *Only Thing That Counts*, 82.

232 FSF progress reports: July 10, 1925; c. May 8, 1926; c. July 21, 1928, *Dear Scott/Dear Max: The Fitzgerald-Perkins Correspondence* (New York: Scribner's, 1971), 118–52.

233 "nice enough": Quoted in Eleanor Lanahan, *Scottie the Daughter of . . . : The Life of Frances Scott Fitzgerald Lanahan Smith* (New York: HarperCollins, 1995) 34.

234 "enchanted sickness": EM to George Dillon, Dec. 15, 1928, LOC.

234 "two fools": Ibid.

234 "always": Ibid.

235 "Lord and Lady of Hardhack": Gladys and Arthur Ficke to EM and EB, Dec. 1928, Beinecke.

236 "Tell him it is a matter": EM to George Dillon, Dec. 29, 1928, LOC.

236 "mess things up": Ibid.

236 "drink wine and laugh": EB to George Dillon, Dec. 1928, LOC.

236 "incredibly happy": EM to George Dillon, Dec. 29, 1928, LOC.

TEN: ᗄ 1929

237 "I'm going to make you": EB to George Dillon, Dec. 1928, LOC.

238 "my troubled lord": EM, *Collected Poems* (New York: Harper & Row, 1956), 631.

238 "I am devoted": EM to George Dillon, Dec. 15, 1928, LOC.

238 "lovely thing": Ibid.

238 "Perhaps I wanted": EM to George Dillon, Feb. 21, 1929, LOC.

239 "This beast": EM, *Collected Poems*, 631.

239 "Oh, sleep forever": Ibid., 681.

239 "Night and day": *Pictorial Review*, Nov. 1931.

239 "a non-union": EM to Stephen Vincent Benét, Feb. 6, 1929, *Letters of Edna St. Vincent Millay* (New York: Harper & Brothers, 1952), 229.

239 "a nervous intensity": *Pictorial Review*, Nov. 1931.

239 "And must I then": EM, *Collected Poems*, 734.

240 "all the natural bonds": Edmund Wilson, *Galahad/I Thought of Daisy* (New York: Farrar, Straus and Giroux, 1967), 126.

240 "Well, don't you think": Ibid., 117.

240 Millay as literary character: Glimpses of Millay can be seen in several of Wilson's works: Rita Cavanagh in *I Thought of Daisy* (1929), Ellen Terhune in

Memoirs of Hecate County (1946), and possibly Sally Voight in the play *This Room and This Gin and These Sandwiches* (1937) (retitled *A Winter in Beech Street*).

240 "very uneven": EM to EW, Feb. 6, 1929, *Letters*, 230.

241 "Whamming": EM to EW, Feb. 10, 1929, *Letters*, 231.

241 Millay's undelivered letters: While never re-sent, the letters were saved and discovered after her death by Norma Millay, who forwarded them to Wilson in 1951.

241 "I could not go": Edmund Wilson, *The Twenties* (New York: Farrar, Straus and Giroux, 1975), 492.

241 "a narrow, stale-smelling": Ibid., 491.

242 "sort of a nerve doctor": Rosalind Wilson, *Near the Magician: A Memoir of My Father* (New York: Grove Weidenfeld, 1989), 32.

243 "dens of loathsome creatures": Edmund Wilson, *Axel's Castle: A Study in the Imaginative Literature of 1870–1930* (New York: Scribner's, 1931), 263.

243 "enjoying a brief nervous breakdown": EW to Seward Collins, Feb. 18, 1929, Beinecke.

243 "couldn't quite make it": Wilson, *Near the Magician*, 31.

243 Millay in Wilson's novel: The assumption that *I Thought of Daisy* was a roman à clef annoyed Wilson, but he never quibbled to John Bishop, who thought the portrait of Vincent unsuccessful, owing to Bunny's relationship with her. In 1957 Crown Publishers submitted a manuscript to Wilson for evaluation, a Millay biography by Robert Farr. Wilson advised rejection of "My Candle Burns at Both Ends," claiming that the author had confused fictional and real events in *I Thought of Daisy*. The character Rita Cavanagh, he maintained, was based on several women, and the rest was invention.

243 "put out her light": ZSF, *Save Me the Waltz*, in *The Collected Writings of Zelda Fitzgerald* (Tuscaloosa: University of Alabama Press, 1997), 44.

243 Lubov Egorova's studio: In a 1932 essay Zelda said that her detailed description of the studio in *Save Me the Waltz* was accurate.

244 "more than anything else": ZSF, autobiographical essay, summer 1930, quoted in Nancy Milford, *Zelda* (New York: Harper & Row, 1970), 175.

244 "Dreadfully grotesque": Gerald Murphy interview, quoted in Milford, *Zelda*, 141.

244 "She no longer read": FSF to Oscar Forel, summer 1930, FSF, *A Life in Letters* (New York: Scribner's, 1994), 197.

245 "extraordinary sweating": FSF to Oscar Forel, Jan. 29, 1931, ibid., p. 205.

245 "a gored horse": ZSF, *Save Me the Waltz*, in *Collected Writings*, 144.

245 "I'm Morley": Morley Callaghan, *That Summer in Paris* (Toronto: Macmillan, 1963), 150.

246 "The boldness": Ibid., 160.

246 "sick with spiritual boredom": ZSF, "The Original Follies Girl," in *Collected Writings*, 296.

247 "In front of the Lorraine": ZSF, *Collected Writings*, 327. The most extensively rewritten of all Zelda's stories, "A Millionaire's Girl" was published in 1931 by the *Saturday Evening Post* under Scott's byline, at his then-standard fee of four thousand dollars.

247 "in the sense": FSF to Dr. Jonathan Slocum, March 22, 1934, *New York Times Magazine*, Dec. 1, 1996.

247 "an extraordinary talent": Ibid.

247 "astonishing power": Maxwell Perkins to FSF, Aug. 5, 1930, *Dear Scott/Dear Max: The Fitzgerald-Perkins Correspondence* (New York: Scribner's, 1971), 168.

248 "the highest paid": Taped interview with Zelda and Scott Fitzgerald, May 28, 1933, by Dr. Thomas Rennie, Henry Phipps Psychiatric Clinic of Johns Hopkins University, F. Scott Fitzgerald Papers, PUL.

248 "Just automatic writing": Ibid.

248 "analysis and subanalysis": Sara Murphy to FSF, summer 1929, quoted in André Le Vot, *F. Scott Fitzgerald* (Garden City, N.Y.: Doubleday, 1983), 246. (Dated summer 1926 in Amanda Vaill, *Everybody Was So Young* [Boston: Houghton Mifflin, 1998].)

248 "what Zelda or Scottie": Sara Murphy to FSF, n.d., quoted in Calvin Tomkins, *Living Well Is the Best Revenge* (New York: Viking, 1971), 130.

249 "magnificent": Julia Sedova to ZSF, Sept. 23, 1929, PUL.

249 Zelda's professional dance career: Only in fiction did Zelda find the strength to accept the offer of a ballet debut. In 1932, while a patient at the Phipps Psychiatric Clinic of Johns Hopkins Medical School, she wrote an autobiographical novel about an ambitious American woman who studies classical ballet in Paris. In *Save Me the Waltz* the characters Alabama and David Knight are virtual carbon copies of Zelda and Scott, just as the closely observed picture of Twenties expatriates is drawn from their own experiences. The story begins in the South before the war, and ends after the Crash, but the core of the novel maps the backstage world of European ballet and depicts Alabama's intensive training, her successful debut in *Faust,* and finally the injury that brings a halt to her career. The Knights and their child return to Alabama's hometown. Even after the one great dream of her life is shattered, Alabama thinks happiness may be possible yet, which is not saying a great deal, because she also believes one can learn to play the piano by correspondence course.

249 "nervous and half-sick": ZSF to FSF, summer/fall 1930, *Correspondence of F. Scott Fitzgerald* (New York: Random House, 1980), 248.

250 "oblivion": ZSF, autobiographical essay, March 16, 1932, quoted in Milford, *Zelda,* 156.

250 "The Fitzgeralds are here": Richard Myers to Stephen Vincent and Rosemary Benét, Oct. 28, 1929, Richard Myers Papers, Beinecke. (In the 1920s Myers worked in Paris for American Express and *Ladies' Home Journal*.)

250 "jockey with me": Callaghan, *That Summer in Paris*, 163.

250 "horrors": Ernest Hemingway to Maxwell Perkins, April 3, 1929, *The Only Thing That Counts: The Ernest Hemingway/Maxwell Perkins Correspondence, 1925–1947* (New York: Scribner, 1996), 97.

250 "Oh, what's this": *New Yorker*, Nov. 29, 1927.

251 "Pay no attention": George Oppenheimer, *The View from the Sixties: Memories of a Spent Life* (New York: David McKay, 1966), 3.

251 "a shit": Ruth Goodman Goetz interview.

252 "hated figs": DP to Helen Droste, Sept. 1929, Columbia.

252 "disgustingly well": Ibid.

253 "but they don't count": Ibid.

253 "The rocks at busy cocktail hour": Robert Benchley to Harold Ross, July 25, 1929, *New Yorker* Records.

254 "that Goddamn book": DP to Helen Droste, Nov. 28, 1929, Columbia.

254 "Mother loved having her": Honoria Murphy Donnelly interview.

254 Parker's Hemingway interview: In a second poem about Parker, "Little Drops of Grain Alcohol," Hemingway vowed to wear glasses to better "kiss the critics' asses" (Hemingway, *88 Poems* [New York: Harcourt Brace Jovanovich, 1979], 86).

255 "it was too late": DP to Robert Benchley, Nov. 7, 1929, Columbia.

255 "a little yippy": DP to Helen Droste, Nov. 28, 1929, Columbia.

255 "big shit": DP to Robert Benchley, Nov. 7, 1929, Columbia.

256 "as long as it takes": Ibid.

256 "When the manuscript is done": Harold Guinzburg to DP, Oct. 11, 1929, Columbia.

256 "as if it were a restaurant": *Pictorial Review*, Nov. 1931.

257 "weak tea and morphine": EB to Eugene Saxton, July 2, 1929, Berg.

258 "deteriorated ghosts": Edmund Wilson, *The Shores of Light: A Literary Chronicle of the Twenties and Thirties* (New York: Farrar, Straus and Young, 1952), 788.

258 "This is awful": *Pictorial Review*, Nov. 1931.

258 "lie on the floor": EM to George Dillon, summer 1929, LOC.

259 "one-street wooden": EF, *Cimarron* (Garden City, N.Y.: Doubleday, Doran, 1930), 381.

260 "Stock Prices Will Stay": *New York Times*, Oct. 13 and 16, 1929.

261 "two people": EF, *A Peculiar Treasure* (New York: Doubleday, Doran, 1939), 326.

263 *Cimarron* characters: In *Cimarron*, Ferber recycled characters from pre-

vious novels. Sabra Venable Cravat behaves like Selina Peake DeJong, while Selina's no-good son, Dirk, became Sabra's disappointing son, Cim, and the virile but unstable Yancey conveyed the essence of the virile weakling Gaylord Ravenal, both of them men who exploit and abandon their women.

264 "good old United States": EF, *Peculiar Treasure*, 339.

264 "This should have depressed me": Ibid.

ELEVEN: ∾ 1930

266 "yammering": EF to Seward Collins, April 6, 1930, Beinecke.

267 "Edna Ferber at her best": *Bookman*, June 1930.

267 "There is no attempt": EF, *Cimarron* (Garden City, N.Y.: Doubleday, Doran, 1930), ix.

267 *Cimarron* reviews: *Saturday Review of Literature*, March 22, 1930; *Outlook*, April 1, 1930.

268 "an extremely offensive personality": Editorial quoted in Julie Goldsmith Gilbert, *Ferber: A Biography* (Garden City, N.Y.: Doubleday, 1978), 361.

268 "a telephone number": Ibid., 358.

268 *Cimarron* filmography: One of the first blockbuster Westerns, *Cimarron* starred Irene Dunne and Richard Dix. A remake with Maria Schell and Glenn Ford was released in 1960.

269 "Are people nicer": *New York Telegram*, Feb. 1, 1930.

270 "the home of horseshit": DP to Robert Benchley, Nov. 7, 1929, Columbia.

271 "slow, even heebs": Ibid.

271 "I'd like to finish": DP to Helen Droste, Nov. 28, 1929, Columbia.

271 "Write novels": DP to Robert Benchley, Nov. 7, 1929, Columbia.

271 "Need of money": *Writers at Work: The Paris Review Interviews*, 1st ser. (New York: Viking, 1958), 76.

271 "mighty much": Franklin P. Adams, *The Diary of Our Own Samuel Pepys, 1926–1934* (New York: Simon and Schuster, 1935), 2:957.

272 "Dotty Darling": George Oppenheimer to DP, July 3, 1930, Columbia. The "21" Club opened as a speakeasy on West Fifty-second Street in 1929. Previously known as Jack and Charlie's Puncheon Club, it had been located across the street from Tony's on West Forty-ninth.

273 "real mess": ZSF, autobiographical essay, summer 1930, quoted in Nancy Milford, *Zelda* (New York: Harper & Row, 1970), 175.

273 "It's horrible": Malmaison report, Craig House Medical Records, PUL.

274 "Ah's mama's": ZSF to FSF, summer 1930, *Dear Scott, Dearest Zelda: The Love Letters of F. Scott and Zelda Fitzgerald*, ed. Jackson R. Bryer and Cathy W. Barks (New York: St. Martin's, 2002), 87. "Stay in Your Own Backyard" was a popular turn-of-the-century tune, in which a black mother warns her offspring not to play with white children.

274 "you can't expect anybody": Richard Myers to Stephen Vincent Benét, May 2, 1930, Beinecke.

274 "exhaustion from work": Malmaison report, Craig House Medical Records, PUL.

274 "a gigantic cocktail": FSF, "The Bridal Party," in *The Stories of F. Scott Fitzgerald* (New York: Scribner's, 1951), 275.

274 The death of Diaghilev: After Serge Diaghilev's death in August 1929, the company dissolved and creditors claimed its assets. However, the company's name would reincarnate as Ballet Russe of Monte Carlo and the Original Ballet Russe.

275 "enormous pressure": ZSF to FSF, summer 1930, *Dear Scott, Dearest Zelda*, 85.

275 "a nervous affliction": Craig House Medical Records, PUL.

275 "unstable": FSF to Dr. Rex Blankenship, May 4, 1934, *New York Times Magazine*, Dec. 1, 1996.

276 "I want to die": Craig House Medical Records, PUL.

276 Zelda's homosexuality accusations: Craig House Medical Records, PUL.

277 "nut farm": Sara Mayfield, *Exiles from Paradise* (New York: Delacorte, 1971), 153.

278 "a constitutional": Craig House Medical Records, PUL.

278 "never follow up anything": Edmund Wilson, *The Shores of Light: A Literary Chronicle of the Twenties and Thirties* (New York: Farrar, Straus and Young, 1952), 380.

279 "Dirt eating": FSF, *F. Scott Fitzgerald's Ledger: A Facsimile*, ed. Matthew Bruccoli (Washington, D.C.: NCR/Microcard Editions, A Bruccoli Clark Book, 1972), 183. Playing with a bowel movement, a symptom associated with schizophrenia, generally indicates severe psychiatric disturbance rising from feelings of self-hatred.

280 "silly life": Arthur Ficke, "Psychoanalytical Notes," c. 1939, Beinecke.

280 "flawless goddess": Arthur Ficke, "Journal Notes," c. 1941, Beinecke.

280 "very cruel": Ibid.

280 "a hell of a lot": EM to Deems and Mary Taylor, May 10, 1930, *Letters of Edna St. Vincent Millay* (New York: Harper & Brothers, 1952), 237.

281 "Love, Eugen": EB to George Dillon, June 28, 1930, LOC.

281 "What makes you think": EW to Floyd Dell, Sept. 10, 1952, Edmund Wilson, *Letters on Literature and Politics, 1912–1972* (New York: Farrar, Straus and Giroux, 1977), 71, quoting a conversation with Esther Root.

282 "the god damn title": EB to Arthur Ficke, c. 1930, Beinecke.

282 "entirely upset": EM to Arthur Rushmore, July 1930, Columbia.

282 "freed of your building problems": Arthur Rushmore to EM, July 16, 1930, Columbia.

283 "into the beets": ZSF to FSF, June 1930, *Dear Scott, Dearest Zelda*, 80.

283 "failli, cabriole": ZSF, *Save Me the Waltz*, in *The Collected Writings of Zelda Fitzgerald* (Tuscaloosa: University of Alabama Press, 1997), 134.

283 "before it is too late": ZSF to FSF, June 1930, *Dear Scott, Dearest Zelda*, 81.

283 "rotten": FSF to ZSF, c. July 1930, ibid., 88.

283 "funereal and unnerving": EW to FSF, Aug. 8, 1930, Wilson, *Letters*, 202.

283 "He lies": John Peale Bishop to Allen Tate, Aug. 9, 1930, *The Republic of Letters in America: The Correspondence of John Peale Bishop and Allen Tate* (Lexington: University Press of Kentucky, 1981), 15.

284 "good to very good": Lubov Egorova to FSF, July 9, 1930, quoted in FSF, *A Life in Letters* (New York: Scribner's, 1994), 186 n.

284 "the saddest thing": ZSF to Scottie Fitzgerald, c. spring 1931, PUL.

284 Accounts of Zelda's eczema: FSF, *Tender Is the Night* (New York: Scribner's, 1934), 183; ZSF to FSF, summer 1930, *Dear Scott, Dearest Zelda*, 83; ZSF to FSF, fall 1930, ibid., 96.

285 "a nightmare": ZSF to FSF, c. 1930–1931, *Dear Scott, Dearest Zelda*, 102.

285 "Miss Bessie": Retitled "Miss Ella," the story was published in December 1931. *Scribner's* rejected an earlier batch of three stories, written in June 1930. Between 1930 and 1932 Zelda continued to produce short fiction, perhaps as many as eight or ten stories, which have been identified from the records of Harold Ober's office. They were submitted to magazines such as *The New Yorker*, *Vanity Fair*, and the *Saturday Evening Post*, but none was accepted.

286 Bleuler consultation: A century after Kraepelin and Bleuler, the causes of schizophrenia remain mostly unknown. There is remission but no cure. The antipsychotic drugs prescribed to control symptoms enable the afflicted to live outside of institutions but do not repair brain abnormalities. Recent biographers of Zelda question her diagnosis. Among the alternate explanations: she suffered a series of manic-depressive incidents accompanied by hallucinations, or she was permanently damaged by her medical treatments at Prangins.

286 "a great imbecile": Oscar Forel to FSF, Dec. 1, 1930, quoted in Milford, *Zelda*, 179.

286 Zelda's reaction to Bleuler's prognosis: ZSF to FSF, Nov. 1930, *Dear Scott, Dearest Zelda*, 97.

287 "Baby's boat": DP to Robert Benchley, Nov. 8, 1930, Columbia.

287 Dottie and Gerald's quarrel: Honoria Murphy Donnelly interview.

287 "loneliness and discouragement": DP to George Oppenheimer, Nov. 13, 1930, Columbia.

288 "I'm tired": *New York Telegram*, Nov. 25, 1930.

288 Breaking news: *New York Post*, *New York Telegram*, *New York Daily News*, *New York World*, for the week of Nov. 24, 1930.

288 "So to Miss Edna": Adams, *Diary*, 2:1000.

288 "Maybe you think": *New Yorker*, Jan. 24, 1931.

289 "photographic": Ibid.

289 New Year's Eve, 1930: Described in Malcolm Cowley, *Exile's Return: A Literary Odyssey of the 1920s* (New York: Viking, 1951), 307–8.

290 "to do better": Adams, *Diary*, 2:1007.

290 "I so happy": Ibid., 1005.

290 "a ghostly rumble": FSF, "Echoes of the Jazz Age," *Scribner's Magazine*, Nov. 1931.

AFTERWORD

292 "an ardent feminist": Julie Gilbert interview.

293 "saying she must resume": Heywood Hale Broun interview.

294 "And You As Well Must Die": EM, *Collected Poems* (New York: Harper & Row, 1956), 579.

295 "afraid of nothing": Martine Jozan Work interview.

295 "unfortunately": Anthony Adams interview.

EDNA FERBER

BOOKS

Dawn O'Hara, 1911
Buttered Side Down, 1912
Roast Beef, Medium, 1913
Personality Plus, 1914
Emma McChesney & Co., 1915
Fanny Herself, 1917
Cheerful, by Request, 1918
Half Portions, 1919
The Girls, 1921
Gigolo, 1922
So Big, 1924
Show Boat, 1926
Mother Knows Best, 1927
Cimarron, 1930
American Beauty, 1931
They Brought Their Women, 1933
Come and Get It, 1935
A Peculiar Treasure, autobiography, 1939
Saratoga Trunk, 1941
No Room at the Inn, 1941
Great Son, 1945
One Basket, 1947
Giant, 1952
Ice Palace, 1958
A Kind of Magic, autobiography, 1963

PLAYS

$1200 a Year, with Newman Levy, 1920
Minick, with George S. Kaufman, 1924

The Royal Family, with George S. Kaufman, 1927
Dinner at Eight, with George S. Kaufman, 1932
Stage Door, with George S. Kaufman, 1936
The Land Is Bright, with George S. Kaufman, 1941
Bravo!, with George S. Kaufman, 1949

ZELDA FITZGERALD

BOOKS
Save Me the Waltz, 1932
The Collected Writings, 1991

EDNA ST. VINCENT MILLAY

BOOKS
Renascence and Other Poems, 1917
A Few Figs from Thistles, 1920
Second April, 1921
The Harp-Weaver and Other Poems, 1923
The Buck in the Snow, 1928
Fatal Interview, 1931
Wine from These Grapes, 1934
Flowers of Evil, with George Dillon (translation), 1936
Conversation at Midnight, 1937
Huntsman, What Quarry?, 1939
Make Bright the Arrows, 1940
The Murder of Lidice, 1942
Mine the Harvest, 1954
Collected Poems, 1956

PLAYS
The Lamp and the Bell, 1921
Aria da Capo, 1921
Two Slatterns and a King: A Moral Interlude, 1921
The King's Henchman, 1927
The Princess Marries the Page, 1932

DOROTHY PARKER

BOOKS
Enough Rope, 1926
Sunset Gun, 1928

Laments for the Living, 1930
Death and Taxes, 1931
After Such Pleasures, 1933
Not So Deep as a Well, 1936
Here Lies, 1939
The Portable Dorothy Parker, 1944

PLAYS
Close Harmony, with Elmer Rice, 1929
The Ladies of the Corridor, with Arnaud D'Usseau, 1954

ACKNOWLEDGMENTS

When I started writing this book in the fall of 2000, I found myself debating in which category it belonged. The first draft did not look quite like a biography to me. Neither did I consider it a collective portrait, because the personalities didn't make up a formal group, not even an informal circle. Certainly, all of these people were linked together: they were young and unspoiled during the years 1920 to 1930, frequently knew each other and lived in the same places, and shared a profession and generally the same concerns. Eventually I realized that the book was turning into a series of vignettes: quick pictures snapped on the fly by a determined shutterbug, two-thirds paparazzo out of John Dos Passos's *U.S.A.* with its nosey "Camera Eyes," one-third voyeuristic descendant of F. Scott Fitzgerald's oculist, Doctor T. J. Eckleburg. In the end, I concluded that the jittery rhythms seemed to suit the lives of my subjects.

I conceived this book because I love the Twenties and I love writers, especially those blessed with the gift of laughter. Dorothy Parker was a funny woman, obviously. But the rest of my heroines could be surprisingly hilarious, too, however many horrible calamities they suffered. They made me laugh and weep for three years.

In the writing I have accumulated many debts. Foremost, I owe thanks to my leading ladies, whose own literary work not only provided inspiration but also opened windows into their world. I was also able to use a trove of letters, diaries, and memoirs left behind by confessional writers such as Edmund Wilson and Franklin P. Adams. Had these fabulous gossips not set down their thoughts, this book would have been greatly diminished.

In personal interviews, a number of people generously shared important knowledge of their families. Heywood Hale Broun spoke with me about his mother and father, as did Anthony Adams and Anne Kaufman Schneider about their parents. Julie Gilbert enriched the book with exceptional insights into her great-aunt Edna Ferber. For recollections about the Fitzgerald, Murphy, and Myers families, my source once again was Frances Myers Brennan, an authentic lady and elegant hostess. A gold mine of information about the French admiral

Edouard Jozan came from his daughter, Dr. Martine Work. Robert Cowley cheerfully answered my questions about his father, Malcolm.

Some of those who gave me their time and memories in previous years are gone. As Frank Crowninshield's secretary at *Vanity Fair*, Jeanne Ballot Winham reported from a front-row seat on the office pranks of the editors Parker, Benchley, Wilson, and John Peale Bishop. The artist Charles Baskerville never forgot the behavior of the Parker dog. Marc Connelly and Margalo Gillmore savored lunches at the Algonquin Round Table more than a half century after the last popover was consumed. At the age of eighty-nine, the newswoman Mildred Gilman Wohlforth readily admitted seducing Parker's lover John Garrett; the actress Lois Moran Young, at the age of seventy-seven, famously admitted nothing about a romantic relationship with F. Scott Fitzgerald. Brendan Gill and E. J. Kahn Jr. dredged up tales of *The New Yorker* and its employees. Parker's dirty talk and unsanitized verse stuck in the minds of the dramatist Ruth Goodman Goetz and the artist Allen Saalburg. Alice Lee Myers led me on a guided tour through expatriate Paris, while Honoria Murphy Donnelly revisited in memory Antibes and her beloved Villa America. (Two people whose acquaintance I first made in the early Eighties, Woodie Broun and Fanny Brennan, died in 2001.)

In addition, I owe an immense debt to the highly talented biographers whose works I have consulted, among them Steven Bach, Daniel Mark Epstein, James Gaines, Brian Gallagher, Julie Gilbert, Malcolm Goldstein, Thomas Kunkel, Eleanor Lanahan, Sara Mayfield, Scott Meredith, Nancy Milford, Stanley Olson, Michael Reynolds, Kendall Taylor, and Amanda Vaill.

A number of scholars, historians, and knowledgeable individuals generously contributed to my research, especially Ann Douglas with her first-rate history *Terrible Honesty: Mongrel Manhattan in the 1920s.* Much-appreciated favors were extended to me by Mary Ellin Barrett, Maryann Chach of the Shubert Archive, Bert Fink of the Irving Berlin Music Company, Andrea Jolles, Michael Macdonald, Steve Mandel, Wendy Meeker, Dorshka Raphaelson, Charles Scribner, Marian Seldes, Nancy Woloch, and Stephen Young of *Poetry* magazine.

For help in finding and using the precious archival sources, I owe thanks to numerous organizations. Those who helped me beyond the call of duty were the admirable special-collections staff of the Beinecke Rare Book and Manuscript Library of Yale University (curator Patricia C. Willis and her efficient colleagues Ellen Cordes, Ngadi Kponou, Lorraine Ouellette, and Karen Spicher); Jean Ashton and Bernard Crystal of the Columbia University Rare Book and Manuscript Library; Sid Huttner and Kathryn Hodson of University of Iowa Special Collections; Dorinda Hartmann of the Wisconsin Center for Film and Theater Research; Mary Ellen Rogan of the Billy Rose Theatre Collection, New York Public Library; Isaac Gewirtz and Diana Burnham of the Berg Collection, New York Public Library; Linda Long of Knight Library, University of Oregon; Vincent

Fitzpatrick of the Enoch Pratt Free Library, Baltimore; Sarah Hutcheon of the Schlesinger Library, Radcliffe; Elizabeth Falsey of the Houghton Library, Harvard University; Margaret Sherry and AnnaLee Pauls of Rare Books and Special Collections, Firestone Library, Princeton University; Pascal Geneste of the Service Historique de la Marine; Robert Feuilloy of the Association pour la Recherche de Documentation sur l'Histoire de l'Aéronautique Navale; Steven Friedman of the Great Neck Historical Society; Timothy Murray and Iris Snyder of Special Collections, University of Delaware Library; Alice L. Birney of the Library of Congress; and Michele McKee of the Kristine Mann Library at the C. G. Jung Center of New York.

In particular I must mention my all-time favorite librarians, Stephen Crook and Philip Milito of the Berg Collection at the New York Public Library.

I'm also obliged to the literary executors and heirs whose kind cooperation contributed to my labors: Anthony Adams, the always-gracious Elizabeth Barnett of the Edna St. Vincent Millay Society, Wolstan Brown, John Donnelly, Laura Donnelly, Julie Gilbert, Carrie Hamilton, Harold Ober Associates, Anne Schneider, and Nan Bright Sussmann.

Biographers require dynamic subjects and reliable sources, but most of all they need a lot of friends. For moral support I would like to thank Erica Abeel, Deirdre Bair, Myron Brenton, Marlene Coburn, Judy Feiffer, Barbara Foster, Kyle Gallup, Janet Gardner, Judith Hennessee, Diane Jacobs, Vanessa Levin, Minda Novek, Lisa Paddock, Carl Rollyson, Florence Rubenfeld, Marlene Sanders, Kenneth Silverman, Sydney Stern, Philip Turner, Ann Waldron, and Brenda Wineapple.

I am grateful to Patricia O'Toole and the Hertog Research Assistantship Program in the Graduate Writing Division of the School of the Arts at Columbia University. My enterprising intern, Amy Greene, did a wonderful job for me.

Special thanks to Holly Peppe, Millay scholar and past president (1987–2000) of the Edna St. Vincent Millay Society, and to Kendall Taylor, author of *Sometimes Madness Is Wisdom: Zelda and Scott Fitzgerald, a Marriage*. To them both I'm indebted in more ways than I can list, not only for professional guidance but also for their personal friendship.

My compliments to an ideal editor, the legendary Nan Talese. This book would not have been possible without her enthusiasm and generosity. For exacting standards in editing, I am especially grateful to the indefatigable Coates Bateman. Thanks also to Frieda Duggan, who deftly steered the manuscript through production, and to Ingrid Sterner, who did the copyediting.

My friend and literary agent, Lois Wallace, is one of a kind. She regularly offers more affectionate advice than I can be expected to use, explains the meaning of life in publishing, and tolerates jokes about the contents of her refrigerator. And she sells my work too. In other words, she's a perfect agent.

ILLUSTRATION CREDITS

All photographs are used by permission.

PAGE 3: Robert Benchley Collection in Special Collections, The Boston University Libraries.

PAGE 39: Al Hirschfeld/Margo Feiden Galleries Ltd.

PAGE 60: Photograph from the F. Scott Fitzgerald Archives at Princeton University Library used by permission of Harold Ober Associates Incorporated as agents for the Fitzgerald Trustees; reproduced courtesy of Princeton University Library.

PAGE 84: Library of Congress, used by permission of The Edna St. Vincent Millay Society.

PAGE 108: New York Public Library.

PAGE 129: Estate of Honoria M. Donnelly.

PAGE 158: The Edna St. Vincent Millay Society.

PAGE 186: Rare Book and Manuscript Library, Columbia University.

PAGE 213: Photograph from the F. Scott Fitzgerald Archives at Princeton University Library used by permission of Harold Ober Associates Incorporated as agents for the Fitzgerald Trustees; reproduced courtesy of Princeton University Library.

PAGE 237: Wisconsin Center for Film and Theater Research.

PAGE 266: Estate of Honoria M. Donnelly.

PHOTO INSERTS

Courtesy of Anthony Adams: Frank Adams portrait; Frank Adams and Esther Root wedding; Anthony Adams with Edna St. Vincent Millay et al; Frank Adams and Harold Ross.

Rare Book and Manuscript Library, Columbia University: Dorothy Parker portrait.

Courtesy of Carrie Hamilton: Ruth Hale portrait.

Courtesy of the Estate of Honoria M. Donnelly: Sara and Gerald Murphy portrait; Villa America terrace; Zelda and Scott Fitzgerald at Antibes; Murphy family; Parker and Murphy drinking sherry; Parker in Switzerland.

Courtesy of Julie Gilbert and Anne Kaufman Schneider: Edna Ferber and George S. Kaufman portrait.

Courtesy of William Marx: Parker, Charles MacArthur, Harpo Marx, Alexander Woollcott, et al.

Courtesy of the Edna St. Vincent Millay Society: Edna St. Vincent Millay portrait; Millay sisters with mother; Millay and Eugen Boissevain on honeymoon; Millay, Boissevain, and Arthur Davison Ficke portrait; Millay, Boissevain, and Cora Millay.

University of Oregon Libraries: Jane Grant portrait; Grant and Harold Ross portrait.

Photofest: Paul Robeson.

Photographs from the F. Scott Fitzgerald Archives at Princeton University Library used by permission of Harold Ober Associates Incorporated as agents for the Fitzgerald Trustees, reproduced courtesy of Princeton University Library: Zelda in tutu; Zelda portrait; Zelda in knickers; Zelda and Scott in Montgomery; *The Beautiful and Damned* jacket; Zelda and baby Scottie; Fitzgeralds in Great Neck; Fitzgeralds on the Riviera; Fitzgeralds in Paris; Zelda's room at Prangins.

Princeton University Library: Ernest Hemingway portrait.

Courtesy of Nan Bright Sussmann: George Dillon portrait.

United Press International: Frank Adams–Esther Root honeymoon.

Wisconsin Center for Film and Theater Research: Edna Ferber and William Allen White; Ferber in Native American costume; Ferber portrait; Ferber returning to New York.

Courtesy of the Edouard Jozan Family: Edouard Jozan portrait.

Beinecke Rare Book & Manuscript Library, Yale University: Edmund Wilson in uniform; Wilson passport photo; Millay and Boissevain in China.

A NOTE ABOUT THE TYPE

This book was set in a digital version of Fairfield Light, designed by Rudolph Ruzicka (1883–1978) for Linotype in 1940. Ruzicka was a Czechoslovakian-American wood and metal engraver, artist, and book illustrator. Although Fairfield recalls the modern typefaces of Bodoni and Didot, it has a distinctly twentieth-century look, a slightly decorative contemporary typeface with old-style characteristics.